CW01192838

Following the Tabby Trail

SOUTH CAROLINA

- Dorchester
- Charleston
- Beaufort
- Port Royal
- *Edisto Island*
- *St. Helena Island*
- *Parris Island*
- *Hilton Head Island*

GEORGIA

- Savannah
- *Sapelo Island*
- Darien
- Brunswick
- *St. Simons Island*
- Woodbine
- JEKYLL ISLAND STATE PARK
- Kingsland
- CUMBERLAND ISLAND NATIONAL SEASHORE
- St. Marys

FLORIDA

- FORT GEORGE ISLAND CULTURAL STATE PARK
- St. Augustine

Following the Tabby Trail

Where Coastal History Is Captured in Unique Oyster-Shell Structures

JINGLE DAVIS   PHOTOGRAPHS BY BENJAMIN GALLAND

The University of Georgia Press   Athens

All sites listed in this book are either on public land or visible from public streets, sidewalks, and waterways. Please be respectful when viewing sites from public vantage points.

© 2022 by the University of Georgia Press
Athens, Georgia 30602
www.ugapress.org
All rights reserved
Designed by Erin Kirk
Set in Arno Pro
Printed and bound by Friesens
The paper in this book meets the guidelines for permanence and durability of the Committee on Production Guidelines for Book Longevity of the Council on Library Resources.

Most University of Georgia Press titles are available from popular e-book vendors.

Printed in Canada

26 25 24 23 22 C 5 4 3 2 1

Library of Congress Cataloging-in-Publication Data

Names: Davis, Jingle, author. | Galland, Benjamin, photographer (expression)
Title: Following the tabby trail : where coastal history is captured in unique oyster-shell structures / Jingle Davis ; photographs by Benjamin Galland.
Description: Athens, Georgia : The University of Georgia Press, [2022] | Includes index.
Identifiers: LCCN 2021062377 | ISBN 9780820357492 (hardback)
Subjects: LCSH: Historic buildings—South Atlantic States—Guidebooks. | Concrete construction—South Atlantic States—Guidebooks. | Tabby (Concrete) | South Atlantic States—Guidebooks.
Classification: LCC NA720 .D38 2022 | DDC 721/.04450975—dc23/eng/20220210
LC record available at https://lccn.loc.gov/2021062377

A Wormsloe
FOUNDATION
PUBLICATION

*For Cash and his beloved
GaGa Barbara*

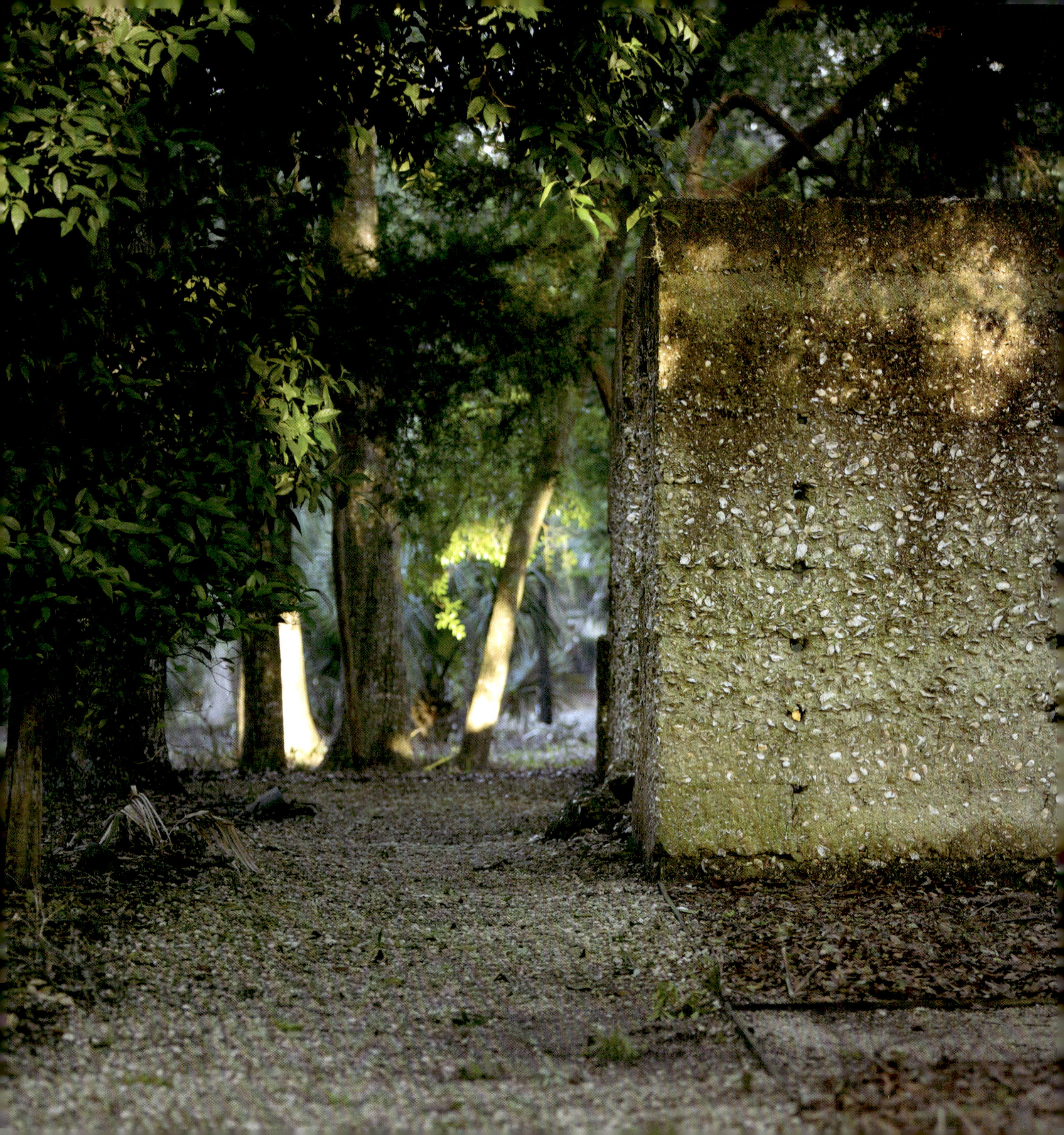

Contents

Preface xi
Introduction 1

PART I *Florida* 7

CHAPTER 1 St. Augustine 11
SITE 1 Fort Matanzas / Pedro Menéndez de Avilés 14
SITE 2 González-Álvarez (Oldest) House / Mary (Maria) Evans Peavett 22
SITE 3 Fernandez-Llambias House / Father Pedro Camps 28
SITE 4 Father Miguel O'Reilly House Museum [short take] 34
SITE 5 Flagler Tabby [short take] 36
SITE 6 Castillo de San Marcos / Chato 38
SITE 7 Fort Mose Historic State Park / Francisco Menéndez 46

CHAPTER 2 Fort George Island Cultural State Park 53
SITE 8 Kingsley Plantation / Anta Madgigine Jai Kingsley 56
SITE 9 Thomson House [short take] 64

PART II *Georgia* 67

CHAPTER 3 Cumberland Island National Seashore 71
SITE 10 Dungeness I and II / Catherine (Caty) Littlefield Greene 74
SITE 11 Miller-Greene House [short take] 80

CHAPTER 4 St. Marys, Kingsland, and Woodbine 82
SITE 12 McIntosh Sugar Works / James Houstoun McIntosh 86
SITE 13 St. Mark's Episcopal Church [short take] 94

CHAPTER 5 Jekyll Island State Park   96
    SITE 14 Horton House / Major William Horton   100
    SITE 15 Hollybourne Cottage / Charles Stewart Maurice   106
    SITE 16 Dairy Silo [short take]   112

CHAPTER 6 St. Simons Island   114
    SITE 17 Hamilton Plantation Slave Cabins / James Hamilton   118
    SITE 18 Retreat Plantation Slave Cabin / Anna Matilda Page King   124
    SITE 19 Fort Frederica / James Edward Oglethorpe   130
    SITE 20 Cannon's Point Plantation / John Couper   138
    SITE 21 Hampton Plantation / Fanny Kemble Butler   146

CHAPTER 7 Brunswick   152
    SITE 22 St. Athanasius Protestant Episcopal Church [short take]   154
    SITE 23 Hopeton Plantation Sugar Mill / James Hamilton Couper   156

CHAPTER 8 Darien   162
    SITE 24 Waterfront Warehouses and Adam-Strain Building [short take]   164
    SITE 25 St. Cyprian's Episcopal Church / Anna Alexander   166
    SITE 26 Ashantilly / William Greaner Haynes Jr.   172
    SITE 27 The Thicket Sugar Mill and Rum Distillery / Mary Letitia Ross   178

CHAPTER 9 Sapelo Island   184
    SITE 28 Chocolate Plantation / Bilali Muhammad   186
    SITE 29 South End House / Thomas Spalding   192

CHAPTER 10 Savannah   197
    SITE 30 Wormsloe State Historic Site / Noble Jones   200
    SITE 31 Fort Pulaski National Monument [short take]   206
    SITE 32 Owens-Thomas House / William Jay   208

PART III *South Carolina*   215

CHAPTER 11 Hilton Head Island   219
    SITE 33 Stoney-Baynard Plantation / Quarters for the Enslaved   222

CHAPTER 12 St. Helena Island   228
    SITE 34 St. Helena Chapel of Ease Ruins   230

CHAPTER 13 Port Royal   234
    SITE 35 Fort Frederick Heritage Preserve / Susie Baker King Taylor   236

CHAPTER 14 Parris Island   242
    SITE 36 Charlesfort–Santa Elena Site / Jean Ribault   244

CHAPTER 15 Beaufort   251
    SITE 37 Seawall [short take]   254
    SITE 38 Arsenal [short take]   256
    SITE 39 John Mark Verdier House / Robert Smalls   258
    SITE 40 Parish Church at St. Helena / St. Helena Cemetery   264
    SITE 41 Barnwell-Gough House / Esther Hawks   272
    SITE 42 Saltus-Habersham House [short take]   278
    SITE 43 Old Baptist Meeting House (Baptist Church of Beaufort) / The Reverend Richard Fuller   280
    SITE 44 Tabby Manse (Thomas Fuller House) [short take]   286

CHAPTER 16 Edisto Island   288
    SITE 45 Tabby Outbuildings at Botany Bay Plantation / Oqui   290
    SITE 46 First Missionary Baptist Church / Hephzibah Jenkins Townsend   300

CHAPTER 17 Charleston   305
    SITE 47 Horn Work [short take]   308

CHAPTER 18 Dorchester   310
    SITE 48 Fort / Francis Marion   312

Acknowledgments   321
APPENDIX Chronological List of Site Construction   323
Illustration Credits   327
Index   329

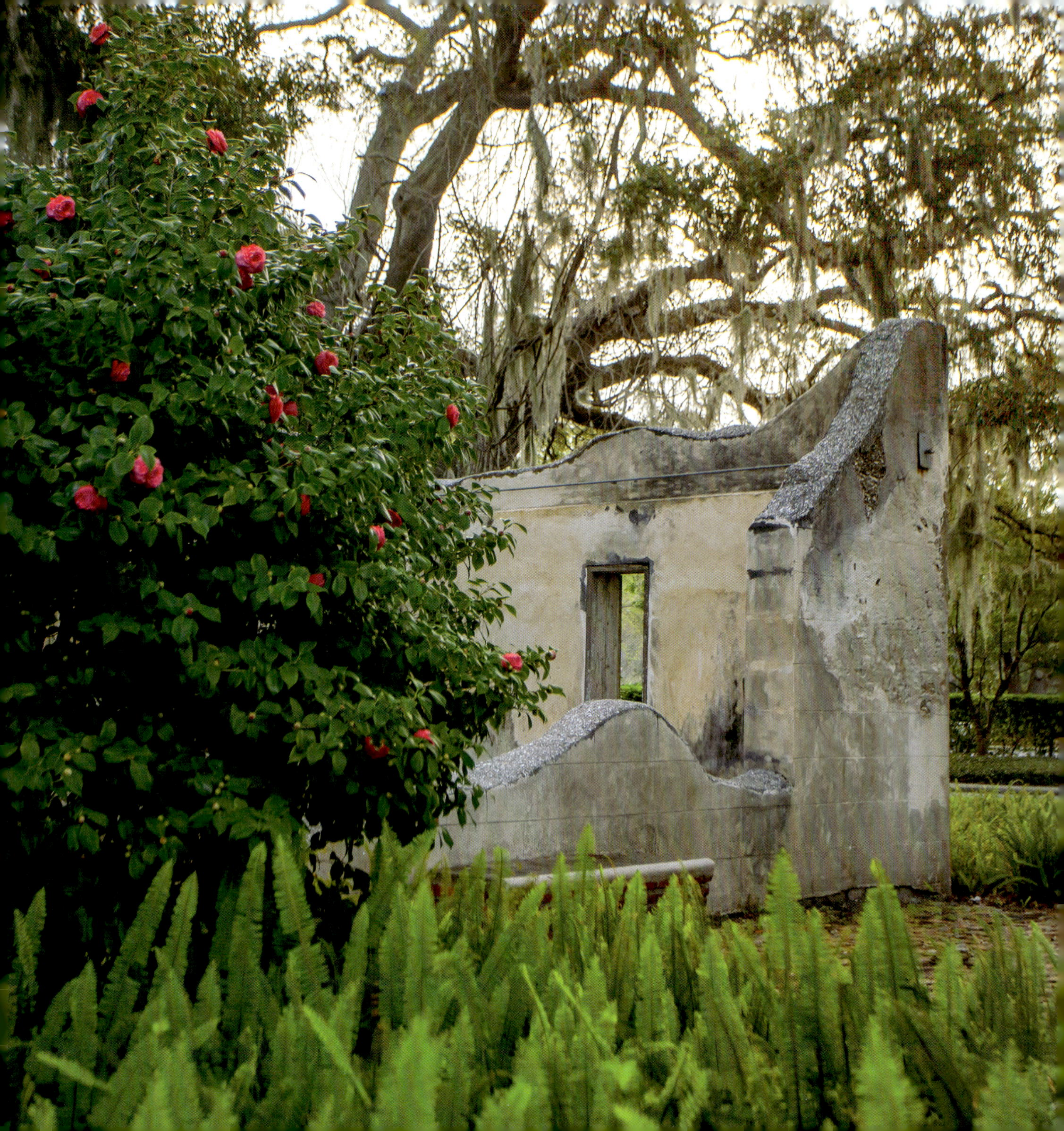

Preface

Although the tabby sites documented in this book can be visited at random, the book follows a trail of tabby that begins at Fort Matanzas, fifteen miles south of St. Augustine, Florida, and ends just north of Charleston, South Carolina, at the defunct colonial town of Dorchester and its well-preserved tabby fort on the Ashley River. The old tabbies in the book were chosen by the author because of their variety, historic significance, physical appeal, and accessibility to the public. All are either on public land or are visible from public streets and sidewalks. Because so many tabby structures are on or near navigable waters, boaters who travel the Intracoastal Waterway can dock along the way to visit historic tabby sites.

For the convenience of travelers, the sites are listed geographically rather than chronologically. A list of the sites in the chronological order of their construction is given in an appendix on page 323.

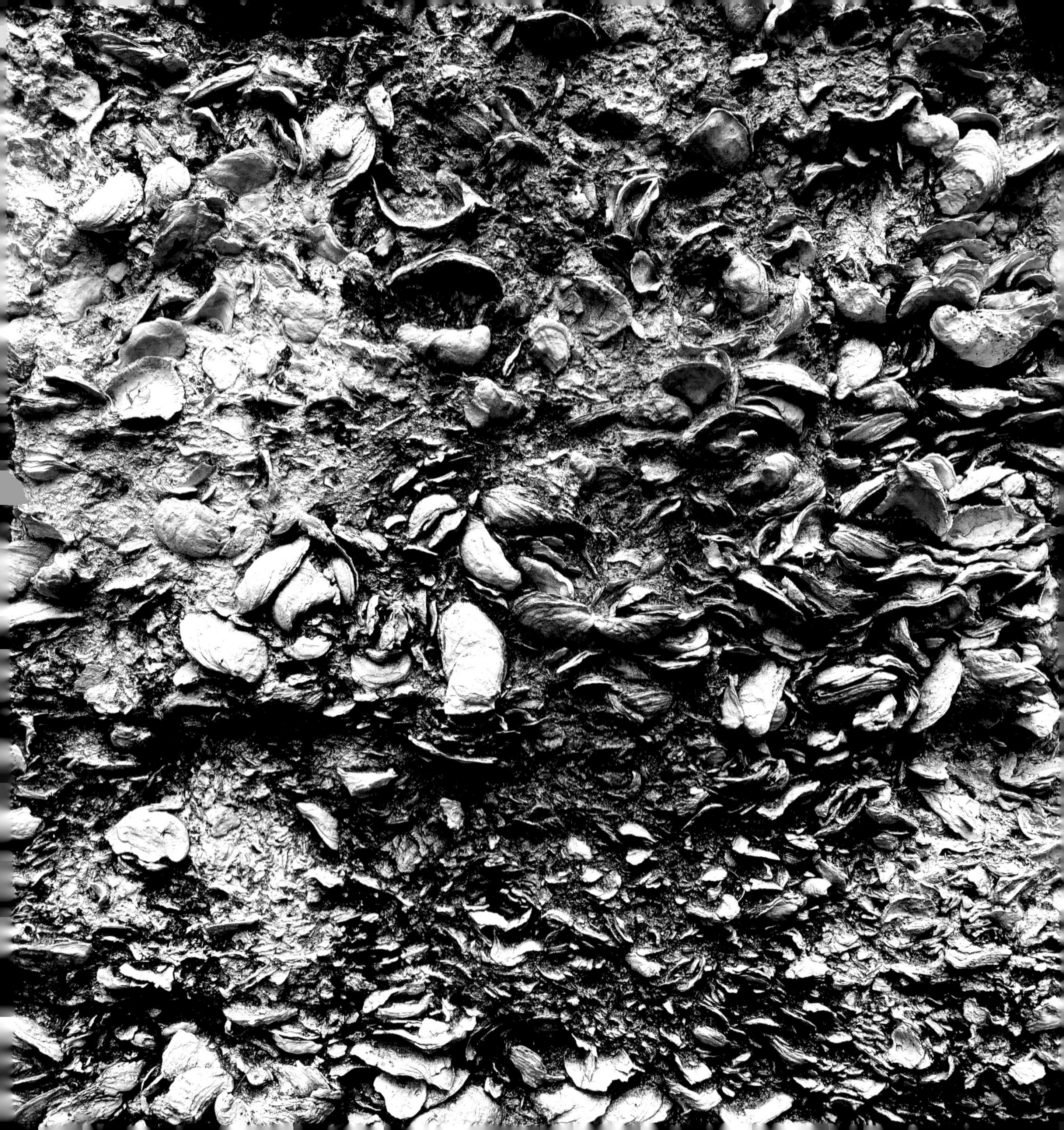

Following the Tabby Trail

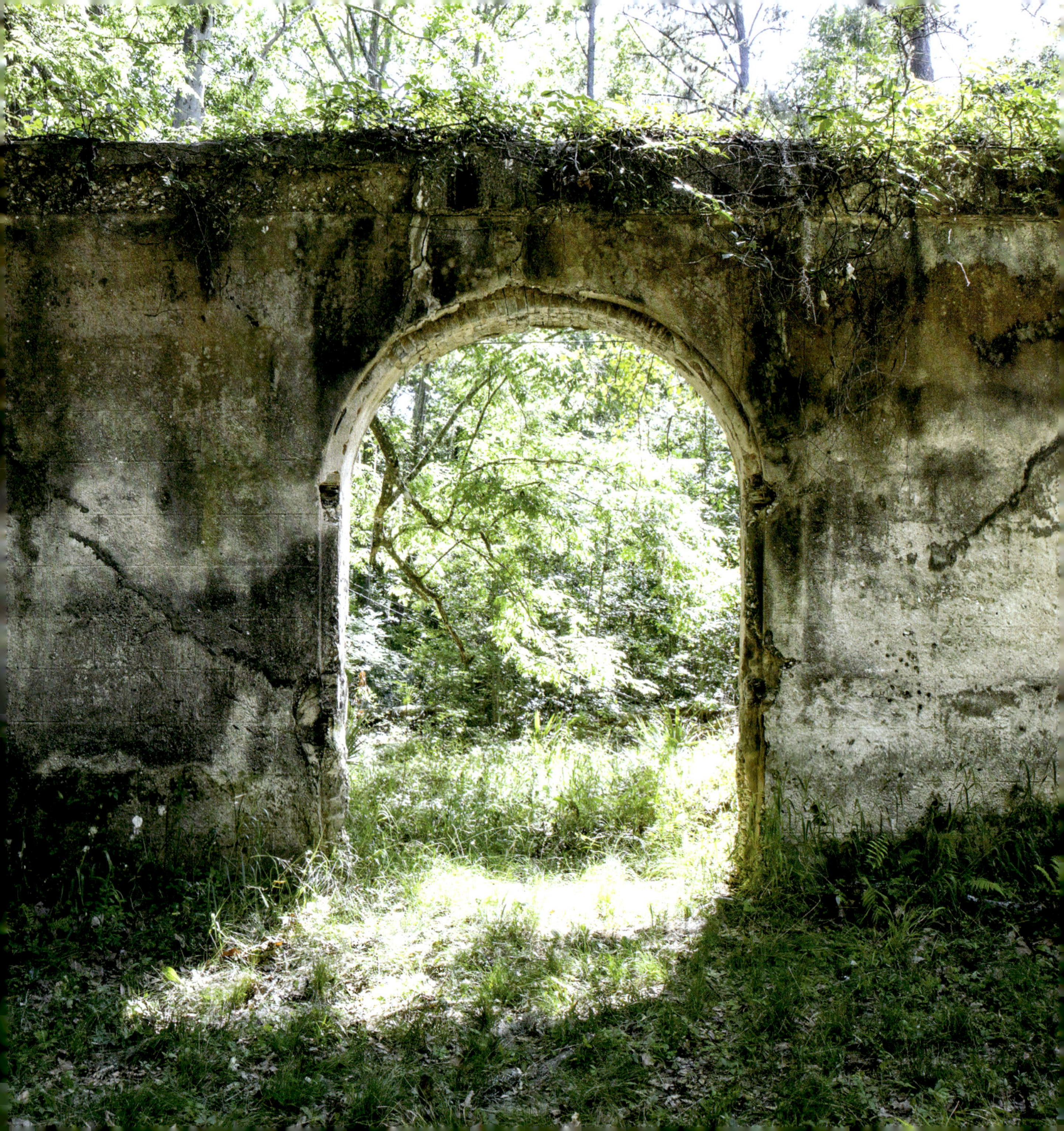

Introduction

AS CAPTIVATING as the time-worn ruins of Europe, intriguing structures built centuries ago of a unique oyster-shell concrete called tabby are historic treasures of the coastal Southeast. Most stand along a 275-mile-long stretch of coastline from St. Augustine, Florida, through the Georgia sea islands and Savannah to Charleston, South Carolina, tucked inside the incurving arc of the continent called the Georgia Bight.

The tabby trail closely parallels the federal Gullah Geechee Cultural Heritage Corridor, established in 2006 to recognize the historic significance of the Gullah Geechee people, their language, and their culture. The corridor runs from St. Johns County, Florida, to Pender County, North Carolina.

Tabby was North America's first concrete. Its chief components were oyster shells burned into lime, which served as the concrete's hardener, and aggregate made from whole or broken oyster shells. It was in use for about two centuries, from the late 1600s until after the Civil War, when enslaved Gullah Geechee were freed from the hard labor of tabby construction. In addition, portland cement became widely available in the United States in the 1870s. It produced a concrete stronger, longer lasting, and more waterproof than tabby.

Portland cement is manufactured of quarried limestone, clay, and other materials that are crushed, mixed with substances such as iron ore or fly ash, and kiln fired to form clinker, marble-sized gray balls. When the clinker cools, it is ground fine and mixed with gypsum and limestone to form the cement.

Although the geographic range of tabby construction was relatively narrow, and its tenure relatively brief, its time and place paralleled one of the most significant periods in North American history. While North Carolina, Virginia, and other sites on the Atlantic Seaboard are often described as the first part of the future United States to be settled by Europeans after contact, the earliest foreign settlements were on the southeastern coast.

It was here that Native Americans, African slaves, settlers from Spain, Britain, France, Portugal, and Minorca, and others mingled different beliefs and traditions, art and architecture, music, food, and languages into the great North American mosaic. All used tabby to build forts, plantation and town houses, slave cabins, churches, chapels of ease, seawalls, docks, barns, wells, garden walls, rice mills, sugar mills, distilleries, indigo-dying vats, mausoleums, and a variety of other structures, many still in remarkably good shape in spite of their advanced age.

Made entirely of indigenous coastal materials, tabby matches the subtle shades of its maritime environment. It mimics the soft grays of wet beaches, Spanish moss, and foggy coastal mornings in much the same way that adobe mirrors the warm tans of the desert Southwest. Apart from their beauty, old tabbies are storehouses of history, solid reminders of historic events and some of the people involved in the earliest days and subsequent growth of the future United States.

Tabby found a foothold on the southeastern coast because it was the ideal building material for its time and place. In North American colonies during the sixteenth and seventeenth centuries, bricks made of clay were rare, expensive, and heavy to transport. Though making and building with the oyster-shell concrete was hard, time-consuming work, tabby's physical components were abundant and free. Before the Civil War, enslaved Africans provided most of the labor.

Tabby had other advantages. It was fire resistant, rot proof, and impervious to termites. It was strong enough to stand up to hurricane winds and coastal floods. Thick tabby walls kept buildings warm in winter, cool in summer. People raised their homes high off the mosquito-ridden coastal lowlands on tabby foundations, drew water from tabby wells, protected their property with tabby seawalls, and cooked and heated with fireplaces and chimneys built of tabby bricks. Early colonists liked the reassuring Old World look of permanence and strength that tabby gave their structures in the unfamiliar, semitropical landscape of the southeastern coast.

Spanish colonists, the first Europeans to establish successful settlements in North America, created—or invented—tabby by combining Old World techniques and New World materials. European builders made lime, the hardener in most early concrete, by burning materials high in calcium carbonate, such as limestone, chalk, gypsum, bones, coral, seashells, and similar substances. They added the lime in small amounts to pounded mud walls to make them stronger and longer lasting.

In Spain, builders constructed *tapia* walls of earth, clay, sand, and aggregate, rammed into wooden forms. They upgraded the name to *tapia royale* when they added lime as a hardener. Early Spanish builders on the southeastern coast called the concrete they made with burned-shell lime and oyster-shell aggregate *tapia de ostione*, or oyster-shell tappy. English colonists may have anglicized the name to tabby.

The southeastern coast lacked the Old World's common lime-burning materials. The region has no native surface stone aside from a semi-rare sedimentary shellstone called coquina, found in only a few outcrops on Florida's Atlantic coast. Spanish builders found an ideal substitute for traditional Old World lime-making materials in ancient oyster shells, rich in calcium carbonate, that had been discarded by the earliest human inhabitants of the region.

After they arrived in North America from eastern Asia, the people who came to be known as American Indians slowly migrated east and south across the continent. The climate was colder and drier then, and they moved in search of freshwater and prehistoric big game such as woolly mammoths, mastodons, and giant ground sloths. These people were nomadic until the Late Archaic period (c. 3000 BCE–1000 BCE), when the climate became warmer and wetter, and the big game, their major food source, began a slide toward extinction.

Because of climate change, great estuaries similar to those of today formed along the southeastern coast. In search of new food sources, the earliest human inhabitants of the region were drawn to the shore by the estuarine abundance of high-protein seafood, including oysters. On the wave-washed sea islands and marsh-fringed mainland of the coastal Southeast, Native Americans established North America's first permanent settlements.

Today, the region is famous worldwide for its long chain of lovely, semitropical sea islands bordered on the east by the Atlantic Ocean and white sand beaches where endangered sea turtles nest on summer nights. Broad fields of unspoiled Spartina salt marsh spread to the west, often in bands more than five miles wide. The marshes and twisting tidal creeks and rivers separate the sea islands from the mainland.

Atlantic tides mingle with freshwater rivers terminating at the coast, forming a maze of sounds, estuaries, and other brackish waterways that provide a rich soup of nutrients essential to the coastal food chain. Oysters are abundant. They line the banks of almost every tidal river and creek in the region. Because of the Georgia Bight's extreme tides, oysters are exposed at the lower stages of the tide.

Indigenous peoples gathered them by hand from the muddy banks of creeks and rivers and from midstream oyster reefs accessible by dugouts. Oysters that spend their lives underwater, as they do in some regions, are harder to harvest without modern equipment. Over thousands of years, Native Americans consumed countless tons of shellfish, primarily oysters, and piled the empty shells along the banks of almost every tidal waterway in the region.

As the population of the area increased, social and ideological interactions became more complex. Native people began shaping discarded shells into giant rings, for reasons still debated by scholars, according to the archaeologist Mike Russo, an expert on shell rings with the National Park Service.

Shell rings are among the most intriguing and mysterious structures of the Late Archaic period. Constructed between 4,500 and 3,000 years ago, some of the rings were huge, more than twenty feet high and almost one thousand feet in diameter. About sixty of the ancient rings have so far been documented along the southeastern coast, including two exposed recently on Edisto Island, South Carolina, by hurricane tides. Most are in South Carolina and Georgia. Northeastern Florida has a few, and they are larger than the rings farther north. Many scholars now consider Late Archaic shell rings the earliest monumental architecture in the Americas, predating the pyramids of Central and South America and the earthen mounds of the Lower Mississippi River valley.

Most tabby was made with those ancient oyster shells. Shells discarded by later coastal Natives during the Woodland period (c. 500 BCE–1,100 CE) and the Mississippian period (c. 800–1,600 CE) were also used to make tabby. At colonial Fort Frederica on St. Simons Island, Georgia, builders included live oysters in their shells in some of their tabby mixes. There is no record of how the soldiers and citizens at Frederica reacted when the oysters spoiled.

After the Spanish settled on the southeastern coast, builders and their laborers gathered the ancient shells by the ton. They burned them for days at high temperatures to make quicklime, an ashy powder so caustic that early warriors used it to burn and blind their enemies. Before the advent of electric lights, stage managers heated quicklime to produce a strong illumination called a limelight. Performers today still take their bows in the limelight, although calcium oxide no longer produces the glow.

Spanish builders slaked, or watered, the quicklime and then mixed it with salt-free sand (tabby crumbles if it is made with materials containing salt), freshwater, and aggregate made of whole, broken, or crushed oyster shells washed clean by thousands of years of rain.

The Spanish used enslaved Native Americans and Africans to build the Castillo de San Marcos in St. Augustine, Florida. Such slavery was officially forbidden under Spanish law, but the law was frequently ignored. In other early settlements in North America, the Spanish conscripted Native Americans for hard labor, but were obligated to later release any survivors to resume their lives. Enslaved Africans and conscripted Natives worked on the giant fortress from 1672 to 1695 alongside Spanish builders and prisoners. They built with blocks of coquina, quarried on nearby Anastasia Island, and tabby made on site.

Construction of the fortification marked the first known use of tabby concrete, although oyster-shell lime had been made in 1580 by Spanish settlers in Florida and South Carolina. Residents there coated their wooden houses with lime stucco to protect them from flaming arrows fired during attacks by Native Americans.

Builders covered tabby structures with stucco topcoats primarily to protect them from rain. They sometimes scored the stucco to resemble more refined and expensive stone blocks. The topcoats were intended to be replaced every few years, but most have long since worn away, leaving the rough concrete, with its oyster-shell aggregate, exposed. Many people today prefer the more rugged look, although the lack of topcoats makes the old tabby vulnerable to weathering.

North America's colonial years were marked by frequent warfare as foreigners fought for land and wealth on the continent. Conflicts that began in Europe, Asia, and Africa spilled over into the coastal Southeast. The region's Indigenous peoples became embroiled in the warfare of foreign nations, and many of their precontact civilizations collapsed as a result. Caught in the middle, they died by the thousands from forced hard labor, starvation, enslavement, and attacks by other Europeans and hostile Natives allied with them, as well as imported diseases, against which they had no immunity.

Some southeastern Native American settlements suffered nearly 100 percent mortality. Members of the large Timucua chiefdom of northeastern Florida and southeastern Georgia were the first known Indigenous people on the continent to succumb to European colonialism. Many joined neighboring Natives in an effort to survive. Others accompanied their Spanish neighbors as they fled to Cuba at the end of the Seven Years' War.

Colonists imported enslaved Africans from scores of West African kingdoms to clear land, harvest naval stores, build houses and other structures, and grow cash crops such as indigo, rice, sugar, and sea island cotton. On the large, isolated plantations of the southeastern coast, the enslaved blended their languages and customs with those of their owners to form a rich creole culture now called Gullah Geechee. Hints of the musical language that resulted, the only English-based creole in North America, still sweeten the speech of older residents in the region. Many Gullah Geechee on the coast maintain African traditions brought to America during the transatlantic slave trade.

Tabby did not begin to receive widespread public recognition as an important historic building material until the late twentieth century. It is still not well known outside the coastal Southeast. Today, many old tabby structures are featured in local, state, and national parks, listed as National Heritage Sites, and included on the National Register of Historic Places. Some tabby sites have been named National Historic Landmarks, the nation's highest designation of historic value.

PART I *Florida*

IN 1565, Spain established St. Augustine on the northeastern coast of Florida, intent on driving newly settled French Protestants out of territory long claimed by Catholic Spain. It was the only one of the earliest settlement attempts to endure; most ended, often in disaster, after a few months or years.

The Spanish king charged St. Augustine's citizens with guarding the Spanish plate fleet as it transported gold and silver from mines in Mexico and Peru to Spain. The heavy, slow-moving ships made tempting prey for pirates and privateers as they rode the Gulf Stream north along the southeastern coast. In addition, Spanish friars used St. Augustine as a home base while they established missions in Indigenous villages in Florida and Georgia to convert the people to Catholicism.

In the late 1600s, enslaved Africans from English plantations in the Carolinas began escaping south to Spanish Florida via an early form of the Underground Railroad. Under Spanish law, slaves had a chance of relatively better treatment and even the possibility of freedom. Many ended up at Fort Mose, a farming community and outpost of the Castillo de San Marcos founded by the governor of Spanish Florida in 1738. The *castillo* was a magnificent tabby-and-coquina fortress built in the late 1600s.

In 1700, English forces from Carolina attacked St. Augustine during the War of the Spanish Succession. Spanish soldiers and citizens took refuge in the *castillo*, but the English torched the town. Over the next sixty years, most townspeople built their houses of fire-resistant tabby in a style mandated by the king of Spain. People entered the houses through courtyards surrounded by high garden walls built for privacy and protection.

The Spanish on the Eastern Seaboard retreated to Florida as the British pushed south. In 1763 during the Seven Years' War, Britain captured Havana, called the "Pearl

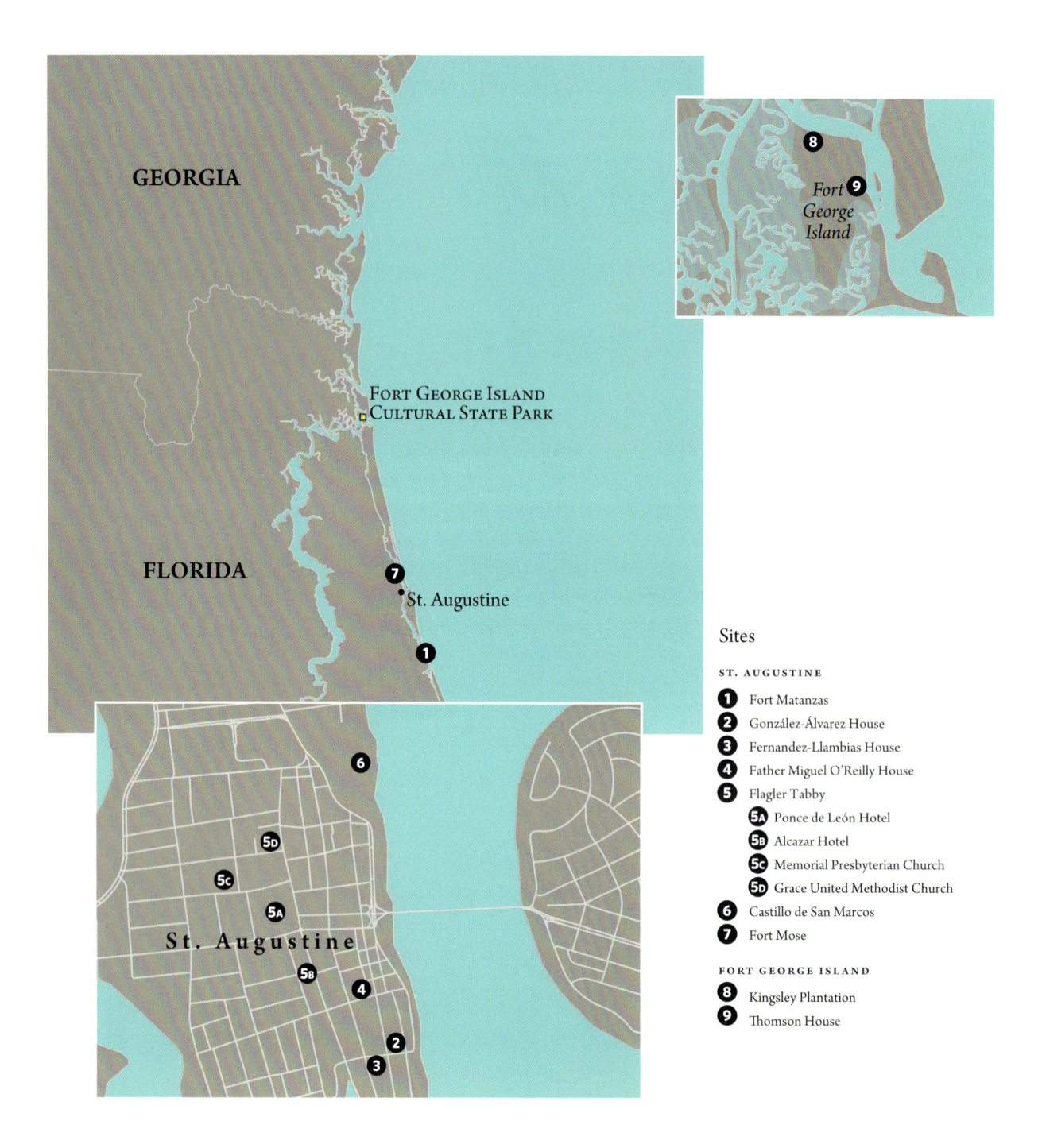

Sites

ST. AUGUSTINE

1. Fort Matanzas
2. González-Álvarez House
3. Fernandez-Llambias House
4. Father Miguel O'Reilly House
5. Flagler Tabby
   - 5A. Ponce de León Hotel
   - 5B. Alcazar Hotel
   - 5C. Memorial Presbyterian Church
   - 5D. Grace United Methodist Church
6. Castillo de San Marcos
7. Fort Mose

FORT GEORGE ISLAND

8. Kingsley Plantation
9. Thomson House

of the Antilles" by the Spanish. Cuba was the largest, and by far the most valuable, island in the Caribbean, so to get it back, Spain traded Florida to the British. During the British occupation of the peninsula, most Spanish residents, along with acculturated Indigenous people and free Africans, left St. Augustine for Cuba and other Spanish territories.

In the Treaty of Paris of 1783, which officially ended the American Revolution, Great Britain ceded East and West Florida to Spain in return for certain concessions, including retention of Gibraltar.

In an attempt to repopulate Florida, officials offered land to anyone who swore loyalty to the Spanish Crown. While St. Augustine regained its Spanish character, the city's hinterlands along the St. Johns and St. Marys Rivers were populated by Anglo-American planters who pledged their loyalty to the Spanish government and its legal system. One such settler, a British doctor from Charleston, South Carolina, imported more than 1,000 people from Minorca and other Mediterranean ports to grow indigo on his plantation, seventy miles south of St. Augustine. The doctor promised them land when their indentures ended; instead, he kept them imprisoned and mistreated them. The workers, collectively called Minorcans, escaped to St. Augustine in 1773, bringing their diverse culture to the already cosmopolitan town.

Early Americans established large plantations in Florida, including a Quaker slave trader who bought and impregnated a thirteen-year-old enslaved girl. He took her to his Florida plantation and called her his wife according to the extralegal system of *plaçage*, in which white Spanish and French men entered ersatz marriages with women of African, Native American, and Creole descent. The slave trader fathered children by other enslaved women. The status of his first African *plaçée* was shown by the apartment that she and their children occupied above the plantation's tabby kitchen near their owner's house. Other enslaved people lived in tabby cabins in the more distant slave quarters.

In 1810, President James Madison and other governmental officials used a rebellion in West Florida as a pretext to annex the area. The attempt failed, but Spanish Florida was devastated by the invasion. Spain was pressured into ceding Florida to the United States in a treaty of 1819.

The coquina-and-tabby Castillo de San Marcos was renamed Fort Marion, for the Revolutionary War hero Francis Marion, the famous Swamp Fox. The United States used the fort for decades as a prison for Native Americans from western plains states.

Some prisoners created unique ledger art, using discarded ledger books to document scenes of their ancestral villages, everyday activities, and horses.

In the late 1800s, the Standard Oil millionaire Henry Flagler built hotels and churches in St. Augustine by combining traditional tabby construction techniques with portland cement instead of burned-oyster-shell lime.

Because many Florida cities and towns today are relatively new, it can be difficult to remember that this part of the coastal Southeast was home to the first part of North America colonized by Europeans and constructed by Africans. St. Augustine, founded in 1565, is now more than 455 years old.

CHAPTER 1   *St. Augustine*

ST. AUGUSTINE is considered the nation's oldest municipality. It predated the first permanent British North American settlement, in Jamestown, Virginia, by forty-two years. In 1566, Martin Argüelles was born to Spanish colonists in St. Augustine. He was the first child of European parents born in what would become the United States, twenty-one years before Virginia Dare's birth in Roanoke, North Carolina, to British immigrants.

St. Augustine even hosted the first Thanksgiving, according to the late Florida historian Michael Gannon. European colonists offered prayers of thanksgiving after they arrived in the New World, often accompanied by a feast. The feast celebrated in St. Augustine in 1565 was held more than fifty years before the better-known celebration at Plymouth, Massachusetts. In his book *The Cross in the Sand: The Early Catholic Church in Florida, 1513–1870*, Gannon wrote that St. Augustine's thanksgiving "was the first community act of religion and thanksgiving in the first permanent settlement in the land."

He noted that the Spanish thanksgiving began with the sound of trumpets and artillery. Pedro Menéndez de Avilés, the town's founder, kissed a cross and reclaimed La Florida for Spain. The territory had briefly been occupied by French settlers after Juan Ponce de León landed on the Florida coast in 1513 and claimed the territory for Spain. Father Francisco Lopez celebrated Mass. Then the Spanish and Indigenous Timucua people sat down together to eat. Spanish foods probably included biscuits from the transatlantic voyage and *cocido*, a stew made with garbanzo beans, pork, and cabbage, and flavored with saffron and onions. The Timucua may have contributed venison, bear, wild turkey, and alligator meat, along with seafood, beans, corn, and squash. The Natives may have tasted Spanish wine for the first time.

The good relationship was fleeting. Within a year, the Timucua had tired of the Spanish pleas for food, women, and supplies. They resented Spanish efforts to conscript them for hard, unfamiliar labor. After little more than a decade, the Timucua were firing burning arrows at the council house they had lent the Spanish.

In 1566, Menéndez established the Spanish town of Santa Elena on today's Parris Island, South Carolina. It was in the same location as Charlesfort, a small settlement established four years earlier by French Huguenots fleeing religious persecution in Europe. The Huguenots had abandoned Charlesfort in less than a year and sailed back to Europe.

Santa Elena served as the capital of Spanish Florida for a decade. It was the first European colonial capital in today's United States. As governor of La Florida, Menéndez built a house there for himself and his family. In 1583, the Spanish abandoned Santa Elena. The capital had already been relocated to St. Augustine, where it remained for almost two and a half centuries.

In the early 1700s, St. Augustine boasted a formal plaza and marketplace, a hospital—albeit one described as a black hole—a gristmill operated by horsepower, and a new residential block on the south side of town. In the market, Native American women sold pottery, baskets, animal skins, tobacco, and dried leaves of the cassina (or yaupon) bush, from which Native people made the famous black drink used in their purification rituals. The women also sold fish, fishnets, dried meat, and corn.

In 1763, Spain traded Florida to Great Britain in return for Cuba and the Philippines, both captured by the British during Queen Anne's War (a phase of the Seven Years' War). Most of the Spanish Floridians, along with Native Americans, free and enslaved Africans, and other Catholic converts, moved to Cuba or other Spanish territories. The exodus marked the end of St. Augustine's first Spanish period.

When the noted botanist John Bartram visited St. Augustine in 1764, not long after the British takeover, he wrote, "Most of the common Spanish houses was [*sic*] built of oyster shells and mortar, as well as garden and yard walls." According to an official British survey at the time, more than 40 percent of the town's 342 private homes were built with tabby, 36 percent were constructed of tabby and coquina, a semi-rare sedimentary stone found in a few places in Florida, and 23 percent were made of wood. In just over sixty years, between the burning of the town by British troops in 1702 and 1763, when the British were granted Spanish Florida, St. Augustine had been transformed from a wooden town into a tabby town.

The houses built in St. Augustine between 1565 and 1821, when Spain ceded Florida to the United States, were described in detail by the late Albert Menucy, an author,

Fulbright scholar, and historian for the National Park Service in St. Augustine. Menucy was an authority on the history of Spanish Florida, and his work is credited with sparking major, ongoing preservation efforts in the old coastal city.

The British period lasted only two decades. Spain fought on the side of the Patriots in the American Revolution, and the new government of the United States returned Florida to the Spanish as a reward.

St. Augustine's second Spanish period began in 1784 and lasted for thirty-seven years. After the British occupation, the once-isolated colonial town became more international than Spanish by forming thriving trade relationships with the United States and the wider world. The population was also more diverse. People of Spanish, British, and African ancestry rubbed shoulders with Minorcans, Italians, Greeks, Seminoles, and newcomers from Switzerland as well as citizens of the newly formed United States.

In 1821, St. Augustine and the rest of Spanish Florida were ceded to the United States, ending Spain's long tenure in the Southeast. The cession was part of the complex negotiations to establish the boundary between New Spain and the United States. Not counting the 21 years under British rule, Spain held territory on the North American continent for 256 years, longer than the United States has been a nation.

During the early twentieth century, the town began building a tourist industry based on its advanced age. Property owners made outrageous claims about the vintage of their houses and other properties in an attempt to appeal to visitors. To attract attention, they added embellishments such as towers with crenellations to their houses. Many of those inappropriate additions and alterations have since been removed and the structures restored to a more authentic look. The old part of town is a National Landmark Historic District, and many of its structures are individually listed as historically important.

St. Augustine is a fascinating place to visit, touristy but not tacky. Even though the British destroyed most of the early eighteenth-century tabby houses, a few houses retain features such as layers of tabby floors dating back to the early 1700s. Many still-standing courtyard walls are tabby.

Today, the coastal city displays its genuine past with pride. Archaeologists, historians, anthropologists, and others have dug beneath St. Augustine's sandy soil and pored over countless historic documents. Scholars have debunked popular myths to give a more accurate, but no less fascinating, portrait of the oldest permanently occupied European town in the United States.

SITE 1

Fort Matanzas

1740

8635 State Road A1A South

Rattlesnake Island National Historic Monument

HISTORIC SIGNIFICANCE: About fifteen miles south of St. Augustine, Fort Matanzas is one of only two fortresses in the world built of coquina stone and tabby. Its name, which means "massacres" in Spanish, dates to 1565 when the Spanish murdered scores of Frenchmen at the inlet where the fort was built 175 years later. The massacre marked the beginning of the long and bitter struggle between Spain and other countries for territory in North America.

The Spanish began building Fort Matanzas in 1740 following a British siege of St. Augustine earlier that year. During the siege, British ships blocked Matanzas Inlet, which feeds into the tidal river providing a back door to St. Augustine. Five Spanish ships from Cuba ran the blockaded inlet to bring supplies to the Spanish soldiers and residents sheltered in St. Augustine's near-impregnable Castillo de San Marcos, but the Spanish knew blockade-runners might not succeed in the future. The inlet needed to be guarded by a fort.

Fort Matanzas was still unfinished in 1742 when the British approached the inlet with a dozen ships. The small fort fulfilled its mission. Spanish soldiers fired cannons from the bastions, forcing the British ships to retreat. It was a golden moment for Fort Matanzas, marking the first and last time its cannons were fired at an enemy.

Today, the outpost on Rattlesnake Island overlooks Matanzas Inlet and the southern end of the Matanzas River.

Three years before the 1565 massacre, the celebrated French sea captain Jean Ribault established a fortified settlement called Charlesfort on today's Parris Island, South Carolina. Ribault sailed back to Europe for additional colonists and supplies, intending to return in six months. He was delayed for more than three years.

In less than a year, the Charlesfort soldiers on Parris Island—hungry, in conflict with the Natives, ill, and discouraged—abandoned the fledgling settlement and headed back to France in a crude boat they built themselves. Two years later, in 1564, Ribault's second in command, Lieutenant René de Laudonnière sailed to the Florida coast and established Fort Caroline near the mouth of the St. Johns River in today's Jacksonville.

Philip II, the king of Spain, was outraged. After Ponce de León landed on the Florida coast in 1513, Spain claimed all the known continent, west to the Mississippi River and

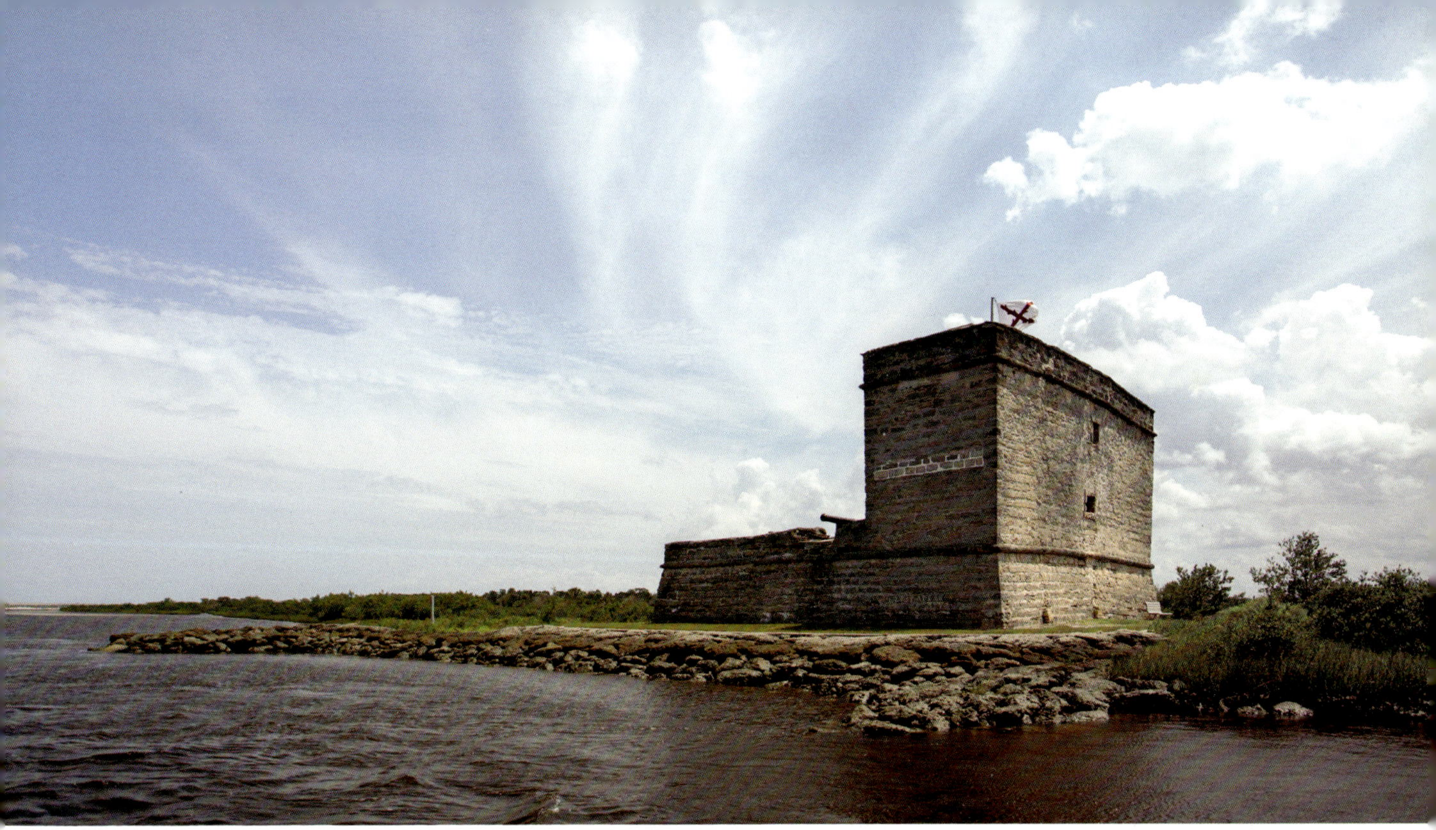

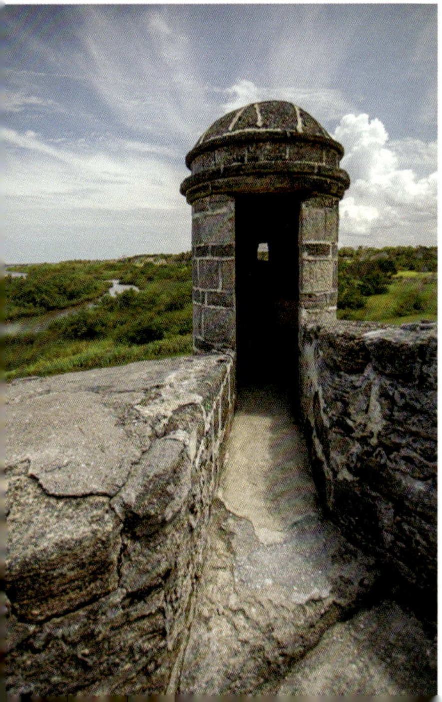

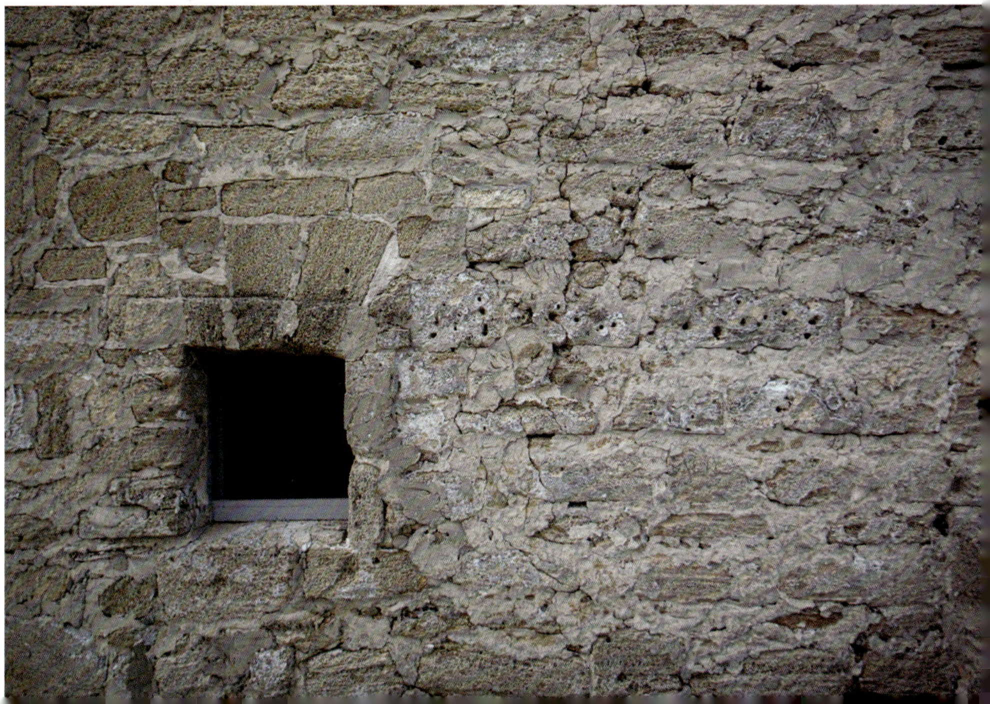

north to Newfoundland. Ponce de León named the territory La Florida.

The Spanish king considered the French settlements a declaration of war. Even more horrifying to his majesty was the fact that the French were Huguenots, that is, Protestants. Although the Huguenots were followers of John Calvin, the Catholic Church branded all Protestants as Lutherans and reviled them as Satan's storm troops.

In Europe, Protestants were being tortured and killed by Catholic inquisitors. Ribault and his Huguenots wanted to start new lives in North America to escape religious persecution. And like the Spanish, the French had other motives: they wanted to claim territory in North America, exploit its riches, and convert the Indigenous people to their faith.

Like Charlesfort, Fort Caroline struggled to survive. Laudonnière had been promised support for his expedition, but only one small shipload of goods ever arrived. He was preparing to abandon the fort and return to France when Ribault finally showed up with the promised supplies and reinforcements in August 1565.

Pedro Menéndez de Avilés and his ships arrived on the coast of northeastern Florida at almost the same time. The subsequent clash between the French and Spanish led to the massacres of the French at Fort Caroline and at the inlet later named Matanzas, south of St. Augustine. Some of the St. Augustine colonists damned their leader's actions as unnecessarily cruel. But others, according to Gonzalo Solís de Merás, the brother-in-law and biographer of Menéndez, approved of the killings: "Because the French were more numerous, they might have destroyed us."

17

Almost two centuries later, the Spanish built Fort Matanzas to guard the inlet, the tidal river, and the back passage to St. Augustine. The fort was later abandoned, and the masonry structure deteriorated until restoration began in 1916. It is now a National Historic Landmark open to the public.

The only way to get to the fort is by boat. Ferry rides and guided tours are available through the National Park Service, which manages the property. Because of shifting sands, the fort now lies about half a mile farther from the Atlantic than it did when enemy ships had to sail within range of the fort's cannons to reach the Matanzas River.

Pedro Menéndez de Avilés, 1519–1574

Pedro Menéndez was the classic Spanish conquistador. He was born to landed gentry in northern Spain and became familiar as a boy with the rituals, nepotism, and backstabbing of the royal court. As a naval officer, he developed connections in high places. When Philip II of Spain married Mary I of England, the daughter of Henry VIII, Menéndez escorted Philip's ship to England for the royal wedding.

Menéndez rose to the rank of admiral in Spain's navy. He gained the king's favor with daring and colorful exploits at sea, which included driving pirates from the Spanish coast. He shared the rich prizes he captured with the Crown. The king chose Menéndez to lead a fleet of ships to the New World to escort Spain's treasure fleet on one of its semiannual trips home from the Americas. Spain had grown wealthy beyond belief from gold and silver mined in Mexico and Peru. The heavy-laden, slow-moving galleons, riding low in the water, were vulnerable to pirates and ships from enemy countries.

Menéndez's only son, Juan, who captained one of the escort ships, was lost during the voyage. Desperate to return to the Americas to search for him, Menéndez began raising funds for the expedition. The Spanish admiral also wanted to claim land for himself and his family in the New World. Catholic to the core, he shared the determination of the Crown and the Church to eliminate the Protestants who were flooding Europe and threatening what Catholics considered the one true faith.

Menéndez signed a contract with Philip II to outfit a fleet of ships to carry tools, supplies, weapons, and about fifteen hundred colonists, including five hundred enslaved Africans, as well as hundreds of horses, sheep, pigs, and other stock to establish at least two settlements in La Florida.

The king granted Menéndez almost unlimited authority as *adelantado*, a sort of self-financed entrepreneur. The license lasted as long as Menéndez succeeded. If he failed, he would not only loose his investment but could be hanged for treason. In addition, Phillip named Menéndez the first governor of La Florida and promised him the noble title of marquis. The king granted him thousands of acres of land and the right to distribute more land to colonists as he saw fit. Since many of Menéndez's relatives were part of the expedition, this allowed him to increase his family's wealth and power.

Menéndez was still preparing for the expedition in 1565 when Philip learned that French Huguenots had founded settlements in La Florida, which Spain had claimed since 1513. The king provided additional funds so that Menéndez could speed up his departure and "kill and burn" any Protestants he encountered in North America.

As soon as Menendez arrived on the coast of northeastern Florida, he attacked the French fleet in the mouth of

Spanish admiral Pedro Menéndez de Avilés (1519–1574), engraving by Francisco de Paula Martí (1762–1827)

the St. Johns River near Fort Caroline. The crews of the French ships cut their anchor lines and escaped to the open sea. Menéndez, whose ships were slower, abandoned the pursuit and sailed south to scout the location for his new settlement.

Against the advice of his top lieutenant, René de Laudonnière, Jean Ribault pursued the Spanish with his ships and most of the soldiers from Fort Caroline. He was organizing offshore to attack the Spanish at the site that Menéndez had chosen for St. Augustine when a violent storm, possibly a hurricane, swept the coast. Ribault's ships were wrecked, and the survivors were strung out along miles of beaches south of St. Augustine. Their only option was to walk back to Fort Caroline.

With most of its soldiers gone, the French fort was vulnerable. Menéndez marched his troops from St. Augustine about forty miles north to Fort Caroline. They traveled night and day through dense woodlands and swamps in the storm's driving rain and high winds. The troops carried twenty long ladders for scaling Fort Caroline's palisades.

When they arrived at the fort, Menéndez and his men stood chest-deep in swamp water all night, waiting to launch a surprise attack at dawn. The undefended fort was an easy conquest. Menéndez had the Huguenots at Fort Caroline put to death, sparing only women, children, and a handful of Frenchmen who claimed to be Catholic or who had skills useful to St. Augustine. Wounded in the attack, Laudonnière hid in the flooded marshes overnight with a handful of other escapees and later sailed back to France.

In a letter to the king of Spain, Menéndez described the capture of the fort and the hanging of "all those we found in it, because they had built it without Your Majesty's permission and because they were scattering the odious Lutheran doctrine in these Provinces." He renamed the French fort San Mateo and ordered the bodies of the slain Huguenots hung on trees outside the palisade. He posted a sign that read, "Not as Frenchmen but as Lutherans," as a warning to other Protestants. Three years later, the French officer Dominique de Gourgues attacked Fort San Mateo. In retribution, he hung the bodies of the Spanish soldiers his troops had killed outside the palisades with a sign saying, "Not as Spaniards but as murderers."

As Menéndez and his troops headed back to St. Augustine, Natives informed them that French shipwreck survivors were gathered at an inlet about fifteen miles south of the Spanish settlement. Father Francisco Lopez, Menéndez's chaplain and chronicler, recorded what happened when Spanish troops reached the inlet and spotted French campfires on the opposite shore.

Menéndez had one of his men row him to the middle of the waterway. A French soldier swam out to meet them. The Frenchman said the shipwreck victims were hungry and "stated that all, or at least the greater part of them, were Lutherans," Father Lopez wrote. By identifying the castaways as Protestants, the hapless French soldier signed their death warrants. Menéndez demanded the surrender of the French. He had them send over their arms and flags and then brought the troops over in small groups. Spanish soldiers took them behind the sand dunes, out of sight of the French waiting on the opposite shore, and killed them "with swords and pikes."

Father Lopez asked Menéndez for clemency for some of the French. "As I was a priest, and had bowels of mercy, I begged him to grant me the favor of sparing those whom we might find to be Christians . . . All the others were executed, because they were Lutherans and enemies of our Holy Catholic faith." A second massacre occurred about ten days later when Menéndez learned that more French shipwreck victims were stranded at the same inlet. The expedition leader, Jean Ribault, was among the French whom Menéndez subsequently massacred at the inlet.

Menéndez witnessed only the first dozen years of the two towns he founded: St. Augustine in Florida and Santa Elena in South Carolina. In 1567 the king recalled him to Spain to prepare an armada to fight the British, a task that would take years. In return, Menéndez was named governor of Cuba, one of the most important Spanish holdings in the New World. He never returned to La Florida.

Menéndez died of typhus in Spain in 1574 at age fifty-five. He made his mark on history by founding the first enduring European settlement in what became the United States. Many consider him one of North America's founding fathers.

SITE 2

González-Álvarez (Oldest) House

c. 1723

14 St. Francis Street

National Historic Landmark

HISTORIC SIGNIFICANCE: The house is the oldest surviving Spanish colonial residence in Florida. It displays the evolution of housing styles over three centuries by Spanish, British, and early U.S. citizens. The house, which has been the subject of numerous scholarly studies, may be one of the best-documented historic homes in the United States. It has at least four layers of tabby floors.

In the late nineteenth and early twentieth centuries, as luxurious new hotels brought flocks of visitors to St. Augustine, residents looked for ways to cash in on the tourist traffic. Visitors were fascinated by historic properties—the older, the better. Having a famous historic figure associated with the site was a bonus.

In 1904, a pioneering female physician, Luella Day McConnell, owned a well in the old part of St. Augustine. McConnell was an adventurous woman. She had spent time in the Klondike during the gold rush and wrote a book about her experiences.

To attract tourists to her St. Augustine property, she enlarged her well and named it the Fountain of Youth. She also circulated the myth that Ponce de León, the first European known to have landed in North America after contact, drank from the well when he discovered Florida in 1513. Scholars say it is unlikely León ever set foot in the St. Augustine area; his fabled landing was probably more than one hundred miles south. Reports that Ponce de León was in search of a spring reputed to cure impotence are probably not accurate, either, but were promulgated by rivals to embarrass the famed explorer.

Today, the privately owned Fountain of Youth Archaeological Park is an attraction that includes the location of the oldest Spanish mission on the continent, Nombre de Dios, which dates back to the founding of St. Augustine in 1565. The site of the mission and its accompanying cemetery have been well documented by experts. But there is no evidence that Louella McConnell's well was the fabled Fountain of Youth, even if such a fountain ever existed.

The owner of the González-Álvarez House jumped on the antiquities bandwagon even earlier than McConnell. In the late 1800s, Dr. Charles P. Carver, a dentist, purchased the property and advertised it as the oldest house in the United States. The resulting flood of tourists disrupted Carver's dentistry practice to the point that he abandoned

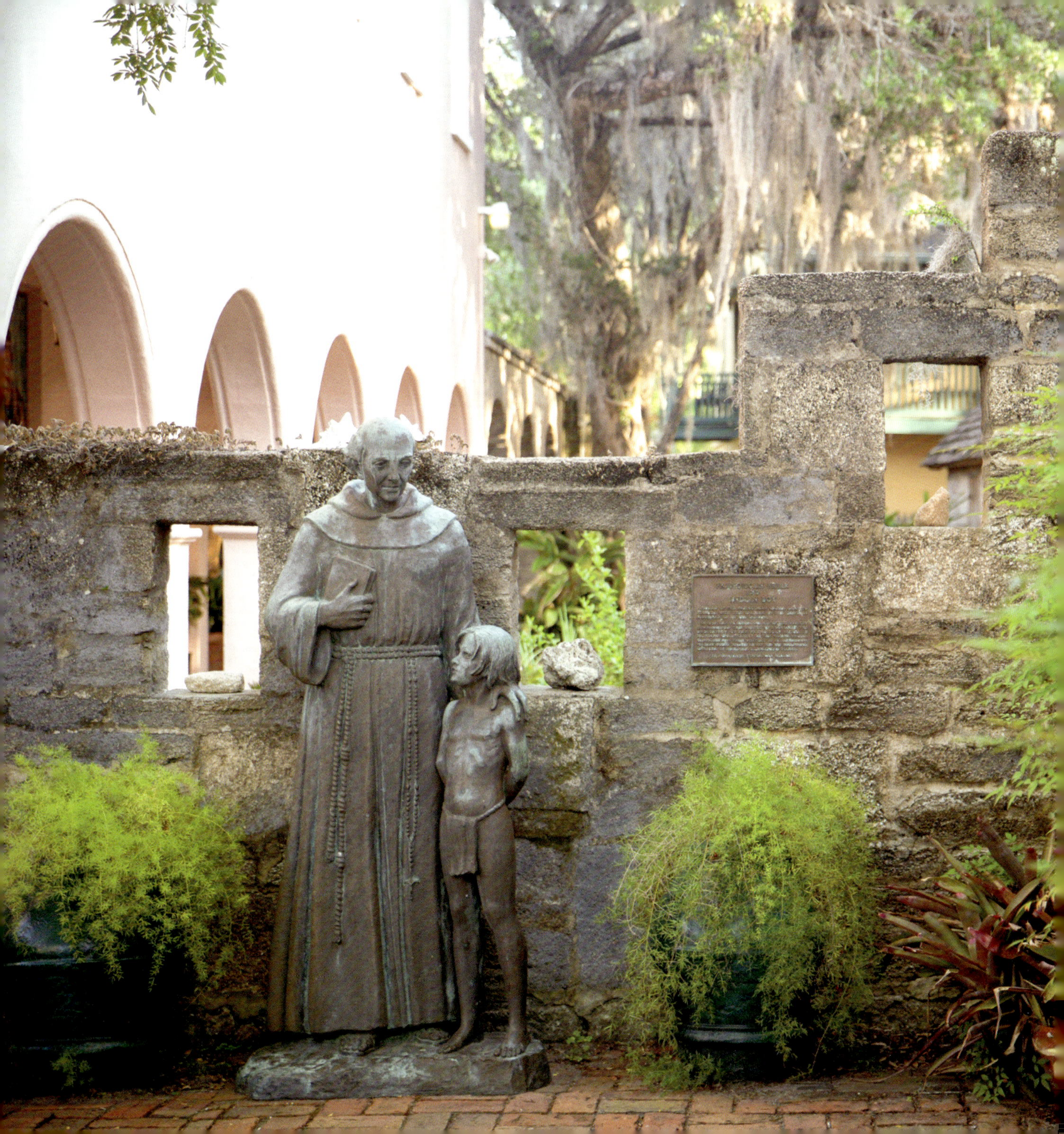

it to give paid tours. Other St. Augustine property owners put up signs proclaiming that their houses were even older than the González-Álvarez House. In 1917, the well-known American humorist Ring Lardner wrote about St. Augustine's obsession with antiquity:

> First, we went to St. George Street and visited the oldest house in the United States. Then we went to Hospital Street and seen [*sic*] the oldest house in the United States. Then we turned the corner and went down St. Francis Street and inspected the oldest house in the United States. Then we dropped into a soda fountain and I had an egg phosphate, made from the oldest egg in the Western Hemisphere. We passed up lunch and got into a carriage drawn by the oldest horse in Florida, and we rode through the country all afternoon and the driver told us some o' the oldest jokes in the book.

The Carvers remodeled the González-Álvarez House to make it more alluring to tourists. They paneled the coquina-and-tabby walls with wood salvaged from a church. They had an eyebrow dormer installed, along with a hip and gable roof covered with novelty shingles. Their finishing touch was a two-story round tower they added to the northeastern corner. The tower's first story was poured concrete topped by a coquina-and-tabby second story with a cornice of conch shells. The tower was roofed with red clay tiles.

Although the home lost its colonial charm, it was transformed into an outstanding example of Queen Anne architecture from the late Victorian period and of local materials in use in the Carvers' time. They owned the home until 1898, when they sold it to the Henderson family, who added an apartment over a garage built to accommodate their car, nicknamed the Red Devil. In 1911, the house was sold to the South Beach Alligator Farm and Museum of Marine Curiosities, which listed the Oldest House as one of its tourist attractions.

Ring Lardner's article may have helped spur research by the St. Augustine Historical Society, which launched an investigation in 1917 to determine which house was the oldest. Society officials concluded that the González-Álvarez House deserved the title and purchased it. Scholars today focus on the fact that the house reflects aspects of history and architecture of national and international significance.

The home's name comes from two Spanish owners: Tomás González y Hernández and Gerónimo Álvarez. González built the original coquina-and-tabby structure in the 1720s and lived there with his family during the first Spanish period, which ended in 1763. Gerónimo Álvarez purchased the house in 1790. He and his descendants occupied the dwelling for almost a century.

Researchers believe the original part of the present structure arose on the ruins of two wooden houses, the earliest built as long ago as 1650. The second wooden structure was destroyed in 1702 when the British attacked St. Augustine and burned the town to the ground. When the British acquired Florida in 1763 and held it for two decades, they enlarged some of St. Augustine's nicer coquina-and-tabby houses, adding second stories with wood-shingled hipped roofs, doors that opened directly to the street instead of into a walled courtyard, and windows with glass panes instead of wooden shutters or grille work.

The original structure built by González was a simple two-room one-story dwelling, twenty by forty feet, built of coquina blocks laid with tabby mortar. The walls were plastered with oyster-shell lime inside and out. The floor was poured tabby treated with linseed oil to make it look like marble.

The house sat vacant for more than a decade until a British officer, Sergeant Major Joseph Peavett, bought the property in 1775. He and his wife, Mary, opened a door directly to the street in order to convert one of the downstairs rooms

Oldest
House
Oldest House Museums and Gardens
Open10am to 5pm
GONZALEZ-ALVAREZ
HOUSE
(THE OLDEST HOUSE)

Oldest
House
Oldest House Museums and
Open10am to 5pm

to a tavern, which catered to soldiers in the barracks across St. Francis Street. After Florida was ceded back to Spain in 1783, some British occupants, including Peavett and his wife, opted to stay in St. Augustine, where they were prospering.

During the second Spanish period, in 1790, Gerónimo Álvarez bought the house when it was auctioned to satisfy debts.

In 1925, concerned about the structure's historic integrity, the St. Augustine Historical Society removed Carver's paneling to expose original wooden beams and coquina-and-tabby walls. A writer for the *St. Augustine Record* described the work: "This paneling was most attractive, but not at all typical of the olden time the structure really represents," the reporter wrote. "The effect is not as pretty, but far more interesting to the seeker after the old, the ancient and the unusual."

In 1959–60, the society undid some of the later additions, based on archaeological research done during the 1950s. Carver's concrete-and-coquina tower from the late 1880s was removed, as was the garage and upstairs apartment. The enclosed balcony and loggia entrance on the east end were left intact because they were added during the British period.

The structure now reflects four hundred years of St. Augustine history—the two Spanish colonial periods, the British colonial period, and the American territorial period (1821–45). The first-floor rooms are arranged the way they would have been when the house was built. The second story reflects the twenty-year British period and the second Spanish period.

The house is now part of the society's Oldest House Museum Complex, which encompasses two museums, a gallery with antique maps and rotating exhibits, an ornamental garden, and a museum store. Guided tours of the complex are offered every half hour.

Mary (Maria) Evans Peavett, 1730–1792

Sergeant Major John Peavett, a well-to-do paymaster for the British Army who was stationed in St. Augustine during the two-decade British period, purchased the house at 14 St. Francis Street in 1765.

His wife, Mary Evans of Charleston, or Maria, as she was called later by the Spanish, was a former tenant of the house. Mary's first husband was Joseph Fenwick, a British soldier. When he was sent to Havana, Mary was one of five women allowed to accompany their husbands to Cuba. The British were fighting the Spanish for control of the strategically located island. It was not uncommon then for wives to accompany their husbands to battle sites. Behind the lines, they cared for ill and wounded soldiers, cooked, did laundry, and made extra money by baking cakes or pies for the troops. After the British captured Cuba, Spain traded Florida to the British in order to get Cuba back.

Fenwick was transferred to St. Augustine in 1763, and the couple rented the house on St. Francis Street. Because of her nursing experience, Mary offered her services as a midwife. Often, she was paid in kind instead of in cash: patients gave her mirrors, thimbles, cloth, knives, and other small items of value. Because of her skill at treating wounds, curing illnesses, and providing relief for pain, knowledge gleaned from nursing soldiers and from her midwifery practice, she was often called on in lieu of a physician.

Midwives were among the few respected female professionals. Mary's work allowed her to meet St. Augustine's townspeople, including influential citizens who helped advance her medical career.

After the British period ended, a handful of English-speaking residents opted to stay in St. Augustine. Although there was a legacy of tension between the Spanish and British, Mary delivered Spanish as well as British babies and nursed Spanish residents. The Spanish began calling her Maria, claiming her as their own. She cemented the relationship by joining the Catholic Church.

Fenwick died in an accident. Unable to afford the rent on the house, Maria found quarters elsewhere. In 1778, she married Sergeant Major Peavett, and the couple purchased the Francis Street residence where Maria had lived with her first husband. They added a frame and masonry second story, a fireplace and chimney, a wood-shingled roof, and windows with glass panes.

The Peavetts made extra money by operating a small tavern downstairs. It was in an ideal location: a former monastery across St. Francis Street had been converted into barracks for British soldiers. Along with Peavett's salary and funds from Maria's midwifery, the thrifty, hard-working couple acquired several rental houses in town as well as large land grants in rural areas nearby.

To lure new settlers to Florida, the British offered tax-free land grants to anyone who would develop the property. The Peavetts intended to establish plantations on their land, but Joseph Peavett became disabled by a series of strokes and fevers, and was confined to an upstairs bedroom for almost a decade. Maria nursed him until his death in 1786.

After Peavett's death, Maria enlarged the St. Francis Street house again with a two-story addition containing three small rooms on each floor. She enclosed the loggia side entrance built by the González family and topped it with a balcony. Maria probably chose the soft gray-green color of the siding.

The oldest house in St. Augustine, shown in a stereograph by George Baker, c. 1886

Depressed and exhausted by her husband's long ordeal, Maria, then fifty-six, rushed into marriage with John Hudson, a charming Irishman twenty years her junior who drank, gambled, and accumulated large debts. Hudson quickly ran through Maria's money and property holdings, and 14 St. Francis Street was auctioned in 1790 to pay Hudson's creditors. He was jailed in the Castillo de San Marcos for insulting the governor and was later killed while attacking a guard.

Maria, who adored her young husband, buried him on rural land she owned, and she lived on the property in near seclusion with her grown foster son until her death a few years later. Her poignant story was told in *Maria*, the second novel in a best-selling Florida trilogy by the noted author Eugenia Price.

SITE 3

Fernandez-Llambias House

c. 1755

31 St. Francis Street

National Historic Landmark

HISTORIC SIGNIFICANCE: The coquina house with its polished tabby floor is among a handful of structures dating back to St. Augustine's first Spanish period. Modified during the British period (1763–84), it exhibits details of both Spanish and English vernacular architecture.

The house is named for two former owners. The first was Pedro Fernandez, who owned it until 1763, when Spanish Florida was ceded to the British for two decades. The house's second name comes from two sisters, Antonica and Ana Llambias, who owned the property during the late 1800s. They were descendants of Minorcans who escaped from a southern Florida plantation run by a British doctor who treated them as slaves and abused them. The Minorcans settled in St. Augustine, bringing their Mediterranean culture to the region.

The Llambias sisters grew a luxuriant garden in their courtyard, planting orange, guava, and banana trees, a pride of India tree, and a large vegetable plot. When saltwater flooded in from the Matanzas River and Maria Sanchez Creek, it covered the courtyard and ruined their beautiful garden.

The original style of the Fernandez-Llambias House was derived from the traditional masonry homes of southern Spain. St. Augustine houses reflect architectural influences dating to first- and second-century Romans and later to the Moors, who occupied Spain for around seven centuries (c. 750–1492).

The style traveled to the Caribbean and to South and Central America with Spanish colonists during the sixteenth and seventeenth centuries. The Spanish Crown dictated not only the layout of new towns in the Americas but also the design of residential construction. In Spanish Florida, the style came to be known as the St. Augustine Plan. It featured rectangular houses with one long side built flush to a narrow front street. High walls surrounded a large rear courtyard. Access to the interior was through a door-like gate in the wall that led into the courtyard.

The Fernandez-Llambias house was a variation on the St. Augustine Plan, with the main entrance located under a covered porch instead of through an open loggia. The original house was a one-story, one-room masonry structure with a poured tabby floor. Scholars say the original roof may have been made of poured tabby slabs surrounded by

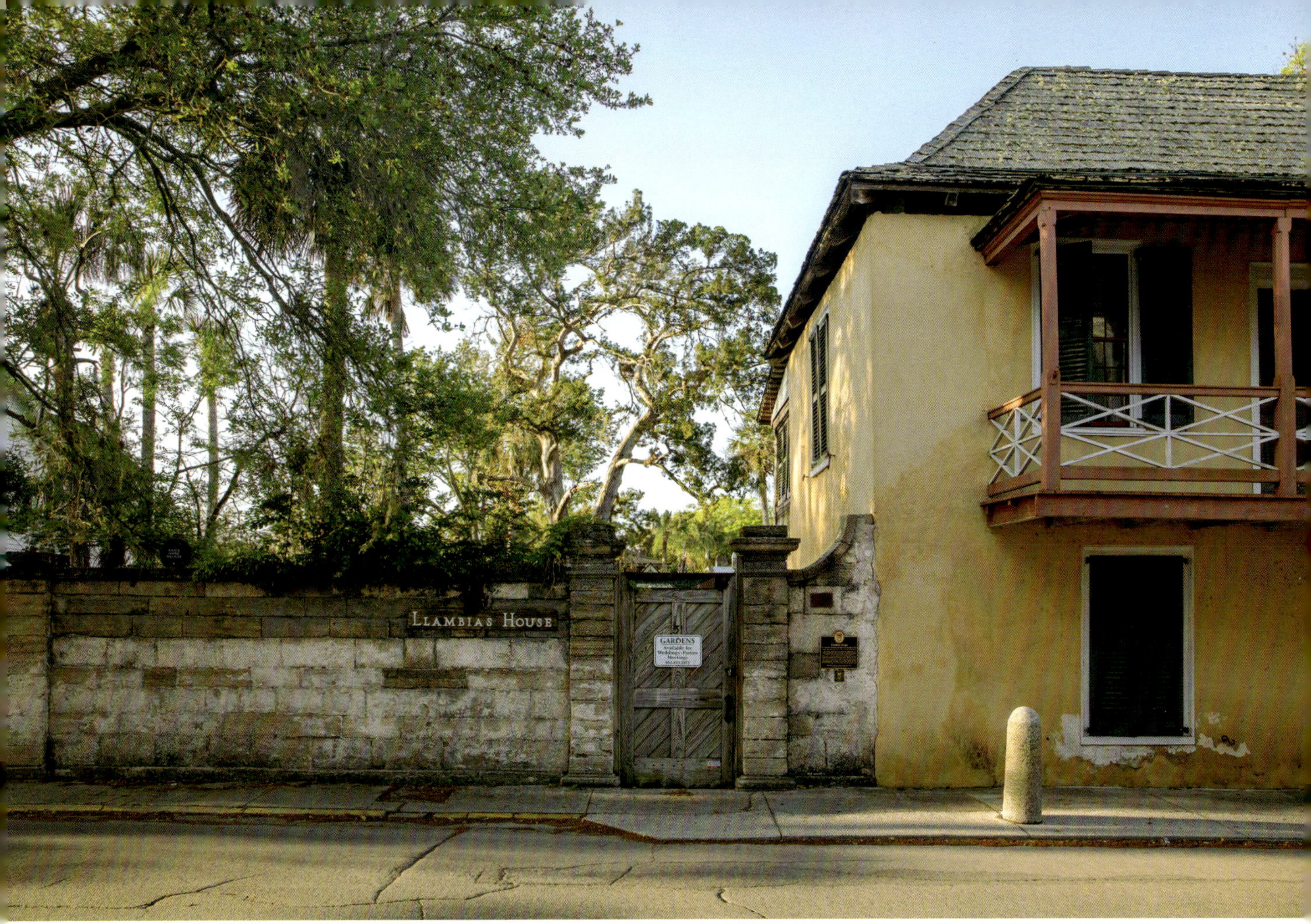
Llambias House
GARDENS

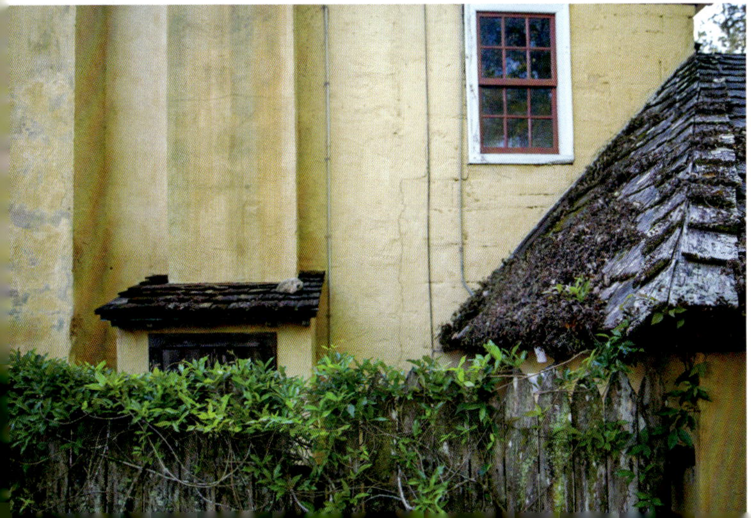

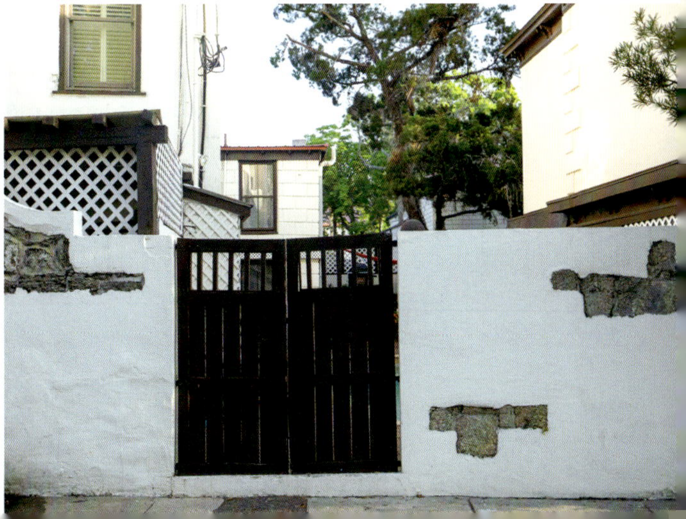

a parapet equipped with rainspouts. The house was oriented to catch breezes in summer and shelter the residents from cold winter nor'easters. There were no windows in the north facade, which featured thicker walls than the rest of the house and offered excellent insulation.

Like other Spanish houses in the town, the Fernandez-Llambias house was designed as a miniature fortress to protect its owners if St. Augustine were attacked. The style also provided the occupants with privacy. Windows were covered with slatted, locally made wooden blinds called *rejas* that could be opened to admit light and air. The *rejas* also allowed people inside to observe activities in the street without being seen.

High walls surrounded the large courtyard, where residents grew fruit trees and vegetables, raised chickens and pigs, and stabled horses. A well provided drinking water. Most cooking was done over braziers inside the house, but in some houses of the same style, a detached kitchen sat at the rear of the courtyard.

When built, the Fernandez-Llambias house was in a poor part of town, across the street from a monastery. When the British took over, they converted the monastery into a barracks, whose free-spending soldiers made the area more affluent. But British soldiers wreaked havoc on St. Augustine's wood and tabby houses, too. After a visit in 1765, the naturalist John Bartram remarked that the soldiers had "pulled down about half the town to make firewood, which was scarce."

At the end of the American Revolution, in 1783, when Florida was ceded back to Spain for aiding the Patriot cause, only nineteen tabby houses were still standing. The mistreatment of property by British troops quartered in private houses prompted ratification of the Third Amendment to the U.S. Constitution, which restricts the military occupation of private dwellings in peacetime.

In 1821, when Spanish Florida became an American territory, a pair of Minorcan brothers named Josef and Peter Antonio Menucy owned the house. They divided each floor into two rooms and built a wooden balcony above the street. The chimney was extended to serve a fireplace on the second floor. The back porch, with its masonry arches, was enlarged to run the full thirty-six-foot length of the house. A staircase gave access to the open second-floor gallery. The new roof was hipped and shingled in wood.

The late Albert Manucy, the highly regarded National Park Service historian and an expert on the houses of St. Augustine, was a descendant of Josef Menucy. Josef was among the indentured Minorcans that Europeans brought to Florida to labor on a Florida plantation. He and other Minorcans fled to sanctuary in St. Augustine in 1777 during the British period.

Father Pedro Camps, c. 1730–1790

In 1768, more than fourteen hundred Europeans set out across the Atlantic during Florida's twenty-year British period. They were indentured laborers hired by Andrew Turnbull, a Scottish doctor-entrepreneur who recruited them from Minorca and other Mediterranean ports in Greece, Italy, and Corsica. Because the majority came from the island of Minorca, off the western coast of Spain, they were collectively called Minorcans. They were the largest single immigrant group to arrive en masse in colonial America.

They were lured to Florida by Dr. Turnbull's promise to give them land and money when they completed their terms of service on his 100,000-acre plantation. The doctor and his investors had grandiose visions of making huge profits by growing indigo at their New Smyrna plantation, about seventy miles south of St. Augustine.

The Atlantic crossing was hard. More than two hundred Minorcans died during the voyage. They were given last rites by Father Pedro Camps, a thirty-eight-year-old Catholic priest who traveled with the Minorcans to provide spiritual support and guidance. The majority of Florida's Spanish Catholics had fled to Cuba at the start of the British period. When the Minorcans arrived at Turnbull's plantation, they were the only Catholics in the area. Father Camps and his assistant provided religious services and counsel for them all.

Turnbull's property was a wilderness located on the aptly named Mosquito Inlet. Backbreaking labor was needed to clear a jungle of untamed tropical growth, and the land was irrigated with a series of hand-dug canals.

Turnbull had expected to recruit about five hundred Europeans, although he was not prepared to accommodate that many. When twelve hundred people arrived, they faced a shortage of housing, food, clothing, and medical care from the moment they stepped off the boat.

Turnbull expected his indentures, including women and children, to start work right away. He ordered his overseers to get the plantation up and running, using whatever means necessary. Turnbull's directive led to terrible abuses. Hundreds of Minorcans succumbed to beatings, starvation, and overwork. Others died from malaria, scurvy, and gangrene.

Workers were whipped often and forced to labor in heavy chains and leg irons if they disobeyed. Even children were brutalized. A ten-year-old boy too ill to work was sent to the fields anyway. The overseer forced the other boys to stone him to death when the child could not complete his tasks.

The Minorcans endured the treatment in part because Turnbull had promised them land at the end of their indentures. Most had never owned property. When their indentures expired, Turnbull instead forced them to sign new contracts. When one man refused to sign, Turnbull sent his pregnant wife to work in the fields, a punishment that likely would have killed her. The worker capitulated and signed.

For a few years, the indigo crop was successful. Later yields dropped because of drought and worn-out land. The doctor's wealthy European investors complained. Turnbull's response was to work his indentured laborers even harder. The plantation's death rate was appalling. Four hundred and fifty Minorcans perished in the first eight months after they arrived. Nine years later, almost 70 percent of the original recruits were dead.

Father Camps and his assistant provided what comfort they could. A year after their arrival, Father Camps encountered two fishermen from Cuba and begged them to smuggle a hastily written note to the bishop in Havana, describing the inhumane conditions on the plantation. After taking more than two years to reply, the bishop offered no help.

When Father Camps's assistant complained to Turnbull about his treatment of the Minorcans, Turnbull shipped him back to Europe. After Father Camps circulated a petition asking for improved conditions, the doctor threatened him with deportation and told him to stick to religious matters. Knowing how much his congregants needed him, the priest complied.

In 1777, Turnbull crossed swords with the Florida governor over other issues. The governor, aware of the rumors about New Smyrna, sent investigators to take depositions from the Minorcans. Appalled by the reports, the governor offered the Minorcans sanctuary in St. Augustine.

Hundreds of Minorcan men, women, and children walked the seventy miles north to St. Augustine, carrying their worldly possessions on their backs. They traveled on the new King's Highway, built by a former Florida governor ten years earlier to accommodate Turnbull and open more of the coast to settlement. The highway, scouted by a Creek native named Grey Eyes, ran as far south as Mosquito Inlet.

Not all of the Minorcans were well enough to walk. Father Camps stayed with the ones left behind and provided medical help and spiritual support. When a ship arrived to take the rest to St. Augustine, Father Camps traveled with them.

He was the only Catholic priest in St. Augustine who spoke Mahonese, the language of Minorca and the common language of the indentured people. Father Camps continued his ministry until his death in 1790. A statue of the him was later erected in the small courtyard west of the Cathedral Basilica of Saint Augustine in celebration of the U.S. bicentennial and to commemorate the two-hundredth anniversary of the arrival of Minorcan colonists in St. Augustine.

Without indentured laborers, New Smyrna failed. Turnbull's investors filed lawsuits. The governor ordered Turnbull jailed for failing to pay a bond, but friends arranged his release. He moved to Charleston, resumed his medical career and lived there as a respected physician for the rest of his life.

In St. Augustine, the governor granted the Minorcans a

four-block area north of the plaza called Little San Felipe. They settled in, at first in mud and palmetto shanties or by sleeping in the open. Although living conditions were hard, they were vastly better than those on Turnbull's plantation. Over the years, the area where they settled grew. It is still called the Minorcan Quarter.

Scholars say the Minorcans' culture, which emphasized self-reliance, a tightly knit community, and equality of the sexes, helped them survive at New Smyrna. Unlike most British and Spanish women of the colonial period, Minorcan females played important roles in society and the church.

The first female lighthouse keeper in the United States was a Minorcan who tended the St. Augustine light, built in 1830, when her husband died and she inherited the job. Because lighthouse keepers were members of the U.S. Coast Guard, she was also the first female to serve in that branch of the military.

The Minorcans and their descendants built good lives in St. Augustine, contributing their skills and culture to the diverse city. They worked as fishermen, net makers, farmers, and craftsmen. The self-sufficient Minorcans were no doubt made more so by their years of misery on Turnbull's plantation.

Over the years, the culture has influenced St. Augustine and the region. More than 26,000 people with Minorcan ancestry now live in St. John's County. Minorcan restaurants serve pilau, a spicy stew containing tomatoes, rice, and seafood or meat, as well as other Minorcan specialties. Hot datil peppers, a signature ingredient of Minorcan cuisine, are still grown in and around St. Augustine commercially and in private gardens, but are rare elsewhere in the country. Local chefs create dishes spiced with datils, and families treasure recipes, passed down through generations of cooks, that feature the peppers.

SITE 3   Fernandez-Llambias House   33

SITE 4   *Short Take*

Father Miguel O'Reilly House Museum

c. 1691–1763

32 Aviles Street

National Register of Historic Places

The oldest parts of the house were built of tabby, coquina, and wood during the first Spanish period, which ended in 1763 when Spain ceded Florida to the British. Some claim an even earlier structure was built on the same site a few years before 1702, when St. Augustine was burned to the ground during a British attack. Portions of that original structure may still exist.

The floor of the Father O'Reilly House was made of poured tabby and the roof was a tabby slab. During a restoration in 2001, the stuccoed walls were opened in places to reveal the original tabby-and-coquina construction. Windows on the first floor had wooden *rejas*, or shutters made with angled slats for privacy, and the second story was floored with wooden planks. A covered loggia led to the main entry from the fenced courtyard.

Father Miguel O'Reilly, an Irish priest, became pastor of St. Augustine Parish after Florida returned to Spanish rule in 1783. O'Reilly purchased the house in 1785 and made it the rectory. An exceptional teacher, he willed his house to the church, specifying that it be used for education.

After the Civil War, eight sisters of the Order of St. Joseph arrived from France to teach the children of the formerly enslaved. Later, nuns of the same order taught the children of Native American prisoners incarcerated in appalling conditions at the Castillo de San Marcos in the late 1800s. The Spanish fort was renamed Fort Marion after Florida was annexed to the United States. The nuns provided their pupils with medicine and made sure they got baths and clothing. An Apache child taught by the nuns later said, "I will never forget the kindness of those good women, nor the respect in which we held them." The sisters still hold title to the structure, now a house museum open to the public.

Father Miguel O'Reilly House

Wooden door set in the coquina wall at the Father Miguel O'Reilly House

SITE 5   *Short Take*

Flagler Tabby

A. Ponce de León Hotel, 74 King Street, 1888
B. Alcazar Hotel, 75 King Street, 1888
C. Memorial Presbyterian Church, 36 Sevilla Street, 1889
D. Grace United Methodist Church, 8 Carrera Street, 1886–1887

National Register of Historic Places

In the 1880s, the Standard Oil millionaire Henry Morrison Flagler launched a Florida tourism industry that continues today. He ran the first railroad down the eastern coast of Florida to Key West and pioneered so much of the state's modern development that admirers claim that "Fl" stands for Flagler rather than Florida.

Flagler built luxury hotels and large churches in St. Augustine with revival tabby made with portland cement instead of burned-oyster-shell lime. Oyster shells and broken bits of coquina stone were used as aggregate. Building with tabby was Flagler's way of celebrating the town's history.

His Ponce de León Hotel was the first large poured-concrete multistory building in the United States and the first one wired for electricity when it was built. Thomas Edison, Flagler's friend, supervised the installation of the generator. Hotel employees had to operate the light switches; guests were afraid to touch them. The hotel's Spanish Renaissance Revival style continues to influence the look of resorts in Florida and elsewhere. Red barrel tiles cover the roof. Louis Comfort Tiffany added stained glass and murals to the interior. The hotel is now the centerpiece of Flagler College.

Flagler's Alcazar Hotel featured a Turkish bath, a three-story ballroom, a casino, an archery range, and the world's largest indoor swimming pool. The hotel is now the Lightner Museum.

Memorial Presbyterian Church honors Flagler's only child, Jennie, who died shortly after giving birth. She is interred in the church mausoleum with Flagler and other family members. Grace United Methodist Church is topped with a terra-cotta spire.

Flagler finished eighth grade before dropping out of school to work in a grain store in Ohio for five dollars a month. Five years later, he joined the sales staff and soon became a partner. While in the grain business, Flagler met John D. Rockefeller, who was then in the same line of work. When Rockefeller decided to start an oil refinery, Flagler joined him. The two formed Standard Oil of Ohio, which soon became one of the largest shippers of oil and kerosene in the United States. Flagler's wealth grew exponentially as the business expanded.

When Flagler's first wife, Mary, fell ill, her doctor recommended a trip to the South. The Flaglers vacationed in Florida and loved it. After Mary's death, Flagler and his second wife returned to Florida. Unhappy with the accommodations in St. Augustine and the transportation options to and from the coastal city, he launched a hotel- and railroad-building campaign, with the goal of creating an American Riviera.

SITE 5   Flagler Tabby   37

SITE 6

Castillo de San Marcos

1672–1698

1 South Castillo Drive

National Historic Landmark

HISTORIC SIGNIFICANCE: The castillo is the oldest masonry fort in the continental United States and the nation's best surviving example of Spanish colonial military architecture. It is one of only two fortresses in the world built of coquina, a semi-rare shellstone, and oyster-shell tabby.

Each of the nine wooden forts built by the Spanish after they founded St. Augustine in 1565 had a short lifespan. Some were swept away by hurricanes; others rotted or fell to termites. Some were torched by accident or by enemies.

One early fort, named San Juan de Pinos—St. John of the Pines—was burned to the ground in 1586 by Sir Francis Drake, the notorious English privateer, who made off with bronze artillery and £2,000 sterling.

In an attack in 1668, pirates murdered sixty St. Augustine residents, kidnapped wealthy young women for ransom, and stole everything of value. Since the invaders were observed making a map of the harbor, the terrified residents believed that the pirates planned to return and occupy St. Augustine because of its proximity to the route followed by Spain's treasure fleet.

Two years later, the British established Charles Towne, South Carolina. The closest British settlement to Spanish Florida, it was a definite threat to Spain's holdings. The danger was too great to ignore. The queen of Spain authorized funds for a masonry fortress.

St. Augustine had always been a poor town. It depended on subsidies from Spain, administered by officials in New Spain—Mexico—that were often delayed for years or never arrived at all. The townspeople were often near death from starvation.

During the twenty-three years that the *castillo* was under construction, Spanish officials often withheld funds and failed to provide needed supplies. The work proceeded with the aid of skilled laborers and convicts from Cuba and Hispaniola, enslaved Africans, freedmen, conscripted Native Americans, European prisoners, and St. Augustine residents. Most were paid low wages or no wages at all.

The Spanish chose coquina for the bulk of the structure. Found only in a few places on Florida's eastern coast, coquina is a soft sedimentary shellstone composed primarily

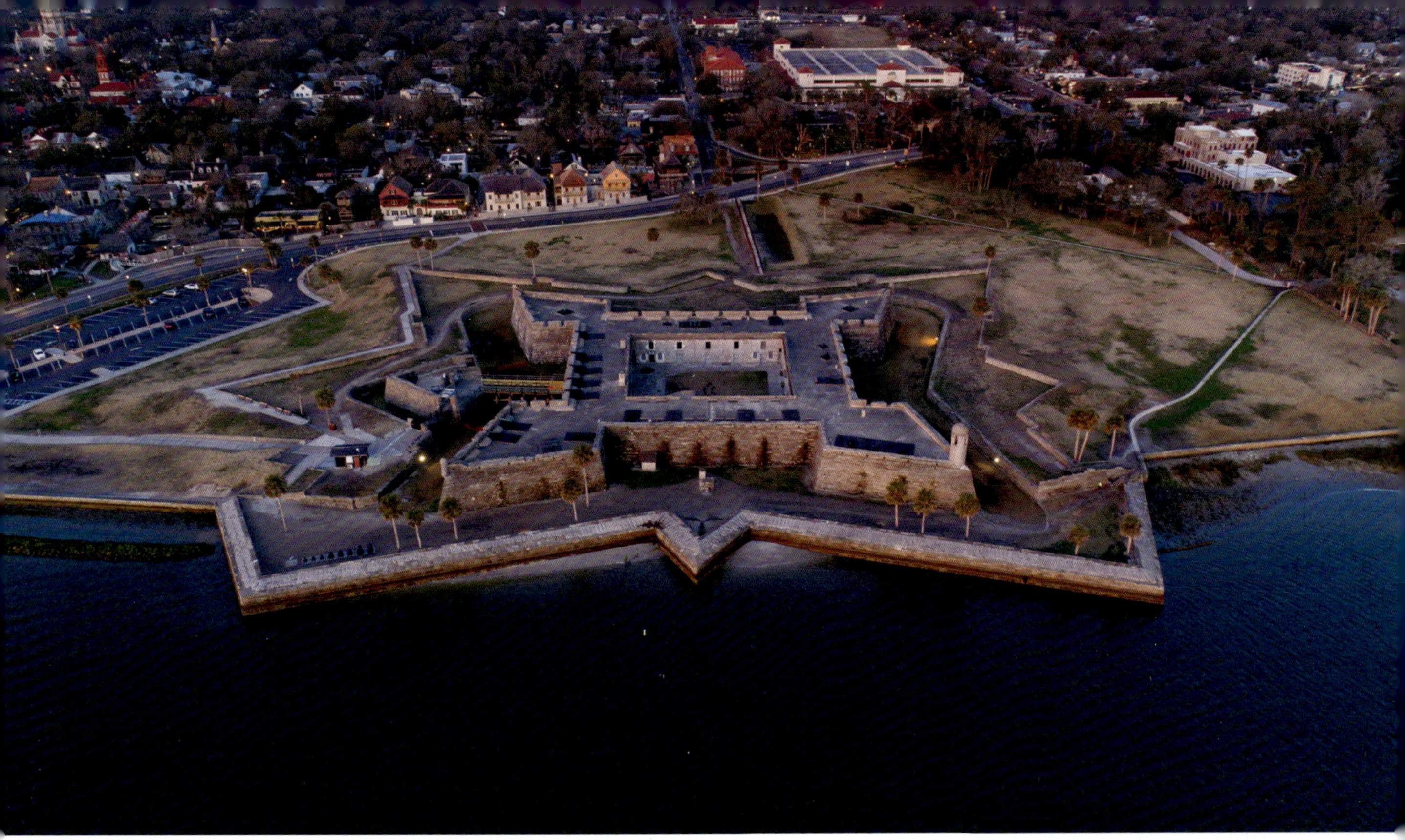

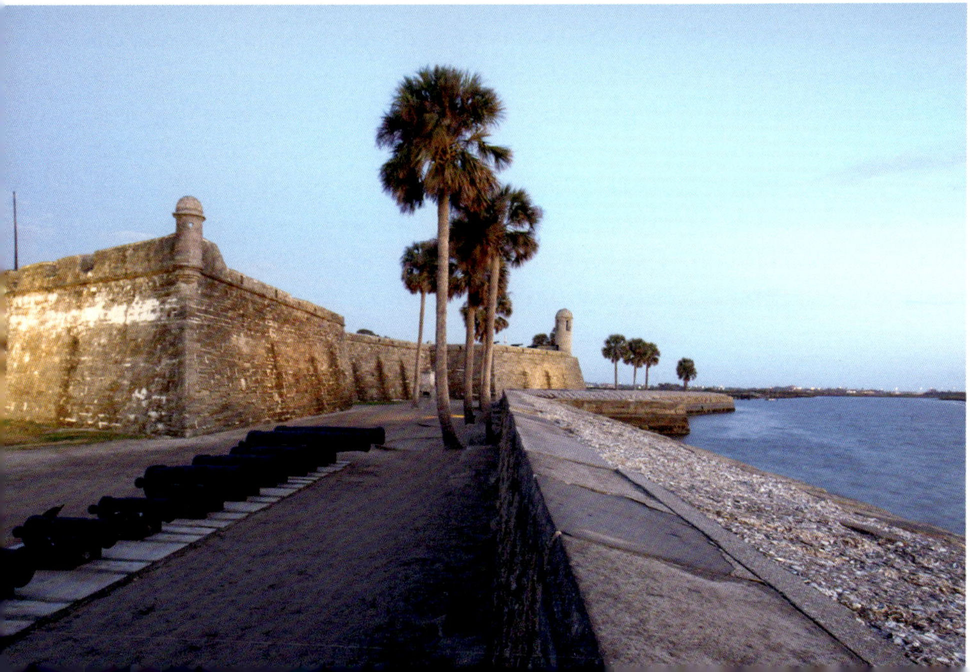

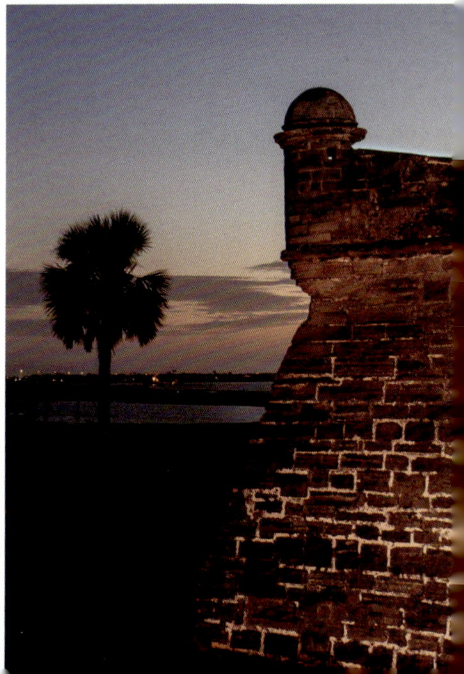

of the small shells of *Donax* clams naturally cemented together by time and pressure. The wet shellstone blocks were quarried on Anastasia Island, across Matanzas Bay from the fort site, barged across the bay, and hauled by oxcart to a staging area. The blocks had to dry and harden for up to three years before masons could lay them. Mortar made from burned-oyster-shell lime was used to cement the coquina blocks together. Tons of tabby concrete were poured for the parapet, the gun deck, and upper floors that shielded the barracks below from cannon fire.

When British troops from Carolina attacked the Castillo de San Marcos in 1702, the Spanish had no way to predict how the coquina-and-tabby fortress would withstand the assault, since it was the first of its kind. Cannon balls fired at masonry forts usually shattered unyielding walls of brick and stone. The porous coquina, on the other hand, absorbed or repelled the cannonballs without sustaining major damage. After witnessing the attack, an observer noted that "the native rock will not splinter but will give way to cannon ball as though you would stick a knife into cheese." The late historian Charles Arnade called the 1702 siege "one of the first large engagements in the international struggle on the North American continent." The siege marked the start of a century of warfare in colonial America.

Unable to breach the *castillo*, the British burned St. Augustine. For this reason, experts believe there are no structures still standing that predate the 1702 battle. When St. Augustine's residents rebuilt, the majority used fireproof tabby for construction. Governmental officials and wealthier citizens purchased quarried coquina, which was considered more upscale, but tabby was the choice of ordinary townspeople because its components were abundant and free.

The *castillo* always did double duty as a fort and a prison. After Florida joined the United States as a territory in 1821, the *castillo* was renamed Fort Marion in honor of the Revolutionary War hero Francis Marion, nicknamed the Swamp Fox.

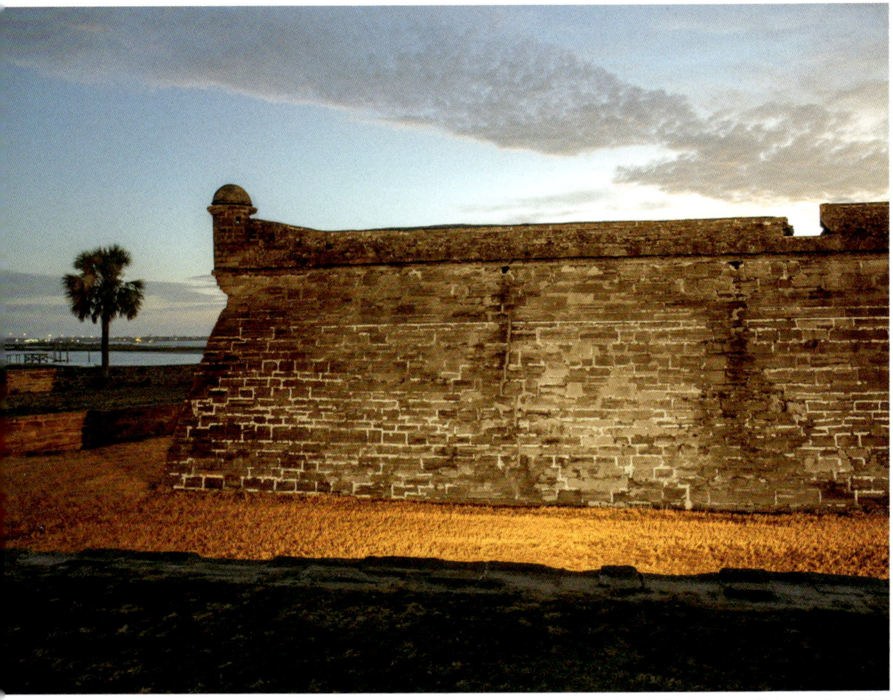
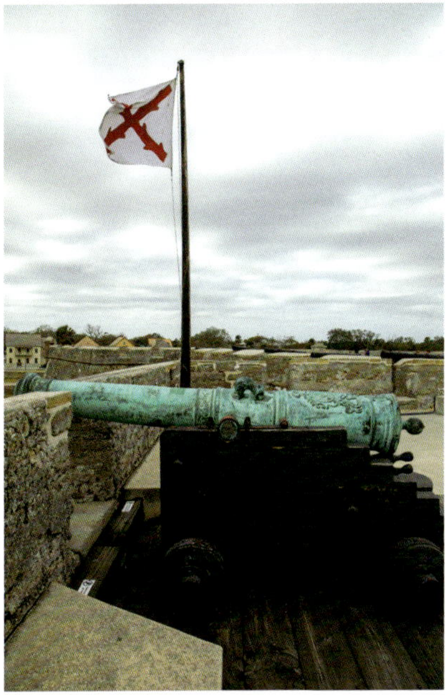
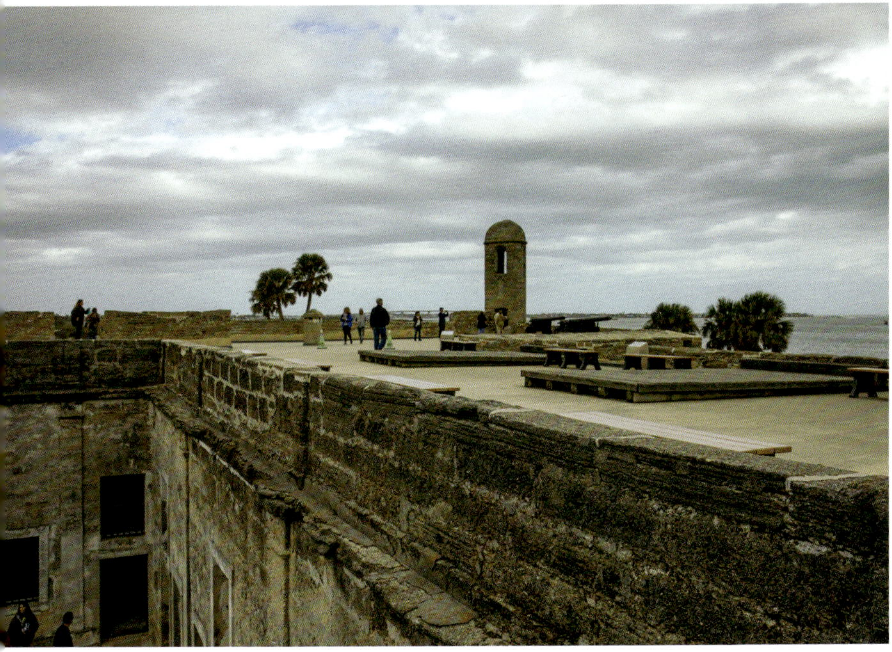
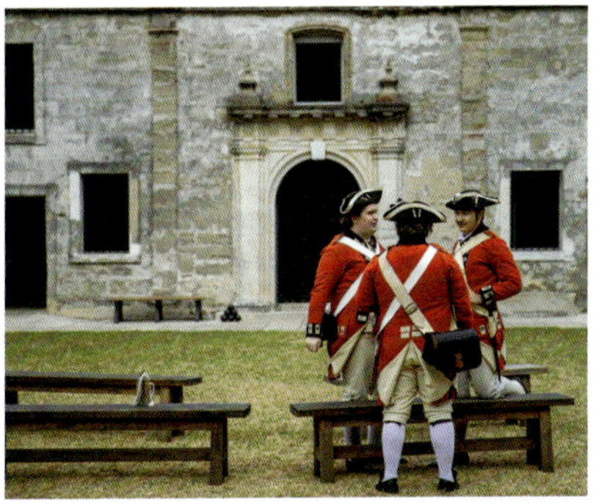
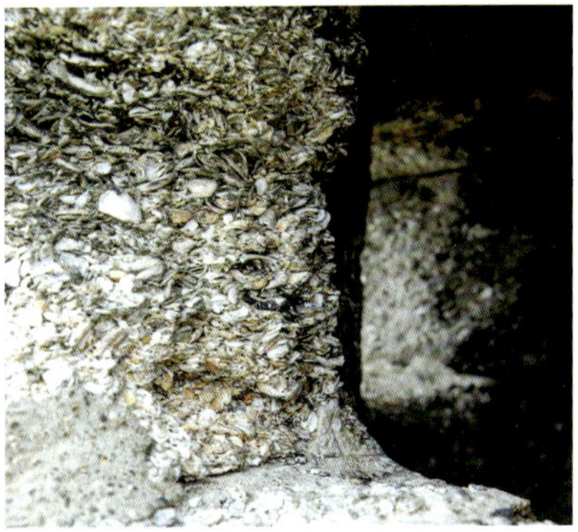

In the late 1800s, thousands of Native Americans—men, women, and children—from the western Great Plains were incarcerated at Fort Marion. Most had committed no crime other than living in the way of a new and rapidly expanding nation.

Because there was little to occupy adult male prisoners, army officers in charge of the fort encouraged them to draw and paint. The military provided pencils, ink, watercolors, and paper in the form of old account books. The art style is known today as ledger art. The finest examples were created at Fort Marion between 1875 and 1878, primarily by Kiowa and Cheyenne artists. In hundreds of drawings and paintings, the artists depicted their former lives on the Great Plains, hunting, farming, fighting, and courting. Horses appear in almost every picture. The artists also recorded their lives as prisoners at the fort.

Ledger art depicts a unique Native American custom called counting coup (pronounced "coo"), which referred to a courageous deed performed by a lone warrior in battle. The warrior who touched an enemy with his hand or struck him with a whip or coup stick without being injured himself scored coup. It was not necessary for coup to result in the injury or death of the enemy. Each act of coup was counted and recorded because it represented the ultimate measure of a warrior's bravery. The most celebrated warriors were not the ones who took the most scalps but the ones who earned the most coup.

Today, the coquina-and-tabby fortress, well over three centuries old, still stands on the shore of Matanzas Bay. The named Castillo de San Marcos was restored by Congress in 1942.

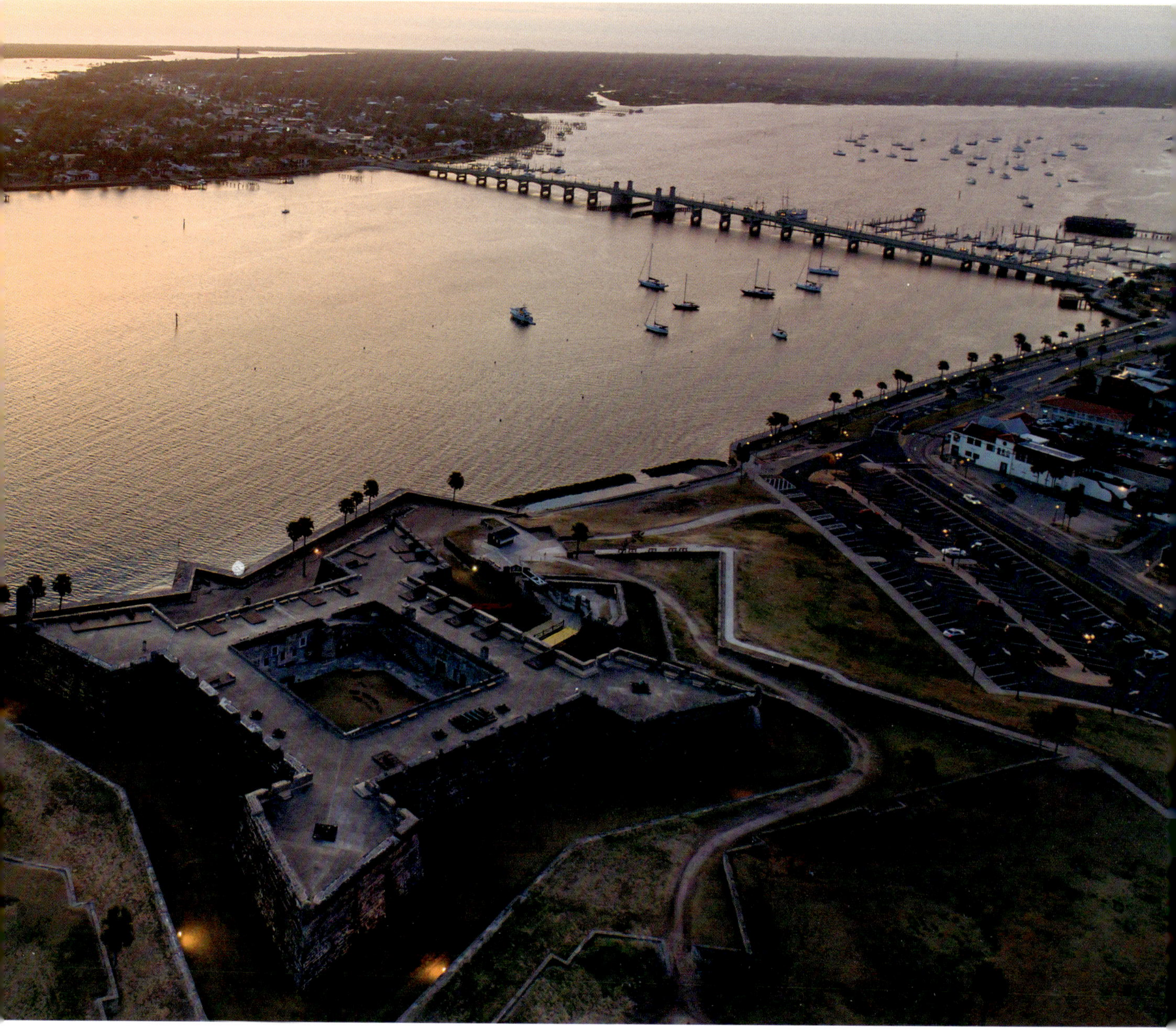

Chato, 1854–1913

The lives of prisoners at Fort Marion were grim. During the late 1800s, more than 500 Chiricahua Apaches removed from Arizona by the federal government were incarcerated at the old Spanish fort, which was large enough to hold only about 150 inhabitants.

Chato, a Chiricahua man believed to have "great medicine," fought for his people and their tribal lands in Arizona. He was a protégé of the famed Apache warrior Cochise. The two men were charged with conducting raids on white settlers in Arizona in the 1870s. Chato surrendered and was sent to the San Carlos reservation (in what is now southeastern Arizona) with other Apaches, including Geronimo, and became a scout for the United States.

In 1883, Chato led a war party that attacked a former Union soldier and judge, Hamilton C. McComas, his wife, Juanita, and their six-year-old son, Charlie. McComas was shot to death; his wife was killed by a blow to her head; Charlie's fate was never determined. After Chato surrendered to an army general in the Sierra Madre, he promised good behavior, a pledge he never violated. He began farming a fourteen-acre spread on the San Carlos Reservation, where he built his home by himself.

Chato was described by a white man as a handsome man who dressed "like a decent white man" in a clean linen shirt and collar, a cravat, vest and trousers, and leather-topped boots. He wore his hair long in the Apache style.

In 1886, the son of the secretary of the interior visited Chato at his farm on the reservation and asked him to come to Washington, D.C., to discuss relocating to a better reservation. In July, Chato led about a dozen Chiricahuas to Washington to meet with President Grover Cleveland and several cabinet members, including L. Q. C. Lamar, the interior secretary, who presented Chato with a silver medal that featured the president's head on the obverse side. The other side pictured a white settler welcoming a Native American to his cabin. The medal was inscribed "peace" and engraved to Chato from Lamar. Lamar's son gave Chato a certificate attesting to his good character. During the meetings, Chato informed the officials that he wanted to remain at the San Carlos Reservation. The officials told him to go home, work, and "behave himself."

On the return trip, Chato and the Chiricahuas were betrayed by the federal government. They were taken off the train and imprisoned at Fort Leavenworth, Kansas. Later, they were transferred to Fort Marion.

Many prisoners at Fort Marion were children and women whose husbands were imprisoned elsewhere. Three wives of the Chiricahua shaman Geronimo were incarcerated at Fort Marion, while Geronimo himself was confined at Fort Pickens in Pensacola, where the dignified old shaman was treated as a tourist attraction. The separation from his family was a violation of the terms under which Geronimo had surrendered.

At Fort Marion, Chiracahua families were torn apart again. Forty-four young people ranging in age from twelve to twenty-two were forcibly taken from their families and sent to the government's Indian Training School in Carlisle, Pennsylvania. Some of the women at Fort Marion kept their children from being taken by hiding them under their full skirts, a tactic that fooled the guards for years. Overcrowding at the fort no doubt helped with the deception.

Carlisle and similar training schools did everything in their power to wipe out Native American culture. The young people were given English names and arbitrary birth dates. They were required to attend Christian church services and barred from wearing native clothing. They learned to read and write in English but not in their Native languages, which they were forbidden to speak.

At Fort Marion, conditions were dreadful. A single well provided drinking water for five hundred prisoners. Only two tubs were available for bathing and washing clothes. When Chiricahua women began slipping out of the fortress to bathe in Matanzas Bay, the guards made them stop.

Chiricahua belief forbade eating anything that swam underwater, yet fish was often on Fort Marion's menu. Rations were insufficient in general and did not include the fruits and vegetables that constituted the bulk of the Chiricahua diet.

When the weather turned cold, the prisoners lacked appropriate clothing to protect themselves from nor'easters that whipped in from the Atlantic. Children had only thin calico slips to wear and had to spend all their time in their tents.

Lieutenant Colonel Lewis Langdon, the army officer in charge of the fort, did what he could to improve the prisoners' lives. Instead of confining them in the dark barracks in the bowels of the fort, Langdon had army tents pitched on the ramparts in sunshine and fresh air. Chiricahua women prepared food for the prisoners over small fires they built in the corners of the ramparts. Male prisoners kept the encampment as clean as possible.

With saddles, blankets, and other personal items stored around the tents, women doing needlework and other handcrafts, coffee boiling and meat frying over campfires, the compound resembled a typical Native American village transported to Florida from Arizona, one army officer observed.

The resemblance was superficial.

Fort Marion's sewage was piped directly into Matanzas Bay, but the fort's porous masonry walls absorbed much

Chato, Apache Chiricahua subchief, photographed by A. F. Randall, c. 1884

of the waste as it washed in with the tide. Even with the copious use of carbolic acid, overcrowding made it impossible to maintain sanitary conditions. Six women, one man, and fourteen children died within the first year of confinement. Langdon, the fort commander, was appalled. He recommended that all the prisoners be transferred to the Indian school at Carlisle, insisting that they could not remain at Fort Marion "until they all die."

Many Chiricahua did not survive years of incarceration at Fort Marion and other southern forts. Those who did were eventually removed to reservations in western states. Chato was moved to Fort Sill, Oklahoma, with his family in 1894. They later settled on the Mescalero Reservation in New Mexico. After being imprisoned for twenty-three years, Chato died in a car accident on the reservation in 1934.

SITE 7

Fort Mose Historic State Park

1738

15 Fort Mose Trail

National Historic Landmark

HISTORIC SIGNIFICANCE: Fort Mose was an outpost of the coquina-and-tabby Castillo de San Marcos and the first community of free Africans established in the future United States. The Spanish awarded its leader, an escaped slave, military honors for fighting against the British. Fort Mose, the premier stop on Florida's Black Heritage Trail, is considered internationally significant as a major stepping-stone in U.S. history. It is part of the National Park Service's Underground Railroad Network to Freedom and part of the Slave Route Project sponsored by the United Nations Educational, Scientific, and Cultural Organization (UNESCO).

After the establishment of Carolina in 1670, St. Augustine became a refuge for enslaved Africans fleeing British plantations in the new colony. Although the Spanish held slaves, the Catholic Church regarded slavery as an unnatural condition and urged better treatment for enslaved people.

Spain's laws forbade the abuse of slaves, allowed them to earn wages and own property, and permitted them to testify in court against harsh owners. Like indentured servants, people enslaved by the Spanish were often allowed to work their way to freedom.

The first documented fugitives from Carolina, two women, eight men, and a nursing toddler, arrived in St. Augustine in 1687 in a stolen canoe. Six of the men were assigned to construction work on the Castillo de San Marcos; two were employed in the tabby blacksmith shop in town. The shop was rebuilt in the 2010s with revival tabby made with portland cement instead of original tabby made with burned-oyster-shell lime. The women worked at the governor's house as laundresses and cooks. All earned wages.

The escapees traveled on a southbound underground railroad that predated Harriet Tubman's better-known counterpart by almost a century. Some escaped in boats, stopping on uninhabited Georgia and Florida sea islands to rest and find food and water; others trekked through the interior, assisted by Natives allied with the Spanish. Africans who staged the largest mainland slave uprising, the Stono Rebellion, aimed to escape to St. Augustine. Twenty-five white people and as many as fifty enslaved people were killed during or after the conflict, which began near the Stono River in South Carolina in 1739.

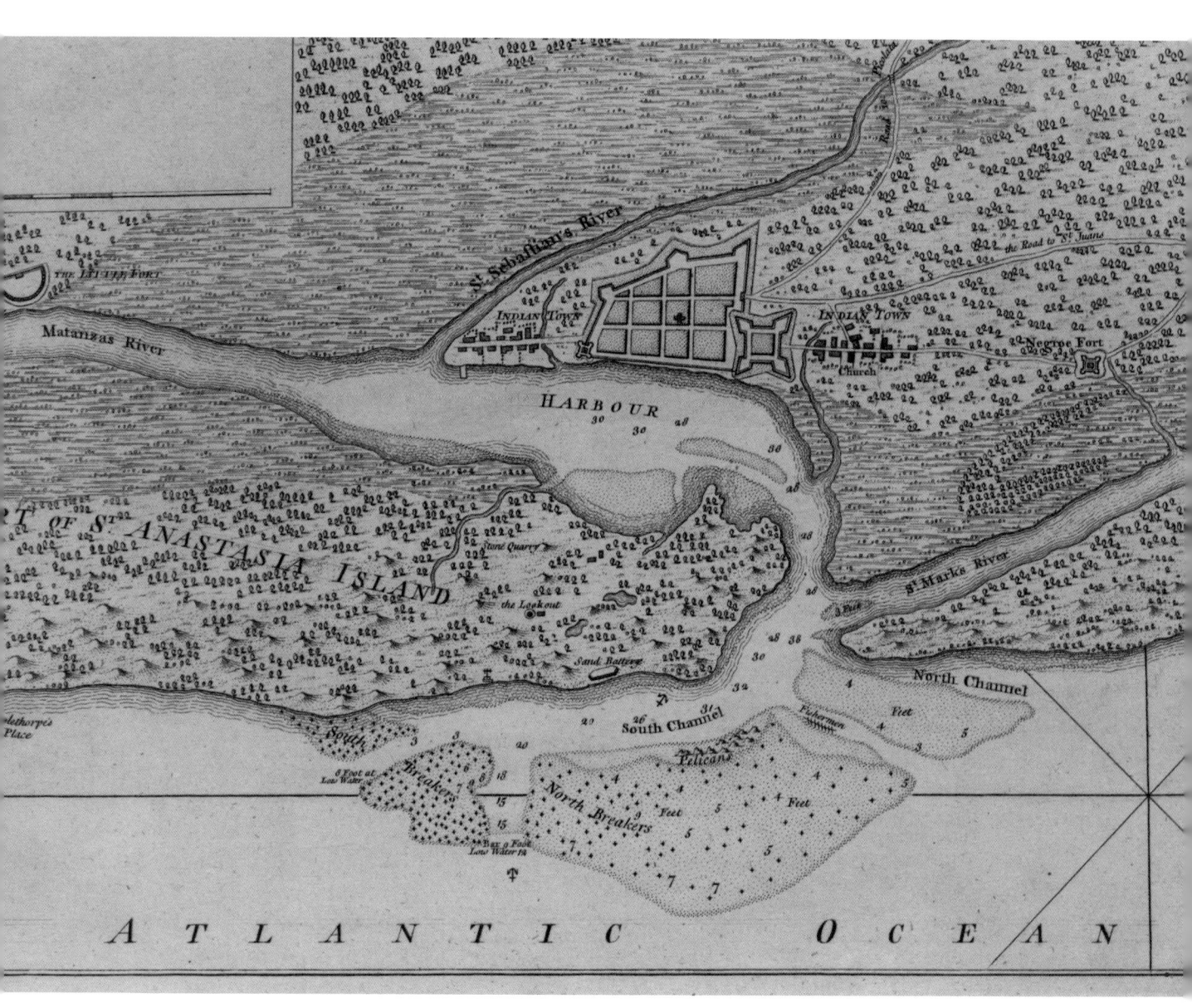

"Plan of the Town and Harbour of St. Augustine," a map by Thomas Jefferys (1699–1775), from *A Description of the Spanish Islands and Settlements on the Coast of the West Indies* (London, 1762), plate 6. This map shows the strategic location of Fort Mose, here called "Negroe Fort." Mose, approximately two miles from the city of St. Augustine, was the northernmost outpost of the Spanish Empire.

In St. Augustine, escaped slaves could gain freedom and citizenship by swearing allegiance to the Spanish Crown and adopting the Catholic faith. Men were required to serve four years in the military. Jane Landers, a historian at Vanderbilt University, is noted for her extensive research on Africans in Spanish Florida. She concluded that the enslaved were better protected legally and socially in St. Augustine than they would be under British rule for another two hundred years.

Africans and Spaniards intermarried. Powerful governmental officials became godparents of African and mixed-race children when they were baptized. Africans worked as craftsmen, artisans, seamen, cattlemen, and soldiers, some of the many occupations in the pioneer town where ability was more important than race. According to Landers, the Africans made important contributions to the overall success of St. Augustine and improved their own lives in the process.

With the blessing and support of the Spanish, escaped slaves often returned to Carolina to raid and burn British plantations, steal goods and livestock, and free other enslaved people. Arthur Middleton, the acting governor of South Carolina, wrote in outrage to officials in London, complaining that the Spanish not only harbored fugitive Africans but also "have found a New way of sending our own slaves against us, to Rob and Plunder us."

By 1738, about a hundred people who had escaped from slavery in British Carolina were living in St. Augustine. The governor of Florida, Manuel de Montiano, set aside land for a fortified enclave north of the Castillo at the site of a former Native American settlement called Mose (mow-SAY). The settlement was named Gracia Real de Santa Teresa de Mose, but it was always called Fort Mose or Fort Moosa by the British.

Fort Mose served as an outpost of the coquina-and-tabby *castillo*. Built with earth-banked walls, it was surrounded by a moat edged with Spanish bayonets, a native plant with sword-shaped, sharp-pointed leaves. Inside Fort Mose's palisades were a guardhouse, a well, and a lookout. A priest who lived in the settlement offered sacraments and taught catechisms.

Among the fort's occupants were Native Americans married to the formerly enslaved. Instead of building Spanish-style houses, Fort Mose residents lived like Native Americans in thatched-roof wattle-and-daub structures.

The archaeologist Kathleen Deagan, curator of the University of Florida's Museum of Natural History, led a team that explored Fort Mose and its successor. Deagan said she found no evidence of coquina or tabby at either outpost except for the remains of a building of later vintage at the second Fort Mose, built after the first outpost was destroyed by British troops.

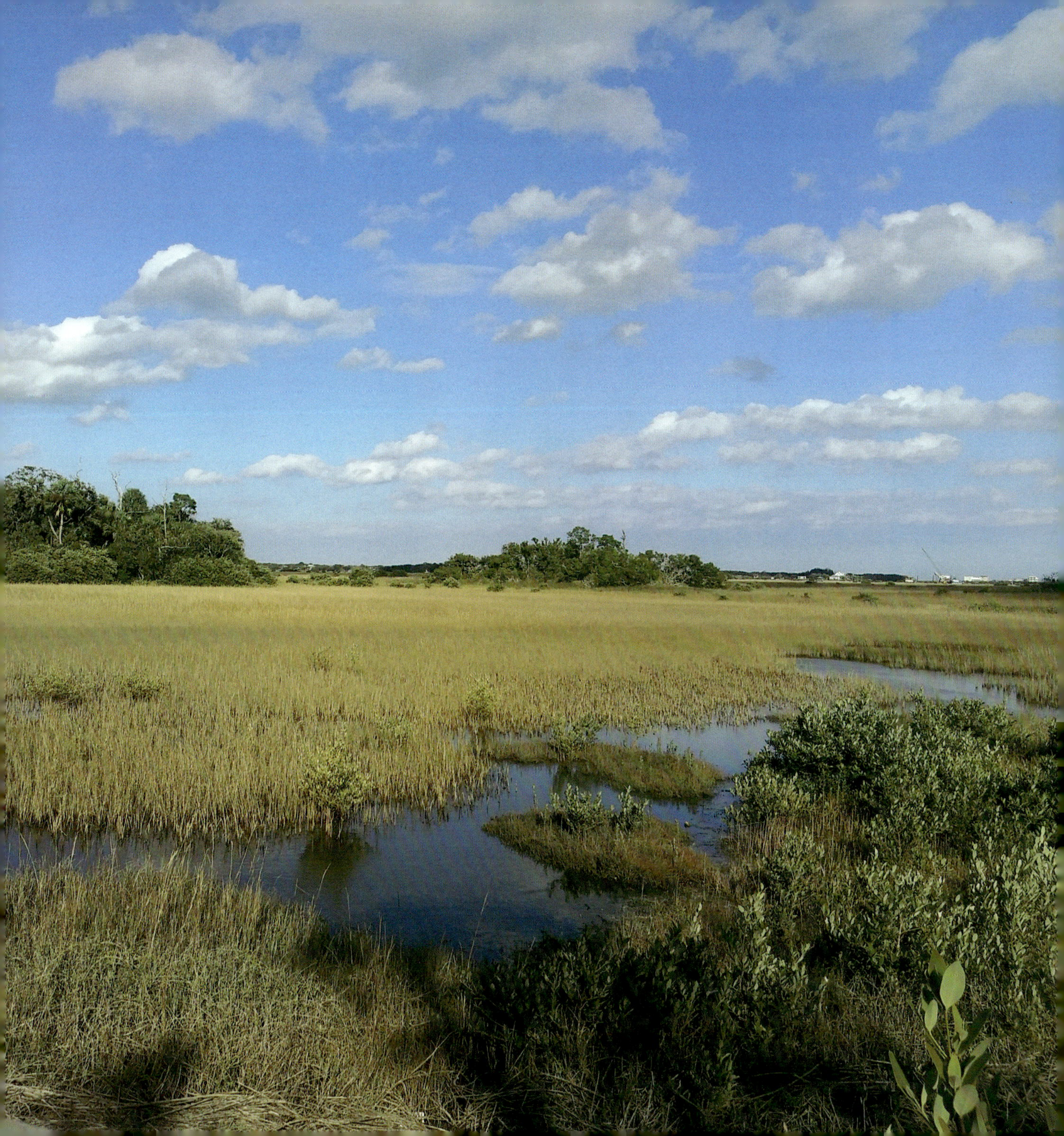

The soldiers of Fort Mose may have trained with other Spanish troops at the Castillo de San Marcos or at Fort Matanzas, built south of St. Augustine of tabby and coquina in 1740. That year, James Edward Oglethorpe, the British officer who founded the Georgia colony, led an attack on St. Augustine in an attempt to dislodge the Spanish from their Florida stronghold. The townspeople of St. Augustine and the soldiers and residents of Fort Mose retreated to the *castillo*. British ships fired cannonballs and mortar rounds at the fortress for thirty-eight days but caused no significant damage.

During Oglethorpe's siege, about 170 British soldiers bivouacked at the abandoned Fort Mose. Security was lax. In a predawn raid, African, Native American, and Spanish soldiers invaded the outpost and killed about one hundred volunteer troops, most of them Highland Scots from the town of Darien, Georgia. Two dying soldiers were mutilated: one was scalped; the other, castrated.

Oglethorpe's troops destroyed Fort Mose during their retreat. Its remains eroded over time into the nearby creek. The second Fort Mose was built a decade later, slightly north of the first. It was larger, with earthen walls on three sides faced with clay and topped with Spanish bayonets. The fort had a dry moat, six cannons, storage houses, a guardhouse, a church, and a sacristy for the priest.

The Spanish honored the Africans who participated in the raid on the first Fort Mose for bravery. Oglethorpe redeemed himself two years later when his troops repulsed a Spanish attack on St. Simons Island, Georgia, in 1742.

At least fifteen African soldiers stationed at Fort Mose fought in the battles of Bloody Marsh and Gully Hole Creek on St. Simons. The battles were little more than skirmishes, but they marked the last time that Spain attempted to reclaim territory north of the Florida Peninsula.

The second Fort Mose was abandoned in 1763 when Spain traded Florida to the British in return for Cuba, which the British had captured during Queen Anne's War. As British settlers moved in, most of the Spanish, freed Africans, and Natives who had converted to Catholicism relocated to Havana and other Spanish-held territories.

The historic site of the second Fort Mose, once on high ground, has been slowly surrounded by marshes and tidewaters formed from rising sea levels. It is now an island, reached by a boardwalk across the wetlands.

Francisco Menéndez (dates unknown)

A young African Mandinga whose birth name and birth date have been lost to time was taken from his home country by slavers, brought to Carolina in the early 1700s, and bought by a British planter.

He was born in a multicultural trading region along the Gambia River in West Africa, and may have been educated in Islamic schools and brought up in a well-to-do household.

He always identified himself as a Mandinga, the most powerful of the African ethnic groups along the Gambia. The Mandinga people established small riverfront kingdoms and grew rich from taxing foreigners and collecting tributes of rice, cattle, poultry, and other goods from their weaker neighbors.

The Gambia was a cultural melting pot. Arabic merchants brought in Islam and education. Catholic merchants and Jews from Portugal found the Gambia a tolerant region in which to settle and trade. During the 1700s, English and French merchants began arriving to buy elephant tusks, beeswax, cowhides, and slaves.

The Mandinga's British slaveholder put him to work with other enslaved Africans and Native Americans. Unlike the British, the Spanish were forbidden to enslave North America's Indigenous people, although they did conscript Natives for hard, unfamiliar labor.

In Carolina, the enslaved cleared land, harvested naval stores, cut timber, and rounded up cattle gone wild in the woods. They learned the local terrain. Some acquired Native languages as well as English and served as guides and translators for their British owners. Because of his multicultural upbringing, the Mandinga may have learned new languages easily.

The Yamasee War erupted in 1715, in part because Carolina traders routinely cheated and abused Indigenous people. The Natives filed complaints with the Carolina commissioner of Indian trade, but the tepid official response did little to curb the offenses. At the same time, the Spanish in St. Augustine were welcoming Yamasee delegations with gifts, hoping to make them allies.

The Mandinga escaped from Carolina with his African wife, but got caught up in the Yamasee War. He fought against the British alongside Native warriors led by Chief Jospo. When it was clear that the British were winning, Chief Jospo, the Mandinga, his wife, and other escaped slaves sought sanctuary in St. Augustine.

The Indigenous Coosa people were allies of the Spanish in Florida. Yfallaquisca, called Perro Bravo, or Mad Dog, was a spokesman for the Coosa chief. He claimed to own the newly arrived Africans. The Spanish objected, but Perro Bravo threatened to kill the Africans unless he was compensated. The acting governor of Florida paid him for the escapees in corn and whiskey.

The Mandinga, his wife, and the others were re-enslaved. The couple may have been owned briefly by the Spanish Crown and perhaps lived in the governor's household. When she was baptized a Catholic, the Mandinga's wife took the name of the governor's wife, Ana Maria de Escovar, as her Spanish name.

The couple were next enslaved by Florida's royal treasurer, Don Francisco Menéndez Márquez and were treated as part of his household. When the Mandinga was baptized, he took the name Francisco Menéndez, who also stood as his godfather. Having a powerful official in that role elevated the Mandinga's status in St. Augustine.

The royal treasurer often conducted diplomatic or military missions to Carolina. Jane Landers, the Vanderbilt historian, thinks it likely that Francisco Menéndez accompanied his owner on those trips because of his knowledge of Carolina's terrain, languages, and politics. In 1725, when Don Francisco led an attack in Carolina, the African Menéndez accompanied him and later led raids on his own.

Still enslaved, Menéndez was named captain of St. Augustine's Black militia. Over the years, he met and exceeded official requirements for freedom and full citizenship. He learned to speak, read, and write in Spanish and had a good grasp of Spanish culture, politics, and social skills. He won citations for bravery in battle. Able to fight with Native American stealth as well as Spanish military skills, Menéndez was a valuable asset to St. Augustine's militia.

He repeatedly petitioned Spanish officials for freedom for himself and his fellow enslaved people. His efforts failed until the new Florida governor, Manuel de

Montiano, learned the worth of the African soldiers. Anticipating war with England, Montiano granted all of the escaped Africans unconditional freedom in 1738, the year the first Fort Mose was built. Menéndez was named commander of the outpost.

After Fort Mose was destroyed in the 1740 British attack, Menéndez and his family moved into St. Augustine, possibly into one of the many tabby houses in town. He wrote to the king of Spain, saying he had been impoverished by his service to the Crown and asking for compensation. When the king failed to respond, Menéndez joined a group of Spanish corsairs, looting enemy towns and ships. He planned to work his way to Spain and petition the king in person for his overdue pay.

In 1741, Menéndez was captured by a British sea captain who accused him of the Fort Mose mutilations and had him tied to a cannon while the ship's doctor pretended to castrate him. The captain then ordered his men to give Menéndez two hundred lashes, followed by a punishment known as pickling: salt and vinegar were poured into his open wounds. Menendez was forcibly, and illegally, taken to New Providence in the Bahamas, where he was sold once again into slavery.

By 1759, he was back in St. Augustine. How he returned is not known, but he resumed command of the second Fort Mose for the next four years.

During the Seven Years' War, British forces captured Cuba. The Spanish, who considered Havana invaluable, traded Florida to England in return for the Caribbean island.

Before the British moved into Florida in 1763, most Spanish residents as well as Africans and acculturated Native Americans evacuated to Spanish territories. Menéndez and his wife and children settled in the small fishing village of Regla across the harbor from Havana. All of Fort Mose's soldiers received cash advances from the government. In recognition of his service, Menéndez was awarded double the amount that the others received. He was also given a slave.

Menéndez died in Cuba, at last a free man. A museum in St. Augustine honors him and the other Africans who escaped to freedom in Florida.

CHAPTER 2 *Fort George Island Cultural State Park*

THE BULK OF FORT GEORGE ISLAND is a state park within a federal preserve. The island is one of seven that form the Talbot Islands State Parks along Florida's northeastern coast. Fort George Island Cultural State Park lies within the 46,000-acre federal Timucuan Ecological and Historic Preserve; the 60-acre Kingsley Plantation, on the island's northern end, is managed by the National Park Service.

The state park offers such activities as hiking, boating, fishing, and bird-watching. The historic Ribault Club, once an exclusive social enclave, is now the visitor center, with exhibits and rental space for special functions.

Like the other sea islands of the southeastern coast, Fort George Island is separated from the mainland by wide bands of Spartina marsh ribboned with tidal waterways. Its topography is flat except for Mount Cornelia, an old dune that rises sixty-five feet above sea level, the highest bump of coastal land south of North Carolina's Outer Banks.

Much of the island is wooded. Spanish moss dangles like tarnished tinsel from the limbs of live oak trees. The dense fanlike foliage of palmetto thickets rattles in the sea breeze. A bluff at Point Isobel on the north end offers a spectacular view of the Fort George River, where flocks of roseate spoonbills feed in the shallows.

Thousands of years ago, Paleo-Indians of the Late Archaic period were the first humans to occupy Fort George Island. The Natives feasted on oysters gathered from tidal waterways, leaving the discarded shells behind. The Rollins Shell Ring on the island is one of the largest of about sixty prehistoric rings discovered to date on the southeastern coast. Because it is vulnerable to human foot traffic, it is off-limits to visitors.

When the French and Spanish arrived in the sixteenth century, the island was populated by Mocama people, the coastal branch of the large Timucua group of northern Florida and southern Georgia.

French Huguenots fleeing religious prosecution in Europe established Fort Caroline on the nearby St. Johns River in 1564. The Mocama people, who welcomed the French, called the island Alicamani (also known as Alimacani). It was home to Saturiwa, the name for both the Mocama leader and the village.

When Spanish soldiers drove the French from the area in 1565, Saturiwa and the Mocama fought the invaders. They later accepted the Spanish and allied with them in battle. The alliances were strengthened as Spanish and Mocama people intermarried and had children.

Alicamani was renamed San Juan Island by the Spanish, who established the mission of San Juan del Puerto at

Saturiwa in the 1570s. Father Francisco Pareja, a Franciscan friar, talented linguist, and scholar was assigned there in 1587 and remained for decades. Pareja is noted for producing the first written versions of Native American languages ever published. Six of his eight books survive.

A French pirate, Michel de Grammont, raided the missions on Fort George Island and Cumberland Island, Georgia, in 1683, stealing—among other things—four bells, two from each mission. When Governor James Moore of British Carolina attacked St. Augustine in 1702, his troops destroyed the mission of San Juan del Puerto, which had lasted for about 130 years.

During digs at the site, archaeologists found the remains of the mission church and friary as well as artifacts, including pottery sherds, religious medals, and two wrought-iron door keys. The remains of the building have been reburied, but a marker at the site describes the mission's historic significance.

In 1736, Georgia's founder, James Edward Oglethorpe, defined the St. Johns River as a distributary of Georgia's giant Altamaha River in order to build a fort on the island, which he renamed for King George II. Oglethorpe was building a series of coastal forts to defend against Spanish Florida and, ultimately, to drive the Spanish from North America. His wooden fort on Fort George Island was just thirty-five miles from the Spanish stronghold of St. Augustine.

In 1763, when Spanish Florida was traded to the British, most of the Spanish-speaking residents fled to Cuba. The British offered potential settlers land grants in Florida in order to repopulate the territory. In 1765, Fort George Island was granted to Richard Hazard of Carolina, who established a successful indigo plantation there. Its location on the island is unknown. When the famed early American botanist John Bartram visited in 1766, he called Hazard "a good kind of a man, and one of the best planters in Florida."

Florida remained under British control for two decades. It was returned to the Spanish by the United States in 1784 as a reward for Spain's alliance with the Patriots during the Revolutionary War.

Three historic figures of note owned the island after the war. One was the Revolutionary War hero John McQueen, the American-born son of a prominent Scottish deerskin merchant. McQueen carried wartime messages from George Washington to the marquis de Lafayette and was a friend of Thomas Jefferson.

McQueen went bankrupt after speculating on large tracts of timberland in South Carolina and Georgia. Facing the prospect of debtors' prison, McQueen left his wife and children in Savannah and fled to Spanish Florida. He took the name Don Juan McQueen and converted to Catholicism. Upset by his religious conversion, his beloved wife refused to relocate to a Spanish-speaking Catholic country.

For serving as an adviser to the Florida governor, McQueen was rewarded with Fort George Island. He acquired additional land grants after leading campaigns against Seminole and British attackers. He became one of Spanish Florida's largest landowners but again struggled to pay his debts. McQueen sold the Fort George plantation in 1804 to John Houstoun McIntosh, a prominent Georgia planter.

Shortly before the outbreak of the War of 1812, McIntosh and other Georgians joined a volunteer army called the Patriots—not the same as the Revolutionary War Patriots—in an attempt to turn Spanish Florida over to the United States. The effort failed, and after the

Spanish government branded McIntosh an enemy, he fled to Georgia in 1814. He first rented and then sold Fort George Island to Zephaniah Kingsley. Florida became a U.S. territory in 1821 and a state in 1845.

John Rollins, a New Hampshire farmer, bought the island in 1869, after the Civil War, and turned it into a tourist resort, using the tabby cabins built by Kingsley for the enslaved as an attraction. Rollins's luxury hotel hosted such luminaries as the banker William Astor and the abolitionist Harriet Beecher Stowe, author of *Uncle Tom's Cabin* (1852).

After a yellow fever epidemic swept the island and the hotel burned down, Rollins grew citrus, packing the fruit cradled in Spanish moss in shipping crates. His daughter, who inherited the island, sold it to private investors in 1923.

The investors built the posh Ribault club on the site of the Rollins hotel. The old plantation house served as a private club for military officers who met there during Prohibition, ostensibly for social rather than alcohol-related reasons. After World War II, the Florida Park Service acquired the bulk of the island.

SITE 8

Kingsley Plantation

1814

Timucuan Ecological and Historic Preserve
Fort George Island Cultural State Park
11676 Palmetto Avenue, Jacksonville

HISTORIC SIGNIFICANCE: In 1968, archaeologists conducted the first study of plantation slave life in the United States, making the Kingsley Plantation the birthplace of African American archaeology. The site includes the oldest still-standing plantation house in Florida, twenty-five tabby cabins for the enslaved, the Thomson House, and a kitchen with a rare tabby floor.

The majority of the tabby structures on Fort George Island date to the time of Zephaniah Kingsley, who rented the island in 1814 and purchased it in 1817 for $5,000. Kingsley, along with several common-law slave wives and their children, occupied the property for almost twenty-five years. The plantation's tabby cabins for the enslaved are the largest group of such buildings from the antebellum era. A historic tabby barn and two-story tabby kitchen on the property date to the early 1800s.

The first plantation house was built by one of the island's early European owners, John McQueen, who often referred to himself as Don Juan McQueen. The son of a Scotsman, he had fled to Spanish colonial Florida with Georgia creditors nipping at his heels.

McQueen's first home burned. He started construction on a larger home between 1797 and 1798 in a style that resembled the houses of British gentry. Its unusual design features a large central room flanked by four square pavilions. The second story has two large rooms and a roof deck. The pavilions were attached to the corners of the main structure and were probably used as bedrooms, each with its own fireplace. They were originally accessed from an exterior porch. Windows on three sides of each pavilion welcomed salt-scented breezes from the river and marshes.

Half of the home's tabby-and-coquina basement served as a warming room for food brought from the nearby kitchen. The basement's other half was used to store clothing and other items doled out to the enslaved at the owner's discretion. A grove of orange and lemon trees surrounded the main buildings. During the mid- to late nineteenth century, when citrus was grown commercially on the island, Spanish moss was used to pack the fruit for shipping.

McQueen, his family, and his neighbors took refuge in the house during attacks by Creeks in 1802. The house was ravaged in 1813 during the Patriot War, when the U.S.

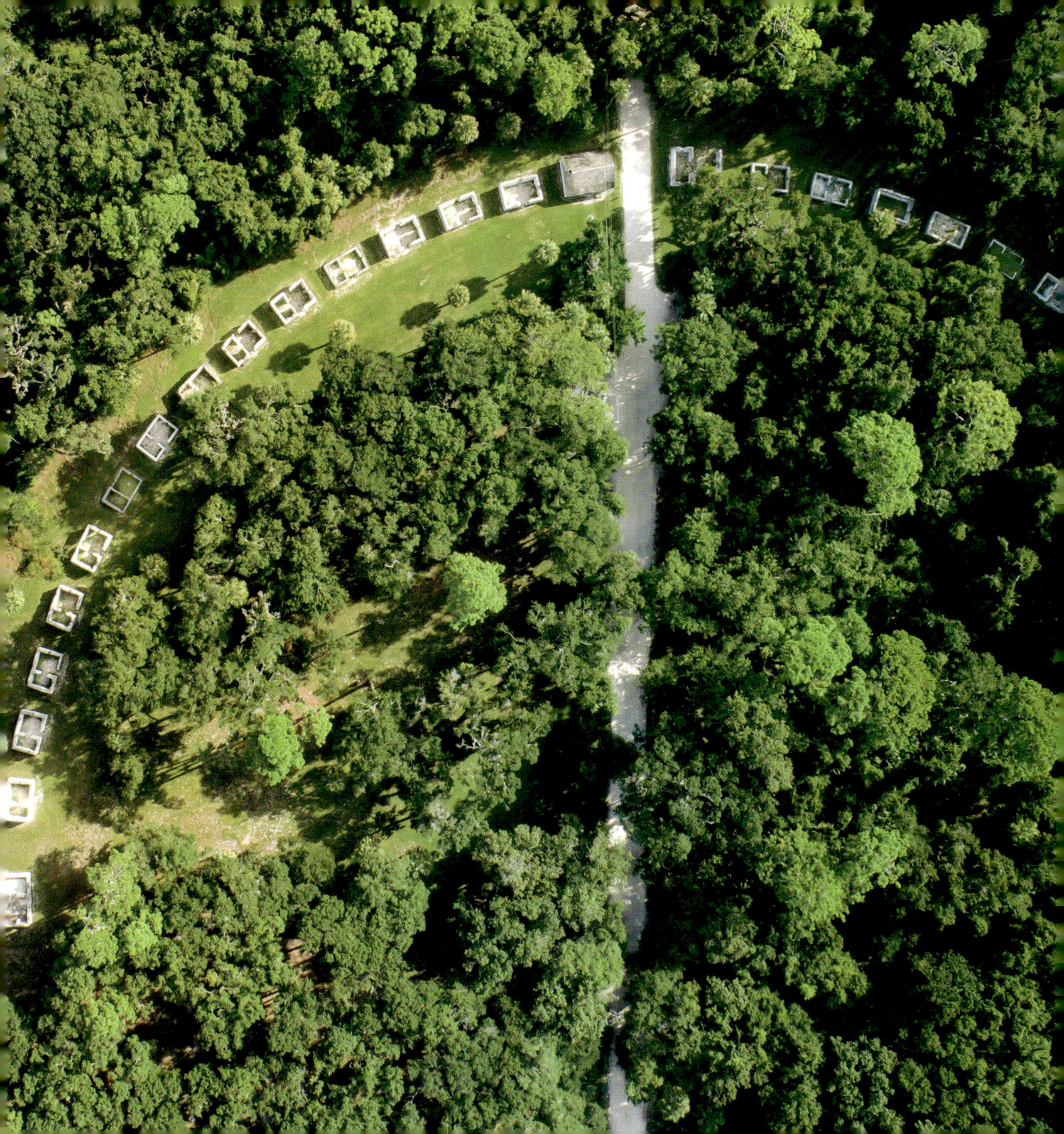

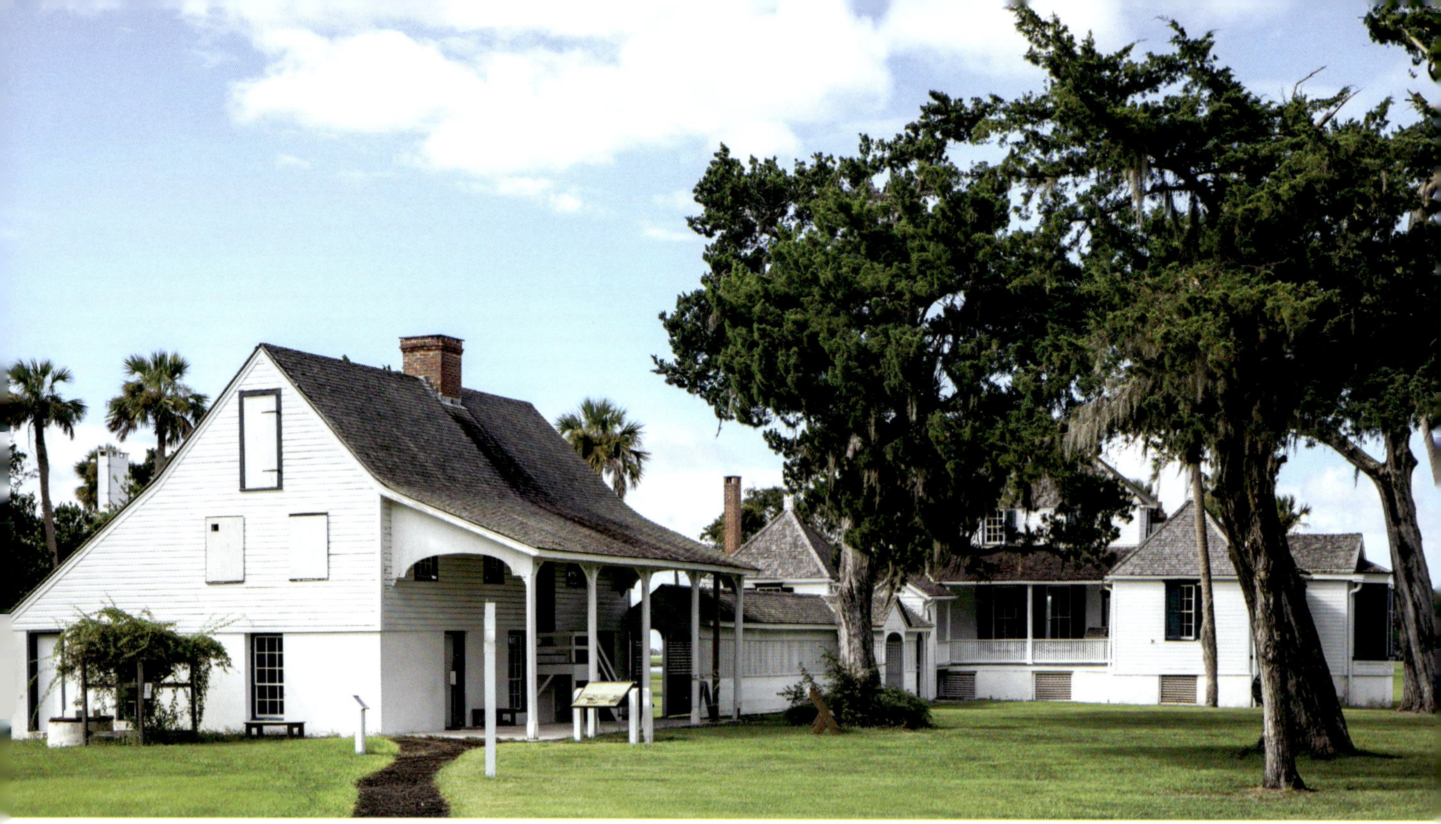

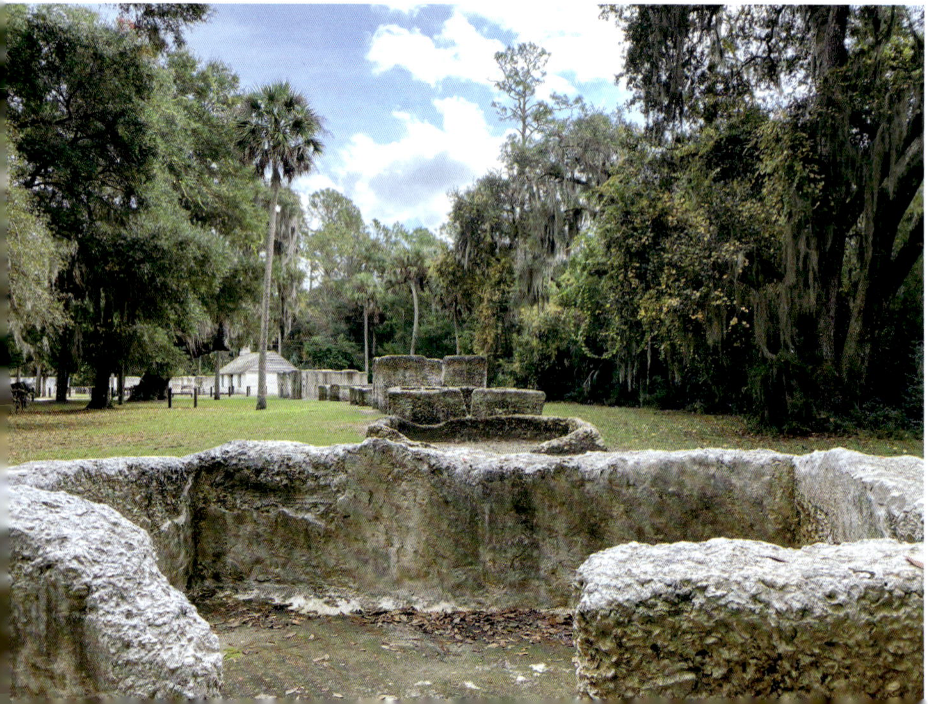

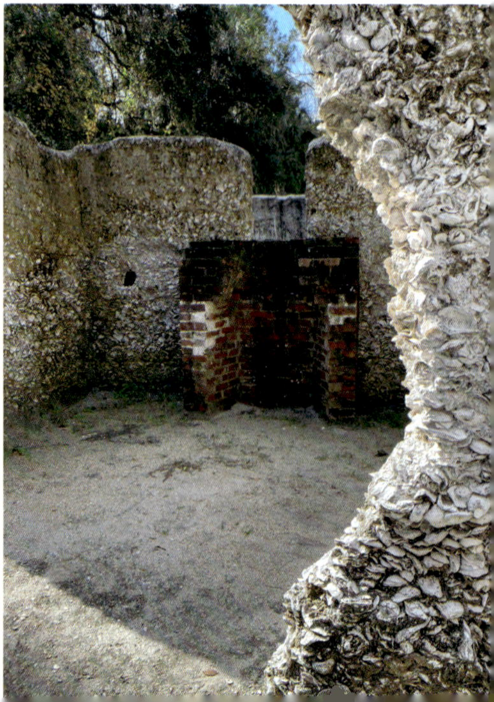

government secretly fomented a fake uprising in an effort to annex Spanish Florida. The attempt failed.

The main house has been remodeled at least nine times. Now listed as the oldest still-standing plantation house in Florida, it is open to the public, by reservation, on weekends.

The kitchen's second story was later occupied by Anta Jai Kingsley, the first of Kingsley's common-law slave wives, whose name he changed to Anna. The building is still called the Maum Anna House. Polygamy was common in parts of West Africa, where Anta Kingsley was born, and wives often maintained separate residences from their husbands.

The twenty-five tabby cabins are situated across a grassy, tree-shaded field far from the main house. They are the survivors of the plantation's thirty-two original cabins, which were arranged in an arc. Each cabin had a tabby floor, a window or two, and a fireplace built of tabby bricks. Some of the cabins had partitioned sleeping rooms; others had a loft over a single room. A few had back porches that faced away from the main house, a feature considered unusual because it allowed the enslaved some privacy from their owner. Each cabin had a door that locked, another uncommon feature.

Charles Thomson, who briefly owned the island in the mid-1800s, started building a house for his daughter, using tabby blocks sawn from some of the cabins. Thomson died before the house was finished, and it was never occupied. The structure, now called the Thomson Tabby House, sits on a shell mound beside the road.

For many years, locals claimed the house belonged to another of Kingsley's common-law slave wives, Munsila Magundo, and their daughter, Fatima. Researchers have since identified Thomson as the builder. The shell midden

SITE 8   Kingsley Plantation   59

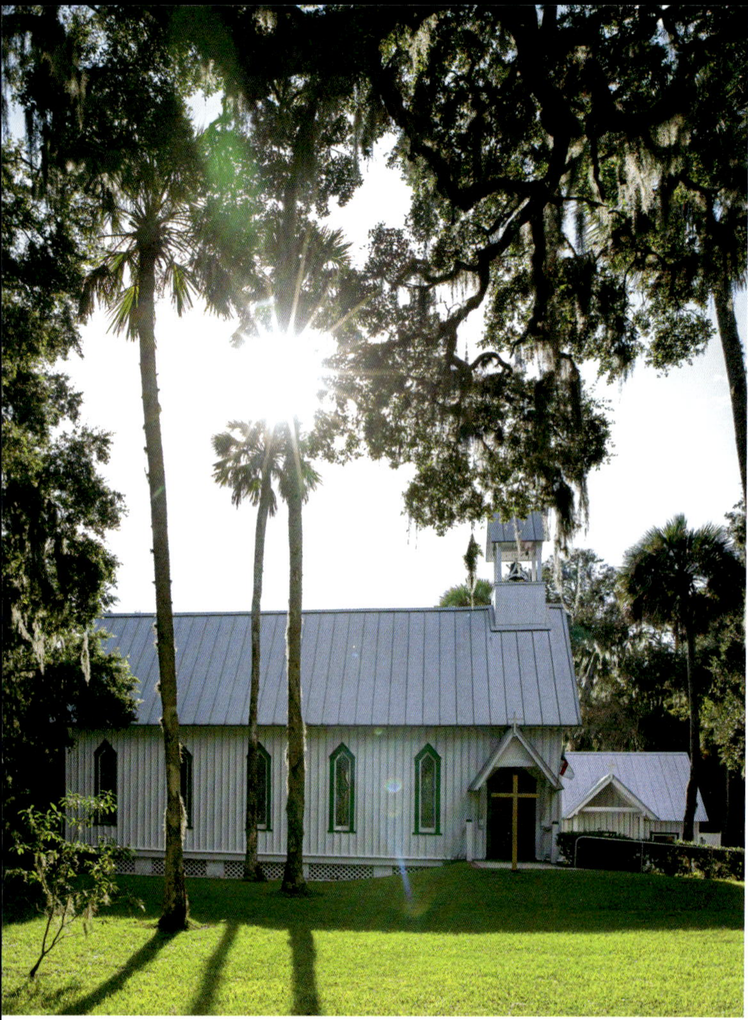
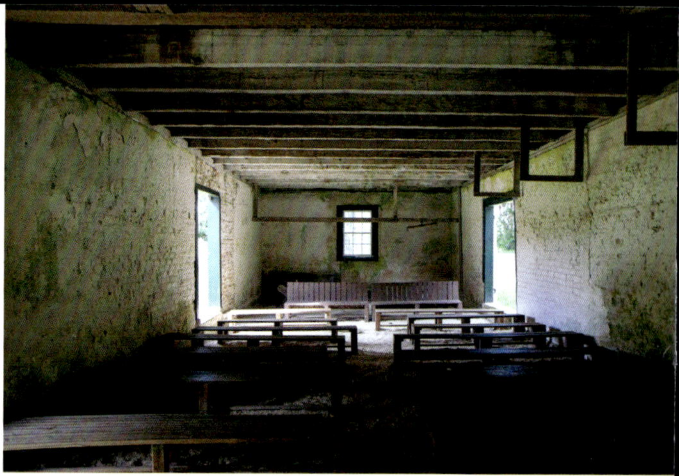
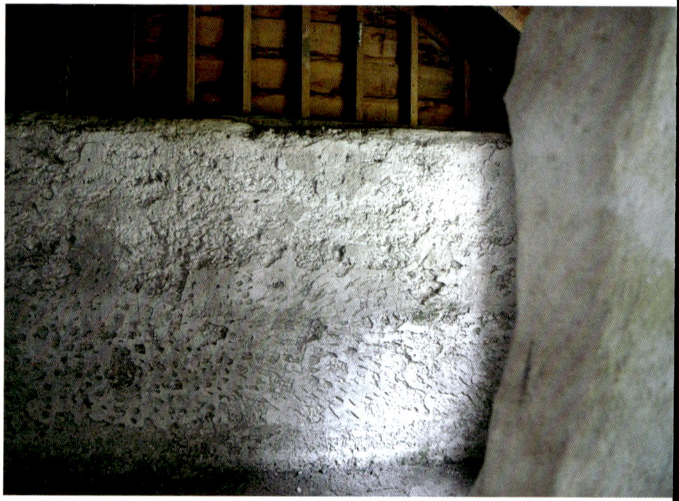
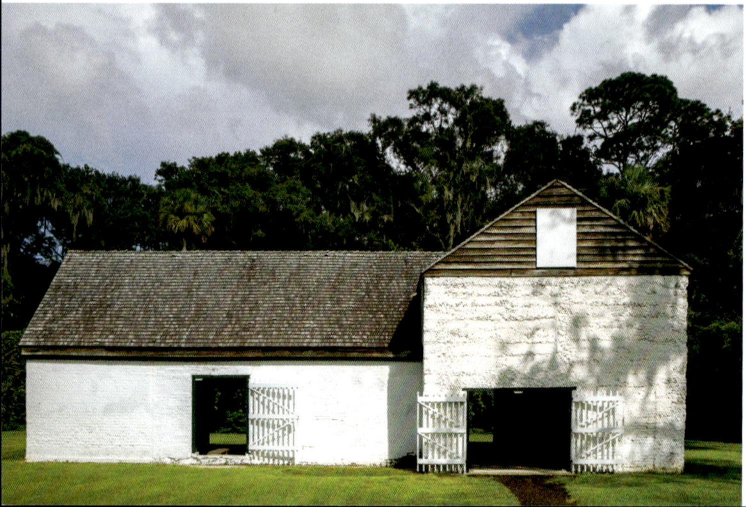
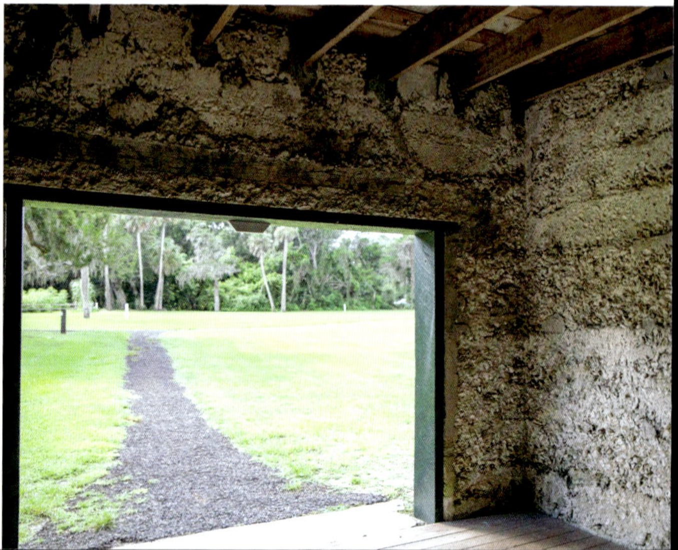

was named the Magundo Mound in recognition of the colloquial name.

After the Civil War, the surviving cabins were occupied by freedmen until the 1890s. John Rollins, another owner of the property, demolished about seven of the cabins and salvaged the blocks and slabs of tabby to build a dock and boathouse. Later, the remaining cabins served as tourist attractions for the private Ribault Club on the island.

In recent years, an expert in the art of restoring historic tabby structures capped the cabin walls to protect them from further deterioration. Graffiti has been removed, and the walls have been replastered with lime stucco. A garden on the property includes indigo plants, once grown and processed to make dye, and a small plot of sea island cotton, the money crop for many coastal plantations.

Today, woodlands cover most of the sixty-acre plantation site, where fields of sea island cotton once flourished. Palmetto Avenue, the long palm-lined drive leading to the property, is unpaved and can be bumpy, but the flanking woods are cool and beautiful. An alternate paved route is not as picturesque, but it is quicker.

Anta Madgigine Jai Kingsley, 1793–1870

At age thirteen, Anta Madgigine Jai was kidnapped from her Wolof community in Senegal and enslaved, according to her biographer, Daniel L. Shafer, a history professor at the University of North Florida. Although descended from a royal lineage, Anta lost the protection of that status after her father lost his battle to lead the Wolof people.

The teenage girl survived the horrors of barracoons (holding pens or barracks) on the African coast before being packed into the dark, cramped hold of a ship with hundreds of other captives. During the long Middle Passage from Africa to the Americas, slave ships lost an average of 15 percent of their human cargo to dysentery, dehydration, yellow fever, seasickness, and mistreatment. Below decks, where there were limited or no sanitary facilities and inadequate ventilation, the stench of human waste and vomit and the moans and cries of the ill and dying would have been unbearable. During the voyage, Anta might have watched the bodies of fellow captives being thrown overboard to scavenging sharks.

After the ship landed in Cuba in the autumn of 1806, Anta was enslaved by Zephaniah Kingsley Jr., then forty-one, who took her to Laurel Grove, his plantation on the St. Johns River in Spanish Florida. He changed her name to Anna and impregnated her. In Florida, Anna was sometimes known as an African princess, probably because of her royal lineage. Kingsley always called her his wife, although they never legally married.

Kingsley was a complex man. A third-generation Quaker, he became a slave trader and planter who advocated slavery as the only way to make southern plantations profitable. He argued in favor of what he deemed humane treatment of the enslaved, saying such treatment made them less likely to rebel or escape. Kingsley fathered children by other women he enslaved, educated and supported his mixed-race offspring, and ultimately freed them all, along with many other slaves he held.

Even in Spanish Florida, where the enslaved were often treated as indentured servants and allowed to work toward

Anna Kingsley planted this allée of palms on Fort George Island's Palmetto Avenue, shown here in 1895. Descendants of these palms still line the road.

gaining their freedom, Kingsley's familial arrangements raised eyebrows. He never attempted to conceal his "co-wives" and children from his kinfolk or other planters.

While Kingsley was away on lengthy trips to import or trade slaves, he left Anna in charge of his properties. He praised her character, intelligence, and industry, describing her as "a fine, tall figure, black as jet, but very handsome." Unlike most enslaved Africans, Anna did not spend her life in bondage. Kingsley emancipated her and their three children when she was eighteen, five years after he purchased her. As a free woman, Anna was entitled to a land grant from the Spanish government. She was awarded five acres on the St. Johns River across from Kingsley's Laurel Grove Plantation. Kingsley gave her a dozen slaves of her own and lent her more slaves to construct a house and outbuildings. Anna began a poultry business, raising ducks and chickens.

Not long after the move, Anna's life was thrown into chaos by the Patriot War of 1812–14, a little-known conflict that occurred at the same time the War of 1812 was being waged between Great Britain and the United States. President James Madison and other governmental officials conspired to foment a rebellion in Spanish East Florida, which they hoped to annex as a new U.S. territory. They intended to recruit rebels from Spanish Florida, but most Spanish residents were happy with their government. Most of the so-called rebels were in fact recruited from southern states, primarily Georgia.

John Houstoun McIntosh, a Scottish planter from Georgia who then owned Fort George Island, signed on to lead the rebellion. Along with volunteers and U.S. troops allegedly sent to protect Spanish towns and people, McIntosh invaded East Florida and pushed south, raising the rebellion flag in every town he captured.

The rebels attacked Laurel Grove Plantation, along with other properties along the St. Johns River, capturing forty-one enslaved people. Anna knew that she and her children would be in serious danger if they were captured. When rebels moved in to attack her new homestead in November 1813, cannon fire from a Spanish gunboat anchored in the St. Johns River drove the invaders into the woods. Anna rowed out to the gunboat and persuaded the commander to take her family, along with her slaves and some of Kingsley's, to safety farther south. To earn their passage, Anna volunteered to lead a party of soldiers to Kingsley's fortified compound to seize the abandoned cannons there. She also promised to destroy her own homestead rather than surrender the property to the enemy.

After the successful cannon raid, Anna slipped back into her home and set fires in trunks filled with combustible materials. The fires were still smoldering when she returned to the gunboat. The Spanish commander was not convinced that she had torched her own property until the buildings burst into flame. The Florida government later awarded Anna 350 acres as compensation for her lost property and her bravery in defying the enemy.

The rebellion ended when Spain threatened outright war with the United States, but it took a year of negotiations between the two countries to reach the terms of the settlement. In the meantime, the rebels, rogue U.S. troops, and renegades continued to raid, pillage, and destroy property in Spanish Florida. Laurel Grove was left in ruins. In 1814, Kingsley rented Fort George Island and bought the property three years later. The seller was John Houstoun McIntosh, who had fled back to Georgia in fear of reprisals from the Spanish government after the rebellion ended.

Kingsley moved Anna and his extended family and slaves to the island and began restoring and improving the old plantation there. He lived alone in the main house; Anna and her children moved into the second story of the tabby kitchen building, which was connected to the main house by a short tabby walkway. Kingsley may have chosen the arrangement so that Anna and his other common-law wives could visit him in private when he wanted their company. Anna was often lonely in what came to be called the Maum Anna House. She pined for her family in Africa, whom she would never see again.

In 1821, after Florida became a U.S. territory, slave laws and the treatment of free people of color became draconian. Interracial marriage was forbidden. Kingsley wrote a spirited defense of slavery but also lobbied for the humane treatment of the enslaved. His views were expressed in a pamphlet first published in 1828: *A Treatise on the Patriarchal System of Society*.

Fearing for the safety of his wives, children, and those he held as slaves, Kingsley sold the Fort George Island plantation to his nephews in 1836 and bought thousands of acres in Haiti, a free Black republic. He moved his wives and most of his mixed-race children there, although two of his daughters with Anna Kingsley had married successful white men and opted to remain in Florida. In Haiti, he treated those he enslaved much as indentured servants and freed them after they completed their contracts.

Kingsley had intended to relocate to Haiti with his family, but died in New York City in 1843. In his will, Kingsley left property to Anna, who returned to Florida to claim it. The will was contested by some of his white relatives, including Anna McNeill, the mother of James McNeill Whistler, who painted her famous portrait.

Anna Kingsley prevailed in court and lived out her life in Florida, near her daughters.

SITE 9   *Short Take*

Thomson House

c. 1854

Fort George Island Cultural State Park
Fort George Road near Palmetto Avenue

National Register of Historic Places

The tabby Thomson House on Fort George Island was under construction by 1854 but was never finished. Charles Thomson, who bought the island that year, intended the house for his daughter and son-in-law, but he died in 1855 before it was completed.

The structure sits high above the road on top of a prehistoric shell mound named the Magundo Midden, which probably provided oyster shells for the tabby. The name for the midden dates to an earlier island owner. For many years, locals claimed the house had been built by Zephaniah Kingsley for one of his common-law slave wives, Munsilna Magundo. Kingsley, who owned Fort George Island in the early 1800s, built extensively with tabby.

Locals claimed that Kingsley had constructed the house for Magundo and their daughter Fatima and willed it to them when he died in 1831. It was said that the dwelling was finished and that mother and daughter lived there. But a local researcher pursuing a ghost story linked with the house discovered that it did not appear on maps of the area before 1854, more than twenty years after Kingsley's death.

There are other indications the structure was never finished. The fireplace was never lined with red-clay brick, and wood grain shows in the spreader pin holes made by wooden ties used in the tabby construction. Usually, builders filled the holes with lime mortar or tabby. In addition, the building's position on a rise indicates a higher degree of engineering skill than was used on the other tabby structures built by Kingsley on the island.

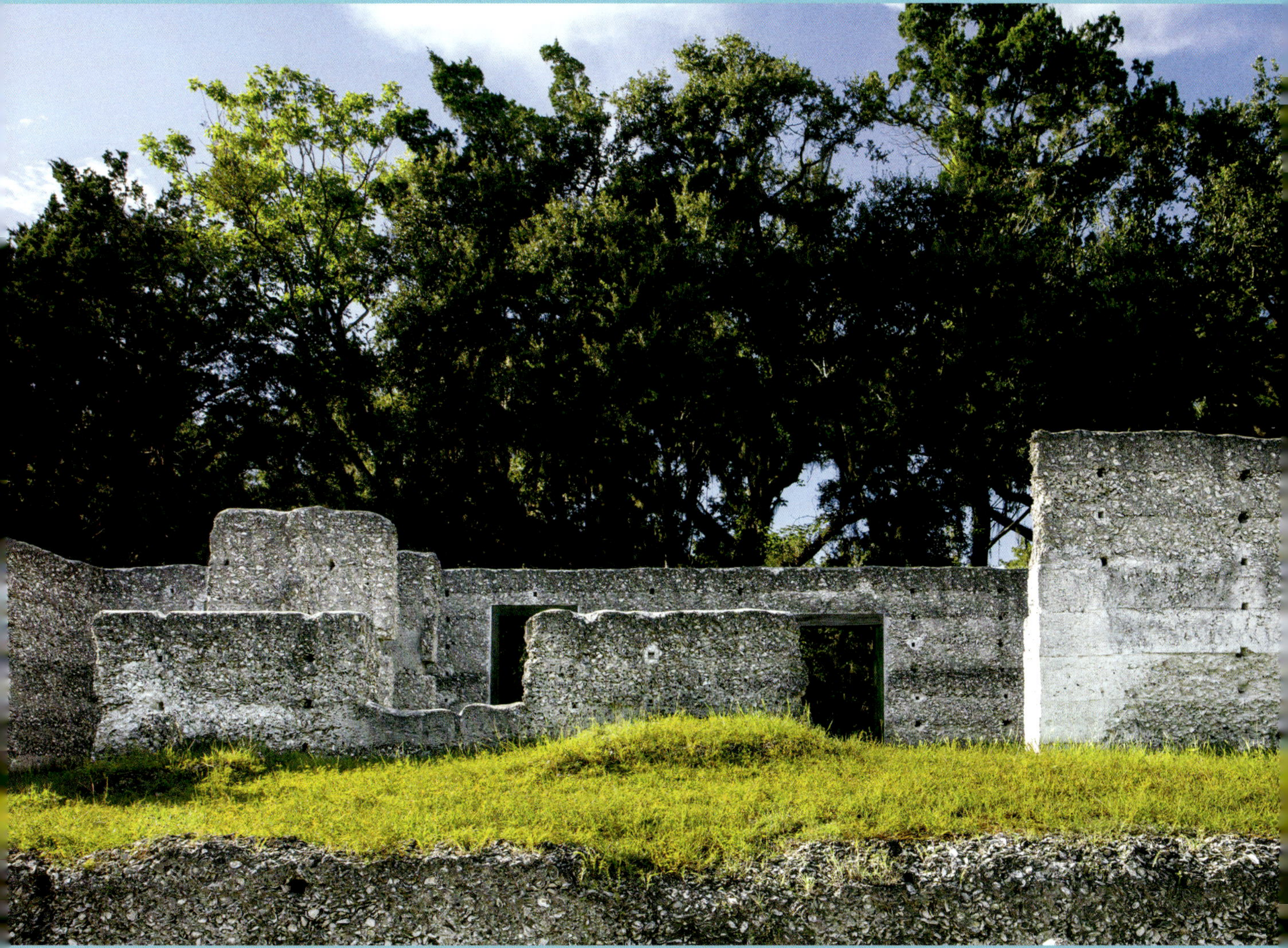

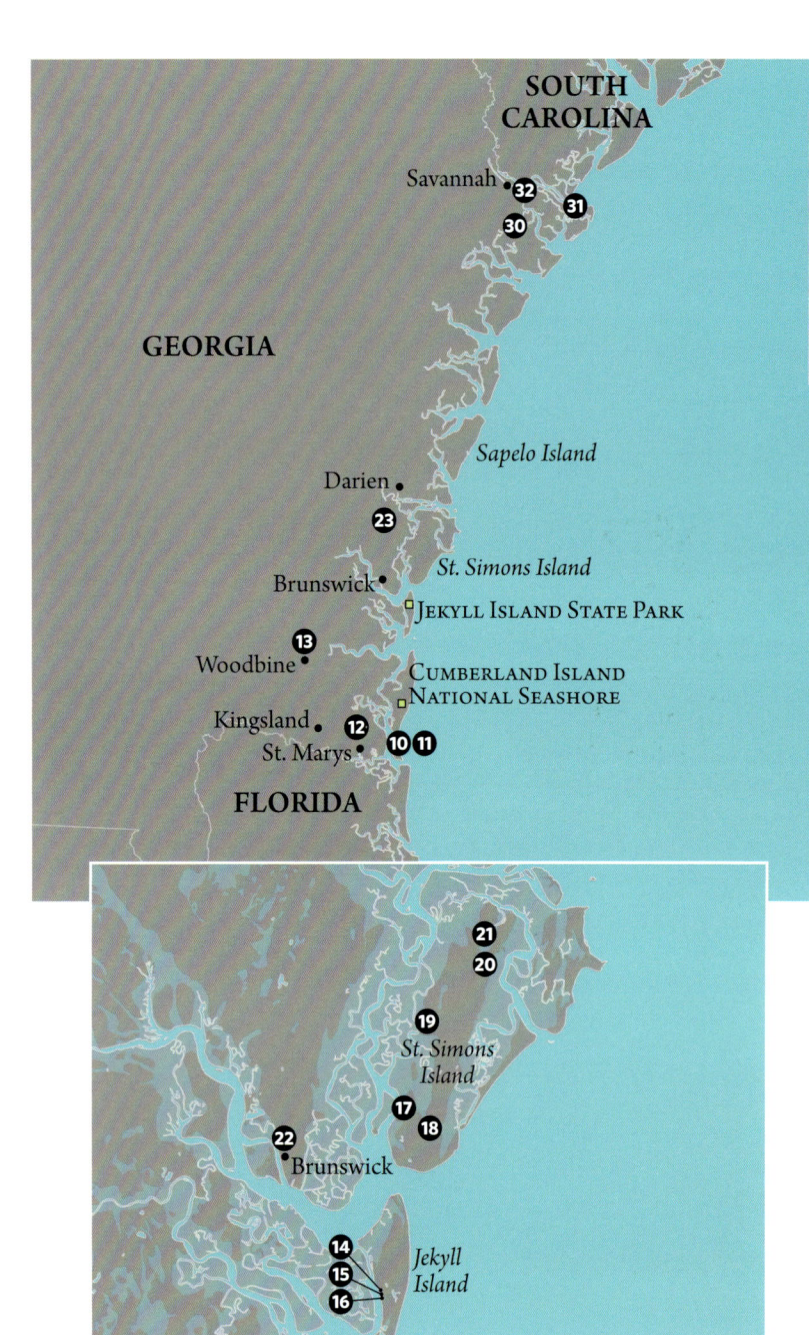

Sites

CUMBERLAND ISLAND NATIONAL SEASHORE
- ⑩ Dungeness I and II
- ⑪ Miller-Greene House

ST. MARYS/KINGSLAND/WOODBINE
- ⑫ McIntosh Sugar Works
- ⑬ St. Mark's Episcopal Church

JEKYLL ISLAND STATE PARK
- ⑭ Horton House
- ⑮ Hollybourne Cottage
- ⑯ Dairy silo

ST. SIMONS ISLAND
- ⑰ Hamilton Plantation Slave Cabins
- ⑱ Retreat Plantation Slave Cabin
- ⑲ Fort Frederica
- ⑳ Cannon's Point Plantation
- ㉑ Hampton Plantation

BRUNSWICK
- ㉒ St. Athanasius Protestant Episcopal Church
- ㉓ Hopeton Plantation Sugar Mill

DARIEN
- ㉔ Waterfront Warehouses and Adam-Strain Building
- ㉕ St. Cyprian's Episcopal Church
- ㉖ Ashantilly
- ㉗ The Thicket Sugar Mill and Rum Distillery

SAPELO ISLAND
- ㉘ Chocolate Plantation
- ㉙ South End House

SAVANNAH
- ㉚ Wormsloe State Historic Site
- ㉛ Fort Pulaski National Monument
- ㉜ Owens-Thomas House

PART II *Georgia*

THOUSANDS OF YEARS AGO, Native Americans settled the Georgia coast, attracted by the rich bounty of seafood in the estuarine waters and marshes. By the time of contact, two groups of Native people were living on Georgia's coastal mainland and sea islands: the Guale (WAL-ee) people north of the Altamaha River and the Mocama people south of the river. The two groups spoke different languages and were traditional enemies, although their cultures were similar.

The first European settlement in today's United States is thought to have been located in Guale territory somewhere on Sapelo Sound, north of the McIntosh County sea island. (Earlier attempts, such as that by Juan Ponce de León in 1521, had failed.) In 1526, Lucas Vázquez de Ayllón, a judge from Hispaniola, founded San Miguel de Gualdape with six hundred colonists. Ayllón imported a number of skilled Africans, the first documented enslaved people in North America, who staged the first slave uprising at the settlement.

Many of the colonists, including the judge, died of unusually cold weather, illness, hunger, or conflicts with Natives. After less than four months, the 150 Spanish survivors fled en masse back to Hispaniola. They probably abandoned the Africans, some of whom may have joined local Indigenous groups. A period skeleton found in the area in recent years shows a mixture of African and Native American characteristics. The exact location of San Miguel de Gualdape has never been determined. In 1540, Spanish artifacts were discovered in an abandoned Native village farther inland by explorer Hernando de Soto during his trek through Georgia and the Southeast. Those artifacts may have come from the short-lived coastal town.

San Miguel's settlers would have introduced the first common European and African diseases to North America, scourges such as smallpox that ultimately devastated Native peoples.

During the late sixteenth and early seventeenth centuries, Franciscan friars from St. Augustine established Catholic missions in Guale and Mocama villages in coastal Georgia. By the mid-1600s, the missions farther north along the coast, along with non-missionized Native villages inland, were under siege by English invaders from Carolina and their Native allies. Pirates and privateers also attacked and pillaged villages and missions.

Residents of several Yamasee villages inland and missions north of the Altamaha River were relocated to the lower Georgia coast, where Spanish soldiers from St. Augustine could better protect them. By 1684, the Native people who had inhabited the coast before contact were gone.

More than 150 years after Spanish colonists built St. Augustine, James Edward Oglethorpe established the colony of Georgia on Yamacraw Bluff, overlooking the Savannah River, about twenty miles from the Atlantic Ocean. Georgia was the last of the thirteen original colonies and the only one governed by a board of trustees.

The Natives whom Oglethorpe met upon his arrival in 1733 were coastal newcomers. Tomochichi, the Native leader who negotiated with Oglethorpe for the high bluff on the Savannah River, was born in the Lower Creek confederation inland but left to found the small Yamacraw band, an offshoot of the Yamasees and Lower Creeks inland. Mary Musgrove, the daughter of a Scots trader and a Native American woman, translated for Tomochichi and Oglethorpe. She later built a tabby house in the fortified town of Frederica on St. Simons Island.

The twenty trustees who, along with Oglethorpe, administered the Georgia colony initially banned slavery, rum, and the ownership of large tracts of land. The trustees wanted to discourage the colonists from creating large plantations such as the ones in Carolina. They expected them to make their living by farming, performing jobs such as blacksmithing or carpentry, and operating taverns and other small businesses.

The colony was founded to give imprisoned English debtors and poor people a fresh start in life, but in reality, most who came to Georgia were from the middle class. Oglethorpe wanted them to create a silk industry. The colonists were ordered to plant imported white mulberry trees to provide food for the silkworms. The industry enjoyed only limited success, in part because unraveling the cocoons proved to be such tedious, time-consuming work. White mulberry trees, along with native red mulberries, still thrive on the coast.

A major aim of the Georgia colony was to protect Savannah and English settlements in Carolina from the Spanish in Florida. One of Oglethorpe's first colonists, Noble Jones, built a fortified tabby home south of Savannah to protect the new town from Spanish attacks.

In 1736, Oglethorpe built a town and a tabby fortress down the coast about seventy miles from Savannah on St. Simons Island. In doing so, he encroached on the debatable land, a swath of coastal and inland Georgia long claimed by Great Britain, Spain, and France and officially off-limits to settlement by all three. For decades the debatable land was home to renegade traders and other scofflaws. After Spanish and British soldiers clashed on St. Simons in 1742, the Spanish never again made serious attempts to regain land north of Florida on the Atlantic Seaboard.

Oglethorpe's right-hand man, Major William Horton, was granted five hundred acres of land on nearby Jekyll Island. After his first house was burned to the ground by Spanish troops retreating from battles on St. Simons, Horton rebuilt it of tabby. The tabby walls of the house still stand.

In 1750, slavery was legalized in Georgia, which led to the development of large rice plantations and the importation and enslavement of thousands of Africans. Rice cultivation was brutal. Enslaved workers lived an average of only sixteen years after being sent out into the muddy rice fields.

The Revolutionary War hero Nathanael Greene, who led the southern campaign, acquired both Mulberry Grove Plantation on the Savannah River and Cumberland Island, the southernmost of the Georgia sea islands, after the war. Greene's wife, Caty, was a captivating woman who encouraged Eli Whitney to develop the cotton gin, a device that helped entrench slavery in the Deep South. She and her second husband built their Dungeness Mansion of tabby on Cumberland, on the oyster-shell foundation of a former Franciscan mission.

Sea island cotton, a Caribbean variety famed for its long, silky fibers, was introduced to North America after the Revolutionary War. It quickly became a mainstay of the southeastern economy. The valuable cotton grows best in a semitropical coastal environment within about thirty miles of the sea.

Because mosquito-borne diseases such as malaria and yellow fever were rampant on the coast during warmer months, many planters and their families retreated to higher ground inland for the season. Enslaved people, isolated on the remote plantations, developed the unique Gullah Geechee culture and language, remnants of which survive today.

In an attempt to acquire Spanish Florida as a U.S. territory, President James Madison and several cabinet members plotted a fake rebellion to make it look as though Floridians were rising up against their government. The effort, which involved the prominent Georgia planter John Houstoun McIntosh, ultimately failed, but Spanish Florida never fully recovered.

During the Civil War, Union General William Tecumseh Sherman burned his way from Atlanta to the coast, liberating the enslaved along the way and leaving a swath of destruction in his wake. He spared the historic city of Savannah from burning and instead jokingly gave it to President Abraham Lincoln as a Christmas present.

The war left the South in ruins. Many enslaved people taken inland by their owners during the war made their way back to their former plantations after ratification of the Thirteenth Amendment officially freed them. General Sherman issued a field order giving the freedmen coastal land, but his order was rescinded by President Andrew Johnson, a southerner who took office after Lincoln was assassinated.

Around 1900, wealthy northerners boosted the coastal economy by building sawmills to process longleaf pine logs harvested from great forests inland and rafted down rivers that flowed to the coast. The lumber was shipped all over the world. Ballast stones dumped by the ships form the foundations of some of the hammocks, or small marsh islands, that lie along coastal waterways.

The commercial fishing industry grew during the twentieth century. So did tourism. Wealthy northern industrialists purchased entire islands on the southeastern coast for private retreats. One writer at the time extolled the "tender beauty" of the sea islands. The Jekyll Island Club, whose members were billed as the world's wealthiest people, bought Jekyll and wintered on the Georgia sea island from 1886 until World War II. Most members stayed in the ornate Victorian clubhouse, but some built large vacation cottages, including one member who built his cottage of tabby.

Since World War II, rapid development on the sea islands, aided by causeway links to the mainland, has boosted the coastal economy but caused environmental damage.

CHAPTER 3   *Cumberland Island National Seashore*

CUMBERLAND IS THE GIANT of Georgia's sea islands; everything about it is supersized. Huge rolling sand dunes, some of them forty feet high, rise above its eighteen-mile-long stretch of pristine beach. In places the mountains of sand have pushed westward to smother swaths of forest. Alligators and water lilies share the eighty-three acre Lake Whitney, one of the largest freshwater ponds on any of the sea islands.

Centuries-old live oaks, soaring magnolias, clusters of semitropical cabbage palms, and vast palmetto thickets are the near-private province of an almost endless variety of wildlife, including almost three hundred species of birds, some migratory. A sizable chunk of Cumberland is designated a federal wilderness area, which limits human activity within its boundaries.

Animals whose ancestors were introduced to the island centuries ago include feral pigs that nurture their young in six-foot-wide nests of pine straw, and horses that graze around millionaires' mansions, in the high marsh, and on the dunes. Sightings of the half-wild horses thrill visitors, but the animals' trampling and grazing damages marsh and woodland vegetation as well as plants that anchor the sand dunes, which protect the interior of the island against hurricanes. The feral pigs feast on the eggs of endangered sea turtles that nest on Cumberland's beach on summer nights.

There is no causeway to Cumberland. People travel back and forth from the mainland town of St. Marys on the ferry operated by the National Park Service, which manages the island. Traditionally, hikers and wilderness campers have explored Cumberland on foot or on bicycles, but a Park Service van and a tram now offer daily tours. Only three hundred visitors are allowed on the island a day, so Cumberland never seems overrun with people.

Cumberland's human history dates back to Paleo-Indians who occupied the sea islands and coastal mainland during the Late Archaic period (3,000–5,000 years ago).

Oyster-shell middens along the island's western shore testify to the abundance of the Natives' favorite seafood.

The Native American settlement of Tacatacuru was one of several Indigenous Mocama villages established on Cumberland before contact. The Mocama, whose name means "people of the sea," were a branch of the large Timucua chiefdom of northern Florida and southern Georgia. They called the island Wissoe for its abundance of sassafras trees. Native Americans used the bark, leaves, and roots of sassafras to make fragrant tea, thicken soups and stews, make poultices, soothe irritated skin and eyes, and reduce fever.

In 1587, Franciscan friars from St. Augustine established a mission on Cumberland, one of the first in North America, and changed the local settlement's Indigenous name, Tacatacuru, to San Pedro. The friars and Natives gathered quantities of shell from ancient middens and piled them up to create a raised foundation for a mission called San Pedro de Tacatacuru.

Father Francisco Pareja, a talented linguist, lived for a time at the Cumberland mission. Scholars believe that it was there that he developed the first writing system for Native American languages. He translated catechisms from Spanish into Timucua and its dialects, including Mocama, so that his fellow friars could instruct the Natives in the Catholic faith in their own languages. Pareja's first book, which dates to 1612, was the earliest ever published in an Indigenous North American language. Pareja wrote eight other similar books; six have survived.

An attack by the British pirate Thomas Jingle in 1684 forced the Franciscans and Native people to abandon the island and flee to St. Augustine.

After James Edward Oglethorpe, a British military officer, founded the Georgia colony, he ordered forts built on the north and south ends of the island, which he renamed Cumberland.

The widow of Revolutionary War hero Nathanael Greene built a mansion called Dungeness on the island in the early 1800s on the raised oyster-shell terrace left over from the Spanish mission. She and her family lived in the tabby structure for years before it burned down. A second Dungeness was built almost a century later by Lucy Carnegie, the widow of Thomas Carnegie of U.S. Steel. The second mansion was also destroyed by fire. The mansions are now referred to as Dungeness I and Dungeness II.

The Carnegies built other mansions on Cumberland. One, Greyfield, is still owned by family members, who operate it as a rustic but elegant inn. A second mansion,

Plum Orchard, is open one day a week for public tours. Its custom-designed wallpaper features the water lilies seen on Lake Whitney.

It is rumored that Oglethorpe built a hunting lodge called Dungeness in the mid-1730s on the site later occupied by the mansions. No trace of such a structure has been found. At any rate, Oglethorpe brought the name "Dungeness" to Cumberland. In 1733, when he negotiated for land in his new colony with Tomochichi, the leader of the Yamacraw people, Oglethorpe took Tomochichi and his nephew and heir Toonahowee to England, where the teenage Toonahowee met the teenage Duke of Cumberland, the third son of George II.

The two boys became friends. The duke presented Toonahowee with a gold watch. In return, Toonahowee asked Oglethorpe to name the Georgia sea island in honor of his new friend. The traditional domain of the Duke of Cumberland in Kent, England, includes a bluff named Dungeness.

Farmers with small plots of land settled on Cumberland's north end during the late 1700s and early 1800s. After the Civil War, a number of people who had lived in slavery on Cumberland remained on the island. One neighborhood, called the Settlement, is home to the First African Baptist Church, established in 1893. John F. Kennedy Jr. and Carolyn Bessette were married at the tiny church in 1996.

High Point, on Cumberland's north end, was home to a popular hotel and other tourist accommodations in the late nineteenth and early twentieth centuries. The Candler family of Atlanta, whose patriarch founded the Coca-Cola empire, has owned property on Cumberland for decades. There is other privately owned land on the island, but the bulk of Cumberland is owned by the federal government. It was named a national seashore in 1972.

Cumberland's National Register Historic District on the south end includes the ruins of Dungeness and a small tabby cottage built in 1803 for Greene's descendants. It is Cumberland's oldest structure. Restored in the late twentieth century by a tabby expert, the cottage is now called the Miller-Greene House.

Dungeness I and II

Cumberland Island National Seashore

National Register Historic District

HISTORIC SIGNIFICANCE: The first Dungeness mansion, completed in 1803 by the widow of the Revolutionary War hero Nathaniel Greene, is the only four-story house in the United States built of tabby made with oyster-shell lime. The spectral ruins of the second Dungeness, built in part of revival tabby made with portland cement by the steel magnate Thomas Carnegie, is now the centerpiece of the Cumberland Island National Seashore's Historic District.

After the Revolutionary War, Brigadier General Nathanael Greene acquired eleven thousand acres on Cumberland, including the Dungeness tract, where he planned to build a large house and establish a working plantation. Greene had fought alongside George Washington at Valley Forge and led the Continental Army's successful southern campaign. He died of sunstroke in 1786 before his planned Cumberland residence was under construction.

His widow, Catherine, called Caty, later married Phineas Miller, the family tutor and Greene's personal secretary. The Millers built the magnificent tabby mansion they called Dungeness House on top of "a large shell mound," one visitor reported. The mansion, which towered above a grove of live oaks, served for decades as a landmark for mariners.

The structure was huge, with more than twelve thousand square feet spread over four floors, not counting the basement, subbasement, and attic. It had four chimneys and sixteen fireplaces. The mansion's shell base elevated the construction site twenty feet above sea level, boosting the roof peak to almost eighty feet. The first-floor tabby walls were six feet thick to support the upper floors. Builders skimmed those walls with a traditional topcoat of lime stucco, but the interiors of the upper floors were left unfinished, with the oyster-shell aggregate visible. Visitors often commented on the incongruity of the Millers' fine antiques and artwork being set against the rough tabby.

The hipped roof was sheathed in copper that weathered to a beautiful blue-green in the sea air. A hurricane in 1815 ripped the roof off; it was replaced at great expense. An observation platform on top of the house offered panoramic views and allowed occupants to identify approaching ships before they reached the island. Pirates were still a problem along the Eastern Seaboard in the early nineteenth century.

A high wall surrounded the mansion and its twelve acres of gardens, where the Millers planted exotic shrubs,

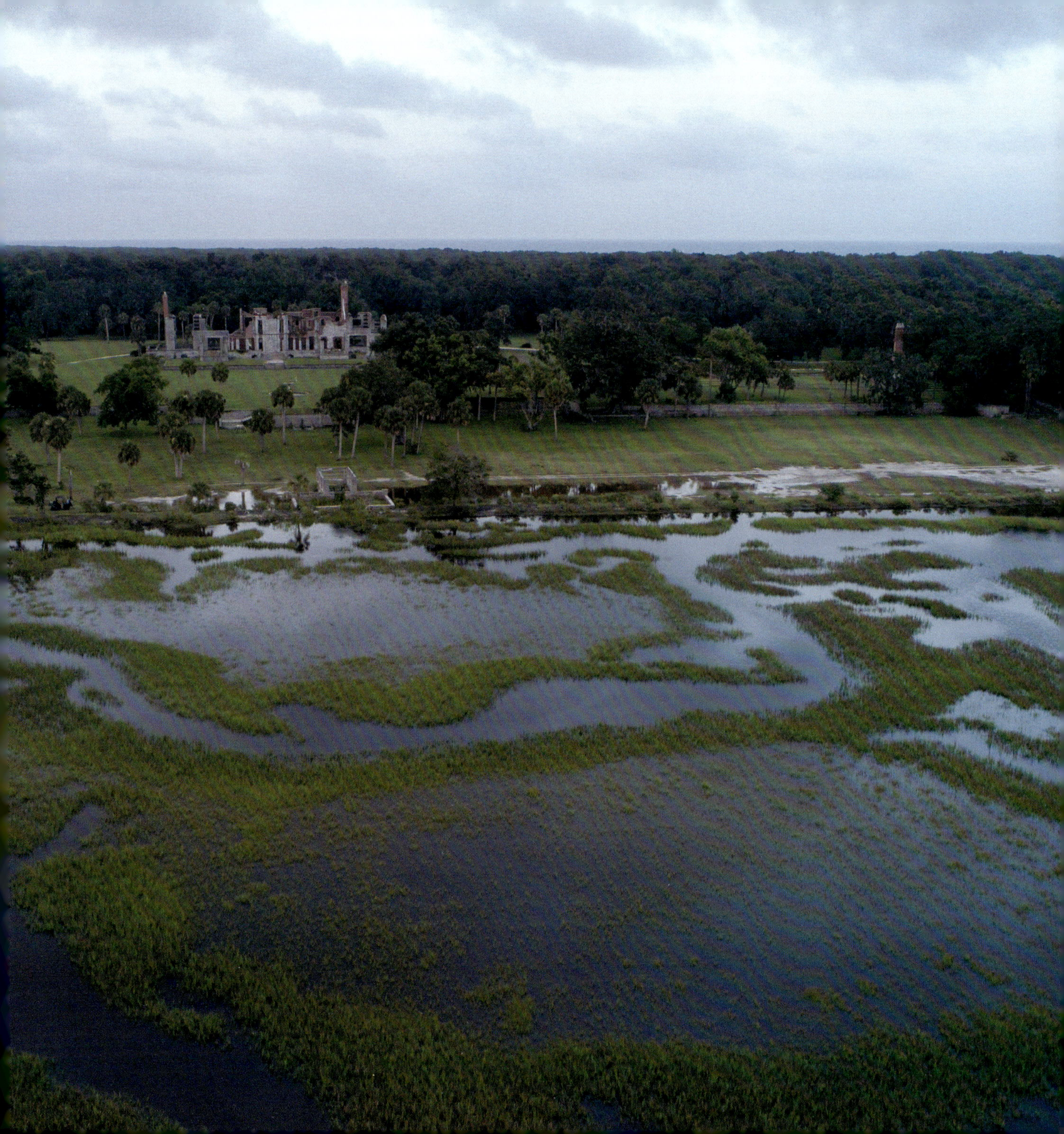

flowers, and fruit trees—plum, pear, olive, date palm, fig, guava, pomegranate, and orange.

The wide central hallway of the house was cooled by ocean breezes. It served as the summer living room, game room, dining room, music room, and library. A sewing room and schoolroom were at the rear of the house. Public rooms were on the first floor; the family's living quarters occupied the second, third, and fourth floors. Bedchambers were named for the rooms below: the music room chamber, the sewing room chamber, and so on.

The Millers moved into Dungeness House in 1803. According to family members, the mansion's upper floors were still unfinished because the couple was eager to move in after years of construction. Others say they ran out of money. Nathanael Greene's estate was burdened with heavy debts after the revolution; most had been incurred because the general spent his own money and borrowed more to feed, clothe, and pay his troops.

The Millers had many notable visitors at Dungeness. Eli Whitney visited often. It was while living at Mulberry Grove, the Greenes' plantation near Savannah, that Whitney invented the cotton gin.

During the War of 1812, the British general George Cockburn, who burned the White House along with much of Washington, D.C., was sent south to free enslaved people and create disturbances to divert American troops from a planned British invasion of New Orleans. Great Britain and the United States signed the Treaty of Ghent on Christmas Eve 1814, officially ending the war, but Cockburn did not receive immediate notice of the treaty and set up his headquarters at Dungeness in January 1815. Even when newspapers reported the war's end, Cockburn stayed on for several months, offering the enslaved asylum on British ships.

During Cockburn's occupation, he banished the Millers and their guests to the upstairs rooms. Even with the enforced separation, a young British officer fell in love with a planter's daughter visiting Dungeness from St. Simons Island, and the couple later married.

Henry "Light-Horse Harry" Lee died at Dungeness House in 1818. Lee, another Revolutionary War hero, was an accomplished rider who headed the cavalry under Greene's command. Lee was the father of the noted Confederate general Robert E. Lee. Henry Lee was traveling along the southern coast by boat when he realized he was dying. He asked to be put ashore at Dungeness, knowing the family of his friend and former military superior would care for him. The Greenes' daughter Louisa nursed him until his death a few months later.

Dungeness I stood until 1866, when its timber framing, flooring, roof rafters, and beams were destroyed by fire.

The wealthy steel baron Thomas Carnegie began building the second Dungeness House on the ruins of the first in the 1880s, but died before the mansion was completed. Lucy Carnegie, his widow, finished the structure. Thomas Carnegie and his brother, Andrew, had founded the company that later became U.S. Steel. The Carnegie mansion was occupied into the mid-1920s, but stood vacant for about thirty years before it burned in 1956. Investigators suspected arson. Dungeness II, built of revival tabby made with portland cement, reflected the Queen Anne and Stick Victorian styles. The east tower was ninety feet high, the outer walls were faced with granite, and the roof was Vermont slate.

Catherine (Caty) Littlefield Greene, 1755–1814

Caty Littlefield of Rhode Island was the New England version of Scarlett O'Hara. She could have been the prototype for the fictional southern belle whose story is told in the novel *Gone with the Wind* against the backdrop of the Civil War. Caty Greene's real life played out in Revolutionary War times. Like Scarlett, she enchanted almost every man she met.

She loved her adoring husband, Nathanael Greene, but also had close—perhaps intimate—relationships with other prominent men. Among her admirers were George Washington, Alexander Hamilton, "Mad Anthony" Wayne, Eli Whitney, and the marquis de Lafayette. Many of Caty Greene's conquests were her husband's close friends or soldiers who served under him. Greene seemed to understand that his wife needed the attention, admiration, and intellectual stimulation of other men. Caty Greene loved parties where she could dance all night with admirers, but she also enjoyed serious discussions of politics, war strategy, and plantation economics with her husband and his associates. She held her own with intelligence, wit, and charm.

The Greenes married in 1774, a year before the first shots were fired at Lexington. Greene rose rapidly to the rank of brigadier general. Throughout the Revolutionary War, Caty Greene traveled to his headquarters at a number of battlefields.

Although the family was stressed financially by the war, Caty Greene always purchased new clothes for her visits. In her fashionable outfits, she flitted around the drab encampments like a bright tropical bird, lifting the morale of the soldiers even when they were starving and barefoot in the snow at Valley Forge.

Her vivacious personality and lively intelligence prompted many men to fall in love with her. Like Scarlett O'Hara, Caty Greene had a bad reputation in polite circles. If Greene thought that Caty sometimes breached her wedding vows—and his letters suggested that he did—he always defended her against suggestions of infidelity.

Caty Greene had few female friends. Wives raged when their husbands fell under her spell. Martha Washington, a genteel, dignified woman, was not disturbed by her

Catherine Littlefield Greene and Eli Whitney, from "Recollections of Washington and His Friends," Century Magazine, January 1878

husband's relationship with Caty Greene, even when the two danced for four hours without pause at a party. Martha was Caty's Melanie Wilkes, the much-admired character in *Gone with the Wind* who defended Scarlett against gossip even when the rumors involved Melanie's husband, Ashley.

When the Greenes' daughter Cornelia was eight, she and her mother stopped to visit the Washingtons at Mount Vernon. Overwhelmed by the honor of meeting the famous General, the little girl burst into tears. The Washingtons were enchanted. After Washington was elected president, he and the First Lady invited Cornelia to spend the winter with them at the presidential manor in Philadelphia. It was an opportunity offered to few fourteen-year-old girls.

After Greene's death, Washington offered to pay for the education of George Washington Greene, Caty and Nathanael's eldest child. So did the marquis de Lafayette, who wanted George to be educated in France. Caty Greene accepted Lafayette's offer with trepidation because her son was only twelve, and France was already embroiled in the turmoil that led to the French Revolution. The boy returned unscathed from France but drowned soon afterward in the Savannah River in a tragic accident.

After the revolution, the Greenes moved to Georgia to assume ownership of two coastal properties: Mulberry Grove on the Savannah River and the acreage on Cumberland. At Mulberry Grove, Greene searched for a tutor on behalf of neighbors and found Eli Whitney, a New Englander and recent Yale graduate. Whitney accepted the job but wrote to his brother that he was traveling south to "the end of the world" and might never be heard from again.

78   Cumberland Island, Georgia

Whitney, a decade younger than his hostess, moved into Mulberry Grove with the Greenes but never took the teaching job, in part because he hated teaching, but also because he soon fell in love with Caty Greene. She admired his genius, encouraged him to follow his passion for invention, and gave him financial support. At the Greene plantation, Whitney heard cotton planters talk of the need for a machine to remove the tiny seeds from upland cotton. A decade earlier, Joseph Eve had invented a gin to process the more delicate sea island cotton.

Caty Greene helped Whitney refine his cotton gin by using a small broom to sweep out seeds and fluff that clogged the gin's teeth. Whitney's cotton gin prompted planters to increase the number of people they kept in bondage, in order to increase cotton production, which entrenched enslavement in the South.

Mad Anthony Wayne, another hero of the Revolutionary War, was a frequent visitor to Mulberry Grove. He met Caty Greene at Valley Forge and never forgot her. Wayne earned his nickname for leading a daring and successful attack on a British fort reputed to be impregnable. He was always known afterward as Mad Anthony.

Wayne's wife rarely traveled with him. During his visits south, he dallied with a Savannah woman, but Caty Green was the woman he loved. Nathanael Greene seemed pleased that his wife and his former fellow soldier enjoyed each other's company. She had been depressed since the death of their baby daughter the year before. Wayne's company helped her heal.

When Wayne visited Caty Greene on nights when the general was out of town, tongues wagged in triple time. When Greene returned from one trip, a local gossip informed him of the rumors. As usual, the general defended his wife, telling the woman that Caty was never alone with Wayne in a household with five children, servants, and Phineas Miller, the Greenes' tutor.

Greene died suddenly of heatstroke at age forty-four. Miller pressed Caty Greene to marry him, but she wanted to enjoy her freedom. She put Miller in charge of Mulberry Grove and the acreage on Cumberland. With young children to support, Greene's estate still weighted with debt, and her discovery that she was pregnant, Caty Greene capitulated and married Miller. The couple built Dungeness House and moved into the tabby mansion along with grown children, grandchildren, other relatives, and friends.

Caty Littlefield Greene Miller was a remarkable woman, independent and bold at a time when such traits were not admired in women. She was widowed again when Miller died of blood poisoning at age thirty-nine after pricking his finger on a thorn. Caty Miller was then almost fifty.

She quarreled with her children and cut several of them out of her will before she died of fever at Dungeness House in 1814, but the bulk of her life was rich with love for her husbands, children, a few female friends, and many male admirers.

They all loved Caty back.

Miller-Greene House

The Miller-Greene House on Cumberland, also called the Tabby House, is the national seashore's oldest structure and one of its most historically significant. Built by enslaved laborers and craftsmen in the late 1700s for relatives of the Revolutionary War hero Nathaniel Greene, the house is located in the historic district near the Dungeness ruins. It is not open to the public.

The cottage was constructed with thick tabby walls and gabled windows in the wood-shingled roof. It probably served as a temporary home for Caty Greene Miller and her second husband, Phineas Miller, while they were building the original Dungeness mansion, a four-story tabby structure. The cottage later served as the gardener's home and as an office for property managers.

The Miller-Greene House was badly weathered when the National Park Service, which administers the seashore, applied a portland-cement stucco in the early 1990s. Agency officials hoped it would prevent further decline. Instead, the house began rapidly deteriorating because the hard modern material was incompatible with the softer, original tabby. Cracks soon crazed the exterior, black mildew bloomed on interior plaster walls, and moisture collapsed part of the ceiling.

Lauren Sickles-Taves Allsopp, one of the tabby experts who did a subsequent restoration in 1997, compared covering the house with portland-cement stucco to putting it in a plastic bag. The modern concrete did not let the tabby breathe, which caused the walls to mildew. After removing the modern stucco and underlying metal mesh, the restorers used tabby blended to match the original material to repair the cottage. They repoured the home's damaged corners to sharp, ninety-degree angles. Then they applied two final coats of tabby stucco to complete the restoration.

There are other structures built with old tabby on the island, including the columns of the large pergola adjacent to the Tabby House.

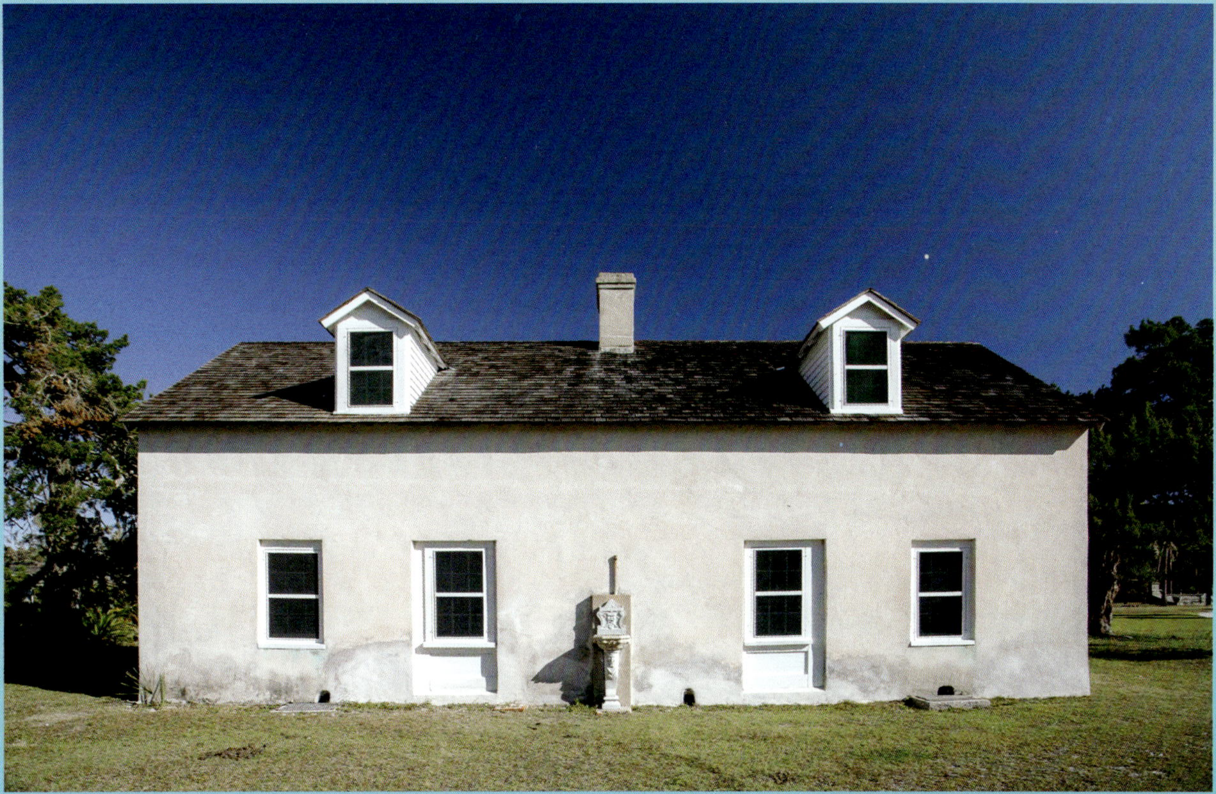
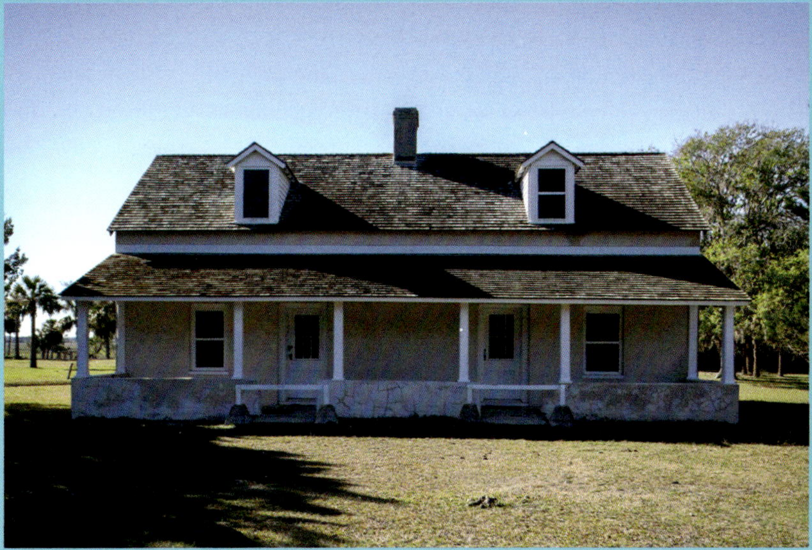
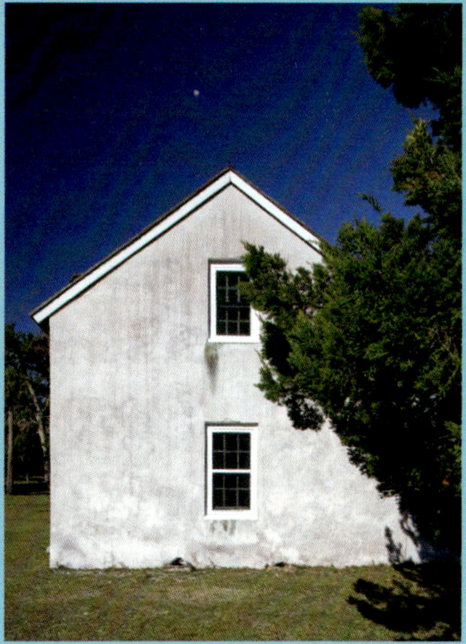

CHAPTER 4   *St. Marys, Kingsland, and Woodbine*

THE FIRST DOCUMENTED VISIT by a European to today's Camden County was made by a French captain named Jean Ribault in 1562, when he was searching for places to establish Huguenot communities. Ribault named the county's two major rivers the Seine and the Somme, which are now known as the St. Marys and the Big Satilla. Ribault described this stretch of coast as the "fairest, fruitfulest and pleasantest of all the world."

There are three incorporated towns in the county: St. Marys on the eponymous river; Kingsland, north of the river and farther west; and Woodbine, north of Kingsland on the Big Satilla River.

The county experienced exponential growth in the later part of the twentieth century when the navy established its billion-dollar East Coast base for giant Trident submarines just north of St. Marys at Kings Bay. Almost overnight, the base transformed Camden's economy from pine-tree-related work to civilian jobs at Kings Bay, which employs more than 9,000 people in addition to navy personnel. From 1980 to 1990, Camden's population jumped from around 13,000 to about 30,000, an astonishing 125 percent growth rate. By 2017, the population had topped 53,000. Millions of dollars in federal funds flowed into Camden and its municipalities to help offset the impacts of the rapid growth.

ST. MARYS

The town at the eastern end of Georgia Highway 40 is the departure point for Cumberland Island National Seashore. St. Marys was built on the site of an abandoned Timucua village called Tlathlothlaguphta. Many early American towns took their names from Native American towns; for understandable reasons, St. Marys did not.

Among the town's first white residents were French-speaking Acadians who had been forced from their homes in Nova Scotia during the French and Indian War. Some, later called Cajuns, settled in Louisiana. Others relocated to Haiti, but during the island's slave revolt in 1781, they dispersed to other locales. A small but visible group settled in St. Marys.

In its early days, St. Marys was an international border town. The St. Marys River separated first the Georgia colony and later the state of Georgia from Spanish Florida, which did not become a U.S. territory until 1821.

After the transatlantic slave trade was outlawed in the United States in 1808, Fernandina, just across the river in Spanish Florida, became a major port for slave importation. Federal troops and gunboats plied the St. Marys River, trying with little success to block the smuggling of enslaved people into the United States.

During the War of 1812, British troops and Admiral Sir George Cockburn—the same Cockburn who ordered the burning of the White House and most of Washington, D.C.— occupied St. Marys. When his forces sailed upriver to destroy an American outpost, they were ambushed and routed by U.S. troops. The Battle of St. Marys, in February 1815, was the final conflict of the war, fought after the treaty ending the conflict was signed, in December 1814. Cockburn claimed he did not receive official notice of the treaty until after the battle.

The live-oak-shaded National Register Historic District downtown features buildings dating to the early 1800s, including the First Presbyterian Church, private houses, and picturesque accommodations. Visitors enjoy strolling through the historic Oak Grove Cemetery.

KINGSLAND

In 1788, the King family bought large tracts of land for a plantation they named Woodlawn. A great-grandson, William King, built his home on the property, which had come to be known over the years as the King's land. When the first passenger train came to Camden County, it crossed King's land. Since William King's home was the only visible structure, the railroad company named the area "Kings Land." "Kings Land" became "Kingsland" when the town was incorporated in 1908.

By the 1890s, Kingsland's economy was deeply rooted in pine trees. The living trees produced turpentine and other naval stores. Cut trees were limbed and trucked to pulp and paper mills in Brunswick, Fernandina, and St. Marys. Almost a century later, in the late 1980s, Camden had become the state's second-largest pulpwood producer, and almost three-fourths of its land was covered in fast-growing varieties of pine. The trees were planted in regimented rows for easy care and harvesting, but the monotonous forests flanking the highways did little to please the eyes of travelers.

In 1908, the small St. Marys and Kingsland railroad began carrying passengers between the towns, but riders sometimes had to share space with cargo. A trolley later took over the passenger route. The first trolley was constructed by a local boat builder on the chassis of a Model T Ford truck with wheels adapted to run on railroad tracks. The vehicle was soon nicknamed the Toonerville Trolley after the popular syndicated comic strip *Toonerville Folks*, which was published during the first half of the twentieth century. The comic strip drawn by Fontaine Fox featured a rickety homemade trolley car. A later, more sophisticated version of the handmade trolley is now on display in St. Marys.

Kingsland's economy got a major infusion of revenue with the opening of the Maine-to-Miami highway through Camden in 1927. The route, designated U.S. Highway 17, was also called the Atlantic Coast Highway, the Coastal Highway, and, in the Deep South, the Dixie Highway. Before the completion of Interstate 95, tens of thousands of snowbirds traveling the route passed through Kingsland in spring and fall like huge flocks of migratory birds. Gas stations, motels, and restaurants popped up like mushrooms along the highway to accommodate the travelers and enrich the locals.

Kingsland won notoriety as southern Georgia's marriage mill when businesses on U.S. 17 advertised, with prominent signs, one-hour blood tests and marriages. The town's downtown commercial district is now on the National Register of Historic Places, but the quickie-marriage signs disappeared years ago.

From the 1930s until the outbreak of World War II, annual horse races were run on the Camden Park Track just west of Kingsland. The events drew thousands of spectators.

WOODBINE

About fourteen hundred acres of land called Piles Bluff on the south bank of the Big Satilla River were granted to four Georgia colonists in 1765. Historians think Woodbine was later founded on or near the same tract.

Woodbine Plantation was a center of activity until the Civil War, when the plantation house burned to the ground. The property was purchased by James King Bidell, who replaced the house and sold some of his land in 1893 to the railroad. He stipulated that the first community built on the property be called Woodbine, the English name for honeysuckle.

A religious group called the Shakers moved south from Ohio in the late nineteenth century to a tiny community north of Woodbine, hoping to expand their numbers and improve their finances in a balmier climate. They were called Shakers because they sang, danced, shouted, and shook during religious activities to "shake off evil." The Shakers purchased a plantation in the White Oak community, where they grew and marketed produce such as pumpkins, corn, sweet potatoes, and rice. Their crops thrived but their membership did not. The Shaker faith prohibited procreation, forcing members to increase their numbers by adoption or conversion. The Shakers abandoned White Oak in the early 1900s and returned to Ohio.

Woodbine was incorporated in 1908. Like Kingsland, the town lay in the path of U.S. Highway 17. The heavily traveled route between northern industrial cities and the tourist meccas of Florida brought a steady stream of traffic through Woodbine. A year later, the county seat was moved from St. Marys to Woodbine. Woodbine's old brick courthouse is one of only two in Georgia built in the Gothic Revival style.

SITE 12

McIntosh Sugar Works

1826–1827

New Canaan Plantation
3600 Charlie Smith Sr. Highway at Georgia Spur 40

National Register of Historic Places

HISTORIC SIGNIFICANCE: The tabby ruins in St. Marys represent an early industrial component of the plantation era, one that helped workers develop the skills necessary for employment during the Industrial Revolution. The mill was the first horizontal sugarcane mill worked by cattle in the antebellum south.

By the late 1700s, planters in the coastal Southeast were looking for ways to augment their incomes. Cotton had worn out their land, and prices for rice were unpredictable. In 1805, Thomas Spalding of McIntosh County, Georgia, became the first planter in the region to grow sugar, not as a replacement for his main crops, grown on Sapelo Island, but as a supplementary cash generator.

Spalding's first cousin, John Houstoun McIntosh, was a descendant of the Scottish Highlanders who colonized coastal McIntosh County in the early 1700s. As a teenager, he ran the family plantations, later consolidating several of his holdings into a large plantation called New Canaan, located just north of the border between Georgia and Spanish Florida. Spalding, a booster of both sugar and tabby, urged McIntosh to plant and process sugar and advised him on the design and construction of his sugar mill. By 1825–26, McIntosh had the tabby mill up and running.

His sugar works were impressive. The main building was a rectangular structure of almost sixty-five hundred square feet, including two porches, each with four large tabby columns that probably helped support the roof beams over the long span of the building's central room. The fourteen-foot-high tabby walls were constructed in a continuous pour, which meant that the form boards were set up so that all four walls were poured at the same time. This eliminated the need for joining walls at the corners of a building, a requirement for structures in which each wall is poured separately.

The sugarhouse walls were fourteen inches thick. Sugar producers believed thick walls were necessary to hold in the heat necessary to produce a good-quality product. The building had three large rooms, each designed for a separate step in the sugar-making process: the two-story milling room on one end, the central boiling room, and the curing room on the other end.

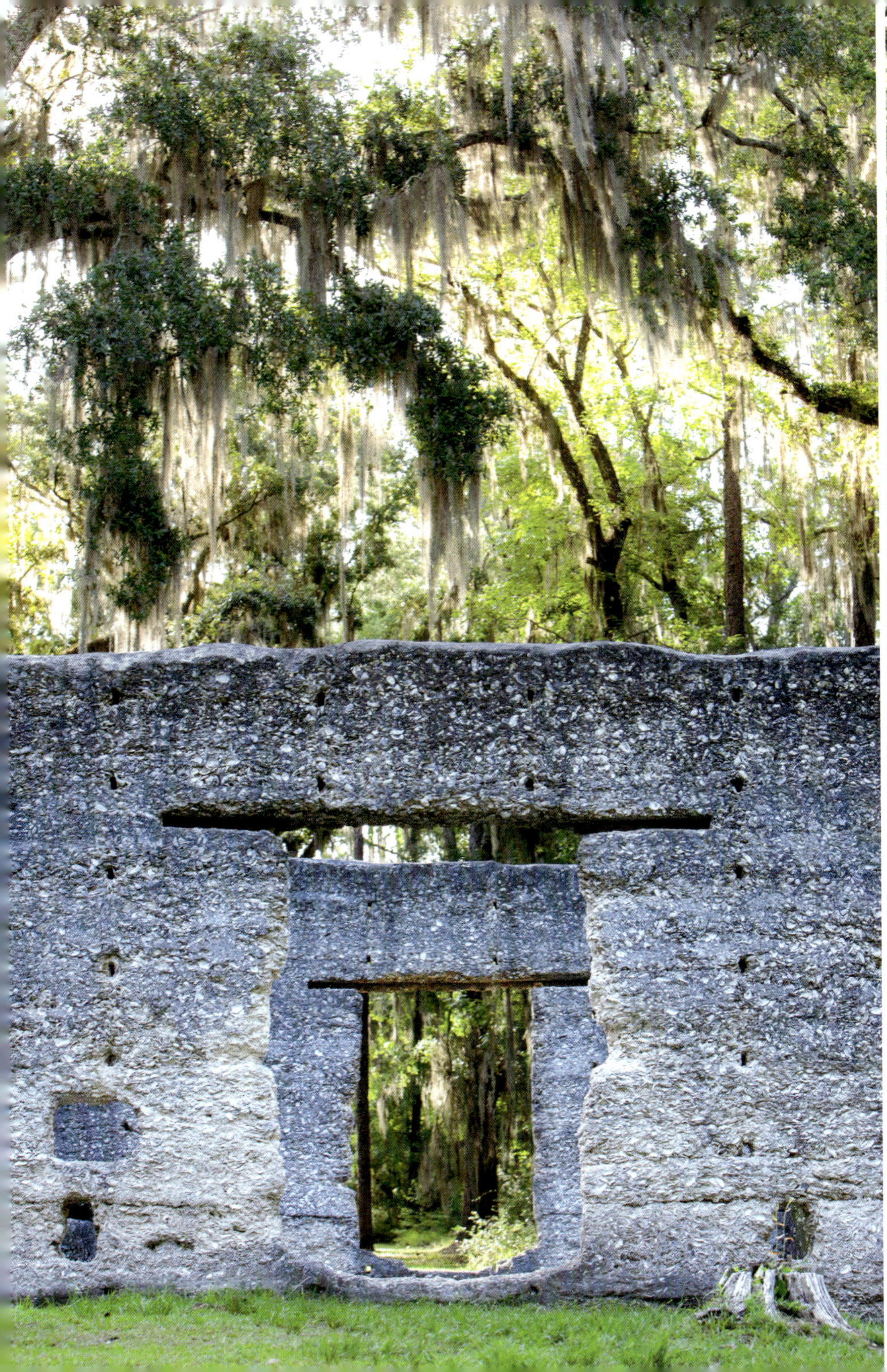
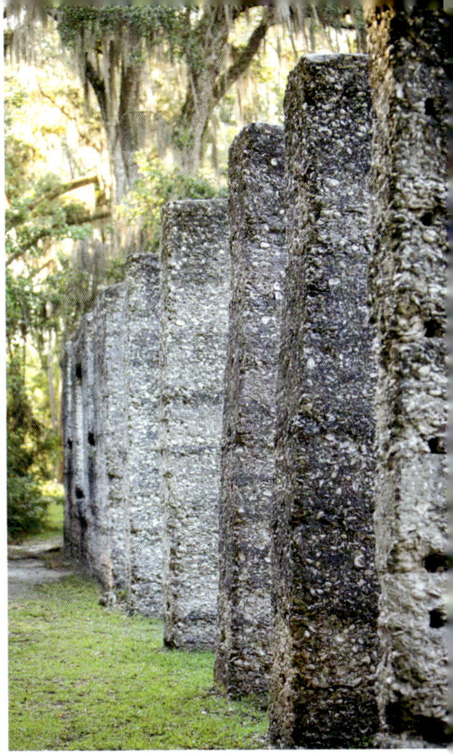
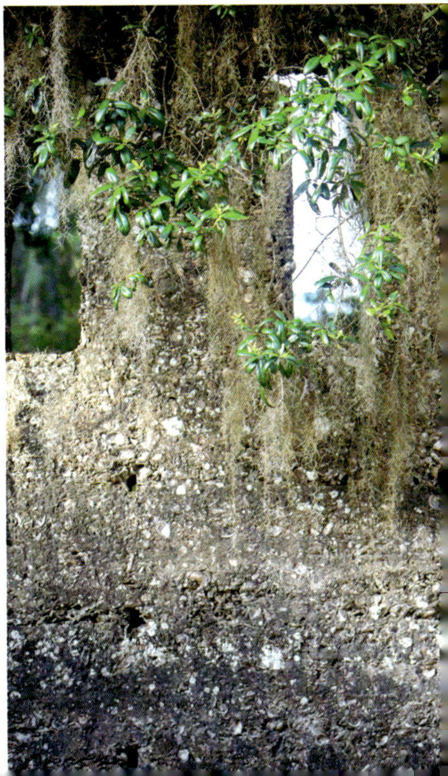

The McIntosh mill was state-of-the-art. Cattle-powered vertical mills were standard at the time, but Houstoun's mill was the first horizontal mill in the coastal Southeast to be powered by cattle rather than steam or water.

Horizontal mills, developed in the late 1700s, were a vast improvement over vertical mills, in which the rollers used to crush the cane stood upright rather than lying flat. Cane stalks had to be fed by hand into vertical rollers, which were notorious for crushing the fingers and hands of the enslaved workers who operated them. With horizontal mills, workers could slide canes down boards into the rollers without fear of injury. Horizontal mills also required less power, produced more juice, adapted well to different sizes of cane, were more durable, and turned out a product faster than vertical mills. The two-story building housed the mill on the first floor; the animals worked on the second floor, plodding around and around to rotate the shaft that powered the equipment.

The sweet juice extracted from the cane went into the central boiling room, where hot fires concentrated the watery juice into syrup. The syrup then moved through what were called Jamaica trains: a series of five or more boiling kettles arranged in a row. The first and largest kettle boiled the raw juice; the smallest and last kettle reduced the syrup to the consistency needed to form sugar crystals.

The syrup was clarified—McIntosh developed a patented process for clarification—and then poured into pans in the curing room. After the syrup granulated, molasses was drained off and the sugar crystals that remained were ready to be bagged and sold.

Molasses was a salable product, as well. Until the twentieth century, molasses was a common sweetener in the United States, in part because it was a by-product of the sugar-curing process and cheaper than crystallized sugar. Molasses was also popular in England, where it was known as black treacle.

Bagasse, another by-product of sugar manufacture, consisted of the crushed cane from which most juice had been extracted. It could be used to fuel the fires of the boiling room or as cattle feed. Today, bagasse is used in the manufacture of a variety of products, including high-quality paper plates. The improved, more efficient mill was a harbinger of the Industrial Revolution.

Growing and harvesting cane needed no special equipment. Thomas Spalding estimated that one enslaved laborer could harvest the cane from two acres in two months: cutting the cane, stripping the leaves, and loading it on flat carts to haul to the mill. Processing sugar, however, required a major investment in labor and materials that only wealthy planters could afford.

The ruins of the McIntosh sugar works show the impressive scope of an early nineteenth-century manufacturing plant. They are in a one-acre oak-shaded park across from the main gates of the Kings Bay Submarine Base, the East Coast home port for nuclear submarines. Like the sugar mill, the naval base was state-of-the-art technology when it was built during the 1990s.

John Houstoun McIntosh, 1773–1836

A descendant of the Scots founders of McIntosh County, Georgia, John Houstoun McIntosh was a teenager when he began running a family plantation in Camden County, just across the St. Marys River from Spanish Florida, shortly after the Revolutionary War. At the time, St. Marys was the southernmost town in the United States.

Spain had once claimed all the known territory in North America, but by the mid-1700s, its holdings on the Eastern Seaboard had shrunk to the Florida Peninsula and part of the panhandle.

Florida had lost most of its Spanish-speaking citizens during a twenty-year British takeover. After Spain reacquired East Florida, the reverse happened: many English-speakers left Florida for the United States. Needing desperately to repopulate the area and boost the struggling economy, Spain offered land deals and grants to anyone who swore loyalty to the Spanish king.

John Houstoun McIntosh had no qualms about buying property in a Spanish colony or swearing a loyalty oath. He purchased more than three thousand acres of undeveloped land in the area of today's Jacksonville, including Fort George Island. He relocated his family to the island and made it his base of operations for other Florida properties. A legacy of the McIntosh tenure on Fort George Island is two unusual teepee-shaped tabby tombs thought to contain the remains of McIntosh's daughter, Mary, and another female relative.

Spanish Florida had long been a refuge for people escaping slavery. It also served as a refuge for displaced Native Americans, most from the Creek and Yamasee chiefdoms. The Spanish called them *cimarrones*, meaning "wild ones" or "runaways" (the term originally applied to

John Houstoun McIntosh, c. 1790s

horses that escaped into the wild), and the name evolved into "Seminoles."

The Spanish governor formed a Black militia to help protect the province from aggressive Americans. The militia fought against the Seminoles during the Micasukee War of the early 1800s and played a pivotal role in the so-called Patriot War of 1812. People escaping slavery who had joined Seminole groups fought with them.

There were frequent skirmishes across the Georgia-Florida border as Seminoles fought with white Georgians, slave raiders from southern states attacked Black Seminole villages in Spanish Florida, and the Black militia raided plantations in Georgia to rescue other enslaved people, steal livestock, and destroy property.

Roughly midway through his presidency, James Madison devised a plot intended to solve the problem of Spanish Florida for his southern constituents and to achieve another goal. His predecessor, Thomas Jefferson, had doubled the size of the new nation with the Louisiana Purchase. Madison saw annexing Spanish Florida as a way to add territory to the United States, eliminate a refuge for runaway slaves, force the Seminoles out of Spanish Florida and Georgia, and destroy the free Black militia.

Unwilling to risk outright war with Spain, Madison and some members of Congress secretly authorized Spanish Florida's annexation. Madison organized the so-called Patriot War, claiming that the rebels were citizens of Spanish Florida rising up against their government. The historian James Cusick dubbed the Patriot War the Other War of 1812 because the two conflicts overlapped. Although it had major consequences, the Patriot War is not a well-known chapter of American history.

The problem for the instigators of the fake rebellion was that most Floridians, including John McIntosh, were prospering under Spanish rule and had no interest in turning against their government. The president appointed George Mathews, the governor of Georgia, to lead the effort. At first, McIntosh refused to join the ersatz rebels, but Mathews persuaded him to change his mind. McIntosh considered the Georgia governor an honorable man and admired him as a war hero who had fought alongside George Washington during the revolution.

McIntosh agreed to lead a contingent of about two hundred armed volunteers, most from Georgia, into Florida, where he hoped to recruit Spanish citizens to join them. Only a few ever did. In March of 1812, McIntosh staged his forces near the free port of Fernandina, just south of the St. Marys River, the Georgia-Florida border near the coast. President Madison sent gunboats into the harbor, ostensibly to keep the peace. Instead, the ships turned their guns on the town, forcing Fernandina's government to surrender. McIntosh declared Fernandina the Republic of East Florida, helped draft the new republic's constitution, and was named its director.

McIntosh raised the Stars and Stripes over Fernandina and then continued south toward St. Augustine, Spanish Florida's capital. With the backing of U.S. forces, the rebels forced other communities along the way to surrender, claiming the occupied territory for the new republic. The overwhelmed Spanish turned to the Seminoles and the Black militia for help. The militiamen fought hard against the rebels, knowing that if Florida went to the United States, they could be reenslaved.

The Patriot War ended after word leaked about the U.S. government's instigation of the so-called rebellion. Madison was criticized by many members of Congress and American citizens. The president withdrew his gunships and ordered his troops to stand down.

Because of McIntosh's high-profile role in the rebellion, the Spanish issued a warrant for his arrest. He leased his Florida property and fled back to Georgia.

Spanish Florida was devastated during and after the invasion. While negotiations over a peace settlement dragged on for more than a year, Seminoles, Black militiamen, faux rebels, and wandering U.S. troops ran riot, looting and burning farms and plantations across East Florida.

In 1817, the First Seminole War broke out, a bloody two-year conflict that began when the United States sent General Andrew Jackson to recapture fugitive slaves. McIntosh joined Jackson's militia as a general. Jackson failed to get the president's sanction to invade Spanish Florida, but the headstrong general invaded anyway.

Survey plat showing one of John Houstoun McIntosh's parcels of land along the St. Johns River and Cedar and McGirt's Creeks, 1830

He and his troops attacked and burned Seminole settlements and forts, leaving a swath of smoking death in their wake. A small group of Seminoles took refuge in the Florida Everglades, where they formed the nucleus of today's Seminole Nation. The rest of the Seminoles were either killed or removed to reservations in Indian Territory (present-day Oklahoma). After serving in Jackson's militia, McIntosh resumed his life as a Georgia planter.

The Spanish in Florida never recovered from the Patriot War and Jackson's attacks. In 1821, nine years after Madison launched the rebellion, the Spanish government ceded Florida to the United States as a territory.

By then, McIntosh was growing sugarcane and building his tabby sugar mill at New Canaan Plantation. He died in 1836 at age sixty-two, and was buried in the historic Oak Grove Cemetery in St. Marys. After his death, New Canaan Plantation and its sugar works were sold. The new owner changed the plantation's name to Bollingbrook and continued to manufacture sugar. During the Civil War, the sugar mill was used to grind and process large quantities of arrowroot into starch.

SITE 13   *Short Take*

St. Mark's Episcopal Church

c. 1900

209 Bedell Avenue, U.S. Highway 17

National Register of Historic Places

Camden County planter J. K. Bedell donated land in Woodbine for the building of St. Marks Episcopal Church in 1898. Two years later, men in the rural community contributed their skills to build the church. Because they wanted the church to be beautiful and long-lasting, they selected the building materials with care. They chose heart pine from the longleaf pine forests inland; ballast stones dumped by sailing ships on the banks of the Satilla River five miles away; and tabby made with portland cement. A cutaway in the exterior stucco displays the stone and tabby underpinnings of the structure.

The ballast stones used to reinforce the building at critical points were dumped during the timbering era of the late 1800s and early 1900s. Great forests of longleaf pine were harvested inland and rafted to coastal sawmills on rivers emptying into the Atlantic. Ships from all over the world sailed upriver to dump the stones they had used for ballast and replace them with freshly milled lumber.

When the Georgia Highway Department built a new bridge across the Satilla in 1953, St. Marks was in the way. The church was moved several feet east of its original location, suffering only one small crack in the tabby walls.

The interior of the church features arches and a bishop's chair made by E. P. Noyes of the nearby Ceylon community. Lights were donated in memory of the Reverend David Watson Winn. The stained-glass windows came from a parish in England, and the gold cross carried by acolytes was given in memory of Dr. Charles H. Lee, a nephew of Confederate general Robert E. Lee.

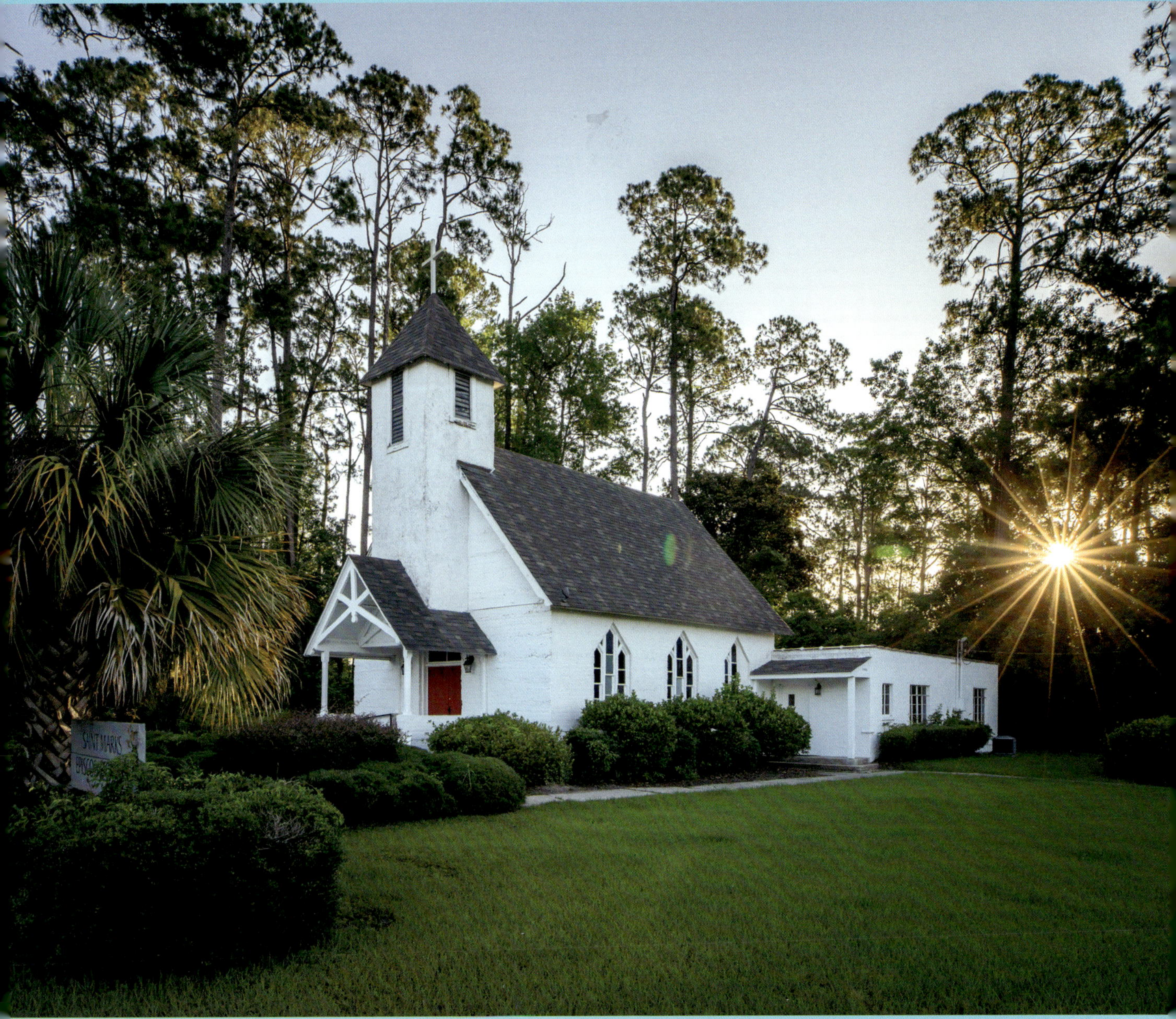
SAINT MARKS

CHAPTER 5 *Jekyll Island State Park*

JEKYLL ISLAND IS ONE OF THREE Georgia sea islands connected to the mainland by a causeway. Exclusive Sea Island in Glynn County is linked to neighboring St. Simons Island by a causeway, but Sea Island's causeway is not open to the public.

The oldest part of the seven-mile-long Jekyll Island, shaped like a swimming shark or a turkey drumstick, was formed by rising seas during the fluctuations of sea levels during the last of the Pleistocene ice ages.

Like the other sea islands of the southeastern coast, Jekyll was sometimes covered by the Atlantic, and at other times left high and dry as a bump on the mainland. Although Jekyll's north end is eroding badly, most of the island's south end is relatively new land that began forming about five thousand years ago during the Holocene epoch.

Settled thousands of years ago by the Paleo-Indians, precontact Jekyll was part of the large Timucuan chiefdom of northern Florida and southern Georgia. Coastal Timucuans, who lived on the islands and a narrow band of mainland, were called the Mocama, or "people of the sea."

Jekyll was claimed at times by France, Spain, and England. The Spanish named it Isla de Ballenas, or Island of Whales, because so many northern right whales gathered around the island in winter months to bear their young. Today, the greatly endangered whales still calve near Jekyll and can on rare occasions be spotted from the beach.

The southernmost English settlement on the North American continent was established on Jekyll in 1736 by Major William Horton, second in command to Georgia's founder, General James Edward Oglethorpe. Oglethorpe gave Jekyll its name to honor an English nobleman who supported the Georgia colony financially. Because of Horton's leadership at Fort Frederica on St. Simons Island, he was rewarded with acreage on Jekyll, where he later built his tabby house. The walls of the house, in remarkable shape after almost three centuries, still stand.

A French nobleman and sea captain, Christophe DuBignon, along with his family and two servants, were living in the Horton home in 1792. By 1800, DuBignon owned all of Jekyll. He operated his sea island cotton plantation with enslaved labor and required all those he enslaved to speak French. Many of them had been purchased on French-speaking islands in the Caribbean. In 1858, the eve of the Civil War, two DuBignon brothers conspired with a wealthy Savannah secessionist to land an illegal cargo of more than four hundred enslaved Africans on the island. The *Wanderer* was the next-to-last documented slave ship to land in the United States.

Jekyll was purchased in 1886 by a group of northern millionaires who established the world's most exclusive winter retreat: the Jekyll Island Club. Collectively, the members were said to represent more than one-sixth of the world's wealth. Today, the restored clubhouse is an elegant hotel flanked by a group of the millionaires' large vacation homes, which club members called cottages to distinguish them from their even-larger mansions in the North. One member, an international bridge builder, used revival tabby made with portland cement to construct his cottage on Jekyll, because he wanted it to last.

In 1910, following a series of national financial panics, a small group of bankers met in secret on Jekyll before the club opened for the season to discuss a new currency-stabilization system. They developed the Aldrich plan, which later led to the establishment of the Federal Reserve System.

In 1915, special telephone lines were run to the island for the first transcontinental call because Theodore Vail, a club member confined to Jekyll with gout, was the president of AT&T. Thomas Edison in New York, his assistant Thomas A. Watson in California, and President Woodrow Wilson in Washington, D.C., all participated in the cross-country call.

The millionaires' club folded after World War II. A former Georgia governor, M. E. Thompson, purchased Jekyll as a park for "ordinary people," to be managed by the agency that oversees state parks. During the late 1940s, Thompson's political rival changed the management structure to an authority whose members were appointed by the governor, an arrangement that remains essentially the same today.

By law, no more than one-third of the island can ever be developed. Jekyll's woodlands, freshwater ponds, and beaches are home to an impressive variety of wildlife, including roseate spoonbills, endangered wood storks, and rare nesting sea turtles. The only sea turtle rehabilitation center in Georgia is on Jekyll. Manatees, listed as a threatened marine mammal, visit Jekyll Creek in the summer months, appearing around island marinas to drink freshwater from dock hoses. Boaters are advised to watch for the slow-moving vegetarians.

Jekyll has fewer than eight hundred year-round residents, but more than one million annual visitors cross the causeway, which spans seven miles of protected marshes between the island and the mainland. A bridge over Jekyll Creek is named for former governor Thompson. A few Jekyll visitors arrive in private boats or fly in by private plane. There is a small airport, but pilots sometimes have to buzz the runway before landing in order to scatter feeding deer.

Shady trails circle and crisscross the island. Bicyclists and hikers often encounter nearly tame white-tailed deer as well as minks, otters, marsh rabbits, and the occasional alligator lazing on a muddy creek bank. Alligators are protected on Jekyll, as are rattlesnakes. Wild turkeys prowl Jekyll's woodlands. Early French explorers named them Indian peacocks because of their iridescent, richly colored feathers.

Jekyll offers amusements including golf, tours of the historic district, a rehabilitated museum, and a water park, as well as popular educational programs for youngsters that include beach seining, marsh exploration, and canoeing in sheltered waters. A new beachfront convention center is part of a $50 million complex that includes a market village.

Accommodations are available at the enlarged Cherokee Campground and at a selection of motels, condominiums, and private homes, many of which have been refurbished or replaced in recent years. Snack bars, casual and upscale restaurants, and shops are scattered around the island, with a concentration in the historic district and the beachfront market.

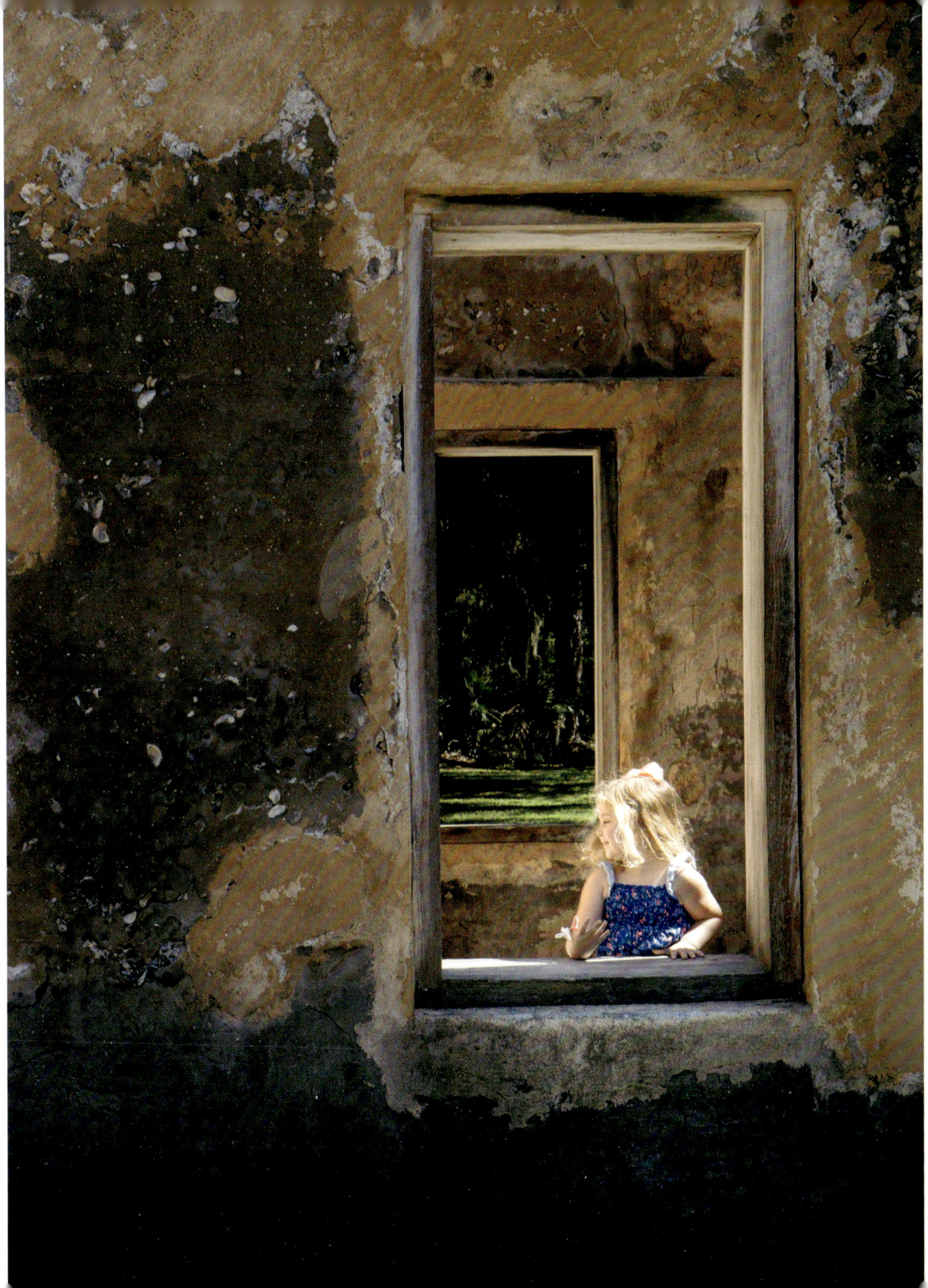

SITE 14

Horton House

1743

375 North Riverview Drive

National Historic Landmark

HISTORIC SIGNIFICANCE: The Horton House is one of only two surviving two-story colonial plantation houses in Georgia. When it was built, it was the southernmost British residence in the American colonies, dangerously close to Spanish Florida at a time when Spain and England were warring over territory in North America.

Major William Horton, second in command to Georgia's founder, General James Edward Oglethorpe, was the first Englishman to live on Jekyll Island. Because his house was less than fifty miles north of Spanish Florida, the location was precarious. England and Spain had fought sporadically for more than a century over land in North America, and Jekyll was located in a stretch of territory called the debatable land, which was claimed by England, Spain, and France.

Horton built his first house in 1736, using wood cut from the maritime forest and processed at the sawmill he set up on Jekyll. When Spanish troops attacked neighboring St. Simons Island in 1742, they burned Horton's house, shot his cattle, and destroyed his crops.

Aware that the Spanish could return at any time, Horton constructed his second house of fire-resistant tabby, completing the structure in late 1743. It was situated on top of an ancient Native American shell mound, just as the first house had been. Parts of the same mound provided the oyster shells needed to make the tabby concrete. The two-story structure was about forty feet long and eighteen feet wide with a red hipped roof and large windows. The floor was tabby, as was the interior wall on the lower floor that partitioned the space into a parlor and kitchen. The exterior walls were given the traditional sacrificial topcoat of tabby stucco; interior walls were plastered with smooth tabby mortar.

The formal parlor, where the Hortons entertained their frequent visitors, was dressed up with wood wainscoting. Each of the downstairs rooms had its own fireplace and opened to a verandah overlooking the garden.

Upstairs were two bedrooms, one for Horton and his wife, Rebecca, and the other for their two young sons and two of his ten indentured servants. The other servants were quartered elsewhere, probably in huts they built themselves. The bedrooms led to a balcony with stunning views of tidal marshes and a small tidal creek that fed into the inland waterway.

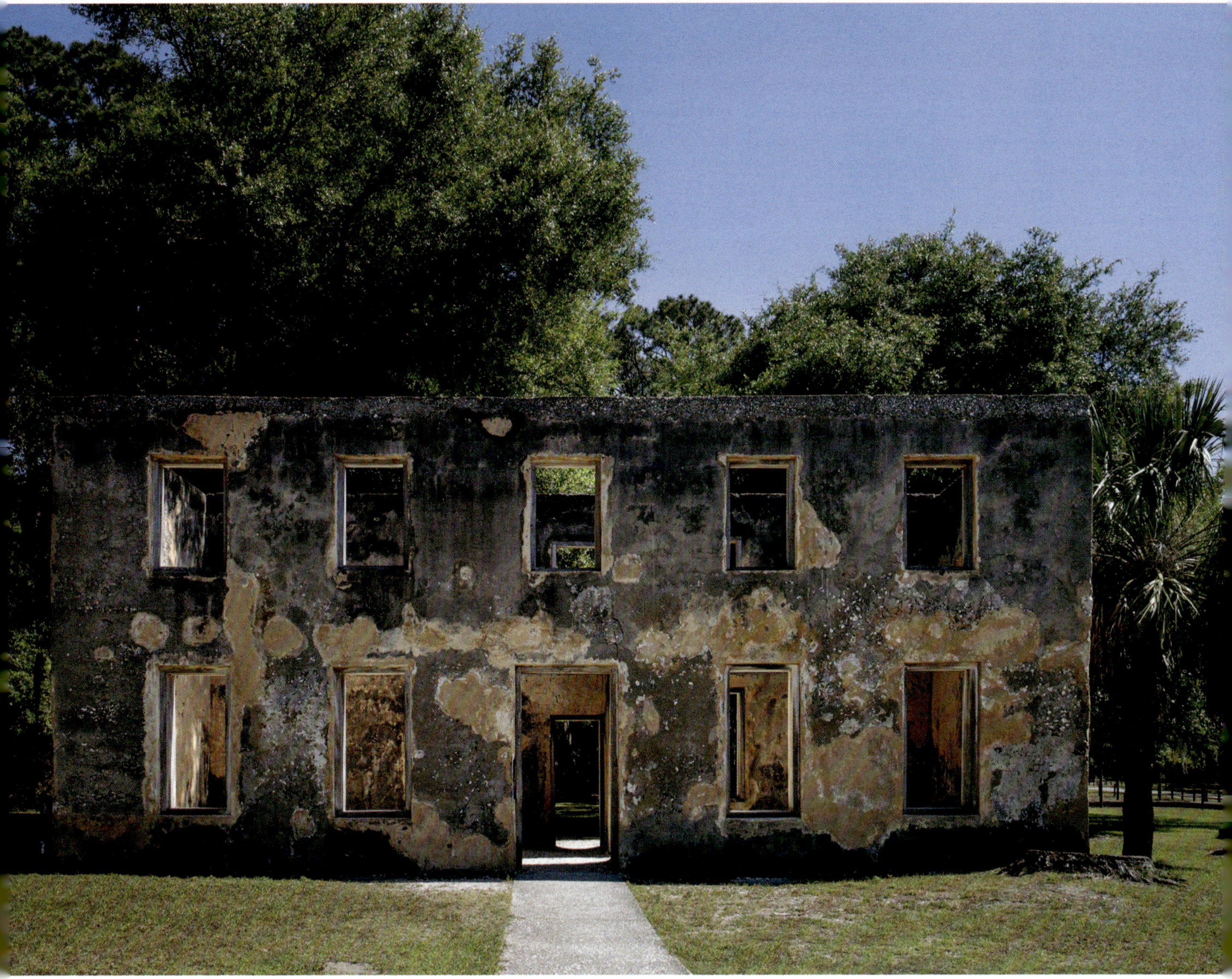

The trustees who founded Georgia intended it to be a dry colony, but the ban on alcohol was flouted from the beginning. The colonists were accustomed to drinking in Europe, often giving beer and ale to their children because of the high calorie content and because drinking water was often polluted. After a dozen years, Oglethorpe persuaded the other trustees to drop the unenforceable prohibition.

Horton may have brewed beer and ale on Jekyll even before the ban was lifted. There is little doubt that he intended to build a brewery. He planted barley and hops and ordered a large copper kettle and "all Conveniences" to set up the operation. If Horton did make beer and ale on the island—there is no evidence of it—his brewery would have been Georgia's first and one of the first in the South. But it was not built of tabby, as the historical marker at the site indicates. The ruins of two tabby outbuildings on the Horton property are probably the remains of a wharf on the tidal creek and a storage building.

After Horton's death in 1749, his widow may have moved inland to live with their son, Thomas, on his Ogeechee River plantation. The tabby house on Jekyll was occupied for a time by Captain Raymond Demere, who commanded a British garrison on the island.

After the French nobleman and sea captain Christophe DuBignon acquired part of Jekyll in 1792, he, his wife, Marguerite, and their family moved into the Horton residence with two servants. He enlarged the tabby house after four grandchildren from his wife's first marriage moved in. Wooden wings were added later to accommodate Christophe and Marguerite's son, Henri, his wife, and their children. Members of the family occupied the house for almost a century.

During the War of 1812, the house was ransacked by troops under the command of the notorious British admiral George Cockburn, who burned the White House. First Lady Dolley Madison and other Washington residents fled for their lives just ahead of the attack. (The president was in Virginia at the time.) In November 1814, one of Cockburn's frigates landed on Jekyll to liberate enslaved Africans and loot and pillage. When the invaders reached the DuBignon house, they took everything of value and trashed the property.

DuBignon, helpless and humiliated, watched as the troops stripped the house of valuables, including silver plate, gold and silver jewelry, cash, personal papers, and gold-framed miniatures of Christophe and Marguerite, the only known portraits of the couple. The soldiers even destroyed the clothes of DuBignon's three-month-old grandson. After the war officially ended, the British staged another raid on the tabby house. They took anything of value still left. By then, the family had taken refuge on the mainland.

The tabby house was damaged by Union cannon fire during the Civil War. After the war, John Couper DuBignon, the grandson of Christophe and Marguerite, refurbished the house and moved in. He had a longtime relationship with Sylvia, an enslaved woman on Jekyll. The couple stayed together for more than twenty-five years and produced six children, five born into slavery. Sylvia took the name DuBignon after the war and lived in the tabby house with the children as John's wife. The remoteness of the island allowed a Black woman and a white man to live together openly.

After Sylvia died, John DuBignon remained on Jekyll. After the island was sold to the millionaire members of the Jekyll Island Club, he built a tiny shack in a cotton field. He died in 1890. He was the last person to live in the Horton House.

The members of the Jekyll Island Club were charmed by the house, which they called Old Tabby, and made efforts to restore and preserve it.

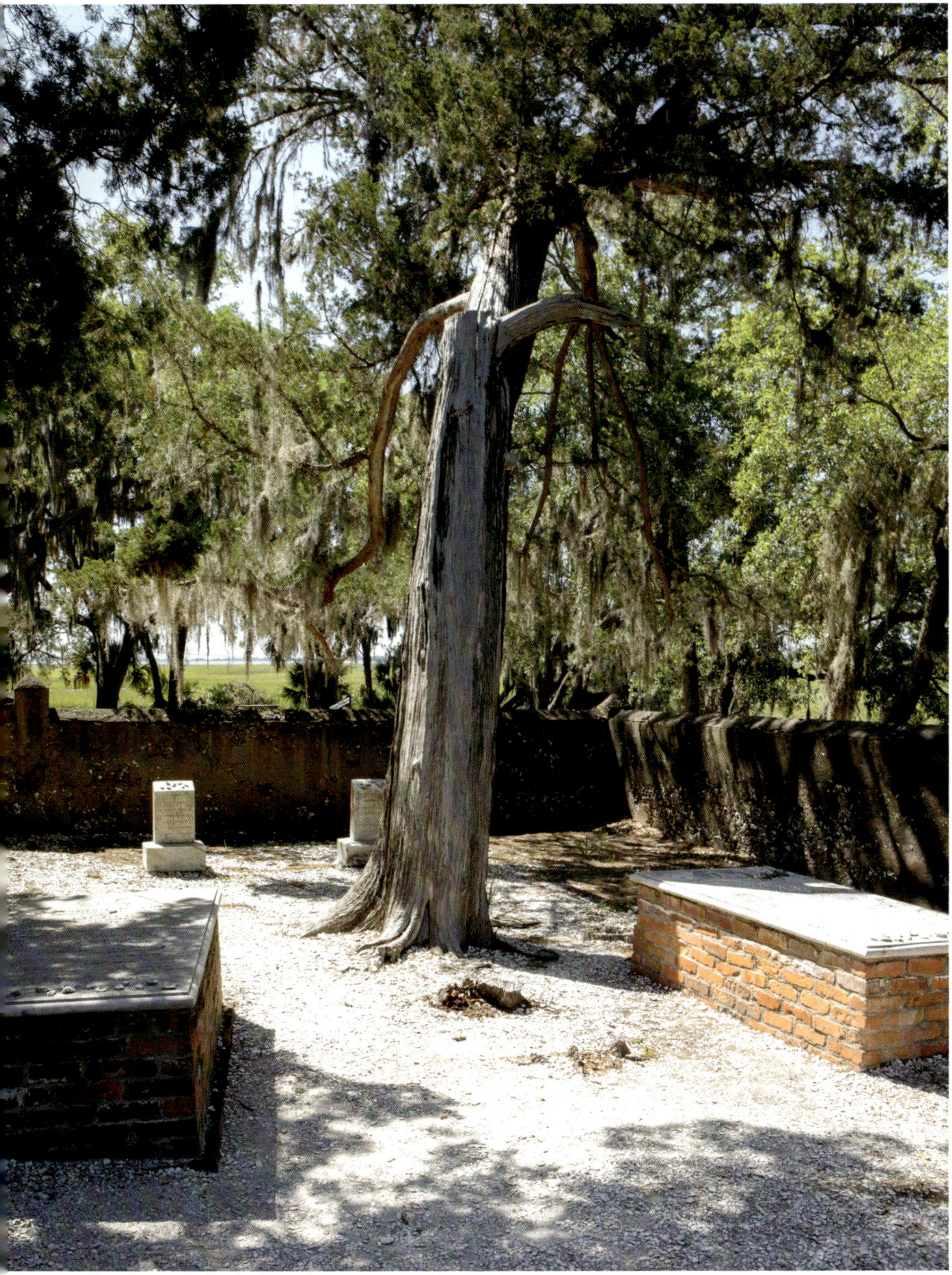
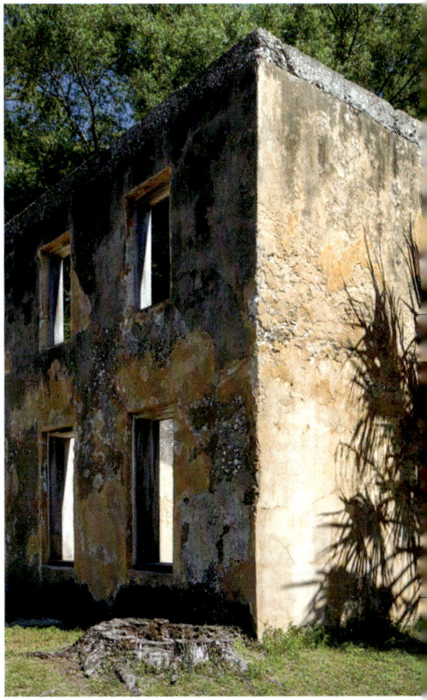
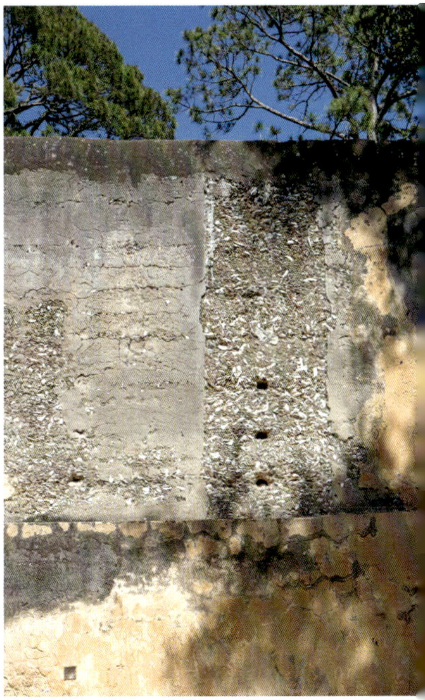

Major William Horton, ?–1748

The major was a redhead with a hot temper, a taste for adventure, and a desire to succeed. In just a dozen years, he became the right-hand man for the Georgia colony's founder, James Edward Oglethorpe. In 1735, Horton left his job as undersheriff of Herefordshire in England to travel with Oglethorpe to America. His wife, Rebecca, and two small sons stayed behind until Horton could establish a home for them in Georgia.

Georgia was an experiment in eighteenth-century social engineering designed by Oglethorpe after he watched a friend die in debtors' prison in London. In Georgia, he hoped that debtors, the "worthy poor," and other ambitious people could work hard and lift themselves out of poverty.

The brothers John and Charles Wesley, later credited with founding Methodism, traveled to Georgia with Oglethorpe and Horton. Even before their ship left England, Horton crossed swords with the Wesleys, who accused one of his indentured servants of drinking and other bad behavior. Oglethorpe sent the woman back home. Although he offered to supply Horton with a replacement, the incident created animosity between Horton and the Wesleys. On the voyage, Horton danced late at night on the deck above the Wesleys' cabin to keep them awake.

The Georgia colonists were not debtors, although the trustees paid passage for at least half of them. Because Horton paid his own way and brought along ten indentured servants, he was eligible for five hundred acres instead of the usual fifty. Horton's grant was on Jekyll Island.

After exploring his acreage on Jekyll for the first time in 1736, Horton pronounced it "exceedingly rich." One of his scouts, excited by Horton's enthusiasm, fired a swivel gun to notify colonists on St. Simons that Horton was pleased with his property. The man kept reloading, each time increasing the amount of powder. On the third shot, the cannon exploded, driving metal fragments into the shooter's head. The boat's crew rowed the injured man back to the doctor at Fort Frederica, but he died the next day.

Horton and his indentured servants cleared land, built shelters, and planted corn, barley, and other crops. The plantation's most successful crop turned out to be cattle. Because Horton traveled often on Oglethorpe's behalf or was needed at Fort Frederica, he relied on his indentured servants to do most of the hard labor. Besides being undoubtedly overworked, they must have been lonely and were no doubt fearful of attacks by the Spanish or hostile Natives. Accustomed to Great Britain's cooler climate, they would have suffered miserably from Georgia's summer heat and biting insects. Four of Horton's servants were unhappy enough to steal his boat and run away. There is no record of whether he retrieved them or the boat.

Oglethorpe sailed to England in 1736, leaving Horton to manage the soldiers and civilians at Frederica. It was a thankless job. The settlers were well aware that Frederica's proximity to Spanish Florida put them at risk. Every time a strange sail appeared on the horizon, they stopped work in the fields, keeping watch until they were sure they were not under attack.

Whenever problems arose, the colonists blamed Horton. They threatened to lock up all of Frederica's weapons, seize all the boats, and chain the storekeepers, even though food shortages at the fort were caused by mismanagement in Savannah. Horton, infuriated, threatened to have one colonist shot, another chained to a scout boat oar, and a third starved to death. When the settlers at Frederica notified Oglethorpe about Horton's behavior, the general was unsympathetic to their pleas. Oglethorpe had endured similar problems when managing the civilians at Frederica. Instead, he praised his right-hand man: "The people [of Frederica] might have starved or abandoned the place had not Mr. Horton given them his own cattle and corn to eat."

When Great Britain and Spain went to war in 1739 (the War of Jenkins' Ear), Oglethorpe sent Horton to England to recruit additional troops for Frederica. In 1740, while Horton was gone, Oglethorpe attacked the Spanish stronghold at St. Augustine. His cannons failed to breach the tabby-and-coquina walls of the Castillo de San Marcos. After a number of his men were ambushed and killed by Spanish soldiers, he retreated, defeated and ill, to his tabby home at Frederica. Oglethorpe was criticized on both sides of the Atlantic for the military failure.

Horton's mission to England was successful. He returned to Georgia with a company of grenadiers (infantrymen armed with grenades) as well as a number of women and children, probably including his wife, Rebecca, and their two sons. Horton was back on Jekyll in July 1742, just a few days before a Spanish fleet from St. Augustine launched an attack on the Georgia coast.

Horton and his men watched thirty-six Spanish ships run the guns of Fort St. Simons on the island's south end and land at Gascoigne Bluff on the island's southwestern shore. The ships carried 3,000–5,000 troops; Oglethorpe had fewer than 1,000. Knowing that his grenadiers were needed on St. Simons, Horton, in a bold move, sailed them in scout boats past the Spanish ships to join Oglethorpe at Frederica.

After the British won skirmishes at Gully Hole Creek and Bloody Marsh, the Spanish commander retreated. On their way back to St. Augustine, Spanish troops landed on Jekyll and destroyed Horton's wooden house and plantation. Horton returned to the devastation, overwhelmed but determined to rebuild. After Horton died of fever in 1749, his widow may have moved inland to their son's plantation on the Ogeechee River. Horton's tabby house on Jekyll was occupied intermittently until the late 1700s, when the DuBignon family moved in. Family members stayed in the house for about a century.

SITE 15

Hollybourne Cottage

1890

379 Riverside Drive

National Historic Landmark District

HISTORIC SIGNIFICANCE: Hollybourne is the only vacation cottage built of tabby at the exclusive Jekyll Island Club, where millionaire industrialists and their families wintered. Hollybourne's owner, an international bridge builder, wanted it to be an architectural wonder, and it is.

From 1888 until World War II, wealthy tycoons of the Gilded Age—men with names such as Astor, Goodyear, Rockefeller, Vanderbilt, Morgan, and Pulitzer—wintered in elegant seclusion with their families and friends at the Jekyll Island Club, billed as the world's most exclusive enclave. The club was limited to one hundred members; they were said at the time to represent an astonishing one-sixth of the world's wealth. Experts today say their economic might was probably underestimated.

The Jekyll Island Club members were people who had everything—except the privacy offered by a remote sea island. Their lives were lived in the public spotlight, like those of rock stars, actors, and politicians today. They were adored, admired, criticized, and reviled. The seclusion of Jekyll allowed them to relax and enjoy themselves in ways they never did off the island. It was claimed that no unwanted foot ever stepped on Jekyll when the millionaires were in residence, generally from December to April.

To accommodate members and guests, the millionaires built a large, ornate, Victorian clubhouse, which opened in 1888. It soon proved to be inadequate to accommodate everyone who wanted to visit or winter on the island. The club's superintendent, Ernest Grob, a young Swiss immigrant who held the post for more than forty years, suggested that some members build their own vacation houses.

Eighteen did. They called their Jekyll dwellings "cottages" to distinguish them from their showplace mansions in New York, Chicago, Boston, and Philadelphia. (The enormous vacation estates in Newport, Rhode Island, were called "cottages" for the same reason.) By any other standard, the cottages on Jekyll Island were mansions: large, comfortable, attractive, expensive. One had seventeen bathrooms. Another housed an indoor swimming pool that was among the first private pools in Georgia. One cottage featured a bowling alley; another had a separate casino with an indoor tennis court and a shooting range, among other amenities.

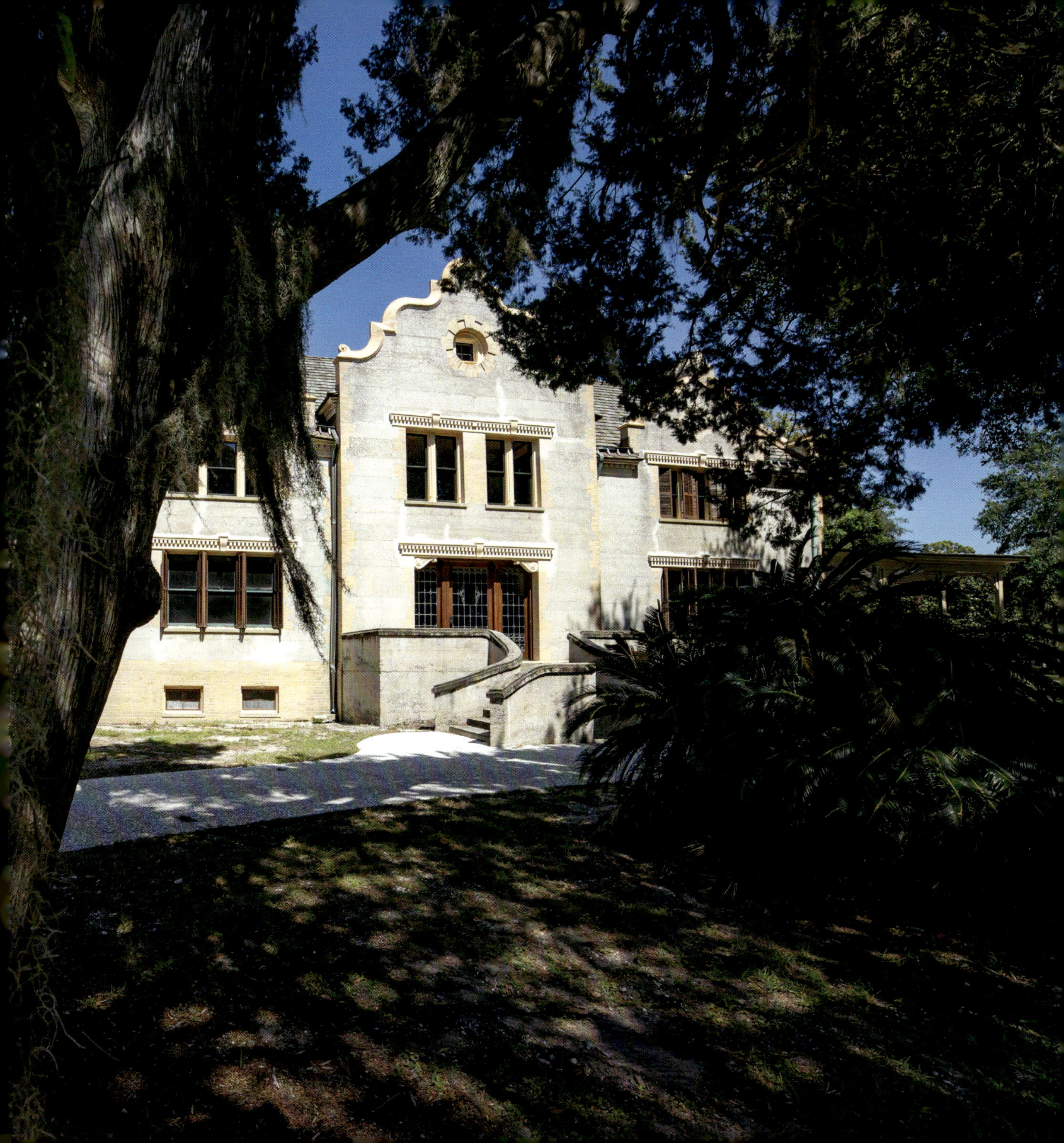

Charles Stewart Maurice was one of the first millionaires to join the club. He and his family loved Jekyll and may have considered the island their true home. The Maurices retained their membership until the club closed, and were the residents most resistant to selling the island to the state after World War II.

Experts consider Hollybourne the most architecturally interesting of the private cottages built by club members, although every cottage is a gem.

Co-owner of the world's biggest bridge-building company, Maurice hired the well-known New York architect William H. Day to design Hollybourne. He wanted a strong, stylish structure built of tabby. Maurice and his wife, Charlotte, were interested in Jekyll's history, and he spearheaded a drive to raise funds for restoration of the Horton House, which club members affectionately named Old Tabby. Maurice, a New Jersey native, may have wanted to honor the history of the southeastern coast and the island by using tabby for his cottage. As a bridge builder, he no doubt admired the strength, versatility, and durability of the oyster-shell concrete. His cottage was built of revival tabby made with portland cement instead of burned-oyster-shell lime.

The style of the four-story cottage that Day designed is called Renaissance Tudor Revival, or sometimes Jacobethan, pseudo-Jacobean, or eclectic Tudor, because it exhibits both Elizabethan and Jacobean influences. The versatility of tabby lent itself to the graceful scrolling Flemish design of the façade's multiple gables. Exterior features include patterned bricks, paired chimneys, and terra-cotta brackets. The cottage has an attic and a basement, the only basement in the original cottage colony that did not require pumps to keep it dry, suggesting that it was built on higher ground than its neighbors.

Maurice designed Hollybourne's underpinnings with materials and techniques used in bridge building. The 11,200-square-foot cottage rests on steel supports and

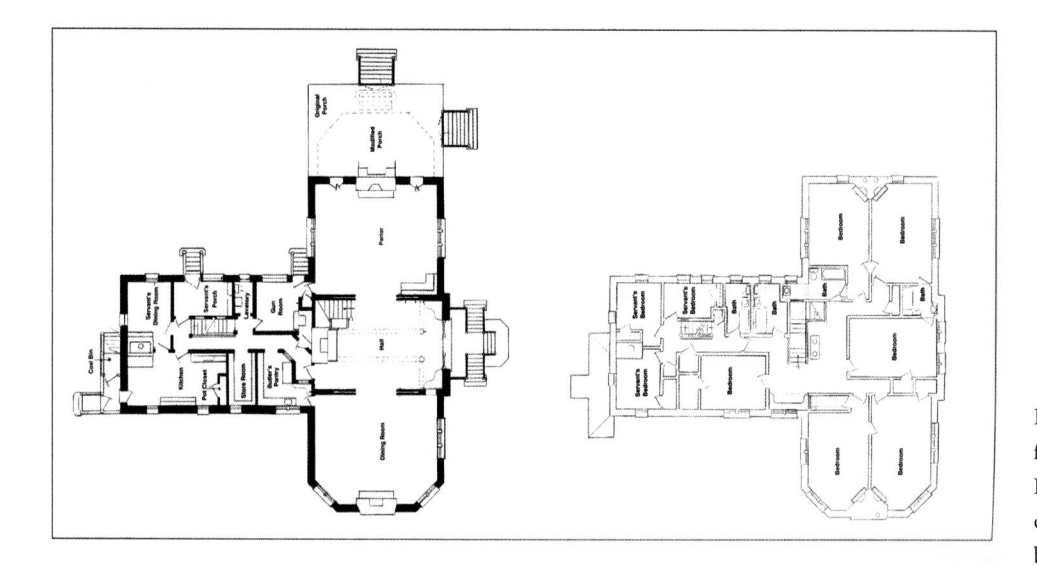

First- and second-floor plans of Hollybourne, based on original drawings by William Day

nineteen brick piers. Maurice wanted large, open rooms; a system of trusses eliminated the need for ceiling beams in the living and dining rooms. On the second floor were five large and four small bedrooms and two bathrooms. Cisterns on the roof supplied water to the rooms below. Three small bedrooms in the rear were occupied by the Maurices' personal servants. Although the Jekyll Island Club was well staffed, many club members brought along their servants for the winter season.

The cottage was decorated in a Victorian style popular at the time, with stuffed birds and small game animals displayed on the mantelpiece. The creatures may have been shot on the island and preserved by the club's resident taxidermist. An animal-skin rug topped the polished oak floors in the entry hall. A spinning wheel by the fireplace may have been used by one of the Maurices as a hobby, but most likely was just decorative. Wicker furniture and leaded glass doors contributed to the light, airy feeling of the interior.

Maurice made a construction decision that caused later problems. Most structural tabby walls were built without an internal support framework. Wet concrete was poured into wooden forms in tiers, with oyster shells pounded into each tier to provide strength. As the tiers dried, the forms were moved up and another tier was poured until the wall reached the desired height.

Maurice evidently thought the tabby tiers needed to be strengthened with an internal wood framework. During the decades when the state allowed the buildings to fall into disrepair, water leached into the framework and began to rot the wood.

The state bought Jekyll in 1947 and refurbished the clubhouse and other structures, but not in a good way. Concrete stairs and pipe railings replaced the graceful staircase and hand-carved balusters in the main entry to the clubhouse, which operated for a time as a hotel. Millionaires' cottages were rented out, some for teenagers' house parties, which was hard on the beautiful old buildings. Appropriate restoration efforts began after two men formed a private partnership to restore the clubhouse to its former glory. The project was a success, and the building is now the Jekyll Island Club Hotel, a stunningly beautiful property.

It took decades for the state to refurbish the cottages. Restoration efforts at Hollybourne were headed for many years by Dick Tennyson, a winter resident of the island, along with a number of volunteers and funds from Jekyll advocacy groups. A missing porch was replaced, funded by the Friends of Historic Jekyll Island. Preservationists suggested leaving some of Hollybourne's rooms in disrepair in order to show visitors how much work goes into proper historic restoration.

Charles Stewart Maurice, 1840–1924

Charles Stewart Maurice did not simply sign up when he decided to join the U.S. Navy. Wanting to prepare for a particular naval career, Maurice enrolled in a polytechnic institute to study marine engineering before he enlisted.

Born in 1840 in New Jersey, Maurice showed an early interest in the principles of building. After serving as a commissioned officer during the Civil War, he declined an offer to teach math at the U.S. Naval Academy in favor of designing steamboat engines. He briefly owned a tannery, but sold it and began supplying timber to a railroad company that used the wood to build bridges.

Designing and constructing train trestles and large bridges was a new industry in the mid-1800s, and it sparked Maurice's interest. He and a partner who had patented a method of building spans of wood and iron formed a company to manufacture and build train trestles and road bridges. The partners pioneered bridge building with iron and later formed a second company to build bridges with steel. Soon they were building bridges all over the world.

The partnership dissolved in 1884 in order to merge with other businesses, including the Union Bridge Company, which built some of the best-known bridges of the era: the Cantilever Bridge of Niagara; the Memphis Bridge across the Mississippi; the Poughkeepsie Bridge over the Hudson River.

Maurice married Charlotte Holbrooke, a socialite and social progressive whose ancestors founded the Plymouth Colony. The couple had nine children.

Maurice hired the New York architectural firm of William H. Day, De Baud and Co. to remodel and expand their home in Athens, Pennsylvania. The Maurices liked the company's philosophy of building "in as quiet a manner as possible," avoiding pretense and flashy newness in favor of structures designed with simple dignity and a homey feeling. Maurice, by then a very rich man, joined the newly formed Jekyll Island Club in 1886. He and Day designed Hollybourne cottage, which was completed in December 1890, just in time for the winter season. Maurice and seventeen others, including family members, friends, and servants, traveled south to celebrate their first Christmas at the cottage. Two employees had left a week earlier to take the Maurices' five horses, four dogs, and a cow to the island.

The Maurices followed the same pattern for the next half century except for two years when the nearby town of Brunswick experienced severe yellow fever epidemics. Since Brunswick was the mainland departure point for

Jekyll, the club closed for the season, over Charlotte Maurice's objections. She believed the first frosts of the winter would have stopped the spread of the disease. She may have been right; yellow fever is a mosquito-borne illness, and mosquitoes are usually killed by freezing weather.

The Maurices, who enjoyed entertaining, hosted friends at Hollybourne Cottage almost every day, serving afternoon tea on the verandah and multicourse dinners in the dining room. Charlotte Maurice kept notes in her diary of the contents of every meal served to guests, probably so that they would not be given the same things to eat on subsequent visits.

Like other club members, the Maurices enjoyed rides around the island on horseback, in carriages, on bicycles, and on small gas- or electric-powered vehicles called red bugs, perhaps in recognition of the tiny mites that live in the long strands of Spanish moss that drape Jekyll's trees. Bites by red bugs, also called chiggers, provoke itching that can last for weeks.

Charlotte and Stewart Maurice were especially interested in island history and began collecting information and stories from various sources. They studied the island's flora and fauna and learned the names of the creatures that frequented the woods, marshes, ocean, and tidal waterways. They gathered seashells from Jekyll's beach, accumulating an impressive collection over a fifty-year period.

Charlotte Maurice spearheaded a campaign to build churches on the island in order to spare club members from having to make the weekly boat trip to Brunswick to worship on Sundays. She invited ministers of every denomination to preach at the Jekyll churches, including a popular Black minister whose service on the island was especially well attended.

Stewart Maurice was a leader in the club's efforts to restore the tabby Horton House, built by Jekyll's first European resident in about 1742.

Charles Stewart Maurice, c. 1890, around the time of the construction of his cottage on Jekyll Island

The Maurices were among the club's most popular members. When Charlotte was stricken with typhoid fever contracted on Jekyll in 1909, everyone worried about her health. She died of the disease later that year at the Maurice home in Pennsylvania. Her death prompted club members to investigate the source of typhoid on the island. Over the next several years, experts reported that the raw sewage dumped by the club into Jekyll Creek infected the oysters that were stored in cages near the sewage outfall. Six more club members came down with the disease before the club finally updated its sewer system.

After the renovation of Hollybourne in recent years, a family descendent was married at the cottage. During the restoration, Charlotte and Stewart Maurice's dining table was discovered and donated to the foundation that provides volunteer workers and helps support upkeep of the property. The bride and her family hosted a prewedding supper at the historic table.

SITE 16 *Short Take*

Dairy Silo

1910

The tabby dairy silo lies in the woods on the western side of Jekyll Island, south of the Horton House site. This structure was most likely part of a late nineteenth-century dairy farm, placing it in the revival-tabby era, when portland cement was used as a binder instead of oyster-shell lime.

Bubbles in the butter prompted picky millionaire members of the exclusive Jekyll Island Club to establish a full-fledged dairy on the island in 1910. At the time, the club was importing butter and other dairy products from Tennessee, and the bubbles raised concerns about the butter's quality. The club's wealthy members, including J. P. Morgan, William Rockefeller, Joseph Pulitzer, Marshal Field, and others, were accustomed to the best of everything and had more than enough money to pay for it.

The dairy barn was located at a distance from the ornate Victorian-style clubhouse and the millionaires' private cottages, in order to prevent bovine odors and sounds from disturbing the members. A dairyman milked the cows in the main part of the barn; butter—presumably sans bubbles—was churned in the smaller part of the structure. Chickens scratched around the barnyard, laying fresh eggs for the millionaires' tables.

To store the cattle feed, the club built a tall silo of revival tabby. The silo's walls are reinforced with iron rods. The structure still stands, hidden in the woods, wrapped in wild grape vines. Deer graze nearby.

The silo is the only relic of the Jekyll Island Club not embraced in the 240-acre National Historic Landmark District. It is located off North Riverside Drive between Jennings Avenue and the church on the unpaved part of Old Plantation Road. A short fire hydrant is a landmark. An unmarked path leads to the structure.

When the dairy on Jekyll closed in 1930, the millionaires' club purchased dairy products from local businesses.

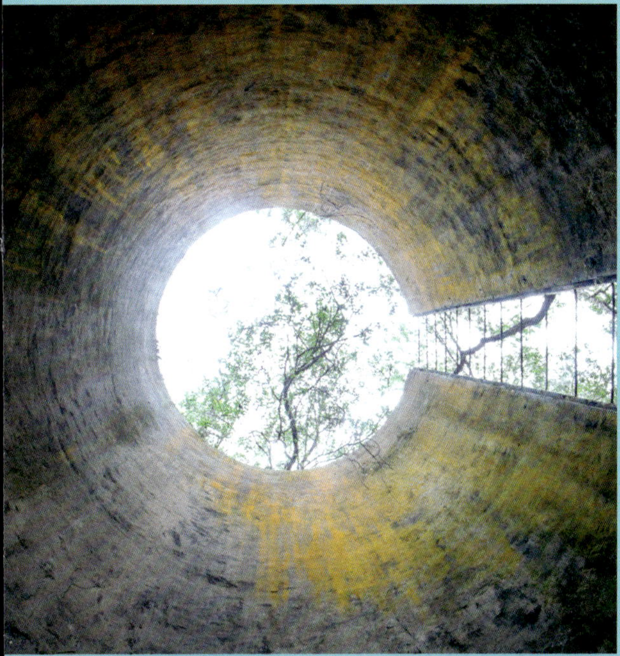
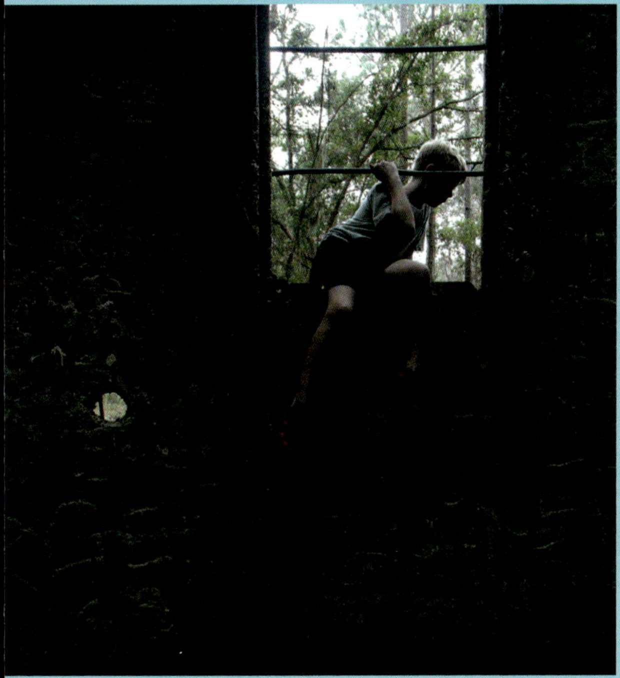
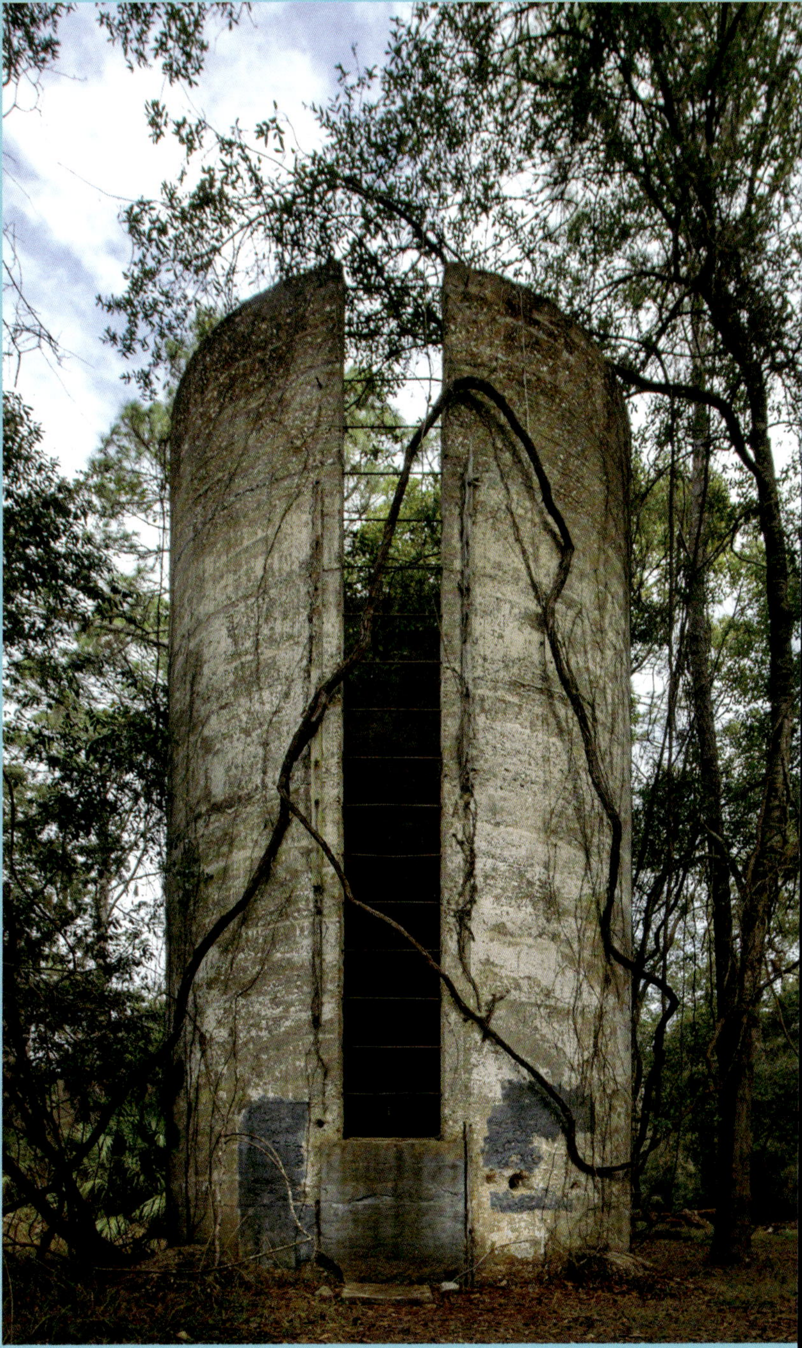

CHAPTER 6   *St. Simons Island*

THE SECOND LARGEST of the Georgia sea islands, St. Simons has a different feel from the other islands that are linked to the mainland by causeways. The island has always been a community rather than a private preserve.

It is less developed than Tybee, more developed than Jekyll Island State Park, and not as upscale as neighboring Sea Island. St. Simons is a blend of all three, and residents and visitors seem to like it that way. There is ongoing concern among islanders about overdevelopment, and resentment of investors who invade the old established neighborhoods, including three historic Gullah Geechee communities.

The island was inhabited thousands of years ago. The Paleo-Indians harvested the rich marine resources of the estuaries. Before contact with Europeans, the Mocama people lived on the island. They were the saltwater branch of the large Timucuan chiefdom of northern Florida and southern Georgia, but spoke their own dialect.

Franciscan friars from Florida established a mission in the Mocama village on the island's south end in about 1604. They named it San Buenaventura de Guadalquini by combining the name of the saint whose saint's day coincided with the mission's first mass and the name of the Native village. Decades later, refugee Guale and Yamasee villages were relocated to the island. One Yamasee village was named San Simón, later anglicized to St. Simons.

From the mid-1600s, Georgia sea islands served as stops on the first underground railroad, which ran south instead of north. Enslaved people who escaped from British plantations in Carolina fled down the coast to Spanish Florida in search of better treatment and possible freedom. They rowed or sailed more than one hundred miles down the inland passage, stopping on islands like St. Simons to rest and find fresh water and food.

In 1736, Georgia's British founder, James Edward Oglethorpe, established the fortified town of Frederica on the island's western shore. He built several fort structures and his own home, Orange Hall, of tabby. Some Frederica colonists built homes of tabby, including Mary Musgrove, the half-Scottish, half-Creek woman who served as the translator for Oglethorpe and the Yamacraw chief Tomochichi when Oglethorpe was negotiating for land for the Georgia colony.

In 1742, Spain made its last serious attempt to reclaim territory north of Florida. Soldiers from St. Augustine invaded St. Simons; Oglethorpe's troops turned them back, securing Georgia for the British. Fort Frederica was decommissioned in 1758 and fell into ruin. Some of the tabby buildings were later sawed into blocks used to build the first St. Simons lighthouse in 1810 on the island's south end.

Before the Civil War, fourteen large plantations sprawled over the island, featuring fields of sea island cotton. Many of the giant live oaks that once covered the island were logged to build the first U.S. warships. One, the famous USS *Constitution*, was nicknamed Old Ironsides.

Several island planters grew rice in diked impoundments built by enslaved people on the Altamaha delta. The planters were wealthy, well educated, and well traveled. They sent their sons to Yale and Oxford, and their daughters to finishing schools in Charleston and Savannah. Some professed to abhor slavery, but they were all slaveholders.

The owner of Hampton Plantation on north St. Simons, Pierce Mease Butler, had more than four hundred Africans auctioned in Savannah shortly before the Civil War to pay his debts. It was the largest sale of enslaved people ever recorded in the United States. It became known as the Weeping Time because so many people were separated from loved ones.

St. Simons was in shambles after the Civil War. Many people formerly held in slavery made their way back to the island, the only home most had ever known, to do the only work they had ever done. The anthropologist John Michael Vlatch says many liberated slaves felt a sense of ownership for the land they had worked for many years. On St. Simons, former slaves formed three Gullah Geechee communities: South End, Harrington, and Jewtown, named for the Levisons, two Jewish brothers who opened a store and wanted the settlement named Levisonton, a real tongue twister. The residents called their community Jewtown instead.

The sawmills on Gascoigne Bluff pulled the island out of the economic doldrums, employing hundreds of Black and white workers to process the logs floated downriver from longleaf pine forests inland. The mill village was a lively place. A school and a church opened on the bluff. Foreign ships anchored in the Frederica River, waiting to dock and load up with lumber. Their crews wandered around the mill village, often singing songs of their homelands. Gullah Geechee stevedores sang their own songs, spirituals, and work shanties. "Pay Me My Money Down," a popular St. Simons work song, was later recorded by such well-known performers as Pete Seeger and Bruce Springsteen.

Visitors from the mainland rode the mill boat to visit friends and enjoy the lively sawmill village. They were forerunners of what later became the island's tourist industry. A new pier was built on the south end of St. Simons, along with a dance pavilion and hotels near the iconic lighthouse. Horse-drawn wagons and later a small-gauge railroad took passengers to a hotel farther north on the island, later home to the U.S. Coast Guard's lifeboat station. Ferries made round trips several times a day between the pier, Brunswick, and Darien.

The first causeway crossed four miles of marshland and five tidal rivers between the mainland and St. Simons in 1924, provoking an island building boom. Residents from Waycross, a town about seventy-five miles inland, built rustic houses near the lighthouse and summered there for decades. New restaurants and hotels opened, including the beachfront King and Prince, still the island's only oceanfront hotel.

During World War II, the King and Prince was commandeered by the navy, which opened a school to train personnel in the advanced technology of radar. The island's new airport was taken over by navy fliers. Nowadays, private jets carry visitors from all over the world to Malcolm McKinnon Airport for conferences and holidays on ritzy

Sea Island, St. Simons' smaller neighbor. The two islands are joined by a short causeway.

The development of Sea Island created thousands of jobs for St. Simons and Brunswick residents. Sea Island today is home to the Cloister Hotel, a cottage colony, and other resort amenities. The Sea Island Golf Club and its elegant five-star, five-diamond Lodge are on larger St. Simons, now home to a number of professional golfers. Every November, Davis Love III, who was inducted into the World Golf Hall of Fame in 2017, hosts the RSM Classic at the Sea Island Golf Club as part of the annual PGA tour.

The pier village on the south end near the lighthouse is a popular tourist destination. Visitors explore T-shirt shops and ice cream emporiums, fish and crab on the pier, prowl the Museum of Coastal History, and climb the spiral staircase to the top of the lighthouse for the breathtaking view.

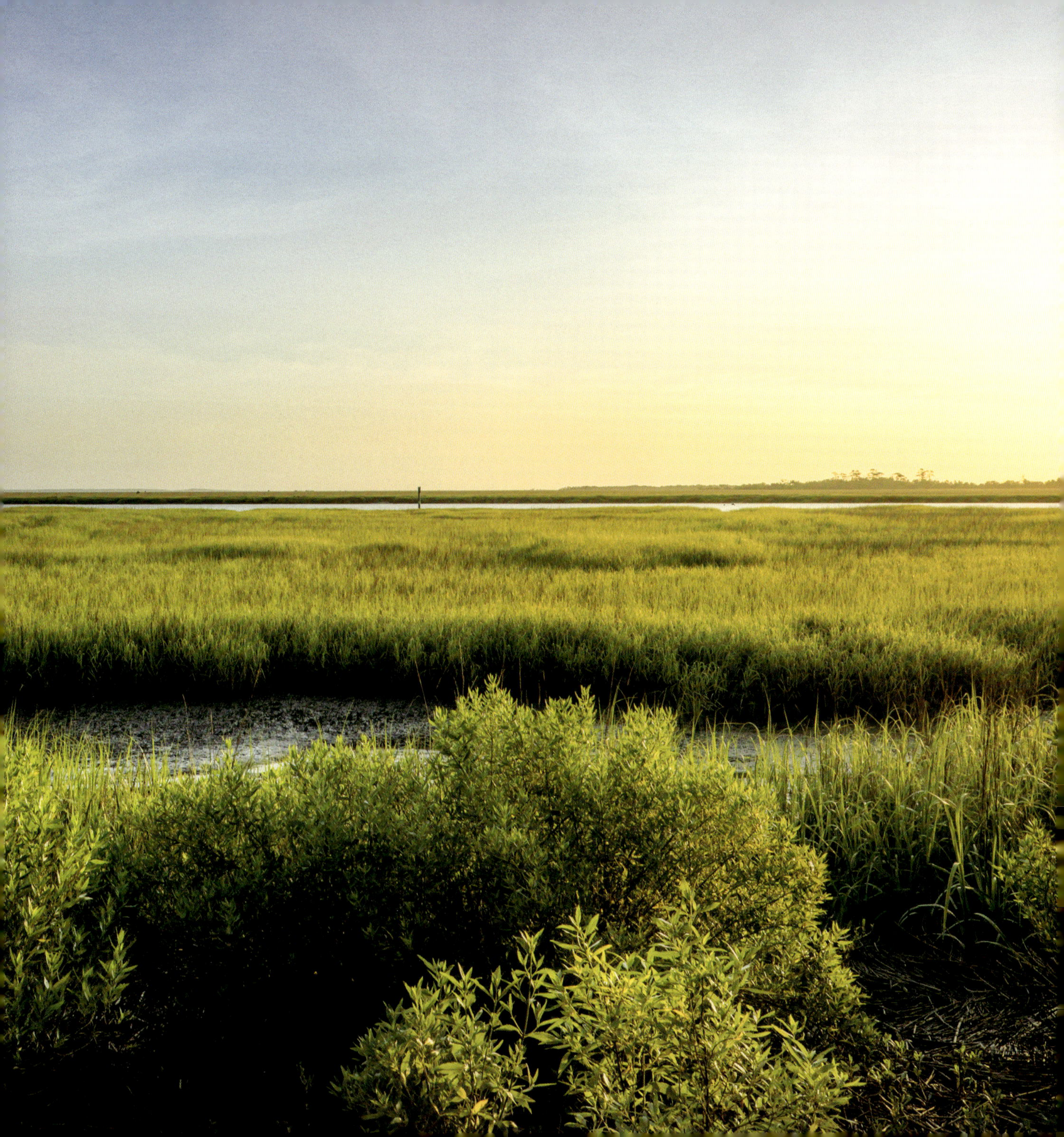

SITE 17

Hamilton Plantation Slave Cabins

c. 1830

100 Arthur J. Moore Drive

National Register of Historic Places

HISTORIC SIGNIFICANCE: Eight tabby cabins on the southwestern side of St. Simons Island were built to house enslaved workers on the plantation founded by James Hamilton, one of the nation's first millionaires. Three cabins have survived; two are now owned by the Cassina Garden Club, whose members raised $400,000 to have them restored.

James Hamilton established his St. Simons plantation in 1793 on Gascoigne (pronounced GAS-coin) Bluff, where the causeway today makes landfall on the island. His tabby home was a plain colonial-style structure set high on a latticed foundation to catch the breezes and offer views of tidewaters and salt marshes. Shutters shielded the verandah from the western sun.

A hedge of flowering yuccas bordered the foundation, and garden walkways were paved with oyster shells. The walkways led through a series of gardens: the rose garden, the cutting garden, and the herb garden, each defined by a picket fence or boxwood hedge.

The remains of Hamilton's two-story tabby barn are now the property of Epworth by the Sea, a Methodist conference center. Three tabby cabins still stand on the bluff. The one on the conference center grounds has been restored and is used for meetings; the other two are owned by the garden club. They are open to the public on Wednesday mornings during the summer; other visits can be arranged by appointment.

Experts date the cabins to 1830. They were designed and built by Hamilton's namesake, James Hamilton Couper, the son of his best friend. They were each meant to accommodate two families. Together, the eight cabins may have housed more than one hundred enslaved people, most of them children. The adult occupants probably did domestic work in their owner's nearby residence.

Although the tabby cabins were small by today's standards, they were state-of-the-art when they were built. Each side of the duplex had a poured tabby floor and two windows downstairs. Windows in the gable ends provided cross-ventilation for the sleeping loft. Doors opened to the river side to catch breezes. The tabby exterior was skimmed with lime stucco to protect it from weathering;

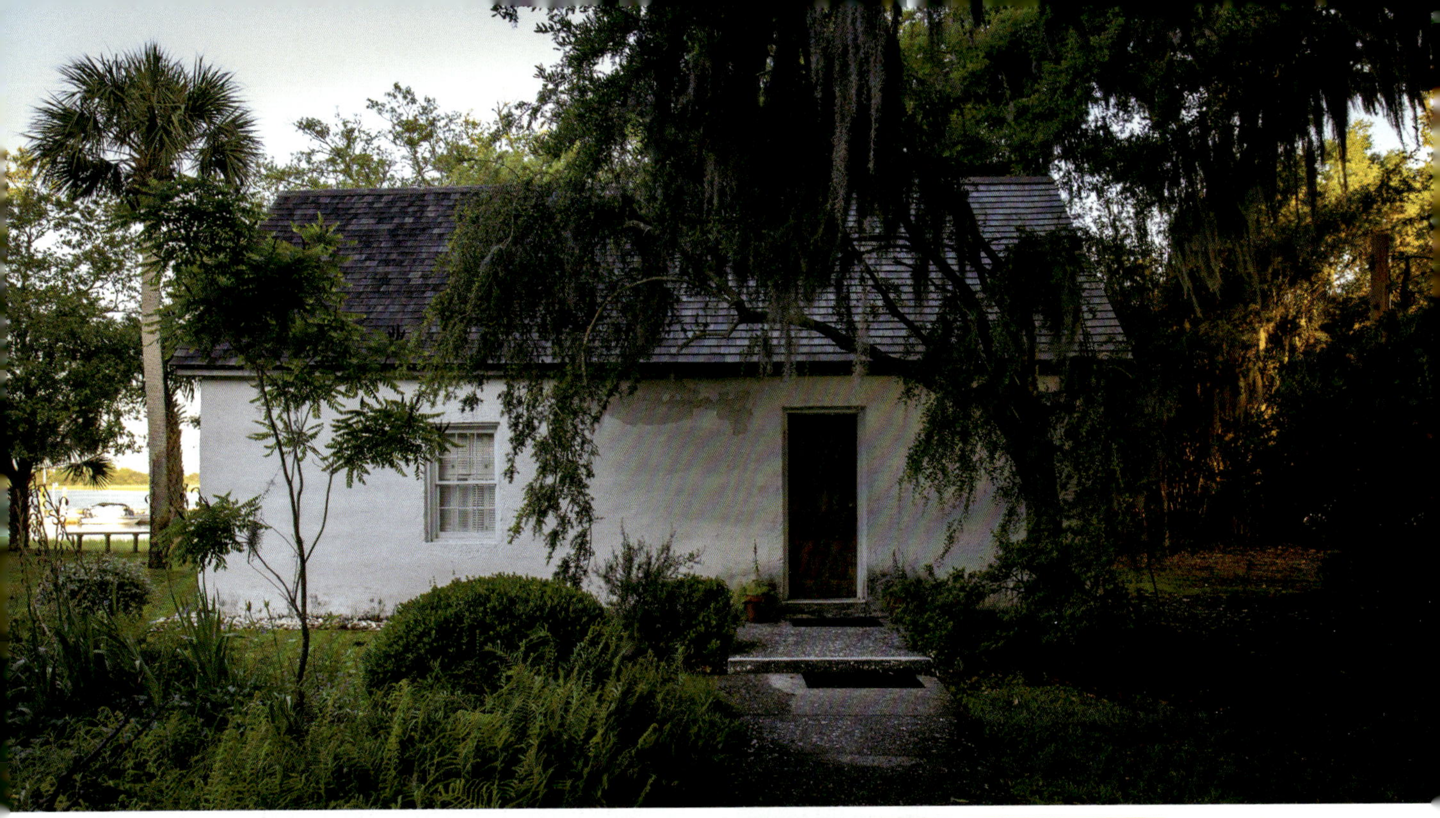
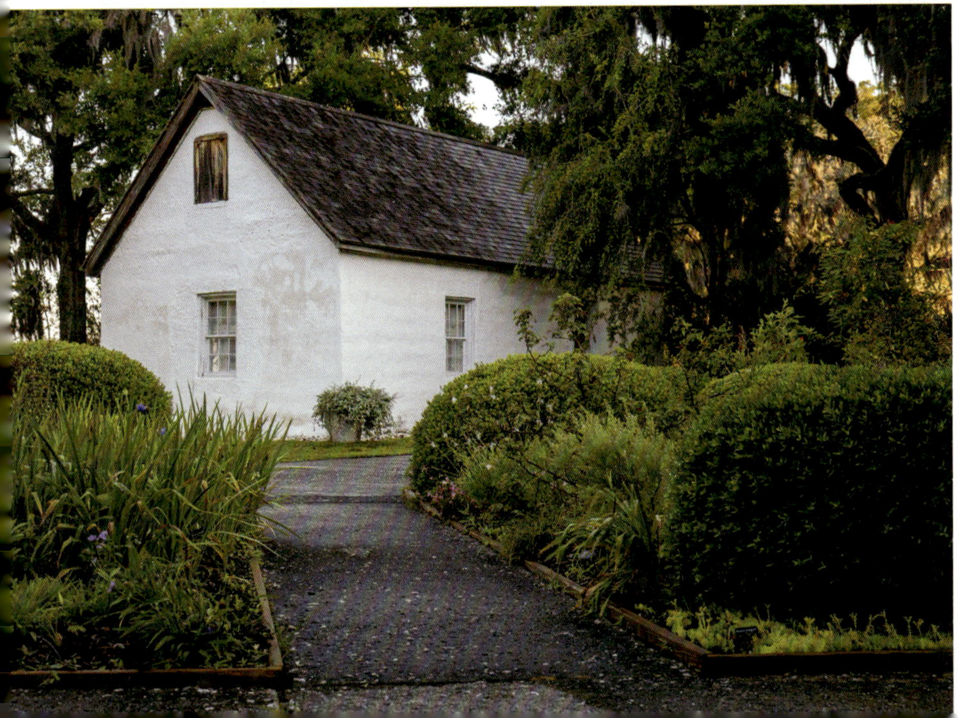
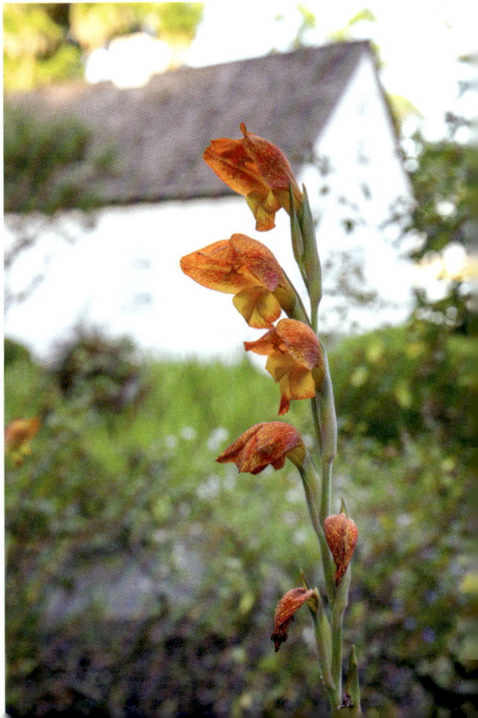

interior walls were stuccoed to shield the occupants from the sharp oyster shells in rough tabby.

The duplexes were divided by central chimneys made of tabby bricks, with a fireplace for heating and cooking on either side. Tabby walls flanked the chimney to provide privacy. The sleeping loft was not partitioned; children of both families shared the space. Adults slept downstairs.

In recent years, garden club members raised $400,000 to hire a Savannah firm that specializes in historic restoration to survey and restore the cabins. The project took five years. An earlier restoration done with concrete made from portland cement had caused the tabby to deteriorate. Some of the windows had been replaced by doors. The doors were removed during the restoration and windows were reinstalled. The restorers left off patches of lime stucco to show the original tabby underneath.

Original materials were retained when possible, including pecky cypress roof rafters. (Pecky is a fungal infection of bald cypress; it does not affect the wood's great strength.) Touches of paint on rafters and trim have faded to a pale blue-gray. The original indigo color, called "haint blue," was believed to frighten away haints, or evil spirits.

Because the south cabin was in better shape than its neighbor, it was restored to resemble period housing for a family of enslaved people. It is furnished simply, with cooking pots, a table and benches, and a loft ladder.

The north cabin was redone to reflect its use in the late 1800s, when sawmills operated on the bluff. The north cabin, now used for garden club activities, displays historic photographs, period memorabilia, and artifacts found on the property.

Tabby walkways lead to surrounding gardens planted with native species, African imports such as okra, benne (sesame) seed, and peanuts, along with flowers appealing to butterflies. Members also grow a few cotton plants, the upland variety, because sea island cotton cannot be grown in many southern states without a special waiver or permit. Sea island cotton, *Gossypium barbedense*, the variety that made coastal planters wealthy, is more susceptible than upland cotton to boll weevils. Sea island and upland cotton were all but wiped out in the 1920s by the voracious beetle, and agricultural specialists aim to prevent a resurgence of the pest.

During the Civil War, the tabby cabins were inhabited either by contrabands—enslaved people from elsewhere who were brought to the island by Northern troops in 1862—or by the troops themselves. Liberated but not yet officially free, the formerly enslaved had limited means of sustaining themselves in the war-torn South.

Union officials set up camps around the South to house the freedmen, who were designated contraband, or spoils of war. That characterization prevented their former owners from reclaiming them. Camps on St. Simons at Gascoigne Bluff and Retreat Plantation housed about five hundred contrabands for almost a year. Some learned to read and write at a camp school established by the formerly enslaved Susie Baker King Taylor, a literate teenager who had attended underground schools in Savannah. Later, at Fort Frederick in Beaufort County, South Carolina, she became a nurse in her husband's regiment, the Fifty-Fourth Massachusetts Volunteer Infantry, the first Union regiment composed of freed Black men.

After the war, the formerly enslaved bought small plots of land on the island or squatted on abandoned parcels. Others were deeded property by their former owners. The Gullah Geechee eked out a living by farming and fishing.

In 1870, the Dodge-Meigs Company, the world's largest timber concern, opened a sawmill on Gascoigne Bluff that provided employment for many islanders as well as workers from the mainland. The mill processed longleaf pine harvested from inland forests that once stretched for millions of acres between New York and Texas. The cut tree trunks were bundled together and rafted downriver to coastal sawmills. Three more mills subsequently opened on Gascoigne Bluff, including one that milled cypress cut in freshwater swamps farther upriver. Ships from all over the world docked at the Hamilton Plantation's former wharf to load up with newly milled lumber.

The tabby cabins were turned into offices for mill officials. One served as a school and a doctor's office. Hamilton's house was occupied by a series of mill executives. At one time, it was converted to a boardinghouse, with dance classes offered in the basement. The house burned in the mid-1880s. By the early 1900s, the once-vast forests of longleaf pine had been depleted, and the mills on Gascoigne Bluff closed.

In 1927, Eugene W. Lewis of Detroit bought Hamilton Plantation. At the time, northern millionaires were buying property, including sea islands on the southeastern coast, lured by the mild winter climate and the area's natural beauty. Lewis's close friend Howard Coffin had bought Sapelo Island and tiny Sea Island, where he built the exclusive Cloister Hotel and a cottage colony in the late 1920s, primarily as a winter resort for wealthy northerners. Lewis and Coffin had both made their fortunes as pioneers in automotive and aircraft development.

Coffin purchased tracts on St. Simons, Sea Island's larger neighbor, to build resort amenities, including a golf course, two yacht clubs, and a riding stable. Lewis enlarged a mill-era house as his residence and had several tabby cabins removed to improve his view. He began spending winters with his family on St. Simons. In tribute to Hamilton's agricultural history, Lewis hired hundreds of Gullah Geechees to plant lettuce, peas, cucumbers, peppers, tomatoes, eggplants, and other vegetables, and to pick, pack, and ship them to northern markets.

Handmade English bricks salvaged from ruined buildings on the bluff were turned into walkways, terraces, and the floor of a tabby cabin that Lewis refashioned into a recreation room.

Lewis' wife, Margaret, restored the lawns and gardens. She made a rock garden out of ballast stones that had been dumped on the riverbanks and in marshes by ships during the mill era. Three small hammocks, or little islands, arose over time on piles of ballast stones. As earth covered the stones, plants grew, including English varieties that had hitchhiked to coastal Georgia as seeds from the stones' countries of origin.

Gascoigne Bluff was named for its first European owner, Captain James Gascoigne, who captained the sloop of war HMS *Hawk*, which escorted the first Georgia colonists across the Atlantic. Today, part of the bluff is a county park with a fishing pier, restrooms, and shady space under the canopy of live oaks for festivals, including one that highlights the Gullah Geechee culture.

James Hamilton, 1763–1829

James Hamilton built Hamilton Plantation on Gascoigne Bluff not long after the American Revolution. He and his good friend and business partner John Couper, whose plantation was on the north end of St. Simons, had emigrated from Scotland as teenagers shortly before the Revolutionary War. Together, they bought large tracts of land, co-owned more than a thousand enslaved workers, and achieved wealth in the new republic. Hamilton turned out to be the better businessman. He worked as a factor, importing seeds, equipment, cloth, and other products, and as a banker-broker, shipping cotton for planters and allowing them to borrow against his credit. The planters repaid the loans with interest.

Hamilton became a merchant in Charleston, South Carolina, and conducted business in Europe, the Caribbean, and the United States. He owned shares in several ships and an elegant home in Philadelphia.

Hamilton Plantation became one of the most profitable plantations on the southeastern coast. When the British actress Fanny Kemble visited St. Simons, she called Hamilton Plantation "the finest on the island." Hamilton's business interests often took him elsewhere, but he served as one of the first vestrymen at Christ Church, established in the mid-1700s at Frederica by Charles and John Wesley. The brothers moved back to England and later founded the movement that grew into the United Methodist Church. The Epworth by the Sea conference center is named for their birthplace in England.

His wealth established, Hamilton sold most of his southern property around the early 1820s and retired to his Philadelphia townhome. He and his wife, Isabella, had a daughter, Agnes Rebecca, and a mentally disabled son, who was institutionalized. When Hamilton died in Philadelphia in 1829, he ranked as one of the nation's first millionaires.

James Hamilton Couper, named for his father's best friend, bought the plantation after Hamilton's death. Couper owned and managed other plantations on the mainland, so he turned the Gascoigne Bluff property over to his brother-in-law, John Fraser.

Only a few years earlier, Fraser had been the enemy. An officer in the British marines during the War of 1812, he had helped liberate thousands of the enslaved along the coast. Replacing those workers cost the St. Simons planters—including James Hamilton and John Couper—a fortune. During the British occupation of the sea islands, Fraser met Ann Couper, James Hamilton Couper's sister. The two fell in love and married after the war. In part because the Coupers were such a popular and well-respected island family, Fraser was welcomed by islanders in spite of his former British service.

Ann and John Fraser moved into Hamilton's tabby house. After Fraser's death, William Audley Couper, another brother, took over management of Hamilton Plantation and occupied the house.

A tragedy occurred while the Audley Coupers were in residence. As the steamship *Magnolia* was pulling away from Hamilton's wharf, passengers lined the deck railings, watching the Couper children playing with a pet fawn near the house. The *Magnolia*'s boiler exploded, blasting crew members and passengers into the river. Some of the victims drowned. Audley Couper turned Hamilton's two-story cotton barn into a makeshift hospital, providing beds by breaking open bales of sea island cotton. Mainland doctors rushed to the island to treat the injured, many of whom had suffered serious burns and broken bones. Couper family members and enslaved people nursed the patients for many weeks until they were well enough to leave.

The *Magnolia*'s passengers later sent the Audley Coupers an engraved silver pitcher in gratitude for their kindness. The pitcher is now on display at the Museum of Coastal History at the St. Simons lighthouse.

SITE 18

Retreat Plantation Slave Cabin

c. 1805

1550 Frederica Road

HISTORIC SIGNIFICANCE: This cabin is the only historic tabby building accessible to the public from Retreat Plantation, one of the largest and best-known antebellum enclaves on the coast. The cabin housed the enslaved who labored at the part of Retreat called New Field.

The tabby cabin that sits at the intersection of Frederica and Demere Roads on the southeastern side of the traffic circle is the sole survivor of a row of eight tabby cabins built for enslaved laborers at New Field, a part of Retreat Plantation, in about 1805. The giant plantation, much of it now home to the Sea Island Golf Club, the Malcolm McKinnon Airport, and upscale subdivisions, sprawled over two thousand acres on the southwestern side of St. Simons, stretching from the lighthouse almost to Gascoigne Bluff.

The eight cabins constituted New Field's quarters for the enslaved. The Tabby House Gift Shop, adjacent to the airport, is privately owned and maintained by the Sea Island Company, which owns the nearby golf club and other properties on the island.

The tabby house is forty-eight feet long and eighteen feet wide with thick tabby walls originally covered, as they are today, with stucco outside and plaster inside. The stucco was designed to protect the porous tabby from the elements; the plaster protected the inhabitants from rough tabby's sharp oyster-shell aggregate. The gabled wood-shingled roof is a replica of the original.

The cabin was built as a duplex to accommodate two families, each occupying space downstairs and a sleeping loft above. Fireplaces in the main living rooms were served by a central chimney.

New Field was about a mile from the main plantation complex at Retreat. The owner's home and outbuildings were clustered on the south end of the island, overlooking the waters of St. Simons Sound and Jekyll Island. The remains of a brick chimney and the corner of a foundation wall are all that remain of the plantation house, which burned years ago. The historic remains of tabby structures at the plantation's main complex, including the hospital for the enslaved, are on private golf club property and are not open to the public.

The plantation house was built in the late 1700s by

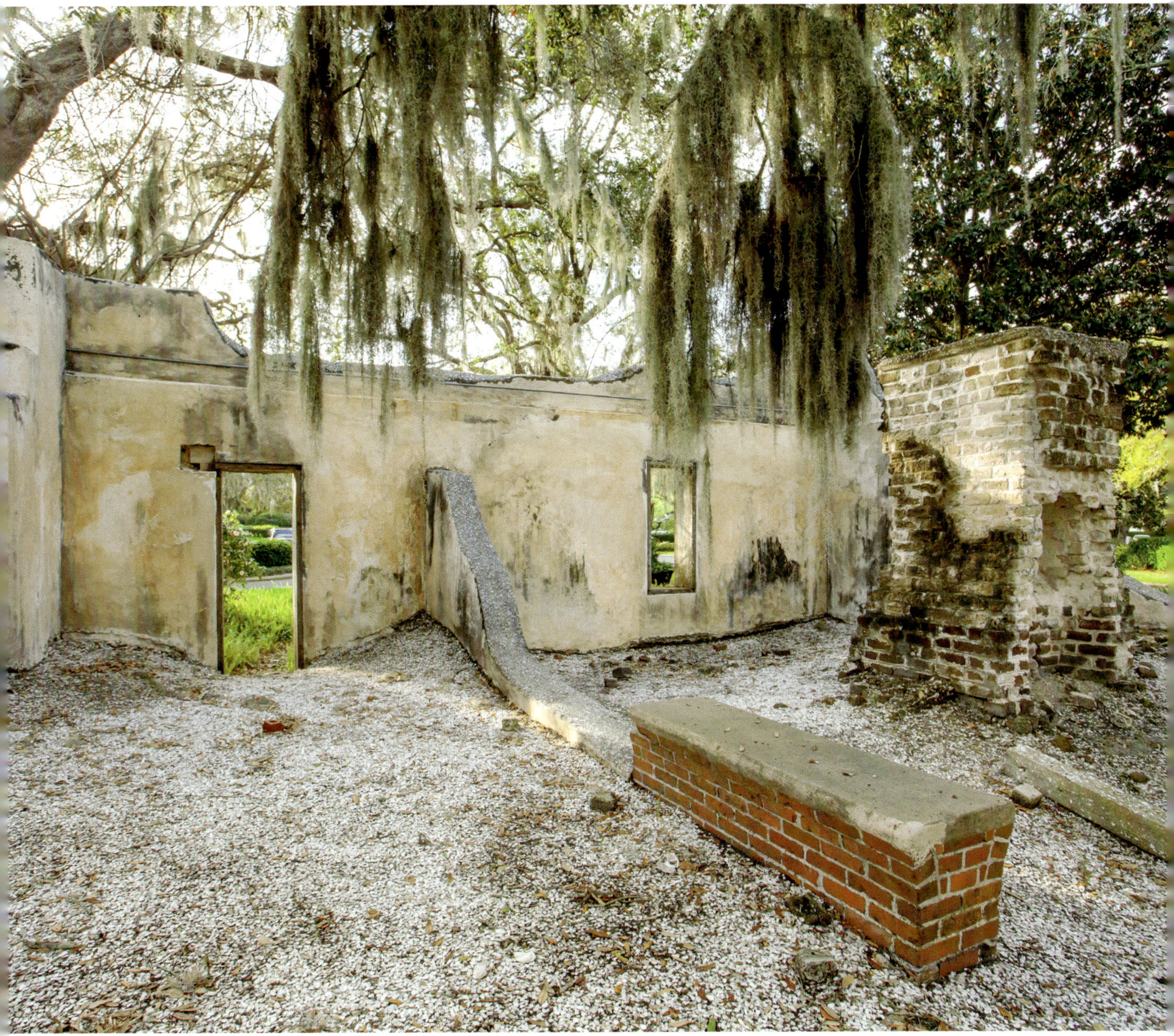

James Spalding, a Scottish immigrant who named the property Orange Grove Plantation. He modeled his home on Orange Hall, the tabby house built on the northwest side of St. Simons by Georgia's founder, James Edward Oglethorpe. Spalding later purchased Orange Hall.

The Orange Grove house was one-and-a-half stories with a raised basement and shuttered porches. It was built of live oak timbers and white pine weatherboards. The window blinds and doors were of native cedar. The home was described by a historian of Georgia's barrier islands as "a roomy eighteenth-century English-style cottage sturdily built to stand the West Indian gales that sometimes blew in from the sea."

Among Retreat's outbuildings were a schoolhouse, a guesthouse, more quarters for the enslaved, and a four-story cotton barn that served as a landmark for sailors for a decade after the island's first lighthouse was destroyed, during the Civil War, and before its replacement was built.

Grasshopper Hall, which housed the sons of the plantation's later owners, was designed like the garçonnières (bachelor apartments) of French Louisiana to give the growing boys privacy but allow them all the advantages of living near the main house.

An important outbuilding was the two-story tabby hospital for the enslaved, built by Major William Page, who bought Orange Grove from Spalding in 1802 and renamed it Retreat. Male and female patients were treated on separate floors. Two full-time nurses trained in basic medical skills and midwifery lived in the attic and cared for their fellow enslaved.

In an attempt to protect the hospital's weathering tabby walls, the Sea Island Company had the building partially restored some years ago, but the restoration was done with concrete made from portland cement. Because Portland cement is harder than oyster-shell lime, it usually hastens the deterioration of old tabby.

The ruins of the main house, the hospital, and other tabby structures lie inside the gated golf course complex where the Sea Island Golf Club's elegant Lodge is located.

The tabby corn barn, built around 1790 by Major William Page, is visible from the west side of Retreat Avenue as it nears the guard gate. It was converted into a clubhouse for the Sea Island Golf Course after the company opened its first nine holes in 1928. Today the corn barn is headquarters for the Davis Love Foundation and the RSM Classic, held on St. Simons in November.

Behind the corn barn is a cemetery where those who had been enslaved at the Retreat, along with their descendants, are buried. The small cemetery is the resting place of one of the island's best-known historic African figures: Neptune Small, who accompanied Henry Lord "Lordy" Page King, the son of Anna and Thomas Butler King, to battle during the Civil War. Small served for almost two years as manservant to the young Confederate soldier, caring for his clothes and cooking his meals. When Lordy King was killed at Fredericksburg, Small risked his life to retrieve the body from the active battlefield and brought it back to Savannah. After the war, King's body was returned to St. Simons for final burial at the historic Christ Church cemetery. Small then accompanied a second King son to war. (He survived.)

The King family rewarded Small by granting him a few acres of plantation land. Neptune Park in the pier village by the lighthouse—once part of Retreat's property—is named in Neptune Small's honor.

Small is credited with planting many of the live oaks that line Retreat Avenue between Kings Way and the entrance to the golf club. Five hundred of the stately trees once lined both sides of the carriage drive from the slave quarters at New Field south to the Retreat plantation house. Traffic is now routed to either side of the Avenue of Oaks because the carriage corridor between the trees is too narrow to accommodate modern traffic.

Floyd White, whose parents had been enslaved, was living in the tabby cabin at New Field during the 1930s when he was interviewed by researchers with the Georgia Writer's Project. The cabin may have been where his family members lived before the Civil War. The writer's project was part of the federal government's Works Project Administration, an effort to employ out-of-work people during the Great Depression. Writers sought out the formerly enslaved and their descendants and compiled the material from the interviews in a book titled *Drums and Shadows: Survival Studies among Georgia Negroes*. White's mother had been enslaved at Retreat Plantation, and his father, Jupiter, had been enslaved at the adjacent Kelvin Grove Plantation.

Anna Matilda Page King, 1798–1859

Anna Matilda Page was the sole surviving child of Major William Page and Hannah Timmons Page of South Carolina. Page was sixteen years old when he signed on with Francis Marion, the notorious Swamp Fox, who led his Patriot troops in an unorthodox style through the woods and swamps of South Carolina during the American Revolution.

After the South Carolina home of the Page family was burned by Tories, Major Page visited friends in coastal Georgia. His daughter, in delicate health as a child, improved in the sea air. Page bought Orange Grove Plantation from James Spalding in 1804 and renamed the property Retreat.

An only child, Anna tagged along with her father as he managed the giant plantation: keeping records, doing the bookkeeping, making sure everything was properly maintained, and overseeing personnel, which included more than one hundred enslaved people. Page decided when crops should be planted, harvested, and shipped to factors for sale. Retreat's crop of sea island cotton was its economic mainstay. Page always selected the best seeds from the previous year's crop to plant the following year.

From her mother, Anna learned to manage the house servants, supervise chores such as sewing and cooking, and tend Retreat's formal flower gardens. One featured a three-hundred-foot walkway bordered by almost a hundred varieties of roses. The walkway led from the main house to the hospital for the enslaved. Other gardens included orange and lemon groves, grape arbors, and olive and date trees, some grown from seedlings in the tabby greenhouse.

Hannah Page and her daughter planted only flowers that smelled good. Retreat's gardens were so fragrant that captains claimed they could catch the scent of flowers even before their ships entered St. Simons Sound.

As an adult, Anna Page expanded her mother's gardens. She planted a cedar "pleasaunce," or pleasure garden, designed to please the sight and other senses. The cedar trees turned out to offer an unplanned advantage: they served as a windbreak to temper winter winds blowing in from the Atlantic.

She laid out oyster-shell walkways that meandered through an arboretum featuring specimen trees and rare shrubs, many of them gifts from foreign countries. The famed ornithologist and illustrator John James Audubon, who took refuge at Retreat when his southbound boat encountered a storm, commented that the grounds of the main house were as beautiful as the mythical fairy gardens of the golden age.

Major Page willed the plantation and fifty enslaved people to his daughter in 1826, a few years after she had married a Massachusetts attorney named William Butler King. The property she inherited was bound in a trust that could not be claimed by her husband, which turned out to be a blessing. King, a politician and society figure who traveled most of the time, suffered major losses in his business affairs. His property and those he enslaved were confiscated to settle debts, but because of the terms of Page's will, Anna King's property could not be claimed by her husband's creditors.

King was not Anna's first love. She had hoped to marry Charles Molyneaux, but his father and hers could not agree on her dowry. Anna Page was heartbroken. Even

Anna Matilda Page King

after she married King, she pined for Molyneaux. She caught sight of him one day during a carriage ride with her husband at a vacation spot in the North. She stood up in the moving carriage, stretched out her arms to Molyneaux, and cried out his name. King showed great restraint—or indifference. He took his wife's hand and said, "Sit down and compose yourself, my dear."

King was a high-profile figure who served in the Georgia Senate and the U.S. Congress and promoted a transcontinental railroad and other civic projects. Two presidents appointed him to special posts, one as collector for the Port of San Francisco. His work and social obligations kept him away from Retreat most of the time, although he fathered ten children on his brief visits home.

In her husband's absence, Anna King took over as Retreat's manager and became one of the best sea island cotton producers in coastal Georgia. Like her father, she experimented with sea island cotton seeds, selecting the best for future planting. Her cotton was famous for its bright white color and long, silky staples. She likewise took charge of the plantation's livestock: horses, hogs, cattle, mules, chickens, ducks, and an ox. She kept Retreat's financial records, distributed food and clothing to the enslaved, and marketed the cotton and other plantation produce. She continued to tend the garden started by her mother. During the Civil War, when St. Simons was held by Union troops, an army colonel described it as "the loveliest tropical garden, though tangled and desolate, which I have ever seen in the South." The officer said the house was bowered in blooming shrubs, flowery scents, and trailing Little Chickasaw roses.

In her spare time, Anna King reared her children and wrote hundreds of letters to relatives and friends. Her collected correspondence paints a vivid picture of her life at Retreat.

She died in 1859, on the eve of the Civil War, shortly after the death of her oldest son, Butler. Her husband and another son died during the war. King family members are buried at Christ Church cemetery.

SITE 19

Fort Frederica

1736

6515 Frederica Road

National Monument

HISTORIC SIGNIFICANCE: Fort Frederica was the headquarters of the British military in colonial America. The fort's soldiers played a pivotal role in the struggle for territory on the continent. Battles fought on St. Simons in 1742 marked the last time that Spain tried to regain land on the Atlantic Seaboard north of the Florida Peninsula.

For almost three centuries, the tabby King's Magazine at Fort Frederica has stood sentinel on the western shore of St. Simons Island, overlooking the Frederica River and the wide stretch of marsh between the island and the mainland.

Another distinctive tabby structure, the entrance to the barracks, stands in an open field like a small medieval fortress, the rest of the building having been lost to time. The barracks formed a ninety-foot square with a courtyard in the center. They were built under the supervision of Major William Horton, Oglethorpe's right-hand soldier, who built a tabby house on Jekyll.

The King's Magazine is a memorable building, with its arched brick vaults and crenellated walls. It was restored in 1904 by builders who used as much of the old tabby as possible. Crenellations may not have been part of the original magazine. The merlons were made of revival tabby with a portland cement binder rather than burned-oyster-shell lime, the only cement available when the structure was first built. Masons used new brick to rebuild the south arch, but the style in which it was laid does not precisely match that of the original north arch.

Albert Manucy, the late National Park Service historian and author who specialized in the architecture of St. Augustine, Florida, examined the ruins of Fort Frederica. He surmised that a sally port, about sixteen feet square, was part of the original magazine but had eroded into the river. The sally port, he said, would have had double doors that opened inward, one facing west toward the river, the other opening through the east wall to the parade ground. Forts in the seventeenth century were built with gates, guardrooms, and magazines near one another. Typical guardrooms at the time included a prison cell and a room for the officer of the day. A tabby gutter, probably planked over with wood, ran through the sally port to drain rainwater from the parade ground into the river. Manucy said he believed the entry gate was a two-story structure,

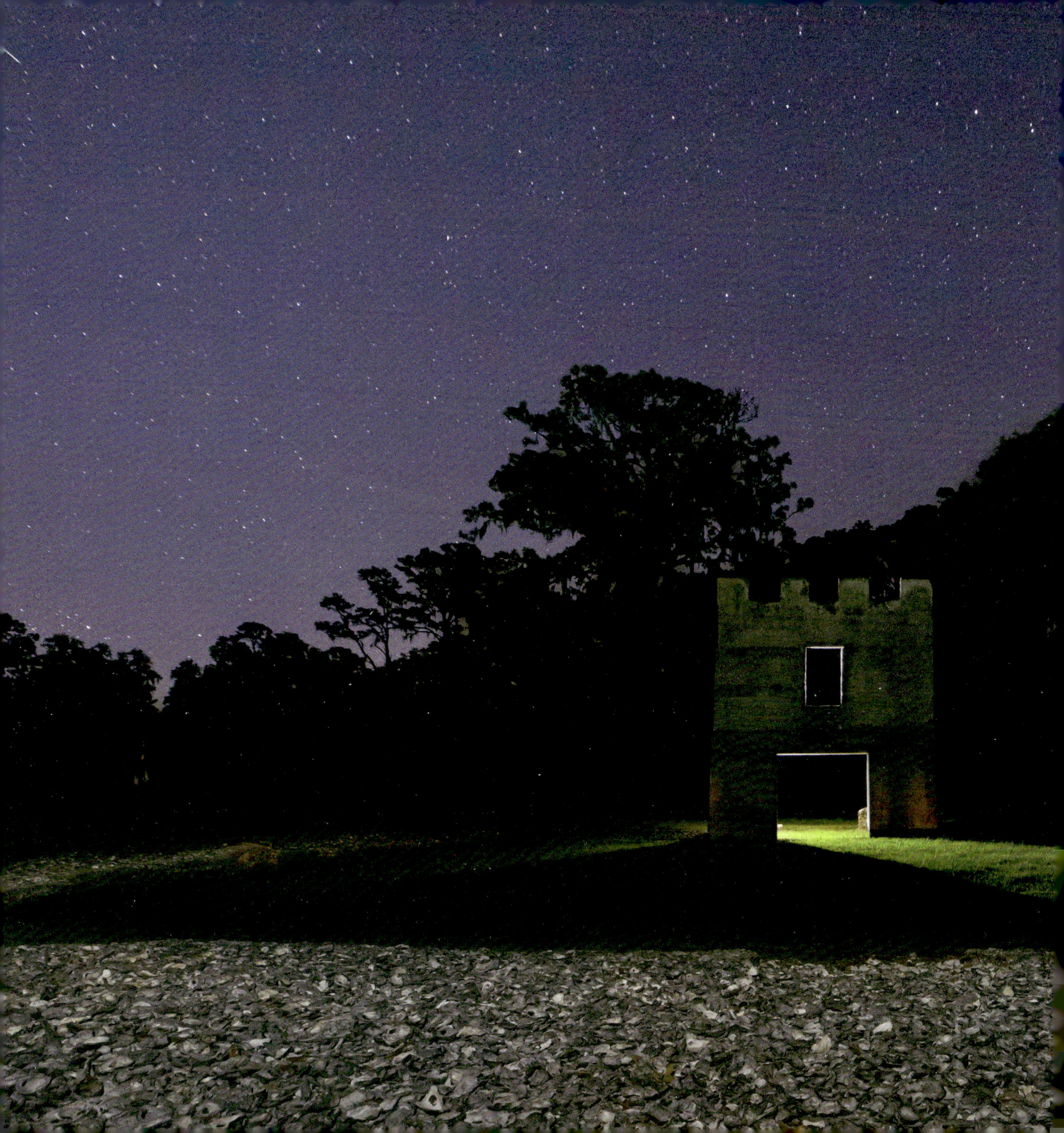

similar or identical to the barracks entrance. Outer doors were strapped with iron bands and studded with nails to repel enemy axes. Ammunition was stored in the arched vaults, which had at least two feet of sand covering the roof. Powder casks were stacked against the west wall for better air circulation.

Broad Street, the town's main thoroughfare, was once lined with the houses and shops of Frederica colonists. The structures are gone now, but their foundations have been excavated to give an idea of what the fortified colonial town might have looked like.

Fort Frederica occupied about forty acres along a straight run of the Frederica River before the waterway curves away from land west into the marshes. The curve forced enemy ships to come into range of the fort's cannons before they could maneuver into position to fire their own guns. Frederica was almost impregnable from the water.

The same tract had been occupied earlier by Yamasees, refugee natives relocated to the island in 1675 because they were under attack inland by Native people affiliated with the British. The Franciscan missionaries who established the temporary settlement named it San Simón, which was later anglicized to the island's present-day name. Oglethorpe designed the star-shaped fort with a quartet of bastions, a spur battery that has since eroded into the river, storehouses, a guardhouse, and a stockade.

The military buildings and the town were surrounded by a rampart, a mile-long earthen wall planted with turf to keep it from washing away in the island's semitropical downpours. The rampart was flanked by a dry moat that Oglethorpe described as a wet ditch. It was fitted with tide gates and could be flooded with river water in case of a land-based attack. Two ten-foot-tall wooden palisades offered even more protection.

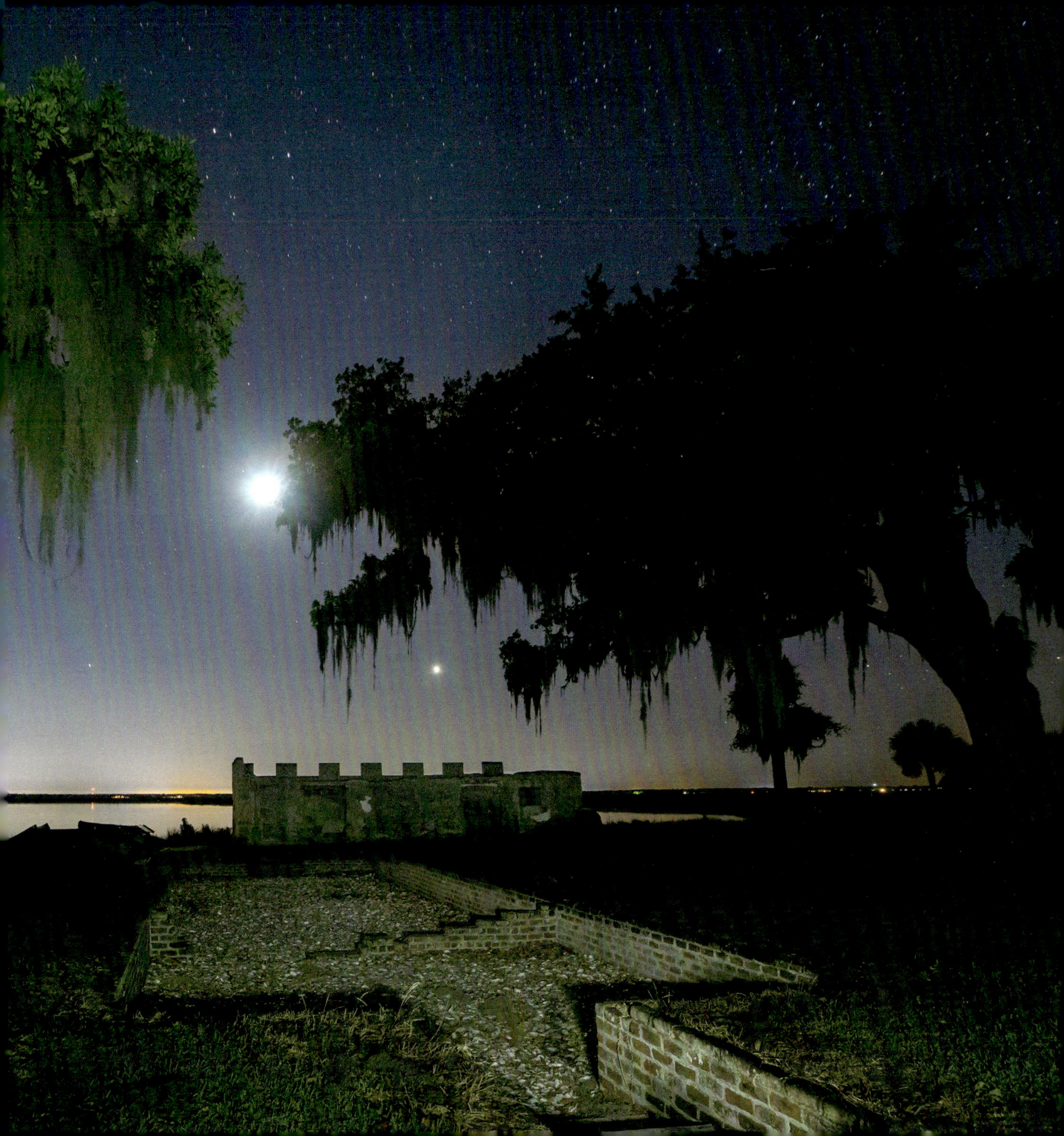

After establishing Frederica, Oglethorpe spent most of his time setting up other military outposts, including the earthen Fort St. Simons on the island's southern tip. A narrow, unpaved military road connected the two forts. Oglethorpe built smaller outposts on sea islands almost as far south as Spanish Florida.

Spain and England were not at war in 1736 when Frederica was founded, but relations between the two countries deteriorated as both struggled for control of the New World.

By 1738, Oglethorpe's regiment consisted of more than seven hundred men housed in Frederica's barracks. The fort was named for Frederick Louis, the Prince of Wales, but because a South Carolina fort bore the name Frederick, the name of the Georgia fort was feminized. Within a decade, Frederica boasted a thousand residents, most of them tradesmen and families. By selling goods and services to the regiment, the townspeople prospered. Many built substantial houses to replace the palmetto huts of Frederica's early years. The town has been described as a smaller version of Williamsburg, Virginia.

Many of the houses had tabby or tabby and brick foundations. Some houses built of tabby were among the oldest masonry homes in Georgia. One tabby house belonged to a woman named Mary Musgrove Bosomworth, a woman of Creek and Scottish ancestry who acted as Oglethorpe's translator when he negotiated for land for his colony with the Yamacraw leader Tomochichi. At one time, Mary Musgrove was considered the richest woman in Georgia. She owned trading posts at strategic locations along major rivers and cattle ranches called cow pens.

Oglethorpe's success on St. Simons was the beginning of the end for Fort Frederica. Once the peace treaty ending the War of Jenkins' Ear was signed between Spain and Great Britain, the fort was no longer needed. British dominance on the Eastern Seaboard was established as far south as Florida. Oglethorpe's regiment was disbanded in 1749. When the soldiers left, so did many of the townspeople who depended on the commerce generated by the military. A fire about a decade later destroyed most of the all-but-abandoned town.

In the early 1800s, a Massachusetts-born timber surveyor named James Gould cut blocks of tabby from buildings at Frederica and hauled them to the south end of St. Simons to build the island's first lighthouse. He served as its first lightkeeper. The lighthouse, which was destroyed by retreating Confederate troops during the Civil War, was rebuilt a decade later of brick.

The Fort Frederica National Monument is open year-round. U.S. Park Service rangers stage lime-burning demonstrations once a year to show visitors how oyster shells were burned in log-cabin-like ricks to make the lime used as the hardener in tabby concrete.

James Edward Oglethorpe, 1696–1785

Because of his military responsibilities in other parts of the new Georgia colony, James Edward Oglethorpe, named a British general in 1736, was often absent from Fort Frederica. He was comfortable with commanding his troops, but disliked trying to govern Frederica's unruly townspeople, who were struggling to make new lives in an alien environment while under constant threat of attack.

Oglethorpe was an unlikely leader for a pioneer settlement. Born to a well-to-do urban family in London and educated at Eton and Oxford, he joined the military to fight against the Turks, who were invading Europe. He ran for Parliament and won the seat formerly held by his father and two older brothers.

After a friend died in debtors' prison in London, Oglethorpe chaired a committee investigating prison conditions. He was appalled. Some of his efforts at prison reform succeeded, and he became known as a humanitarian. To help destitute people escape the slums of London, Oglethorpe and others lobbied for a new American colony where debtors and the "worthy poor" could work to improve their lives.

Instead of choosing slum dwellers to be Georgia's first settlers, however, Oglethorpe and twenty other trustees who governed the new colony selected successful farmers, merchants, carpenters, tailors, bakers, and others who could help the fledgling settlement survive. Some of the chosen were wealthy enough to travel with ten indentured servants.

Frederica's residents, a contentious group, created problems for their neighbors and for Oglethorpe, who disliked adjudicating civic disputes. The general complained that he had more trouble with the eighty colonists at Frederica than he did with the entire Spanish Armada.

Two young Anglican clerics, John and Charles Wesley, were ill treated by the Frederica colonists. Born in Epworth, England, the brothers traveled to Georgia with Oglethorpe in 1736, eager to convert both the colonists and the Indigenous people to Christianity. Although period illustrations depict the Wesleys preaching to Native Americans, they never did. The trustees appointed John Wesley to remain in Savannah as minister of the Georgia colony and sent Charles Wesley to St. Simons to be Oglethorpe's secretary, the secretary for Indian affairs, and Frederica's minister.

Many of Frederica's residents were not religious, which made Charles's job difficult. Most of the colonists disliked the young minister's piety and rigidity. For example, when Charles learned that a Frederica toddler had not been baptized by triune dunking, or total immersion three times, he insisted that the rite be repeated in the Frederica River, still chilly in early spring. The mother refused, but Wesley pestered the father until he allowed the toddler to be dunked. The forced baptism did not endear Charles to either parent.

At Frederica, Charles fell victim to two mean-spirited housewives who falsely confessed to the young minister that they had engaged in sexual relations with an "important person" at Frederica. As the women intended, Charles assumed that the important person was Oglethorpe. The women then went to Oglethorpe and accused Wesley of spreading vicious rumors about him and them. Oglethorpe, who at first believed them, was outraged. He shunned Wesley, as did the other colonists after the tale spread all over town. Even the washerwoman refused to do the young minister's laundry.

After Charles Wesley fled Frederica, his brother John replaced him. The colonists spurned him as well. Both Wesleys returned to England in despair of ever converting the colonists. They later founded Methodism, which evolved into the United Methodist Church.

There was ample cause for the colonists to be contentious. Most hailed from the cool British Isles, and Georgia's semitropical heat would have been hard to endure. The Frederica River, a southern outlet for the giant Altamaha, was fresh enough for bathing, but baths had to be taken early, before the alligators were active. With grim humor, the colonists nicknamed sand gnats "merry-wings" and called the bites they inflicted "American chicken pox."

The colonists were always alert to danger, which kept them in a constant state of anxiety. Whenever a sail appeared on the horizon, they stopped work and scrambled to get ready to repel an attack.

Like the Wesleys, about a third of the original colonists abandoned Frederica in the first five years. Oglethorpe and the trustees had miscalculated the ability of colonists to grow enough food to support themselves after a year or two. They had also misjudged the fertility of the sandy coastal soil.

Ongoing tensions between Great Britain and Spain exploded into war in 1739. Initially called the War of Jenkins' Ear, it started as a conflict over trade agreements in the Caribbean. Oglethorpe attacked St. Augustine in 1740, but his cannons failed to breach the coquina-and-tabby walls of the great Castillo de San Marcos. Ill and in disgrace, the general retreated to Orange Hall, his tabby house on St. Simons. He was castigated on both sides of the Atlantic.

General James Oglethorpe in military dress, to commemorate his armed attempts to keep Spanish forces out of Georgia, mezzotint by Thomas Burford, c. 1757

Two years later, in 1742, the Spanish attacked St. Simons with an estimated 4,500–5,000 troops. Oglethorpe, outnumbered five to one, sent an urgent message to the Carolina governor for reinforcements. The governor, one of the general's harshest critics, was sure that Oglethorpe's message was a false alarm. The Spanish invasion began in midsummer. The armada ran the guns of Fort St. Simons without harm because the inexperienced British soldiers were such poor shots. The fleet landed on the southwest side of the island at Gascoigne Bluff, several miles downriver from Fort Frederica.

The Spanish discovered Oglethorpe's narrow Military Road but doubted that it was the main route to Frederica. The Spanish commander dispatched a scouting party to investigate. British troops and Spanish scouts first engaged at Gully Hole Creek near Frederica. When the sounds of battle reached Oglethorpe, he rushed to join the fight. In hand-to-hand combat, he captured two Spaniards and helped rout the other Spanish scouts.

A dozen Cuban grenadiers from Havana were killed in the skirmish. One British soldier died of heat exhaustion. Oglethorpe chased the scouts for several miles to a point where the Military Road crossed a stretch of high marsh on the east side of St. Simons. He posted soldiers in the woods and returned to Frederica for reinforcements. The Spanish leader had already sent reinforcements. When they reached the marsh crossing, the British launched their ambush but then began to retreat in panic. Oglethorpe returned just in time with more troops. Meanwhile, the Spanish had run out of ammunition and were also in retreat.

The history-changing battles were minor skirmishes. When the second battle ended, seven grenadiers lay dead in the marsh. The British later boasted that the marshes ran red with blood, an obvious exaggeration. The Spanish named the conflict the Battle of the Grenadiers, but it was soon dubbed the Battle of Bloody Marsh, a name that the British may have intended to offset their crushing defeat at what they called the Battle of Bloody Moosa (Fort Mose) in St. Augustine two years earlier.

The Spanish stayed on St. Simons another week. Oglethorpe sent a letter to a Frenchman who had deserted to the Spanish, pretending to be a British friend. The letter, written in French, informed the deserter that Frederica was vulnerable but that two thousand British reinforcements were on the way. The Spanish commander was skeptical until three British scout boats appeared on the horizon, sent by Carolina's governor to assess the situation. The Spanish leader assumed the scout boats represented the vanguard of the British troops and ordered a retreat back to St. Augustine.

The two minor battles fought on St. Simons ended Spain's two-century-long claim to Georgia territory and established British dominance in the Southeast north of the Florida Peninsula.

In 1743, Oglethorpe left for England, never to return. Conditions deteriorated at Frederica. The settlers abandoned their farms. A soldier's wife opened a brothel. Drunken soldiers broke into houses. After an attempted rape, one colonist commented, "Sodom and Gomorrah were more deserving of protection by the Almighty than Frederica."

Oglethorpe officially disbanded the regiment in 1749. When word reached St. Simons, the soldiers stayed drunk for three days.

SITE 20

Cannon's Point Plantation

1794

Cannon's Point Preserve
Cannon Point Road off Lawrence Road

National Register of Historic Places

HISTORIC SIGNIFICANCE: Cannon's Point, one of the largest of the dozen large antebellum plantations on St. Simons Island, operated with the labor of hundreds of enslaved workers. Tabby foundation walls, tabby pilasters that supported the verandah, and two partial chimney stacks built on tabby foundations are highlights of the picturesque brick and tabby ruins.

When John Couper and his wife, Rebecca Maxwell Couper, first moved to the point, they lived in the small house built by Daniel Cannon, a carpenter from the nearby town of Frederica. Cannon came to the island with Georgia's founder, General James Edward Oglethorpe, in 1736 to help build Fort Frederica as a defense against the Spanish in Florida. Cannon's small, one-room house, built in 1738, had a tabby basement, chimneys with heavy bases of tabby brick, and a tabby stoop.

The Coupers were known for their hospitality. The family entertained often, and guests sometimes stayed for months, even years. One newly married young couple who honeymooned at Cannon's Point settled in until after their second child was born.

Unlike the white-columned mansions of inland planters, the houses of planters on the southeastern coast resembled plantation houses in the West Indies. They were raised well above ground in order to catch breezes, elude mosquitoes, and survive floods.

The Coupers built their house in stages on the north end of Cannon's Point overlooking the Hampton River and the Altamaha delta, where planters grew rice in muddy, diked fields. For the first stage, builders used a technique called post-and-tabby to make the walls, pouring tabby around posts that may have supported Cannon's home. (They dug the oyster shells to make the tabby from large shell middens along the river.) Builders capped the walls with two or three runs of tabby brick. The builders then constructed a pair of two-and-a-half-story clay brick chimneys on heavy foundations of tabby brick inset with arches to relieve the weight. A dairy room occupied one corner of the porch. They built a separate, larger extension next to the first house, finishing it in 1804.

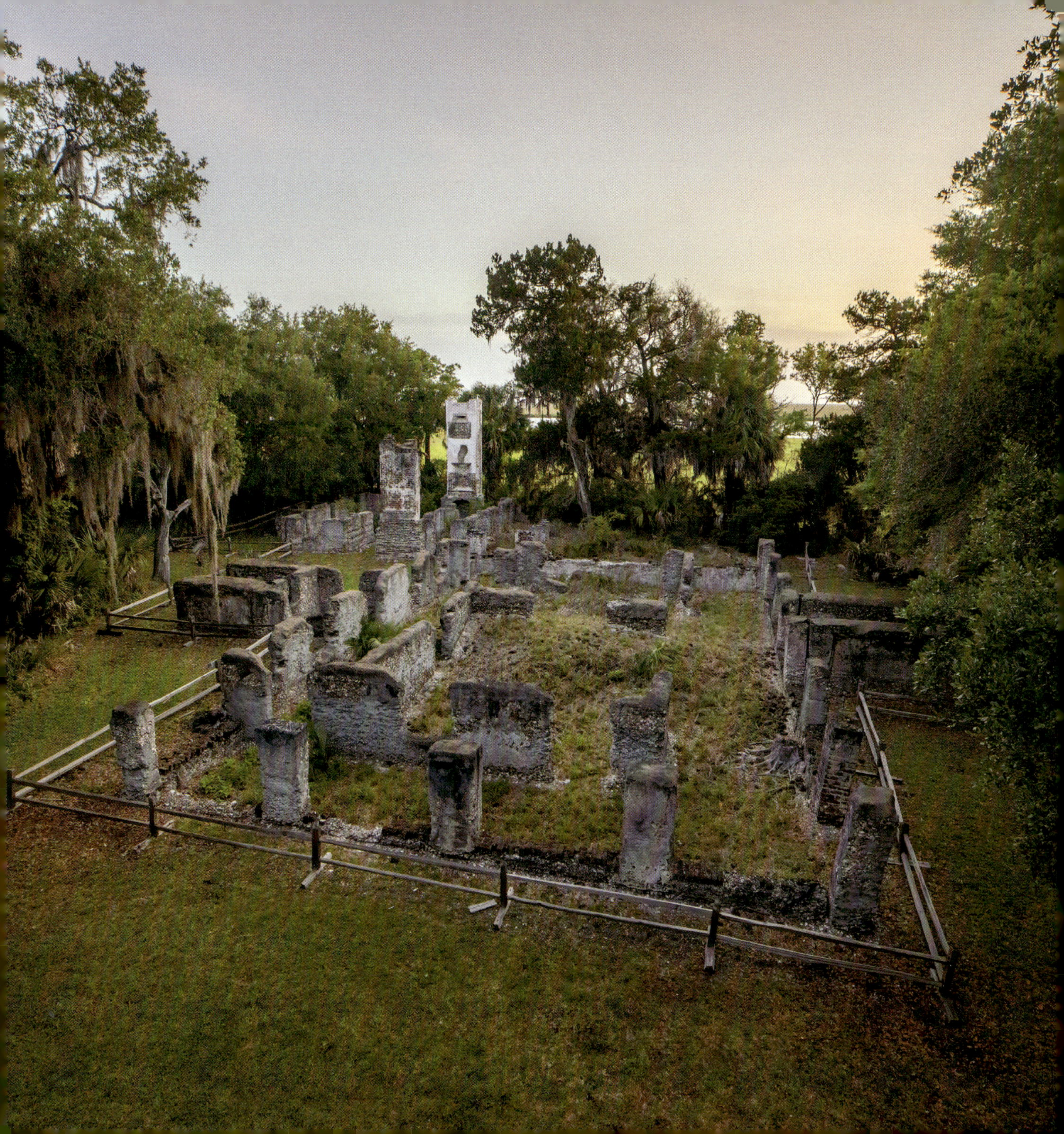

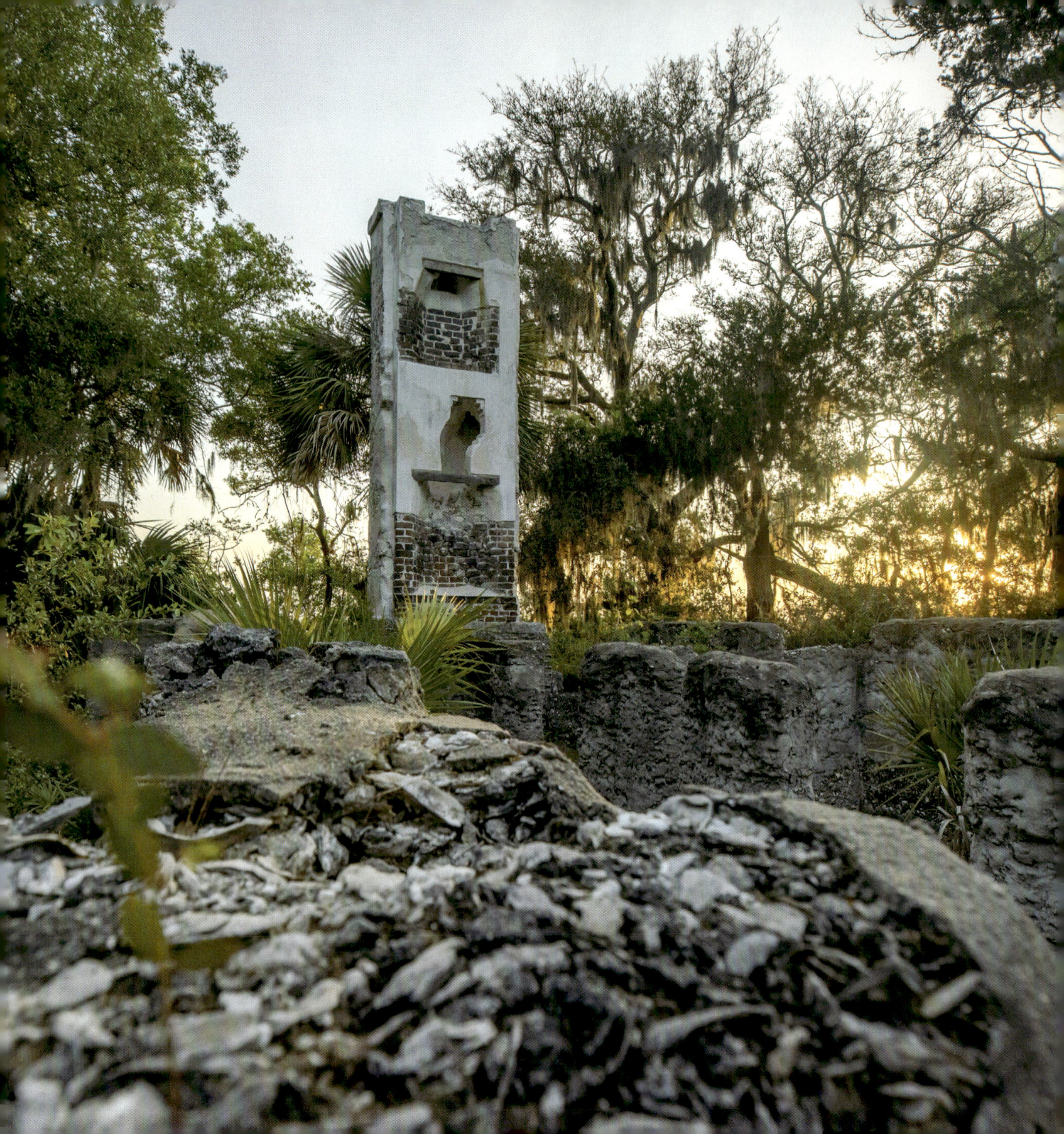

The British actress Fanny Kemble, the wife of Pierce Mease Butler, who owned Hampton Plantation, described the Coupers' residence as "a roomy, comfortable, handsomely laid-out mansion."

The extension was larger than the first house, three stories tall with a tabby ground floor topped with two wooden stories plus a loft with dormer windows. A verandah ran around three sides of the house. Double tabby walls enclosed the first-floor staircase. Poured tabby pilasters supported the verandah. A nineteenth-century painting by Couper's grandson John Lord Couper shows the wooden part of the house painted pale yellow or cream with white trim. Lord Couper was killed in action during the Civil War. His painting is now on exhibit at the Museum of Coastal History on St. Simons.

Two sets of tabby steps rose to a wide second-story verandah that wrapped around three sides of the house, offering views of gardens and the river. The Coupers and their guests spent a great deal of time on the verandah to escape the stifling heat inside the house in warmer months.

The tabby kitchen was housed in a separate building to protect the house from fire and its inhabitants from kitchen odors and the clanging of pots and pans. The Coupers were said to have the most elaborate kitchen on the Georgia coast, although their chef, Sans Foix, was only the second best in the region. He was trained by the best: Cupidon, the chef for one of the French aristocrats who owned Sapelo Island. Couper, who had tasted Cupidon's cuisine, invited him to become the chef at Cannon's Point. After Cupidon and his family were freed in their French owner's will, they moved to Couper's plantation. Together, Cupidon and Sans Foix prepared sumptuous meals and trained some of the enslaved workers as chefs for other planters. Abraham-Fire-All became the chef for Couper's son, James Hamilton Couper, at Hopeton Plantation on the mainland.

After Cupidon died, Sans Foix graduated to top chef. His specialty was deboning a raw turkey and reassembling it to look intact. His technique was a closely guarded secret that Sans Foix kept by dismissing the rest of the kitchen staff during the procedure. As an extra precaution, he concealed his deboning in progress under a cloth.

The historian Bessie Lewis of Pine Harbor, in neighboring McIntosh County, gave a wonderful description of Sans Foix's domain:

> In the great kitchen he was in supreme command, with two or three lesser helpers to do his bidding. The pots and kettles suspended on the cranes and hooks in the big fireplace—there were no stoves—held savory stews and vegetables. In the tin "kitchens" placed in front of the fire whole quarters of meat would be roasting, to be basted at just the right moment. Broilers would be used over the red-hot hickory or myrtle coals, and bake ovens

with lids for coals on top held delicious cakes. The long-handled toasters and waffle and wafer irons stood beside the fireplace, ready for use in their turn. Often corn wafers baked for dinner were kept in rows laid on either side of the chimney to keep them hot and crisp, and a good child could run in and be given a hot buttered wafer to sustain him until the serving of the meal.

Only rarely were there fewer than two dozen people at the Coupers' table. After-dinner toasts were traditional, and Rebecca Couper's orange shrub was a toasting favorite. Her recipe called for steeping eighteen chips of sour Valencia oranges with three quarts of brandy for two weeks in a stoppered stone bottle. Two quarts of spring water were boiled gently with a pound and a half of the finest sugar. The mixture was clarified with an egg white, strained, and boiled until reduced by half. When the sweet syrup cooled, it was blended with the orange-flavored brandy.

A number of structures, some built of tabby, were located on Cannon's Point, including an icehouse, a workshop, storage buildings, houses for ginning and storing sea island cotton, an overseer's tabby home, and eight cabins for the enslaved. Although dirt floored, they had clay and stick chimneys and glazed windows. The cabins nearest the main house were for single families; the four farther south were duplexes.

Archaeologists who studied the site found a building they tentatively identified as a hospital for the enslaved near the main house. Such a hospital was usually sited near the owner's house so that a planter's wife could oversee its work and recuperating patients could work in the planter's vegetable garden.

None of the cabins survived the hurricane of 1804. Everyone on the plantation survived, but the storm destroyed a chimney on the Coupers' house and wrecked part of the verandah.

Two prehistoric shell rings at Cannon's Point were excavated during the 1970s by researchers from the University of Florida. Both are now surrounded by marsh. Extensive shell mounds on the point were raided to make tabby and, later, to pave roads and driveways on St. Simons and neighboring Sea Island.

The property, owned for almost a century by the Sea Island Company, was purchased by the St. Simons Land Trust in 2012 for $25 million. The trust created a preserve to protect the historic ruins and the island's last maritime forest. To see the tabby ruins, visitors must hike or bicycle about two and a half miles on an unpaved trail to the north end from the parking area. A tabby cabin once occupied by enslaved people is the first site along the trail.

John Couper, 1759–1850

At age sixteen, John Couper and his closest friend, James Hamilton, left their homes in Scotland and sailed for Savannah. They arrived in 1775 on the eve of the Revolutionary War. Couper was indentured to a mercantile company in Savannah whose owners, like many other Georgians, supported the British cause. When war broke out, Couper moved to Spanish Florida with his Loyalist employers, who fled to escape the wrath of Georgia Patriots called the Liberty Boys.

Couper clerked for his employers in St. Augustine, which prospered during the war as an international trading center. Couper returned to Georgia when his indenture ended in 1783. He and Hamilton opened successful stores in Savannah and Sunbury. In Liberty County, Couper married Rebecca Maxwell, who later inherited one-third of her Scottish father's considerable estate. Couper and Hamilton began investing in land, including Cannon's Point on St. Simons Island.

Couper planted sea island cotton at Cannon's Point, selecting the best seed to plant the following year and producing a high-quality crop, but his joy was nontraditional agriculture. He grew lemon and orange trees, Persian date palms, and exotic plants from around the world; many were sent to him by Hamilton, who often traveled internationally on business. He grew so many different varieties of grapes that one family member described Cannon's Point as "very grapey." It was not intended as a compliment. Thomas Spalding of Sapelo Island, who grew the first commercial sugarcane in Georgia, received his first stalks from Couper's experimental garden.

When Thomas Jefferson heard of Couper's agricultural successes, he arranged for him to purchase two hundred olive trees from France. Because Jefferson did not offer to pay for the trees or the shipping costs, Couper delayed ordering them for a decade. Once he did, his olive grove thrived, and Cannon's Point produced a fine-quality olive oil.

USS *Constitution*, the frigate nicknamed Old Ironsides during the War of 1812 after its battle with HMS *Guerriere*. The *Constitution*, one of the six original frigates of the U.S. Navy, was commissioned by the Naval Act of 1794.

In 1804, when Vice President Aaron Burr fled to adjacent Hampton Plantation after killing Alexander Hamilton in a duel, the hospitable Coupers sent him an assortment of French wine, sweetmeats, and pickles. Burr was visiting Cannon's Point on the day a major hurricane hit the island. The violence of the storm forced the Coupers and Burr to abandon the waterfront plantation house and take shelter in another building. Although the hurricane destroyed most of the plantation's cotton crop, worth $100,000 (roughly $2.2 million today), Burr said Couper just laughed off the loss.

Couper's sense of humor and dry wit endeared him to everyone. He often joked that he and Hamilton had migrated to America "for the good of our country." Couper was the youngest of three sons of a distinguished Scottish minister. One brother was a noted surgeon whose experiments with bleach aided the British textile industry. His other brother held the Chair of Practical Astronomy at the University of Glasgow. John Couper preferred to fish, entertain, read, and enjoy his wife and five children.

One of John and Rebecca Couper's sons, James Hamilton Couper, was named for John Couper's best friend and business partner. A Darien doctor, James Holmes, noted that the father was "full of fun and humor, and he delighted in a good joke." The son, Holmes said, was "all dignity and studied propriety, and seldom unbent to youthful ways." John Couper often referred to his staid son as "the old gentleman." James Hamilton Couper grew up to be a brilliant man and innovative planter in spite of—or perhaps because of—his serious nature.

John Couper was always civic minded. In 1794, he donated one of the giant live oak trees on Cannon's Point to the U.S. Navy to be used as the stern post for the frigate

USS *Constitution*, nicknamed Old Ironsides. Live oaks were prized by shipbuilders because large, curved parts could be carved intact from the limbs. Such parts were stronger than those that had to be pieced together. Couper was proud of the fact that the frigate's sternpost came from Cannon's Point. He had the stump encircled with an iron band engraved with the words "U.S. Frigate, *Constitution*, 1794." The stump remained at Cannon's Point for more than a century. It was displayed at the International Cotton Exhibition in Atlanta in 1895 and never returned.

Couper believed a lighthouse would improve commerce for the port in Brunswick. To support the project, he charged the government one dollar for four acres on the south end of St. Simons, where the island's first lighthouse was built in 1810.

Couper served as a judge for the Inferior Court of Glynn County. During his tenure, a major scandal broke out involving legislative corruption in West Georgia land grants. At the time, Georgia stretched from the Atlantic Ocean to the Mississippi River. In 1795, four land-speculation companies bribed Georgia legislators to pass a law that would allow them to buy millions of acres along the Yazoo River in today's Mississippi for less than two cents an acre—a total of $500,000. The corrupt sales came to be known as the Yazoo land frauds. Most Georgians were outraged when the frauds were exposed; the corrupt lawmakers were voted out of office and had to flee the state to escape angry mobs.

The following year, Couper was elected to the legislature, which staged a public burning of the law that had permitted the fraudulent sales. Since the companies had resold much of the land to innocent third parties, the financial tangle was not settled until the federal government paid off purchasers in 1814.

Before the War of 1812, Couper chaired the committee that drafted a resolution condemning the presence of British warships along the coast. Members sent the resolution to President James Madison, asking for three gunboats to be stationed near St. Simons, but their request was not granted. British ship captains offered freedom to the enslaved; about sixty of those held by Couper escaped, along with a number of other enslaved people from other coastal plantations.

The Coupers helped fund the first Christ Episcopal Church on St. Simons in 1820. When church wardens argued over the purchase of an organ, Couper sent an enslaved man named Johnny to play the bagpipes for the officials, along with a message saying that he hoped they would "try the pipes as a compromise." He was probably joking.

The loss of valuable crops over the years forced Couper into bankruptcy in 1828. His old friend James Hamilton, who had become one of the nation's first millionaires, bailed him out. Couper lived to be ninety-one. After spending more than fifty years at Cannon's Point, he spent his final years at Hopeton Plantation on the mainland with his son, James Hamilton Couper.

SITE 21

Hampton Plantation

1774

Hampton Point Drive

HISTORIC SIGNIFICANCE: Hampton Plantation was established by Major Pierce Butler, an original member of the U.S. Senate. Butler's grandson and heir arranged the nation's largest slave sale to pay debts. His wife, the actress Fanny Kemble, wrote her famous abolitionist journal after a visit to Butler's plantations on St. Simons Island and on the Altamaha delta.

Hampton Plantation, owned by Major Pierce Butler from 1774 until his death in 1822, and later by his grandson Pierce Mease (Maze) Butler, is located on the westernmost of two broad peninsulas that form the north end of St. Simons Island. The 1,700-acre plantation was dedicated to the production of sea island cotton. Now home to a subdivision called Hampton Point, the property is dotted with the tabby remains of plantation buildings, including a walled garden or entry complex to the main house, five tabby slave cabins, and the tabby building that housed the plantation's cattle-powered cotton gin. All of the old tabby is on private property, but most is visible from the public road.

In the winter of 1838–39, the celebrated English actress Fanny Kemble visited Hampton with her husband, Pierce Mease Butler. She described the major's house as an "imposing-looking old dwelling" built of wood and tabby on the Hampton River, approached by an avenue of live oaks.

As the third son of an Irish nobleman, Pierce Butler was unlikely to inherit a title, land, or other assets. His father bought him a commission in the British Army when he was twelve; at age fourteen, he was fighting against the French in Canada. During the American Revolution, Butler left the British Army and fought on the side of the Patriots. He settled in South Carolina and married Mary "Polly" Middleton, the daughter of a wealthy slave trader and planter. When his father-in-law died, Butler and his wife inherited valuable property.

Slavery was initially banned in the Georgia colony, but after it was legalized in 1750, wealthy planters from South Carolina and the West Indies migrated to Georgia, seeking land not worn out by years of planting.

Butler bought 1,700 acres on north St. Simons and named it Hampton Plantation. The land has a long human history. It was occupied thousands of years ago by Paleo-Indians who lived on the southeastern coast. They discarded tons of oyster shells that were used to make tabby during the colonial and plantation eras.

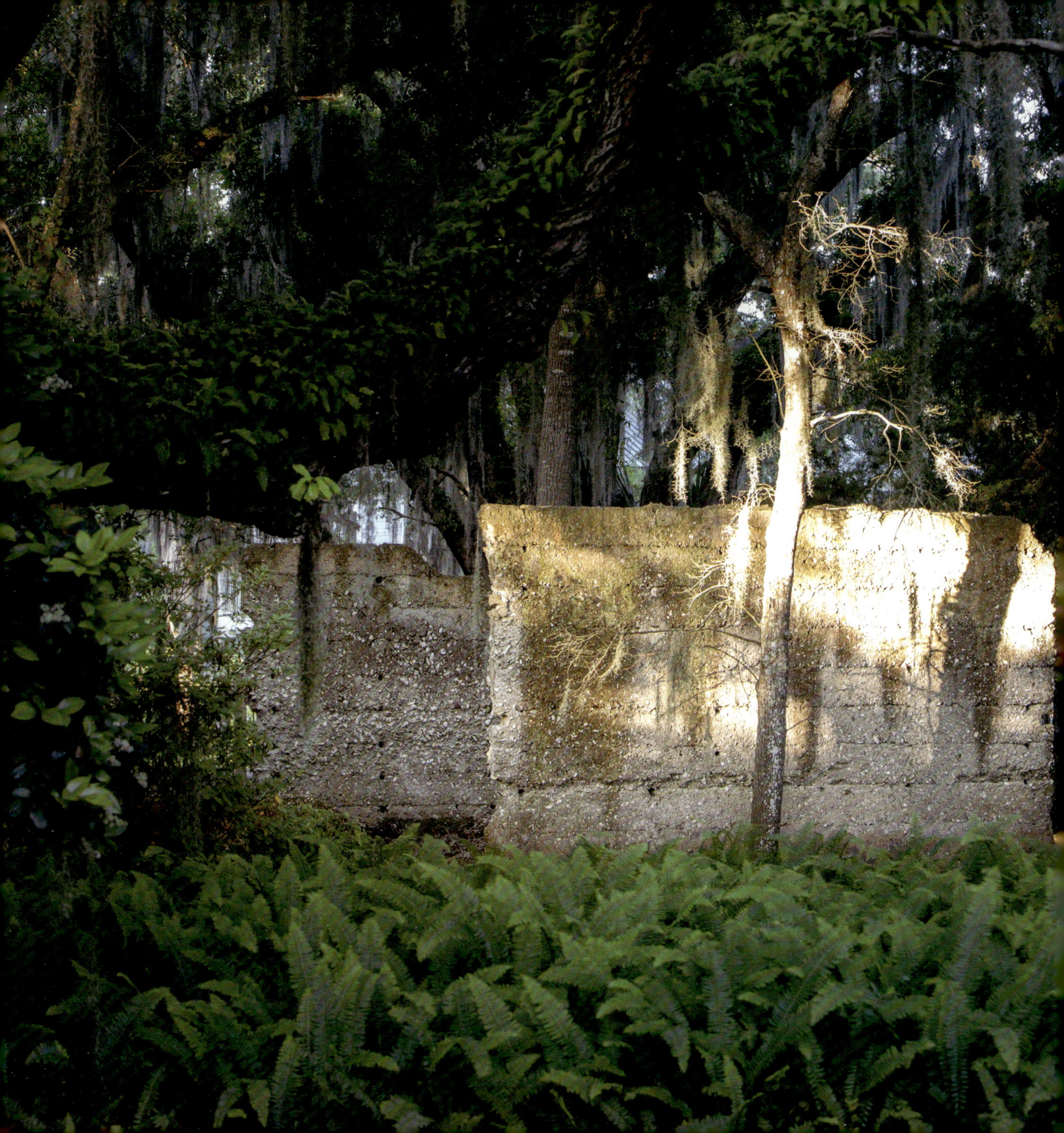

In 1736, when the British general James Edward Oglethorpe founded Fort Frederica on St. Simons, he stationed soldiers and their families on riverbanks around the island in hope of thwarting a possible attack from Spanish Florida. The settlement that became Butler's plantation was called Newhampton, later shortened to Hampton.

At its zenith, from the late 1700s to the 1830s, Hampton was one of the most productive agricultural operations on the southeastern coast. Major Butler, who owned fine houses in Philadelphia and Charleston, and was involved in national politics, depended on managers to run his Georgia properties.

Butler also owned Butler's Island, 700–1,000 acres of diked land on the Altamaha delta between McIntosh and Glynn Counties. It was the largest tidewater rice plantation on the Georgia coast. Building the dikes was brutal work. About five hundred enslaved men and women dug tons of mucky delta soil, wading through ankle-deep water and mud for much of the day, battling mosquitoes, snakes, alligators, and other dangers.

At times, as many as a thousand slaves worked Butler's plantations, making him one of the largest slaveholders in the South. Butler expected his managers to run his Georgia plantations with military efficiency and discipline. His slaves were forbidden to socialize with others on nearby plantations, because he considered their owners too lenient and thought their slaves might be a bad influence. Nor could Butler's slaves attend special church services held for them at Christ Episcopal Church, whose congregation dates to Oglethorpe's time. Some slaves may have spent their entire lives on Butler's property.

Everything needed at Hampton was produced on site by enslaved artisans and laborers. Cobblers made shoes from leather tanned from cowhides after the animals raised on the plantation were slaughtered for beef. Blacksmiths crafted cooking pots and other kitchenware as well as farm implements. Dressmakers stitched simple clothing for the slaves and linens for residents of the main house. Skilled carpenters crafted fine furniture for their owner and built fences and other wooden structures. Even elderly slaves were expected to work. One old woman was given the task of leading a goose by a string tied around its neck to a pasture where it grazed for an hour every day.

The enslaved woke before dawn to the foghorn bellow of a large whelk shell blown by the head driver. Like almost all sea island slaves, Butler's worked on the task system. Each one was assigned a daily task according to his or her ability. When the work was done, the slaves could spend the rest of the day fishing, hunting, making nets, tending their own small gardens, raising pigs, ducks, and chickens, and telling stories to their children. Researchers say the task system helped preserve the Gullah Geechee culture. Slaves elsewhere in Georgia and other inland areas usually worked in gangs that toiled from daylight to dusk, leaving them little time to themselves.

The white managers who stayed longest at Hampton were Roswell King Sr. and Jr. of Connecticut, employed by Butler from 1802 until 1820, when Roswell King Sr. and his son Barrington moved inland and founded the town of Roswell near Atlanta. Roswell Jr. succeeded his father as overseer of Butler's plantations for a time. During their tenure, the Kings made Hampton and Butler's Island two of the most profitable plantations on the Georgia coast, but did so at great human cost. Slaves were flogged for minor infractions. Those caught attempting to escape were fitted with heavy iron ankle cuffs that weighed them down and rubbed their skin raw.

After Vice President Aaron Burr killed Alexander Hamilton in a duel in 1804, he was indicted for murder in New York and New Jersey. He took refuge at remote Hampton for five weeks until the furor in the North died down. As usual, Major Butler was not in residence, but he and Burr had served in the U.S. Senate together and were political allies, even if not friends. During his time at Hampton, Burr survived the major hurricane of 1804, which devastated the Georgia coast. He described the storm later in letters to his daughter, Theodosia.

During the hurricane, Hampton's head slave driver, Morris, saved the lives of more than one hundred slaves on Little St. Simons Island, across the Hampton River from St. Simons. The slaves wanted to flee in their boats to the larger island, but Morris used his whip to force them into the hurricane house, where they all survived. Many Georgia slaves drowned during the storm, including a number on low-lying Butler Island.

Butler would have suffered a huge financial loss except for Morris's action. The major presented his head driver with an engraved silver cup and offered Morris his freedom. Since the offer of freedom did not extend to Morris's wife and children, he opted to remain a slave.

Colonel Robert Gould Shaw, the young white commander of the Fifty-Fourth Massachusetts, the first Black regiment in the Union army, was stationed with his troops at Hampton in 1863 after the Georgia coast was occupied during the Civil War. In letters to his mother, Shaw complained that he and his troops were ordered to burn the nearby town of Darien. A few months later, Shaw and his men participated in the Union attack on Fort Wagner, on Morris Island, South Carolina. Shaw and about half of his regiment died in the assault and were buried together in a mass grave. Their story is told in the 1989 film *Glory*.

Fanny Kemble Butler, 1809–1893

The famed British actress Fanny Kemble married Major Butler's grandson, Pierce Mease Butler, who inherited the island plantations with his brother, John. Kemble visited St. Simons for a few months during the winter and spring of 1838–39 with her husband and their two young daughters.

Frances Anne "Fanny" Kemble, born into a family of distinguished actors, wanted to be a writer. During her lifetime, she published journals, plays, essays, and poems that won critical acclaim. Desperate family finances prompted her to pursue an acting career in her late teens, and she was a natural from the moment she stepped on stage. As Shakespeare's Juliet, she packed theatres in Europe and the United States. Later in life, overweight and matronly, she continued to captivate audiences with her dramatic readings. The American-born writer and intellectual Henry James considered her one of the most fascinating women he had ever met.

When Mease Butler saw the young Kemble perform on tour in America, he courted her until she married him. The union was stormy at best. Kemble, passionate, outspoken, and temperamental, was a woman ahead of her time. She thought men and women should be equal partners in marriage, not a view popular with her husband or most other men of the era.

In addition, Mease Butler had a well-deserved reputation as a playboy and gambler. He continued those activities after their marriage and the birth of their daughters, Frances "Fan" and Sarah "Sally." Kemble left her husband on several occasions but returned for the sake of the girls. Her journal also suggests she loved him, at least some of the time.

The most heated arguments between Kemble and Mease Butler came over the issue of slavery. Two years after they married, he needed to hire a new manager for the Georgia plantations. Kemble was determined to go south with him to see for herself the system that financed their lavish lifestyle. Mease Butler, who often boasted of how well his slaves were treated and how much they loved him, thought a firsthand tour might soften or even change his wife's abolitionist sentiments. It proved to be a serious miscalculation.

The couple arrived in Georgia with their daughters in December 1838, after the end of the fever season. Kemble was captivated by the lush beauty of St. Simons, describing it as a fairyland. She was appalled, however, by the realities of slavery. She wrote about her experiences in her daily journal, detailing the four months she spent on the Butler Island rice plantation and at Hampton Plantation on St. Simons.

She listened to slaves' complaints, observed their grim lives—she described a group of slave cabins as "miserable hovels"—and tried to help them. She may have done

Pierce Mease Butler family

more harm than good; slaves were punished for talking to her, and Mease Butler soon forbade her to bring their complaints to him.

Possibly because she knew about or suspected her husband's philandering, or perhaps simply because she related more easily to women, Kemble focused her attention on the female slaves. In one entry, the twenty-three-year-old actress asked a married slave woman why she submitted to the white overseer. The woman said she had no choice: "We do anything to get our poor flesh some rest from de whip." The sexual exploitation of slave women by white men was the grim reality of slavery that shocked Kemble most.

Enslaved women faced horrifying consequences whether or not they refused their owners. Julia Maxwell King, the wife of Roswell King Jr., had two slave women on St. Simons, Scylla and Judy, "strung up and lashed" for bearing children fathered by her husband. She personally supervised the initial whipping and then banished the women to the desolate stretch of impounded marsh on Little St. Simons called Five Pound Tree, where slaves were often sent as punishment. Julia King ordered the slave driver to flog the women daily for a week.

Mease Butler was responsible for the largest single sale of human beings ever conducted in the United States. The sale occurred in 1859, well after Kemble had divorced her husband and moved back to England. He had more than 436 slaves auctioned in Savannah to raise money to pay his debts, many incurred from gambling. Although Butler specified that the slaves were to be sold in family groups, the two-day auction is still referred to as the Weeping Time by Gullah Geechees on the Georgia coast. Many slaves were wrenched away from grandparents, aunts, uncles, grown siblings, cousins, sweethearts, and lifelong friends, as well as the only home many had ever known. Butler made

Hand-colored lithograph of Fanny Kemble, after a painting by Sir Thomas Lawrence, c. 1830s

more than $300,000 from the sale (roughly $9.5 million today), enough to satisfy his creditors and treat himself to a European trip.

One of the most famous antebellum-era books of all time, Fanny Kemble's *Journal of a Residence on a Georgia Plantation, 1838–1839*, describes the months she spent on Butler's Island on the Altamaha delta and at Hampton on St. Simons. Published during the Civil War, it became an overnight best seller in England and the northern United States, but was reviled in the South well into the twentieth century.

Resentment of Kemble was long-lived, especially on St. Simons, where much of the abuse she reported had occurred. Although the journal has long been credited—or blamed—with dissuading Great Britain from supporting the Confederate war effort, England had already become disenchanted with the southern cause by the time Kemble published it in 1863.

Kemble's journal is still in print.

CHAPTER 7 *Brunswick*

IN 1736, the town and fort of Frederica were built on St. Simons Island. Two years later, a Frederica colonist named Mark Carr, a captain in the colony's Marine Boat Company, established a 1,000-acre plantation in what became the mainland town of Brunswick, opposite St. Simons.

In 1771, Carr's plantation, Plug Point, was purchased by the Royal Province of Georgia to establish the town of Brunswick. Built on a peninsula flanked by the East, Turtle, and Brunswick Rivers, the town echoed Oglethorpe's design for Savannah. It was laid out in a grid with neighborhoods and commercial areas centered on green spaces. In 1789, when President George Washington named Brunswick one of the five original ports of entry for the former British colonies, the designation helped the town flourish. Less than a decade later, Brunswick was named the county seat of Glynn County.

Brunswick was named for the Duchy of Brunswick-Lünenburg, a region in the Electorate of Hanover, the ancestral German home of the family of George III, the monarch when the town was founded. Many of Brunswick's streets and public squares bear English names: Gloucester and Newcastle, both named for English dukes; Egmont Street, named for the Earl of Egmont; and Hanover Square, named for the Electorate of Hanover.

Glynn Academy, one of the nation's oldest public high schools, opened in Brunswick in 1819. In the 1820s, the town boasted a jail, a courthouse, and about thirty houses and stores. Three local entrepreneurs—Urbanus Dart, William R. Davis, and Thomas Butler King—formed a company to build a canal from Brunswick to the Altamaha River to connect the port with shipments of cotton from inland plantations. After struggling through a recession in the 1830s, Brunswick found its economic footing with the opening of the Brunswick-Altamaha Canal and a railroad. The city was incorporated in 1856. Before the Civil War, Brunswick grew to almost five hundred residents, large enough to support a newspaper and a bank.

During the war, Confederates burned Brunswick's wharves and the Oglethorpe House hotel to keep them out of Union hands. Residents evacuated inland, the canal and railroad shut down, and the city was abandoned.

Brunswick prospered after the war when one of the largest sawmills in the United States opened four miles away on St. Simons. Brunswick's port, formed by the confluence of the three rivers bordering the peninsula, continued to expand. Railroads connected the port to other Georgia cities and the rest of the country.

The well-known Georgia-born poet Sidney Lanier, who suffered from tuberculosis, came to live with an uncle in Brunswick, hoping the coastal climate would help cure his disease. He wrote his famous poem "The Marshes of Glynn" while sitting in the shade of a tree overlooking the marsh. A live oak in the area has been designated the Lanier Oak. The bridge over the Brunswick River on U.S. 17, the highest bridge in Georgia, bears Lanier's name, as do streets, subdivisions, and other area locales.

The elegant Oglethorpe Hotel, which replaced the Oglethorpe House, opened in 1888. It served as a stopover for millionaire members of the Jekyll Island Club, who purchased the Glynn County sea island and wintered there in luxury from the late 1800s until World War II. Because of the hotel's patronage by members of the Jekyll Island Club, a national magazine predicted that Brunswick was destined to become the nation's most exclusive wintertime resort. Many locals mourned when the beautiful old brick structure was razed in 1958 in the name of urban renewal and replaced by a chain motel and a budget department store.

A number of residents died during a yellow fever epidemic in 1893. More were killed in hurricanes in the late 1800s that flooded much of the Brunswick peninsula. Residents saved their horses and other livestock by leading the animals to higher ground in Halifax Square, one of the city's green spaces, until the floodwaters receded. As the city recovered from the epidemic and the storms, its port expanded and fishermen developed an oyster industry.

During World War II, Brunswick's population tripled when workers from all over the South poured into the city to build Liberty ships, which transported food, fuel, and other supplies to Allied troops in Europe. At the start of the war, German submarines torpedoed cargo ships off St. Simons, Jekyll, and Cumberland Islands, which led to the establishment of the Glynco Naval Air Station, the world's largest blimp base. Hangars built to store the huge aircraft were billed as the largest wooden buildings in the world. The blimps escorted almost 100,000 Liberty ships and other cargo vessels to protect them from German submarines. While the blimps were on guard, not a single ship was lost to the enemy.

The war brought Brunswick and the rest of the nation out of the Great Depression. New industries in town employed thousands of people to manufacture paper and chemicals, and to catch and process seafood. Brunswick began calling itself the Shrimp Capital of the World. The port expanded from the docks downtown to Colonel's Island, which handles containerized cargo and automobiles. Huge ships enter and leave the port through St. Simons Sound between Jekyll and St. Simons Islands. Regular dredging to maintain the ship channel has accelerated erosion on the two islands' beaches.

Many houses and commercial buildings in Brunswick's Old Town have been restored to their former glory and are now included in the National Register District. Mary Ross Park, on the Brunswick River, offers concerts, farmer's markets, and other entertainments. The park is named for a Brunswick historian whose pioneering research during the early twentieth century revealed much of Georgia's Spanish history.

The city hosts the annual Brunswick Stewbilee, a contest to choose the restaurant that makes the best Brunswick stew, traditionally a concoction of smoked wild game, corn, butterbeans, and tomatoes, simmered for hours over an open fire. Brunswick claims that the stew originated in Glynn County, but Brunswick County, Virginia, disputes the claim. The two locales often engage in well-publicized but good-natured arguments over which made the first Brunswick stew.

A number of commercial buildings downtown were built of revival tabby concrete made with portland cement. In the early twentieth century, many were owned by Jewish merchants who operated businesses on the ground floor and lived in luxurious apartments upstairs, some of which still contain Victorian features such as elaborately carved woodwork.

SITE 22   *Short Take*

St. Athanasius Protestant Episcopal Church

c. 1885

1321 Albany Street

National Register of Historic Places

Two important historic figures are associated with the picturesque tabby revival church in New Town, Brunswick.

Anson Green Phelps Dodge was a wealthy northerner who rebuilt historic Christ Episcopal Church on St. Simons Island after the Civil War, along with three Episcopal churches for Black island residents. Dodge is the protagonist of the novel *The Beloved Invader*, part of a best-selling trilogy by the late Eugenia Price.

Dodge helped obtain funds for St. Athanasius Church after learning that St. Marks Episcopal, a nearby church for white people, was holding evening services for Black congregants in its Sunday-school room. Dodge funded a pastor for St. Athanasius and preached there sometimes himself.

Anna Alexander, the first Black female Episcopal deacon in the United States, was born on St. Simons Island to freed slaves shortly after the Civil War. She was inspired to build an Episcopal church and school for African Americans after making frequent visits to St. Athanasius during the early 1900s. The results of her efforts, the Good Shepherd Church and School, are in Pennick, a tiny post–Civil War community about ten miles north of Brunswick. At the time, there were no school buses to take Black children back and forth from Pennick to the segregated public schools in Brunswick.

The St. Athanasius School opened around 1900 in a new, two-story tabby building adjacent to the church. The school building was later razed. The stained-glass windows at St. Athanasius honoring heroes of the civil rights movement were added later.

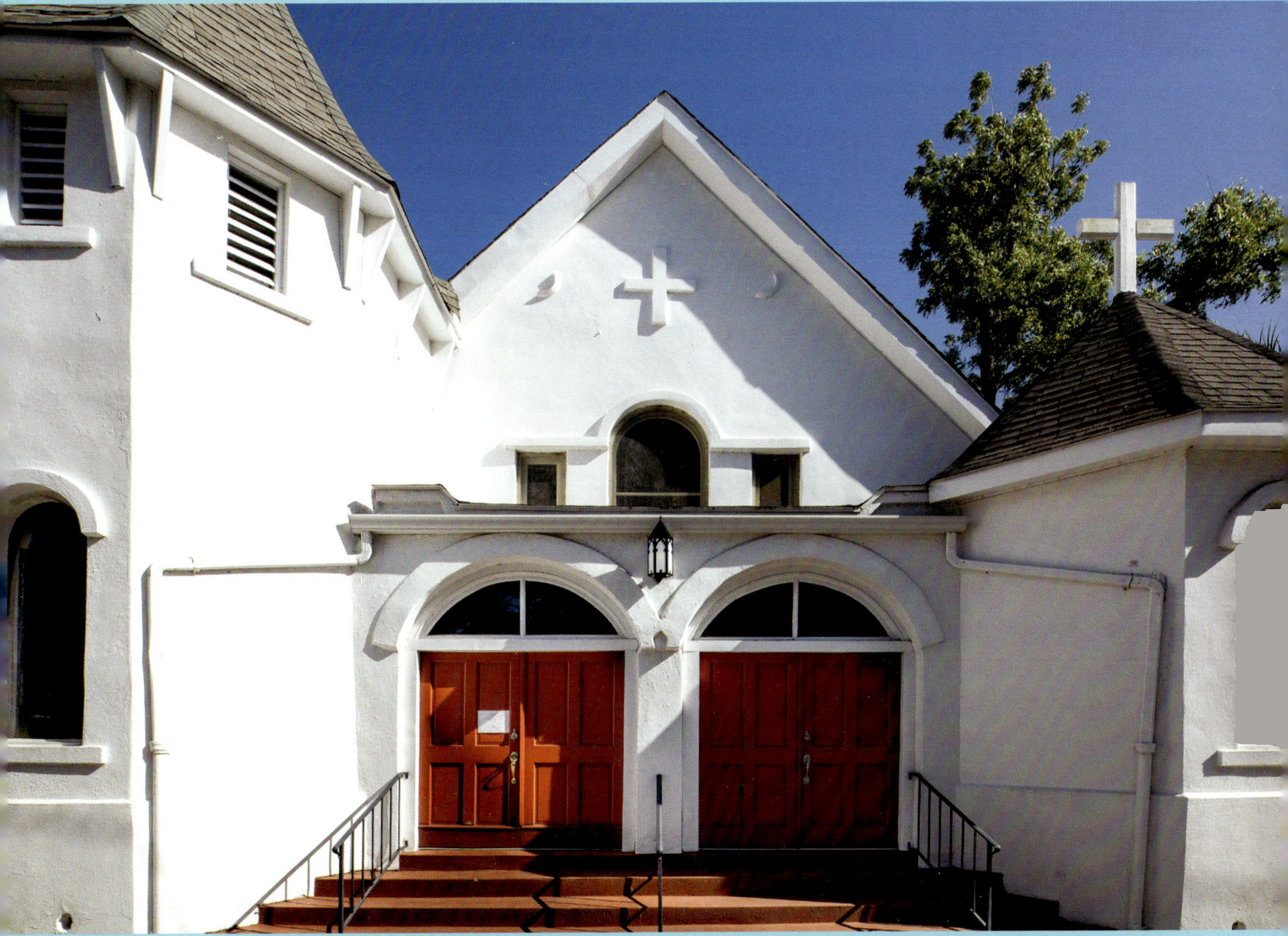

Hopeton Plantation Sugar Mill

1830

Altama State Wildlife Management Area
6853 Georgia Highway 99

HISTORIC SIGNIFICANCE: Hopeton Plantation was a prosperous antebellum operation whose innovative owner, James Hamilton Couper, used tabby extensively to build a variety of structures, including his elegant three-story house. He also built Georgia's largest sugar mill; its remains are among the still-standing tabby on the property.

The plantation's original name was Hopeton-on-the-Altamaha. It was a 3,986-acre plantation on the south bank of the giant Altamaha River in northern Glynn County. The name was later shortened to Hopeton and, in 1914, renamed Altama Plantation by its new owner. It is located just west of I-95. The State of Georgia acquired the property in 2015 and designated it a wildlife management area.

The original plantation was named for William Hopeton, who was granted two thousand acres of riverfront land in 1763 by George III. It was purchased in 1805 by James Hamilton and John Couper, Scottish immigrants and good friends who co-owned several plantations and property elsewhere in Georgia and in other states. The plantation was later acquired by Couper's son and Hamilton's namesake, James Hamilton Couper.

For several years, sugar was Hopeton's main crop. The tabby mill, completed in 1830, was 240 feet long, almost 40 feet wide, and 26 feet high. Couper used tabby to build his mill after corresponding with sugar producers in Louisiana, the West Indies, and Europe, and studying the designs of their mills. The equipment used to grind the cane and extract the sweet juice was powered by a steam engine that was also used for threshing and pounding rice.

The Hopeton sugar mill was the only one on the Atlantic coast with three furnaces and two sets of kettles with six kettles in each set. The kettles held cane juice at various stages of concentration as it was being cooked down in the boiling house before being moved to the cooling house and then to the curing house, where it crystallized into sugar.

For a variety of reasons, including tariffs, sugar was not a successful crop for Georgia planters. Hopeton's fields did not meet Couper's expectations for the quantity of cane he hoped to produce. Droughts, too much rain, early frosts, and tropical storms often damaged the crops.

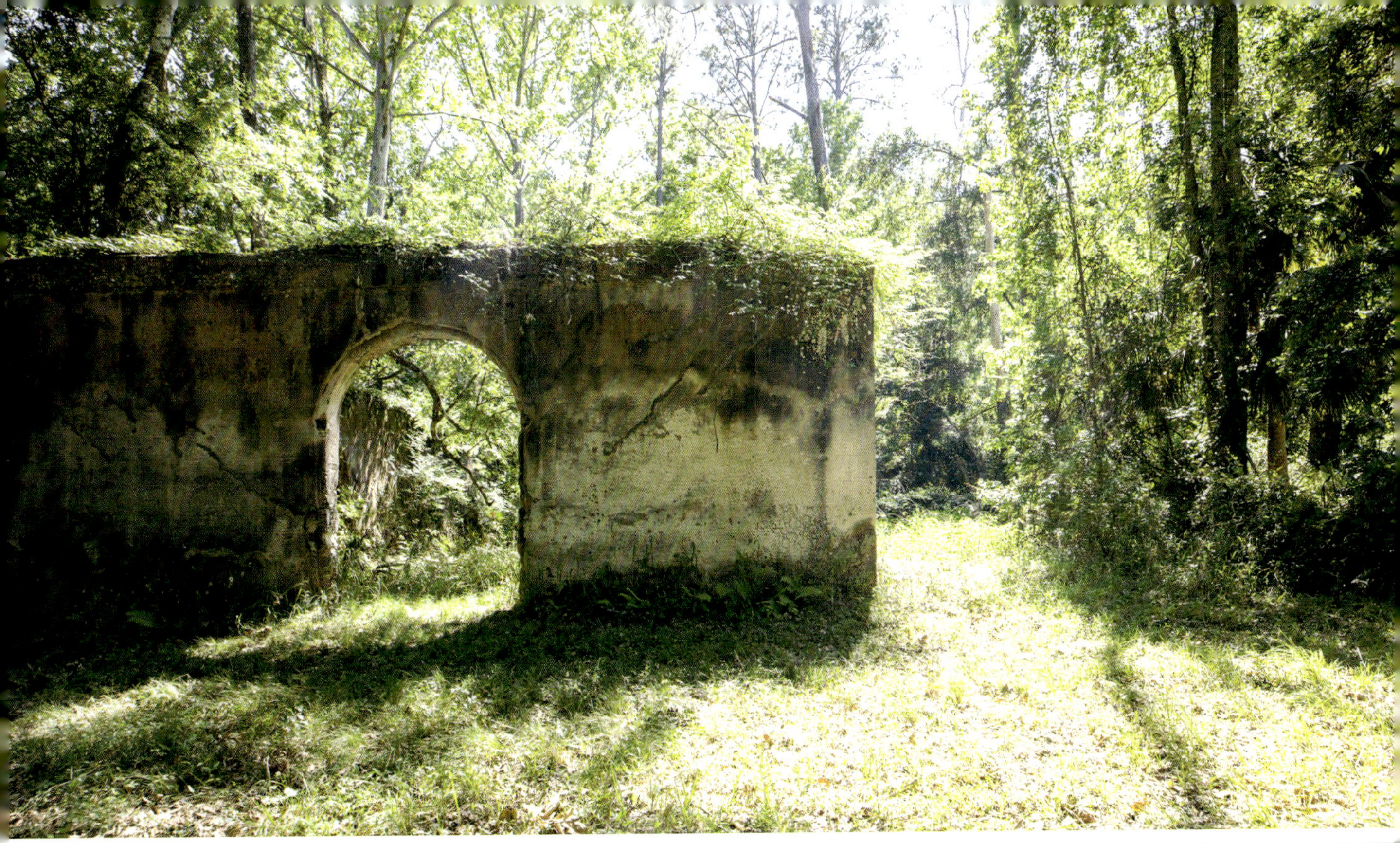
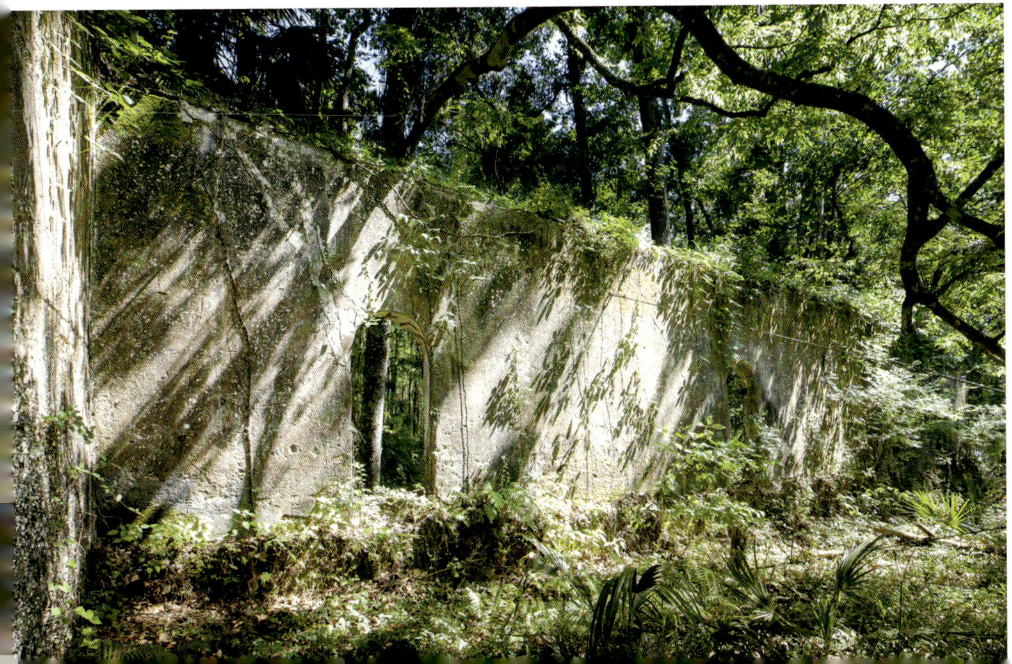
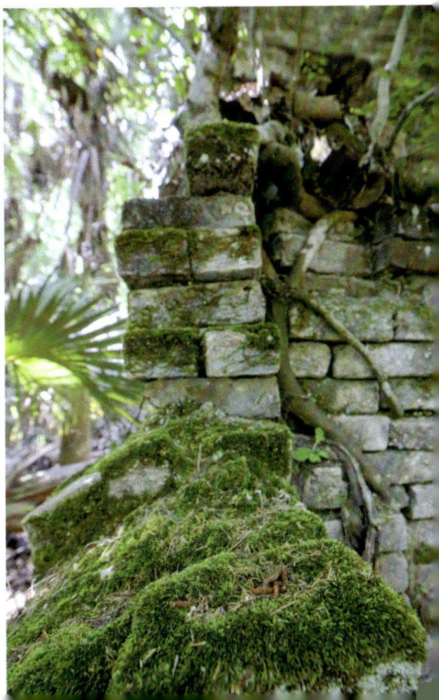

Just after Couper built his mill, sugar producers in Louisiana developed a method of boiling cane in vacuum containers, which reduced the amount of heat required to cook the sugar. The vacuum method also produced a better-quality product. With further improvements, Louisiana soon cornered the nation's sugar market. After 1839, sugar was grown at Hopeton only to provide molasses for the slaves and the family table.

Couper designed and built the elegant three-story Italian-style tabby house on the property, which was surrounded by formal gardens that suited their owner's staid personality. The white stucco exterior was punctuated by green shutters. The twenty-four-room mansion had curved windows on the top floor. Dignitaries from the United States and abroad were frequent guests. The renowned editor of the *Southern Agriculturist* described Hopeton as "the best plantation we have ever visited."

Couper built other tabby structures at Hopeton: his two-story retirement home, slave cabins, and a slave hospital.

Steam heated and spacious, the hospital also served as a nursery for children under twelve. A head nurse and her attendants supervised the children and the hospital's operation. Doctors attended to slaves who needed specialized medical care.

Hopeton's slave cabins were well built, originally of wood but later of tabby, which needed little maintenance and was more comfortable for the occupants; tabby cabins were cooler in summer, warmer in winter. The cabins stood in two rows, shaded by live oaks. Unlike the double-pen cabins that James Hamilton Couper designed for Hamilton Plantation on St. Simons, each of his Hopeton cabins was designed for one family. Each cabin had a central living space with a fireplace, two sleeping rooms, and a loft for the children.

Hopeton was a model of crop diversification and experimentation. Couper planted sea island cotton, sugarcane, and rice as money crops, and corn, peas, and other produce to feed people on the plantation. He focused on one cash crop at a time, depending on the market and the need to rotate crops.

Couper traveled to Holland in 1825 to observe water-control structures in the low-lying country, which was in permanent battle against the tides. Hopeton's system included a complex of canals, ditches, floodgates, and dikes patterned after those used by the Dutch. Couper's father, John, who owned Cannon's Point Plantation on nearby St. Simons Island, commented that his son's rice operation was "perhaps the only thing of its kind in America." The diked fields were a success, but after they were abandoned, they created an ideal mosquito-breeding habitat. The dikes have been opened in recent years to allow water to flush the fields.

Two other innovations at Hopeton were a canal, three miles long, fifteen feet wide, and four and a half feet deep, and a portable railroad. Fed by the Altamaha River, the canal was used to irrigate Hopeton's fields and deliver harvests on flatboats to plantation mills and the cotton gin. Flatboats also carried supplies to the plantation house. The canal, which looped back to the river, had massive floodgates at either end to control water levels. At the canal entrance, four pairs of floodgates were fixed in a structure seventy-five feet long. Flatboats exited the other end of the canal to carry the plantation's products across the four-mile-wide Altamaha delta to Darien, where the goods were shipped to market. The flatboats brought supplies back to Hopeton.

The railroad, which ran only within the plantation's boundaries, had wooden rails that could be reconfigured. One of the earliest private railroads of its kind, it was used to pick up sugarcane and rice from the fields and transport the crops to the canal flatboats that ferried them to the mills. The railroad moved sugar from the mill's cooling room to the curing room, where molasses was drained off.

At one time, sea island cotton was Hopeton's mainstay, but when prices plummeted during the 1830s, cotton was phased out.

After Georgia's ban on slavery was lifted in 1750, a number of South Carolina planters immigrated to coastal Georgia in search of new rice-growing acreage, bringing thousands of slaves with them. After the bottom fell out of cotton prices, rice became Georgia's most lucrative coastal crop. During the last quarter of the eighteenth century, rice exports constituted the basis of Georgia's prerevolutionary plantation economy.

Over the years, Hopeton's fields produced more rice than any other plantation in the South except for a larger spread owned by the governor of South Carolina.

Tidewater rice, which required an elaborate water-control system, was grown in diked fields. Building the dikes was brutal work for the slaves. At Hopeton, about five hundred men and women dug tons of mucky delta soil, wading through ankle-deep water and mud for much of the day. They piled the muck into dikes and then built wooden tide gates so that the fields could be flooded and drained according to the needs of the crop. Enslaved workers on rice plantations died regularly of injuries, overwork, snakebites, alligator attacks, and mosquito-borne diseases such as malaria and yellow fever. The average life span of an enslaved person compelled to work in the rice fields was just sixteen years after he or she began that brutal work.

Coastal planters believed that slaves from the western coast of Africa were immune to malaria. And while it is true that some had inherited a gene that gave them partial immunity, the rest were just as vulnerable as their white owners, who fled the mosquito-ridden lowlands in warm months.

James Hamilton Couper, 1794–1866

By all accounts, James Hamilton Couper was a remarkable man. He designed Christ Church on Johnson Square in Savannah. He led the surveying party that mapped the border between Georgia and Florida. Couper took the type specimen of the Eastern indigo snake from south of the Altamaha River in Wayne County, Georgia, to the herpetologist John Edwards Holbrook, who in 1842 was the first to describe it. The snake is now endangered and federally protected. The snake's scientific name, *Drymarchon corais couperi*, honors Couper.

At age twenty-two, Couper assumed management of Hopeton-on-the-Altamaha. The plantation's name was shortened to "Hopeton" during Couper's tenure and later changed to Altama Plantation when it was purchased by William DuPont in 1914. DuPont, a wealthy businessman and banker, trained Thoroughbred racehorses on the property and spent winters there. The house he built was modeled after James Hamilton Couper's tabby plantation house.

The plantation's heyday was during Couper's tenure. Sent to boarding school in Connecticut at age eight with

The Eastern indigo snake, *Drymarchon corais couperi* (named in honor of James Hamilton Couper), is the longest native snake species in North America.

a personal slave, Couper later attended St. Marys College in Maryland and graduated with honors from Yale. He was well versed in agriculture, archaeology, architecture, conchology, geology, herpetology, history, languages, ornithology, surveying, and paleontology. His library at Hopeton contained more than five thousand books, some rare and valuable.

Couper toured Europe in 1825, visiting Scotland, his father's birth country, as well as England, France, Italy, and the Netherlands. He learned crop rotation from European farmers and dike construction in Holland. When he returned from Europe, his father, John Couper of St. Simons Island, was in serious financial straits. After crop failures caused by hurricanes and insects, John Couper had borrowed money at high interest rates in order to replant. His income was further reduced by the War of 1812 and the Embargo Act, which prevented shipments of Couper's cotton to lucrative markets in Liverpool.

During the war, British troops helped sixty of John Couper's slaves escape, a loss to the planter estimated at $15,000 (roughly $250,000 today). His chief creditor was his friend and longtime business partner James Hamilton. John Couper turned over his share of their co-owned properties to Hamilton in order to settle his debts. Hamilton, in turn, sold half of Hopeton and half of the plantation's slave force to James Hamilton Couper. After Hamilton's death in 1829, James Couper bought the rest of Hopeton from his heirs. James Couper spent most of his time at Hopeton, one of four large plantations he co-owned or managed on the mainland and on St. Simons.

Couper was thirty-three in 1827 when he married the sixteen-year-old Caroline Wylly of the Village plantation on St. Simons, which adjoined his father's property at Cannon's Point. Mary Houston, a teenager who attended the wedding, said she thought she detected a "resignation of expression" on the bride's face. Houston commented that James Couper was invariably courteous but was always stiff, formal, and probably not much fun.

James and Caroline Couper entertained visitors from all over the world at Hopeton. Their house was expensively furnished but comfortable, and Caroline was described as the perfect hostess. Many visitors came to see a model plantation in operation. Some who came from countries where slavery was banned were curious to see how Couper treated his slaves.

Couper, who controlled the lives of about fifteen hundred Africans on the four plantations, was known as a strict master. One of his slaves, Okra, built an African-style hut with mud walls and a roof of palm fronds at Hopeton. Couper made him tear it down, saying he did not want an African structure on his land. Slaves traditionally used drums, often to accompany nighttime burial processions. Like other slave owners, Couper banned the drums. Planters feared their slaves could use them to transmit secret messages or plot uprisings. On the other hand, he approved the use of the lash "only sparingly." Fanny Kemble, the British actress who married a St. Simons planter, reported that James Couper withheld meat from his slaves because he said it made them savage.

Before the Civil War, James Couper lobbied without success to keep Georgia from seceding from the Union. Six of his sons joined the Confederate army when war broke out. Two died of camp illnesses; one was seriously wounded and became a recluse after the war. Long imprisonment by the Union was described as "damaging" to a fourth son.

Couper's debts mounted during the war. Saddened by the loss of his sons and depressed by his financial circumstances, Couper died in 1866.

CHAPTER 8   *Darien*

THE SMALL TOWN OF DARIEN perches on a high bluff on the north side of the Darien River, the northernmost branch of the giant Altamaha. As the river approaches the incoming tides of the Atlantic, it splits into branches that braid and meander across a grassy four-mile-wide delta before emptying into the ocean.

When Great Britain and Spain were fighting for territory in North America, South Carolina established Fort King George in 1721 on the Darien River bluff to protect British settlements from the Spanish coming up from Florida. The small fort, then the southernmost British outpost in North America, was staffed by South Carolina rangers. It predated the founding of the Georgia colony in 1733 by General James Edward Oglethorpe.

After establishing Savannah about fifty miles north of Fort King George, Oglethorpe recruited Highlanders from the west coast of Scotland to settle Darien, which the Highlanders first called New Inverness. They later changed the name in memory of a failed Scots colony on the Isthmus of Panama, historically known as the Isthmus of Darien. When Oglethorpe visited the following month, the industrious Highlanders had laid out the town, installed a battery with four cannons, and built a guardhouse, a storehouse, and several huts. Fort King George was disbanded that same year.

In 1736, the Highlanders founded the First Presbyterian Church. For more than a century, it remained the only church and the only recognized faith in town. Although churches of many denominations were established later, Darien is often considered the cradle of Presbyterianism in Georgia. Two previous churches burned; the present church, at 403 Jackson Street, was built in 1899 of revival tabby made with portland cement. An educational building and fellowship hall have been added since then. The old church is open to the public.

Oglethorpe and the other Georgia trustees initially banned slavery in the colony, along with rum, lawyers, and Frenchmen, but Georgia colonists, envious of the riches that slave labor was producing for their counterparts in Carolina, lobbied for slavery to be legalized. Prominent Darien Highlanders signed a petition opposing it in 1739, but slavery was legalized a dozen years later.

Highlanders from Darien fought the Spanish in Oglethorpe's attack on St. Augustine, Florida, in 1740. A number of troops were killed or captured in the Battle of Fort Mose, the outpost of the Castillo de San Marcos established by former African slaves in 1738.

General Lachlan McIntosh, who gave the county its name, commanded the Georgia forces during the American Revolution.

The Bank of Darien, chartered in 1819, became one of Georgia's most powerful banks because of the value of the upland and sea island cotton, rice, and naval stores exported from the town. The products were stored in two-story tabby warehouses that lined the lower bluff. Darien was incorporated and designated the county seat in 1820. The town's prosperity lasted until the Civil War. In 1863, Union troops torched Darien, burning the town almost to the ground. The only buildings to survive were the tabby parts of the warehouses on the lower bluff and the tabby Adam-Strain Building on the upper bluff on Broad Street.

After the war, Tunis Campbell, an agent of the Freedmen's Bureau and a McIntosh County property owner, became the most influential Black politician in Georgia. Born in New Jersey in 1812 to free Black parents, he trained as a missionary and later established schools and preached against slavery.

During his work as a hotel steward in New York City and Boston, he wrote the *Hotel Keepers, Head Waiters, and Housekeepers' Guide* (1848) to instruct others in running a first-class hotel. The book is mainly noteworthy as a guide to interracial social skills. Campbell urged workers to be well educated, prompt, clean, and competitive, and counseled managers to recognize the dignity of their employees and pay them well. White employers in the North described Campbell as a man disposed "to elevate the condition and character of persons of his color."

Before the Civil War, Campbell often appeared on the lecture stage alongside Frederick Douglass, the famed writer-abolitionist. During the war, Campbell traveled south to Port Royal, South Carolina, to work with liberated slaves called contrabands, who were housed in temporary camps protected by Union troops. After the war, he supervised coastal land that had been temporarily granted to former slaves by General William Sherman. When the claims were rescinded, Campbell bought 1,250 acres in McIntosh County and formed a collective of Black landowners to subdivide the property and profit from its sales.

As an official of the Georgia Republican Party, Campbell worked to register voters. He was elected a justice of the peace, a delegate to the state constitutional convention, and a state senator. Campbell organized McIntosh County Blacks to protect themselves from abuse from their former owners and other whites. His actions made him a controversial and despised figure in the coastal county and beyond. His home was burned, he was poisoned, and his family lived in fear.

After a change from the liberal Republican state government to one that lobbied against Black civil rights, Campbell was convicted of malfeasance in office, jailed in Savannah, and leased as a convict to a labor camp for a year. After he was freed, he returned to the North and wrote a book about his sufferings in Georgia. Campbell died in Boston in 1891.

After the war, the timber industry salvaged Darien's economy. Huge rafts of longleaf pine cut from forests inland were floated downriver to sawmills on the bluff. Ships from all over the world sailed up the Darien River to load and transport the freshly milled pine to distant markets. Darien became a premier southern port for timber shipments. Sawmills and docks provided employment for hundreds of workers, Black and white.

By the early 1900s, the longleaf pine forests had been depleted, and the sawmills shut down. Darien residents turned to the coastal estuaries for their living, developing a robust seafood industry. Georgia white shrimp, blue crabs, fish, and oysters were brought to Darien docks for processing and sale.

Shrimp boats still dock at the bluff downtown, offering a picturesque scene for traffic passing over the U.S. Highway 17 bridge. Every spring, priests and ministers stand on the bridge to bless the shrimp boats during the annual Blessing of the Fleet festival.

Darien's premier industry now is historic tourism.

SITE 24 *Short Take*

Waterfront Warehouses and Adam-Strain Building

Broad Street–Fort King George Street

National Register Historic District

The two-story tabby warehouses that once lined Darien's lower bluff were built between 1812 and 1824. In their heyday, they stored a fortune in rice, cotton, and naval stores.

After slavery was legalized in Georgia in 1750, Carolina planters left their worn-out land and relocated to coastal Georgia to grow sea island cotton and rice. Shortly before the Civil War, the small town of Darien exported more than six million pounds of rice, much of it grown in impoundments on the adjacent Altamaha delta.

Rice grown on the delta represented almost one-third of all the rice produced on the Georgia coast.

Before the Civil War, McIntosh County became one of the wealthiest locales on the Atlantic Seaboard. Darien, the county seat, was a major shipping port for upland cotton barged down the Altamaha as well as for sea island cotton, rice, and other locally produced goods.

Sailing ships traveled up the Darien River, the northern branch of the Altamaha, to load up with goods to deliver to markets in England and elsewhere. When Darien was torched by Union troops in 1863, the wooden sections of the warehouses went up in flames, leaving only picturesque tabby ruins on both sides of the U.S. Highway 17 bridge.

The Adam-Strain Building, constructed of tabby on the upper bluff on Broad Street around 1813, was a ship's chandlery and mercantile store. The only commercial building to survive the burning of Darien, it is listed on the National Register of Historic Places and was identified in 2008 as one of the state's Places in Peril by the Georgia Trust for Historic Preservation. The west wall of the privately owned structure seems on the verge of collapse, and the rest of the building is in poor repair. When its former owner announced plans to raze the building, the people of Darien and advocates of historic preservation objected. The building was sold in 2019 to a couple who are restoring it.

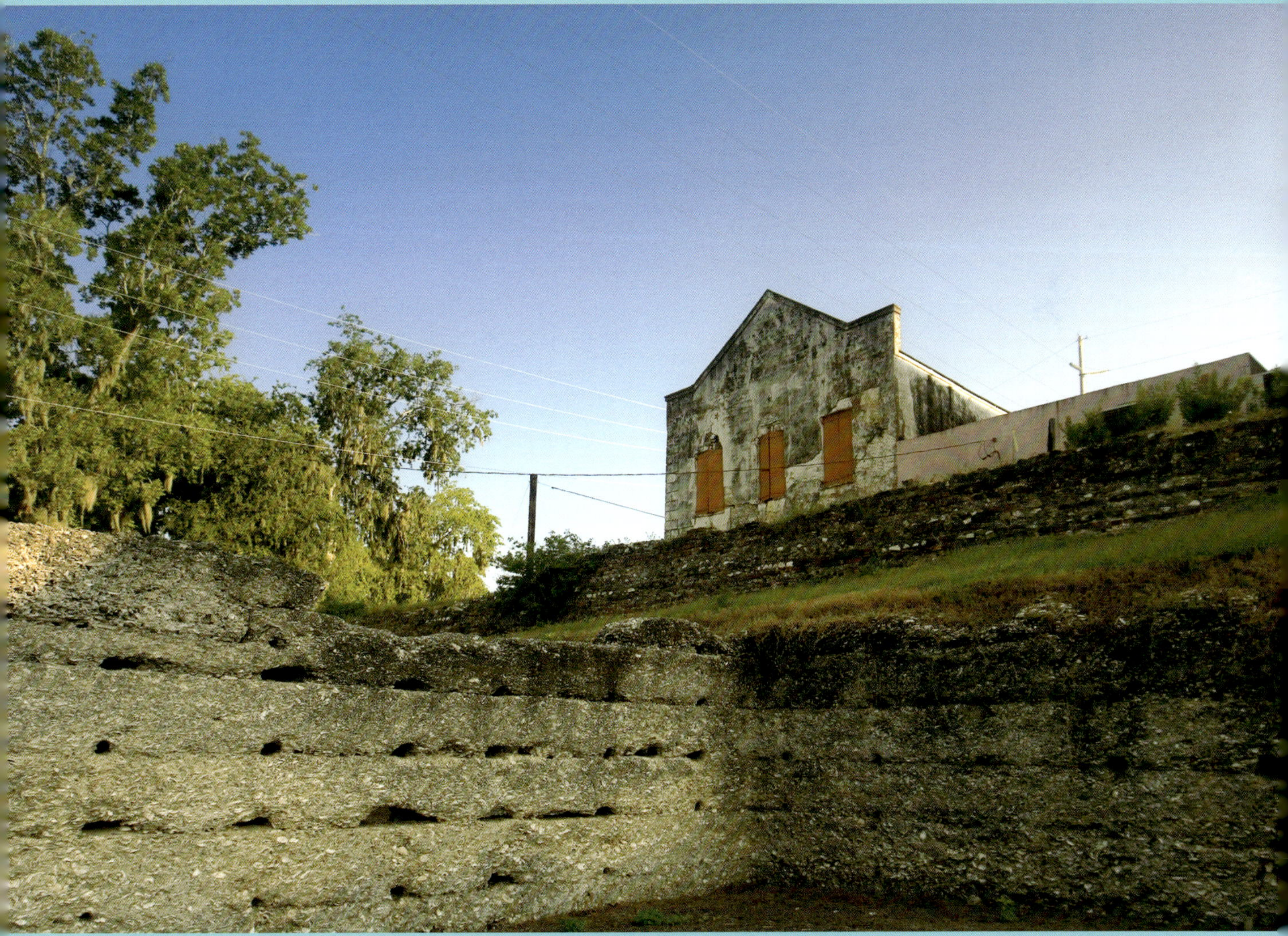

St. Cyprian's Episcopal Church

1876

401 Fort King George Drive
Vernon Square–Columbus Square

National Register Historic District

HISTORIC SIGNIFICANCE: The church is one of the few traditionally Black Episcopal churches in Georgia and one of the few nineteenth-century tabby buildings still being used for its original purpose. It was built by freedmen after the Civil War. The first Black female Episcopal saint in the United States had close ties to the church.

St. Cyprian's Episcopal Church in Darien's Vernon Square–Columbus Square National Register Historic District was built by freedmen of revival tabby after the Civil War on land donated by their former owner's daughter. Some of the builders were skilled masons; others were experienced carpenters. They provided all the labor for the church building as well as for the pews and other furnishings.

Buttresses were added to the sanctuary's walls, perhaps for aesthetic reasons. Many large churches and cathedrals were built with buttresses to provide walls with extra support. St. Cyprian's is a small church with a one-story sanctuary. Its walls could have supported their own weight.

The sanctuary is connected to a large square belfry, which was added later as funds became available. The lower part of the belfry is tabby; the upper part is wood. The sanctuary's arched windows and doors are trimmed with brick. A red entry door provides a bright note of welcome, in contrast with the soft gray tabby.

The church sits on a high bluff overlooking the Altamaha delta, where many of St. Cyprian's first congregants once labored on antebellum rice plantations. The largest rice plantation on the Georgia coast, on Butler's Island, was a 700-acre delta spread owned by Pierce Mease Butler, whose daughter Frances "Fan" Butler donated the land for St. Cyprian's. Her mother was the famed English actress Fanny Kemble, an ardent abolitionist. She and Butler divorced in part because Kemble objected to the way his slaves were treated.

After the war, Fan Butler came to Georgia with her father to try to revive his rice and cotton plantations. They were not successful. Although most of the freedmen were destitute, few were willing to return to the rice and cotton fields, even for wages. Many may have harbored ill feelings for Mease Butler, who was responsible for the largest

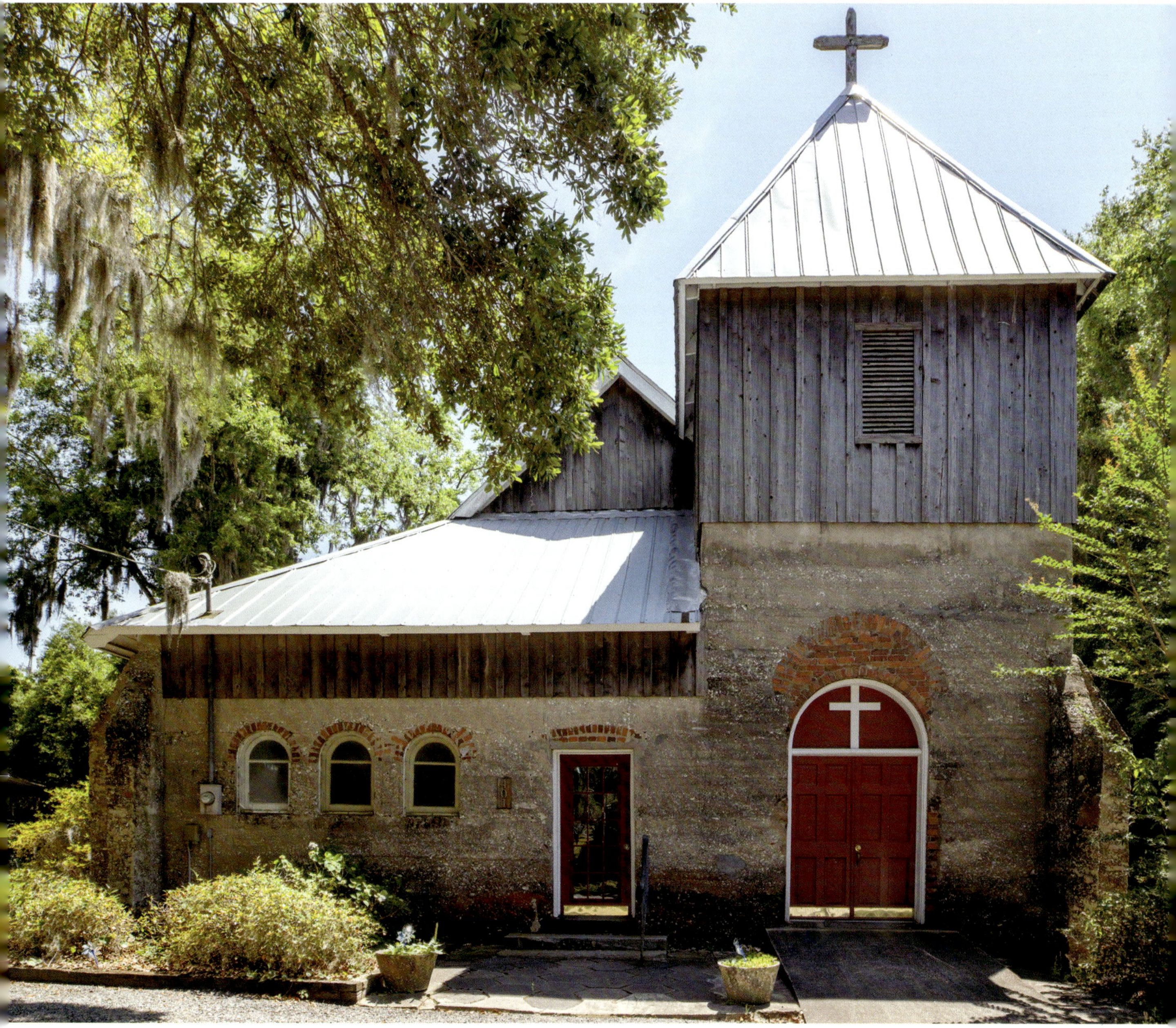

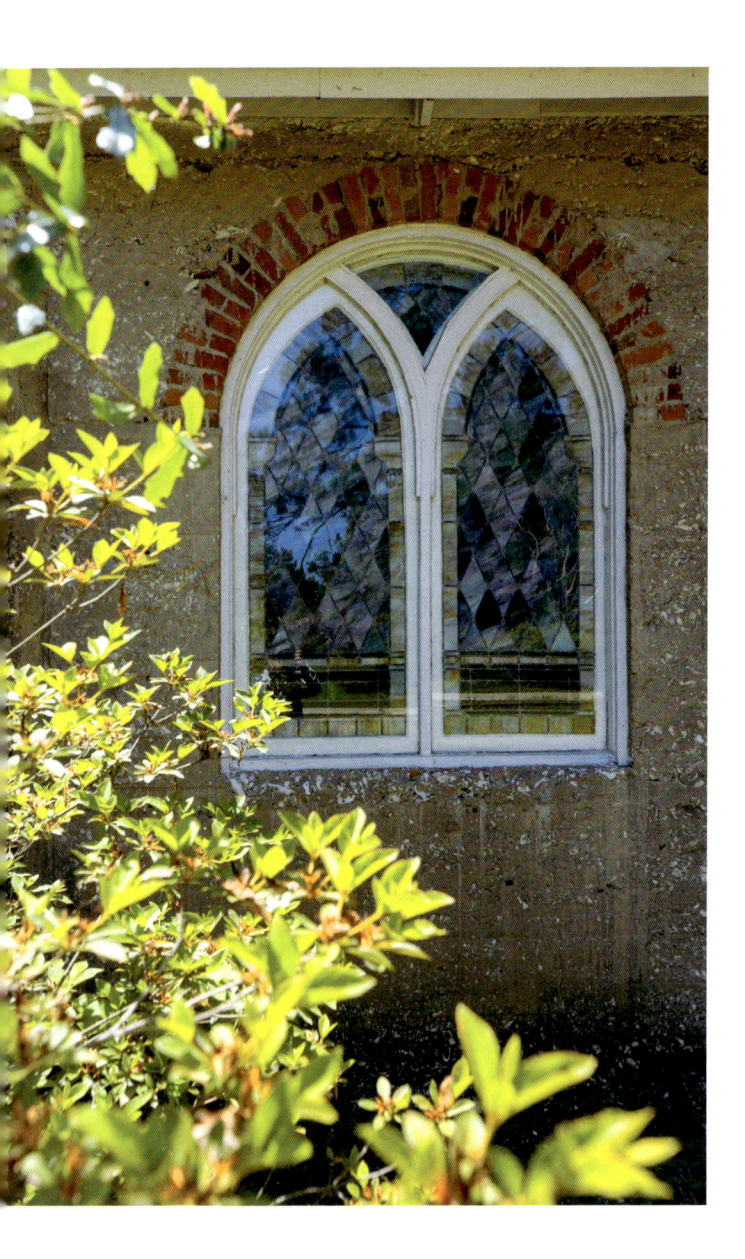

single slave sale in the nation's history. (For an account of the auction, see the section on Fanny Kemble in Site 21: Hampton Plantation.) After the war, most of the people who had been sold traveled long distances back to the Georgia coast to be reunited with family members and lifelong friends.

William Dusinberre, who wrote about slavery on Butler's Island, narrated the horrors faced by enslaved workers in rice fields. He reported that half of all children born to slaves on Butler's Island died before their sixth birthday; 60 percent died before age sixteen. Many were killed by malaria and yellow fever, mosquito-borne diseases that were endemic in the rice fields on the low-lying Altamaha delta. (For details of the miserable conditions faced by enslaved workers in the rice fields, see the account in Site 21: Hampton Plantation.)

Butler slaves dug a mile-long canal called the Rifle Cut through the delta marshes as a shortcut for flatboats that carried the rice to mills on Butler's Island and in Darien. The canal was said to be so straight that a bullet fired from a rifle at one end could travel straight through to the other end.

After Pierce Mease Butler died, in 1867, Fan Butler continued to try to revive her father's plantations, again without success. After she married the Reverend James Wentworth Leigh of England, he began holding services for former slaves on Butler Island and at Hampton Plantation on north St. Simons. Perhaps because Leigh had never been a slave owner, the freedmen liked him and his church services. In 1884, Leigh began preaching to African Americans on the mainland in Darien. At the time, there were no roads through the delta, and mainland congregants had to row long distances to attend Leigh's services on Butler's Island and St. Simons. Soon Leigh and his Darien parishioners decided to build an Episcopal church in the small riverfront town.

Fan Leigh donated the land for the church, and she and her husband solicited donations from wealthy people in England and the northern states to help with building expenses. Construction began in 1875. St. Cyprian's was consecrated the following year and named for Cyprian of Carthage, a Black African bishop and an early Christian writer from the third century. He was martyred under the Roman emperor Valerian and was later canonized as an Episcopal saint.

It is notable that the first Black female Episcopal saint in the United States, Anna Alexander, had close ties to St. Cyprian's Episcopal Church. Probably born the year the Civil War ended, she was the daughter of slaves who had worked in Butler's rice fields and on his cotton plantations.

For a time, St. Cyprian's was served by ministers from St. Andrew's, the white Episcopal church in Darien. From 1892 until 1914, the church had a Black pastor: the Reverend Ferdinand Meshack Mann, the husband of Anna Alexander's sister Mary. During his tenure, St. Cyprian's established a school for Black children from Darien and nearby communities. The school operated for many years.

In 1877, the Leighs relocated to England, where he accepted a position as the Very Reverend Honorable Dean of Hereford Cathedral. The Leighs kept in touch with members of St. Cyprian's. When their daughter Alice married, Fan Leigh sent money to St. Cyprian's for a reception and dinner for members who had known and loved "Miss Alice."

Anna Alexander, c. 1865–1947

Anna Ellison Butler Alexander was born shortly after the Civil War to Aleck and Daphne, newly freed slaves at Hampton Plantation, the cotton plantation then owned by Pierce Mease Butler on the north end of St. Simons Island.

Daphne was the daughter of an enslaved woman named Minta and Butler's white overseer, Roswell King Jr. Aleck was taught to read by the British actress Fanny Kemble during the months she spent on St. Simons in 1838–39 as Butler's wife. Daphne and Aleck took the surname Alexander after emancipation.

Anna Alexander attended services at St. Cyprian's and later helped establish a school there for Black children and taught at the school with two of her sisters. After she moved to the tiny Pennick community, settled by former sea island slaves in the pine barrens in west Glynn County north of Brunswick, she would walk fifteen miles to the Altamaha delta and then row herself through a series of delta rivers to Darien, reversing the journey on the way home. She would also walk ten miles from Pennick to Brunswick to attend St. Athanasius Church. On her travels, she always dressed in her Episcopal deaconess habit: a black dress with a spotless white collar and cuffs, a shoulder-length black veil, and a large silver cross on a chain around her neck.

The lack of an Episcopal church for Black congregants in Pennick inspired her to found the Good Shepherd Episcopal Church and School there in September 1884.

Born to recently emancipated slaves on St. Simons Island, Anna Ellison Butler Alexander (1865–1947), c. 1907, the year that she became the first African American deaconess in the Episcopal Church

Congregants first met in a brush arbor and then in abandoned shacks. With the help of her brothers and other congregants, Anna Alexander built the church and, in 1902, a one-room school next door, "with her own hands." She lived in an apartment above the school for the rest of her life.

She later worked at a segregated Episcopal Church camp on St. Simons and received permission to bring some of her Black students to the retreat, according to Jan Saltzgaber, a former history professor and Episcopal deacon who now lives on the island and has researched Alexander's life.

The Gullah Geechees who settled in Pennick after the Civil War were not tenant farmers; they owned the land they worked. The area was also home to poor white farmers. The small congregation of the Good Shepherd Episcopal Church donated proportionally more to needy people around the world than any church in the diocese. After an earthquake in Japan in 1923 that killed more than two hundred thousand people, Alexander's congregation donated its building funds to help the victims. Children at the church whose parents were poor regularly donated pennies and nickels to charity because Alexander taught them that Christians have a responsibility to help anyone in need.

Anna Alexander died in 1947. A large granite cross in front of the church now marks her grave site. Her remains were moved after the small cemetery where she was first buried was all but lost in the woods.

Alexander's former students still remember her as a small, slender woman who was often too busy to smile. They describe her as a strict but loving teacher who insisted that Pennick children learn to read and write even though many of their adult relatives could not. One former student, Samuel Homes, said she came to his house before he started school to insist that the grownups teach him and his siblings their ABCs. "They said, 'Sure will,' and after she left, Auntie said to Uncle, 'What that fool woman talking about, their ABCs?' She didn't know her ABCs either," Holmes remembered, laughing. Holmes said he and his family memorized groups of letters until everyone could read and recite the alphabet. "We'd go around hollering A-B-C-D-E-F. She'd come and check up on us," Holmes remembered. He and others appeared in a 2002 video made by the Episcopal Diocese of Georgia on the hundredth anniversary of the founding of the church and school.

Anna Alexander encouraged her students to attend college at a time when it was rare for rural Blacks in the Deep South to attend high school, much less institutions of higher learning. She personally drove several students to colleges that accepted Blacks. Her former students excelled, entering professions such as medicine, engineering, and teaching.

She was consecrated as the first Black Episcopal deaconess in the United States in 1907. In 1998, the Episcopal Diocese of Georgia named her a saint and designated September 24 as her feast day. She was named a saint by the General Convention of the Episcopal Church in 2018 and is listed in the national church calendar, Holy Men, Holy Women.

SITE 26

Ashantilly

c. 1810–1820

1712 Bond Road

National Register of Historic Places

HISTORIC SIGNIFICANCE: Thomas Spalding, who owned most of Sapelo Island, built Ashantilly as his winter residence on an ancient sand dune ridge near Darien. The house is named for the barony of Ashantilly in Scotland, which Spalding's father inherited. Like Spalding's South End House on Sapelo, Ashantilly was built of tabby. Although the home was altered by subsequent owners and rebuilt after a fire, the centuries-old building is still structurally sound.

Thomas Spalding built his mainland home, Ashantilly, during the early decades of the 1800s, around the same time when he built South End House, his home on Sapelo Island. Both mansions were completed no later than 1820, and possibly well before then. They marked the beginning of a tabby building revival that Spalding sparked in coastal Georgia during the early nineteenth century.

Ashantilly's footprint was similar, but not identical, to that of South End House. The island home was one story, built low to the ground to help the structure withstand hurricane winds. The mainland home, nicknamed Old Tabby, was on higher ground, built on a dune dating to one of Georgia's prehistoric shorelines. The old shorelines formed during the ice ages, when sea levels would periodically drop far enough to expose the continental shelf and then later rise high enough to inundate the coastal plain. The oldest and highest of the old shorelines, about seventy miles inland, is called the Wicomico. Dunes left over from the former sea islands are now known as Georgia's sand hills.

Ashantilly had a two-story central core supported by a system of tabby vaults, designed by Spalding, that ran east to west under the floors.

The walls were built of solid tabby poured in two-by-twelve-inch layers in a formwork of boards. The flat roof, held up by massive live oak beams, was a poured tabby slab with a cornice and parapet designed to protect the roof from wind damage. Although the slab roof was strong, it was not waterproof and needed to be coated with tar every year or so to keep it from leaking.

Spalding sited Ashantilly so that the front rooms could capture sunlight all day long through the front façade's floor-length windows. Views from the mansion were of massive live oaks draped with Spanish moss and magnolias sporting fragrant white blooms as large as dinner plates.

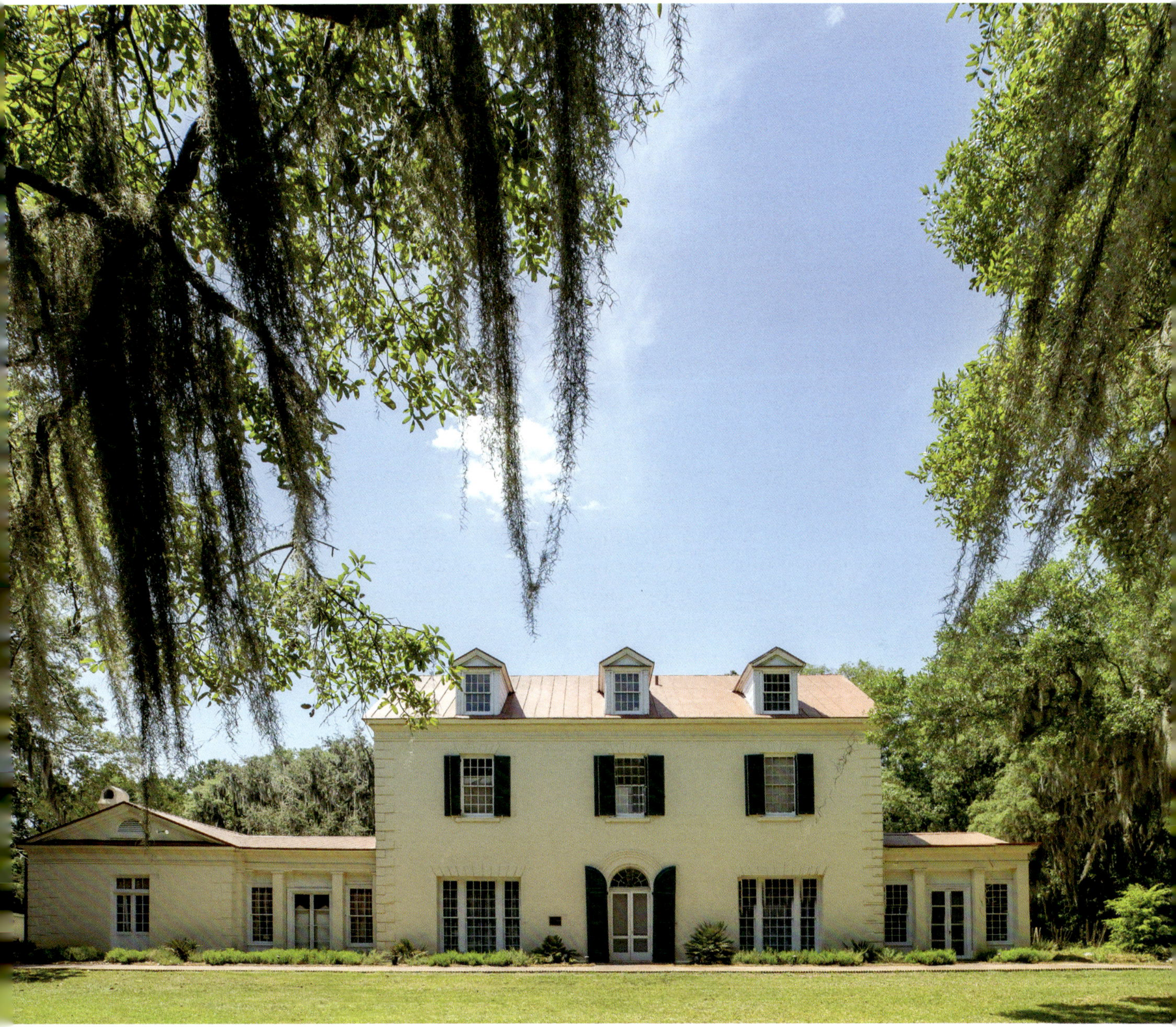

The original Ashantilly was built in a simple neoclassical style. The central core featured a dramatic two-story entry hall flanked on either side by large parlors. One-story wings accessed by open loggias lined with marble columns connected the house's smaller rooms to the core block. Interior rooms were well proportioned and spacious. Details such as wainscoting and cornices were hand carved.

Spalding may have later added a flat-roofed piazza to the façade of the central core. The roof was supported by terra-cotta columns from Italy. The columned piazza and side loggias gave the home the airy look of an Italian villa.

Spalding probably refined Ashantilly's design during the year and a half that he, his wife, Sarah, and her mother spent touring Europe. There he studied several architectural styles, including Regency, which was becoming popular at the time. The original Ashantilly exhibited both neoclassical and Regency elements.

During their trip abroad, the Spaldings purchased numerous design elements for both Ashantilly and South End House. They chose Italian marble for floors and mantels and Greek statuettes of robe-draped females holding chandeliers for the parlors and dining rooms. Each statuette was three feet high, standing on a marble pedestal.

Many chandeliers were needed to illuminate the large, high-ceilinged rooms of both houses in order to keep them from looking gloomy.

The Spaldings imported other accessories from Europe: mirrors and artwork from Italy, the foundational holdings of his extensive home libraries from England. Instead of selecting the other furnishings for their Georgia residences themselves, Spalding gave carte blanche to a friend in Europe to choose the individual furniture pieces. One was a massive sideboard, each leg of which was carved from a single tree. Spalding later complained that his friend had bought too much, but someone who knew him well said he did not think Spalding was "at all displeased" by the excess.

After Spalding's death in 1851, his son Charles inherited Ashantilly but lived there only briefly. Charles Spalding found the upkeep of the mansion daunting, especially the need to retar the roof every year. He built a wooden house across the street and abandoned Ashantilly, which sat empty for decades. The home suffered from a leaky roof and the loss of its exterior coat of stucco. During the Civil War, the abandoned mansion was occupied and damaged by Union and Confederate troops and perhaps by displaced people, including liberated slaves with nowhere else to go.

The Spalding family cemetery was adjacent to the mansion. In 1867, Charles dedicated land around the cemetery to St. Andrew's Episcopal Church in Darien, to be used in perpetuity as a burial ground. Now called St. Andrews Cemetery, the wooded burial ground offers a lovely view of tidal marshes and Black Island Creek.

The Wilcox family purchased Ashantilly in 1870. Their renovation included a hipped roof with wooden shingles. The William G. Haynes family bought the mansion in 1918. A fire destroyed the interior walls and floors in 1937, but the sturdy tabby walls survived the blaze, as did Spalding's vaulted foundation. Haynes family members began a long-term restoration that included replacing the hipped roof with a gable roof more compatible with the original house.

Ashantilly is now owned and operated by a private trust. The Ashantilly Center Inc. is a nonprofit educational enclave and studio that reflects the Haynes' interest in the art of letterpress printing and books, the history and culture of the South, and the environment. The center works in partnership with organizations that offer native plant sales, beekeeping classes, and wildflower gardening. Center events include lectures, cemetery walks, Darien walking tours, and an artist-in-residence program.

William Greaner Haynes Jr., 1908–2001

William G. "Bill" Haynes was a talented artist, an ardent environmentalist, and an exceptional printer who practiced the almost-lost art of letterpress printing for most of his adult life. His imprint, the Ashantilly Press, consistently produced high-quality, award-winning books. His first printing was done on a press in the large south room at Ashantilly. As the business grew, he built a print shop on the grounds of the main house.

After Ashantilly burned, Haynes spent the remainder of his life lovingly restoring the house. He left a greater imprint on Ashantilly than any other owner besides Thomas Spalding, who designed and built it.

Exterior door connecting the right wing of Ashantilly to the main house. This photo was taken by L. D. Andrew as part of the Historic American Buildings Survey in December 1936; fire gutted the mansion the following year.

Haynes moved to Ashantilly with his family as a ten-year-old boy. After graduating from high school in 1927, he studied art in New York City and lived there with his sister, Ann Lee, a commercial artist. He returned to McIntosh County during the Great Depression and joined the Civilian Conservation Corps as an artist. When Ashantilly was gutted by fire in 1937, the family was forced to find other living quarters. Their old tabby home sat empty for two years until the Depression ended. Haynes inherited just enough money to begin the long process of restoring the large historic property on a limited budget.

During the restoration, Haynes prowled the shops of salvage and antique dealers in Savannah and Charleston to purchase mantels, doors, and other period pieces to replace the ones lost in the fire. He replicated the plaster molding in the living room by pulling a profile stencil through wet plaster in traditional fashion, working on long ladders to reach the high ceilings.

Work on the mansion came to an abrupt halt when Haynes was drafted into the army at the start of World War II. His military service took him to Brazil and other distant lands. He produced *A Journal of a Voyage to Australia and New Guinea*, a two-volume book handwritten in calligraphy and illustrated with charming watercolor sketches of people he had met, places he had visited, and events he had witnessed during his time abroad. The journals defined what would become his artistic style.

Haynes returned to New York after the war. At Cooper Union, he studied typography and letterpress printing. He learned to select type, design pages, and use color, as well as to carve woodcuts for illustrations. During summers, when school was out, Haynes continued the Ashantilly restoration. In the summer of 1946, he purchased the small handpress and type that he later used to print his first book, *Anchored Yesterdays*, by Elfrida De Renne Barrow and Laura Palmer Bell (1956), a history of Savannah. In New York, he continued to add different styles of type to his collection. After art school, he worked for an advertising agency and then returned to a job he had held earlier at the New York Public Library.

Haynes later worked for the publishers of the Frick catalogue, a compendium of paintings, sculptures, and decorative pieces in New York's Frick Collection. Working with experienced Frick designers and typographers for three years, he polished his work to his own perfectionist standards. For the next four decades in Darien, those standards were reflected in Haynes's work.

While he was still at Cooper Union, Haynes met Natalie Erdman, whom he married. The couple returned to Darien in 1955 to live full-time. Neither of his sisters ever married, and both returned to Ashantilly after they retired to live with their brother and sister-in-law.

Haynes named his printing operation the Ashantilly Press. Within a year, he produced a map of Fort King George, built in 1721. It was the first British stronghold in what later became the colony of Georgia. The fort, founded by British troops from South Carolina, overlooks the Darien River, a branch of the Altamaha. It is now a state historic site.

Haynes' silk-screened four-color map, considered a work of art even when it was produced, is now a collector's item. So are the thirty hand-printed, limited-edition books he produced over the next thirty-five years. Haynes illustrated each book with prints pulled from wood blocks he carved himself. Many of the books relate to the area's history and environment, including *Anchored Yesterdays*, an account of Savannah's early days, which was printed in Ashantilly's south room. A larger press occupied the same room until Haynes built his print shop on the grounds of the main house.

Because all the type was set by hand and each page was printed separately, Haynes rarely printed more than five hundred copies of his books, which received a number of prestigious awards. The Ashantilly Press also printed posters and cards, and for thirty years Haynes hand printed the weekly church bulletin for the Darien Presbyterian Church. He also rang the church bell every Sunday morning to announce the eleven o'clock service.

Soft-spoken but passionate about worthy causes, Haynes was an ardent advocate for historic and environmental preservation at a time when protecting natural and cultural resources was still a new concept. He was always protective of the giant Altamaha River and the tidal marshes between the McIntosh County mainland and the distant sea islands: Sapelo, Blackbeard, and Wolf. Haynes was a major force behind the establishment of the Lower Altamaha Historical Society.

In his later years, Haynes lost his hearing. Before he retired in 1991, he and his sisters founded the nonprofit Ashantilly Center, placing the mansion and its eighty-acre grounds in a permanent trust.

SITE 27

The Thicket Sugar Mill and Rum Distillery

1816

Georgia Highway 99 at Tolomato Island
Carnochan Drive

HISTORIC SIGNIFICANCE: Tabby ruins at the former sugar plantation called The Thicket mark the location of a sugar mill and Georgia's first rum distillery. Tabby slave cabins on the plantation each housed two families. The Thicket's owner, a Scotsman named William Carnochan, came to the United States from Jamaica, where he had grown sugarcane and distilled rum.

In the 1600s, African slaves on Caribbean sugar plantations discovered that molasses made from sugarcane could be fermented and distilled into rum. In the early 1800s, William Carnochan migrated to McIntosh County from Jamaica, intending to mill sugar and distill rum in Georgia.

Carnochan and the wealthy entrepreneur Thomas Spalding of Sapelo Island formed a partnership. Using Spalding's sugar mill on Sapelo as a model, Carnochan established a large sugar plantation that he named The Thicket. He built his sugar works and distillery on the banks of a tidal creek a few miles northeast of downtown Darien.

When he moved to Georgia, he may have brought slaves who were experienced in processing cane juice into rum.

Spalding was already processing sugar in the mill he designed and built on Sapelo in 1809. He was the first to plant sugarcane and process it on a commercial scale in Georgia. His Sapelo mill was the first of many tabby structures he built on the island and the McIntosh County mainland. He planted one hundred acres of cane on Sapelo in 1805. The plants thrived in the sandy soil and warm, humid climate. Spalding's mill overlooked the marshes on Sapelo's western shore. Carnochan's sugar mill faced east, overlooking the creek subsequently named for him. Both mills overlooked the same wide stretch of marsh that separates Sapelo from the McIntosh County mainland.

Carnochan's vertical cane press was housed in an octagonal building forty-one feet in diameter. The press was powered by oxen, mules, or other work animals that were led up a ramp to the second floor and harnessed to a horizontal sweep. As the animals plodded around in a circle, the sweep turned a vertical shaft, rotating the rollers that crushed the cane in the room below, extracting the sweet juice. From the cane-press building, the juice flowed to the adjacent boiling house through a gutter inside the walls. The juice then poured into large purification vats called receivers, and from there it was transferred to copper boiling kettles and cooked

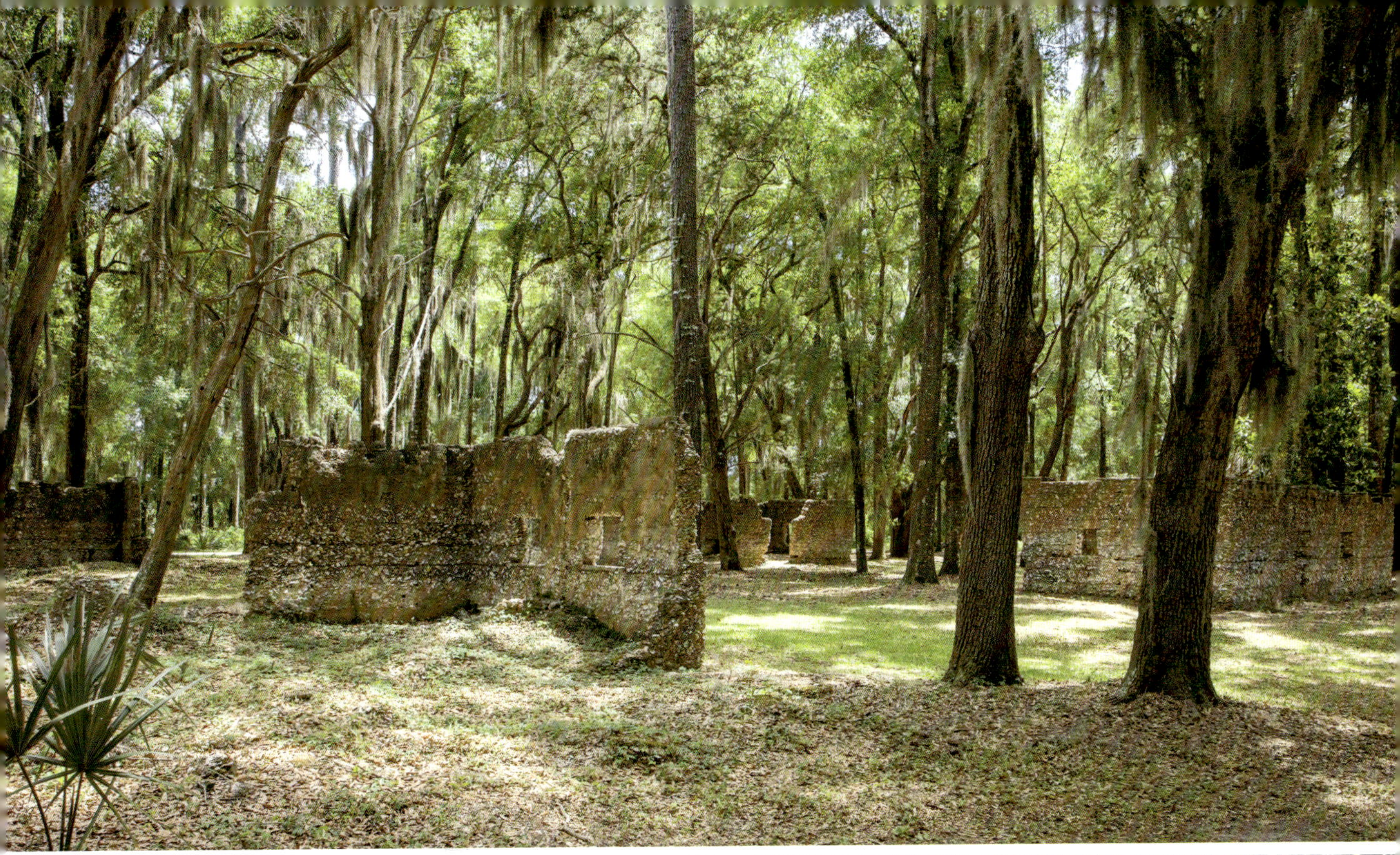
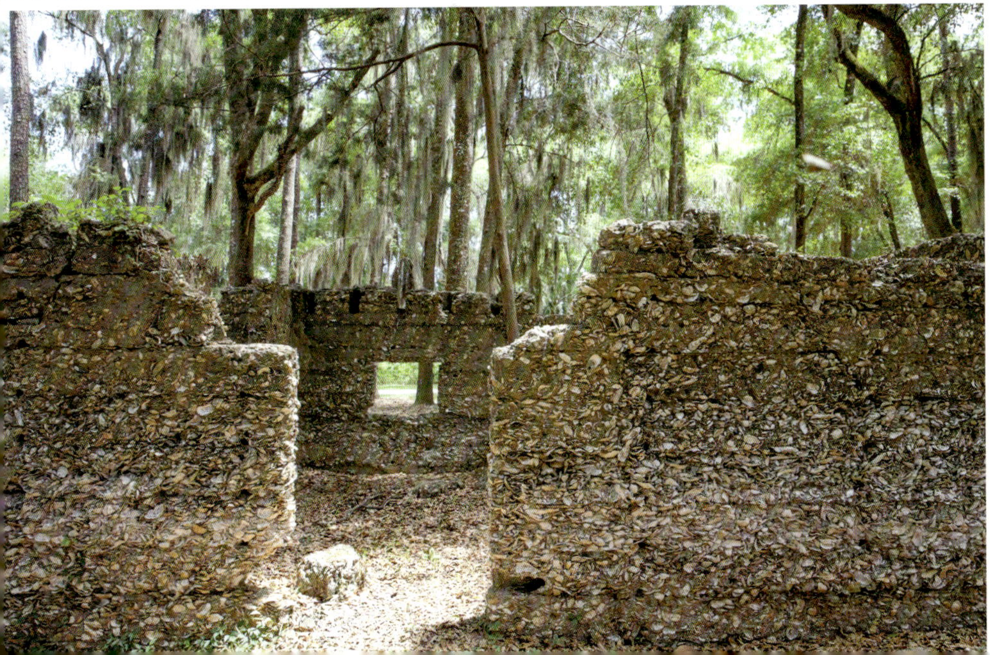
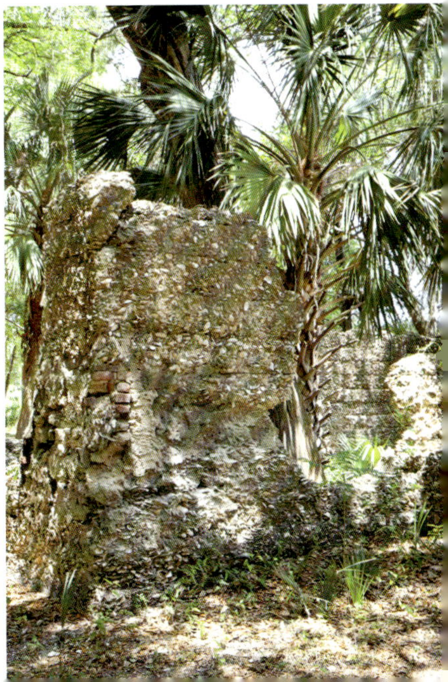

down until syrup began to form. Cypress coolers were used to help the sugar crystallize. What was described as a "thick turbid mass" of sugar and molasses then traveled to the curing house, where molasses was drained by gravity into a central gutter, leaving the sugar crystals behind. Most of the sugar and molasses was sold in Savannah and Charleston.

At the Thicket, the boiling and curing buildings were arranged in a large T shape estimated to be 100 feet long and 30 feet wide. Spalding's sugar works served as a prototype for those of several other planters in coastal Georgia. James Hamilton Couper of Hopeton Plantation in Glynn County built his first sugar mill from Spalding's design, but when Couper increased his sugar acreage, he needed a mill more powerful than one powered by animals. He built a huge steam-powered mill—again using tabby—that was praised as the finest ever built in Georgia.

Today, residents of Sapelo and the McIntosh County mainland are planting a historic variety of sugarcane in an effort to revive the sugar industry and make cane syrup—and perhaps rum—on a commercial scale.

Only rubble remains of the tabby sugar mills on Sapelo and at The Thicket. The boiling house on Sapelo, now called Long Tabby, has been restored and houses the island's post office and other government offices.

The Thicket's rum was stored in a tabby warehouse that Carnochan and Spalding built on the banks of the Darien River. The Savannah firm of Carnochan & Mitchell advertised the product for sale in 1817: "14 puncheons of 4th proof Georgia rum, equal in flavor and quality to Jamaica." The ad announced that a "constant supply" of rum could be purchased in Savannah or at the distillery in Darien "on very accommodating terms to country merchants and others."

Carnochan's sugar works and distillery operated from 1816 until 1824, when a powerful hurricane swept away the roof of the cane barn and the upper story of the cane-press building. Other buildings were damaged, and the cane crop was destroyed. Carnochan did not have a chance to rebuild. He died the following year at age fifty-one.

By the start of the twentieth century, erosion had toppled large chunks of Carnochan's tabby distillery into Carnochan Creek, later renamed Crum Creek, which changed course after his death. Part of the distillery and other tabby ruins are in a small park maintained by the Tolomato Island Homeowners Association. The ruins are on private property but may be viewed from the nearby public street.

Carnochan's distillery represented Georgia's link with an early American tradition. Rum played an important role in the history of the United States and in the transatlantic slave trade. During the colonial era, New England distilleries made rum the mainstay of the region's economy.

Rum provoked many colorful expressions and folktales. One involves the body of Admiral Horatio Nelson, who died during the Battle of Trafalgar off the coast of Spain in 1805. His body was reportedly returned to England in a barrel of rum, which was intended to preserve the remains. Some stories claim the preserving liquid was French brandy. When the barrel arrived at its destination, it contained nothing but the body. According to the legend, sailors on board the ship carrying Nelson's body drilled a hole in the bottom of the barrel and drank all the preserving liquid. One of rum's many nicknames is Nelson's Blood.

The Royal Navy mixed rum with beer or water and issued a daily ration to sailors, called a tot. The diluted rum, named grog, was intended to keep the sailors from getting drunk. Surprisingly, the practice continued until 1970. Now, only the queen, a member of the royal family, or, in rare cases, British admiralty boards may order tots to be issued on special occasions such as royal birthdays, weddings, or anniversaries. The nautical phrase "splice the mainbrace" indicates that double tots will be forthcoming.

In Jamaica, where Carnochan learned to make rum, a distillation called John Crow Betty is now rated as one of the ten strongest alcoholic drinks in the world.

In the Caribbean and on the hot Georgia coast, distillers always lost part of their product to evaporation. The lost spirits are called the angels' share.

Mary Letitia Ross, 1881–1971

Mary Ross was a brilliant historian from Camden County, Georgia, who pioneered the study of early Spanish history in coastal Georgia. Ross was criticized harshly after she misidentified several tabby ruins, including Carnochan's, as the remains of Spanish missions established on the sea islands and mainland of Georgia and Florida from the late 1500s to the early 1600s.

In 1925, Mary Ross and her mentor, Herbert Bolton, a professor at the University of California, Berkeley, coauthored and published a landmark book called *The Debatable Land*, which explored the Spanish colonial history of the region. Before then, little was known about the Spanish on the Eastern Seaboard, even though they were the first Europeans to claim territory on the North American continent, from 1513 until 1821. Spain was a major presence in the coastal Southeast for more than two and a half centuries after St. Augustine, Florida, was settled in 1565.

Bolton, an expert on Spanish colonial history, was one of the country's most respected historians. His research focused on Catholic missions established after 1769 by Franciscan friars in the West. The Franciscans had founded missions on the Atlantic coast almost two hundred years earlier, but almost nothing was known about that chapter of the nation's history. Bolton encouraged Ross, his graduate student at Berkeley, to research the Spanish era in Georgia.

Ross spent years collecting documents from the Archives of the Indies in Spain, assisted by an American woman who lived in Seville. She amassed more than a thousand documents, all written in archaic Spanish, and then spent the rest of her life translating and interpreting them. Ross is known as an impeccable researcher who was a pioneer in the field of Georgia's Spanish history. Her library and more than eighty cubic feet of papers, correspondence, and documents are now housed at the Georgia Department of Archives and History in Morrow, south of Atlanta, where the material is open to researchers.

But a serious error in the book that Ross wrote with Bolton in 1925 upset her so much that she vowed never to publish another word. She misidentified several tabby ruins in coastal Georgia as the remains of Spanish missions. Ross reported that the remains of the nineteenth-century sugar mill and distillery at The Thicket were once part of the sixteenth-century mission of Nuestra Senora de Guadalupe de Tolomato, founded in 1595 in the Native American village of Tolomato. The village was one of the centers of the Guale-Tolomato chiefdom. When the first Europeans arrived, Guales were the Indigenous occupants of the northern part of the Georgia coast. Guale territory stretched south from the Ogeechee River near Savannah to the Altamaha River. Mocama people of the large Timucuan chiefdom lived south of the Altamaha.

Sculpture of a pelican by Jim Swain, Mary Ross Waterfront Park, commissioned by Keep the Golden Isles Beautiful in 2017. The steel-mesh body of the bird is filled with plastic and aluminum litter collected along the waterfront by KGIB volunteers.

Mission Tolomato and the Native village were actually five miles south of The Thicket on land later occupied by Fort King George, another historic site in McIntosh County. None of the mission's structures were built of tabby. Mission Tolomato lasted less than two years. It was burned to the ground during a Native uprising in 1597, and the occupants were relocated to St. Catherines Island farther north on the coast.

John Tate Lanning, another brilliant Bolton protégé, who taught at Duke University, perpetuated the misconception of tabby missions a few years after the Bolton and Ross book with his own scholarly tome, which included drawings and descriptions of what Georgia's Spanish missions might have looked like. The drawings were inspired by the later Franciscan missions of the West, with bell towers, arched walkways, and courtyards.

Regional and national publications, including the *Atlanta Constitution*, the *New York Times*, and *National Geographic*, produced feature articles about Georgia's Spanish missions, illustrated with photographs of romantic moss-draped tabby ruins and speculative drawings that captured the public's imagination. Ruins of old buildings built of oyster-shell tabby were soon being touted as a "unique asset" that could be exploited to attract tourists and new residents to coastal Georgia.

The publicity kicked off a mini land boom. In Glynn County, weathered tabby walls on the Altamaha delta north of Brunswick were misidentified as the ruins of Mission Santo Domingo de Talaje, and the site was designated a state park. But the only Spanish mission identified to date in Georgia is the one on St. Catherines Island. The noted archaeologist David Hurst Thomas of the American Museum of Natural History in New York has spent decades leading teams of archaeologists exploring the remains of Mission Santa Catalina de Guale, established in 1598.

Thomas said the books published in the 1920s by Ross, Bolton, and Lanning about Spain's Catholic missions in Georgia caused a furor among descendants of early British settlers, who "objected to such a complimentary view" of the Spanish as the earliest Europeans to settle in North America after contact. They considered their Protestant British forebears the true European founders of Georgia and the rest of the country. "Everyone knows that America's colonial history began at Roanoke, Plymouth and Jamestown—not at St. Augustine or on the sea islands of Georgia," Thomas wrote facetiously in his book *St. Catherines: An Island in Time* (1988).

Thomas says that the identification of some of the old tabby structures as Spanish mission ruins "positively electrified" members of the National Society of the Colonial Dames of America in the State of Georgia when Ross, Bolton, and Lanning published their conclusions. The organization hired a team of experts headed by the noted historian E. Merton Coulter to investigate and refute what they called "the Spanish mission myth." Coulter enlisted the help of Marmaduke Floyd of Savannah and James A. Ford of the Smithsonian Institute, who researched the subject for a decade in the late 1920s and 1930s. They conducted archaeological studies, reviewed documents, and interviewed longtime coastal residents whose older relatives had linked the tabby to the antebellum period. The team proved beyond doubt that not a single tabby ruin in coastal Georgia dated to the mission period.

Researchers now believe that the Franciscan missions of coastal Georgia were built of wood, thatch, and other materials more fragile than tabby.

Memorial to Mary Letitia Ross in a park named for her in Brunswick, Georgia

Tourism promoters, developers, and governmental officials were outraged. When Floyd helped prove that the ruins being promoted as the Mission Santo Domingo de Talaje were actually the remains of Elizafield Plantation, he was fired from his state job. Members of the Colonial Dames were vindicated, although Ross's identification of Spanish missions on the Georgia coast was no myth.

Ross and Bolton were ridiculed for their error. Bolton, an established scholar, weathered the storm in faraway California, but Ross, who had moved back to her home in Brunswick, was crushed. She believed she had ruined her reputation as a historian. Even worse, she feared she had damaged the reputation of the mentor she revered. She continued her scholarly research for another thirty years, but she kept her vow and never published another word.

A waterfront park in downtown Brunswick is named in her honor.

CHAPTER 9   *Sapelo Island*

MOSTLY STATE-OWNED SAPELO is a 16,500-acre mostly natural wonder. It is flanked on the east by the Atlantic Ocean, Nannygoat and Cabretta beaches, and Blackbeard Island, and on the west by wide Spartina marshes and sun-spangled tidal waterways. Doboy Sound flows past Sapelo's southern reaches; Sapelo Sound caps the island's north end.

Forests of live oak and pine, magnolia and palmetto, cover most of the interior. The island is largely undeveloped except for the small Gullah-Geechee community called Hog Hammock, the University of Georgia's Marine Research Institute, a tabby mansion called South End House, offices occupied by the Georgia Department of Natural Resources, and Chocolate, the extensive tabby remains of an antebellum plantation.

The red-and-white-striped lighthouse, built in 1820 on the south end, was raised by ten feet in the 1850s. It was restored in 1998 and relit, and is now listed on the National Register of Historic Places.

The Sapelo Island National Estuarine Research Reserve occupies six thousand acres on the island's western shore.

Sapelo is one of several large Georgia sea islands not linked to the mainland by a causeway. Visitors, Hog Hammock residents, and scientists travel back and forth on a state-run ferry that runs between the mainland dock at Meridian off Georgia Highway 99 and Marsh Creek Landing on the Duplin River on Sapelo's western shore. The ride takes about half an hour, and the views of Spartina marshes, tidewaters, dolphins, and wading birds are spectacular.

There is a visitor center at the Meridian dock and another, smaller center in Darien. Among their offerings are sweetgrass baskets hand woven by Hog Hammock residents.

On the northwest side of Sapelo—the word is a variation of "Zapala," the name of a pre-Columbian Guale village on the island—a large aboriginal shell ring and two smaller rings date back 4,500 years. The shells were deposited by Paleo-Indians in the Late Archaic period.

In the decades leading up to contact, Sapelo was occupied by people of the small Guale chiefdom, which stretched along the Georgia coast between the Altamaha and Ogeechee Rivers. The Guale's main village was on St. Catherines Island farther north, but Sapelo had at least two Guale villages: Chuculate, on the northwest side, and Zapala, on the northern tip. Franciscan friars formed a mission on the island and named it San Jose de Zapala.

During an archaeological investigation in 2016, researchers found Spanish majolica pottery and sherds of Native American pottery that showed Spanish influence.

They also found a whelk shell carved to make a decorative cup that may have been used in black drink ceremonies. Native Americans in the Southeast believed the black drink, made from the toasted leaves of the native cassina bush, kept them in a state of ritual purity. When consumed to excess, the highly caffeinated liquid induced vomiting, thus cleansing the body.

The Spanish mission period began in the coastal Southeast in the late 1500s and continued until 1684, when the British and their Native American allies forced the Franciscans and missionized Natives to abandon the coast. The friars retreated to the Spanish stronghold of St. Augustine, taking most of the missionized Natives and pagan refugees with them. Some Guale people allied with the Yamasees in Carolina. The Yamasees were an ethnically mixed confederation of Native groups that had banded together after many of their original members died out. The Georgia coast was never again occupied by its Native people. Other Indigenous people, including the Yamacraw and the Creek, moved in to fill the void.

After James Edward Oglethorpe arrived to settle Georgia in 1733, he negotiated with the Yamacraw chief Tomochichi for land for the thirteenth and last American colony. Oglethorpe got most of the property he wanted, a stretch that ran south from the Savannah River to the Altamaha River. The Lower Creeks, who claimed the coast, reserved several sea islands, including Sapelo, as hunting preserves.

Later, after the Natives had ceded their hunting islands to the British, Georgia colonists received land grants on Sapelo and other sea islands.

A group of French noblemen, eager to escape their home country during the lead-up to the revolution, bought Sapelo in 1789, along with other coastal property. They intended to harvest live oak timber and raise crops and livestock with slave labor. The partnership ended in tragedy. One partner was killed by another in a duel, and a partner died of yellow fever a short time later. A partner who returned to France lost his head to the guillotine.

Most of Sapelo was bought in 1912 by the Detroit millionaire Howard Coffin, a pioneer in automotive and aeronautical engineering. Coffin restored Thomas Spalding's South End House and other island buildings. The tobacco magnate Richard J. Reynolds Jr. purchased the bulk of Sapelo in 1934. He modernized South End House and donated land and facilities to the University of Georgia for estuarine research. Scientists on the island who studied coastal marshes established the value of the watery fields of Spartina grass, which led to state legislation that protects them. Reynolds's widow sold Sapelo to the state in transactions in 1969 and 1974.

Feral pigs and cattle brought over by island planters still run free in the woods, in the high marsh, and on the beach. A black bull named Butthead once enjoyed hanging out in the Gullah Geechee community of Hog Hammock.

SITE 28

Chocolate Plantation

1790–1875

N 31°29.978 and W 81°15.174 [no street address; no named street]

National Register of Historic Places

HISTORIC SIGNIFICANCE: The Chocolate property was purchased in the late 1700s by a group of French noblemen who formed the Sapelo Company. The tabby at Chocolate dates to the early nineteenth century when a Danish sea captain and slave trader built the main house, outbuildings, and rows of slave cabins of tabby. A later planter added the large tabby barn.

Early Sapelo property owners included Patrick Mackay, who grew crops on the island before the Revolutionary War, and John McQueen, a colorful figure who fled to Spanish Florida to escape creditors in Georgia and took the name Don Juan McQueen. In 1974 the late Eugenia Price published a best-selling novel about McQueen.

The first recorded use of the plantation's unusual name was in 1797 when the French noblemen who bought Sapelo Island listed the property as Chocolate in official documents and correspondence. The name had probably been in use even earlier. Experts think it is a derivative of Chucalate, a prehistoric Guale village that was once on or near the same site. Modern historians discount an older theory that Chocolate derived from Gullah Geechee slaves mispronouncing the name Le Chatelet, the home of one of the Frenchmen on Sapelo.

The nobles were eager to get out of France. On the eve of revolution, starving commoners were raging in the streets of Paris, burning chateaux owned by noble families and pillaging monasteries around the country. The nobles who purchased Sapelo knew it was only a matter of time until they would be targeted.

The Sapelo Company failed in less than a decade, in part because of mistrust and incompetence among the principals. Only one had ever worked for a living: Christophe Poulain DuBignon, a successful sea captain for forty years. DuBignon wisely traded his shares in the Sapelo Company for part of Jekyll Island, where he established a sea island cotton plantation and created a dynasty that lasted almost a century.

Richard Leake and Edward Swarbreck bought the Chocolate tract in 1801 from the Sapelo Company's agent. When Leake died the following year, Thomas Spalding, who was married to Leake's daughter, bought most of

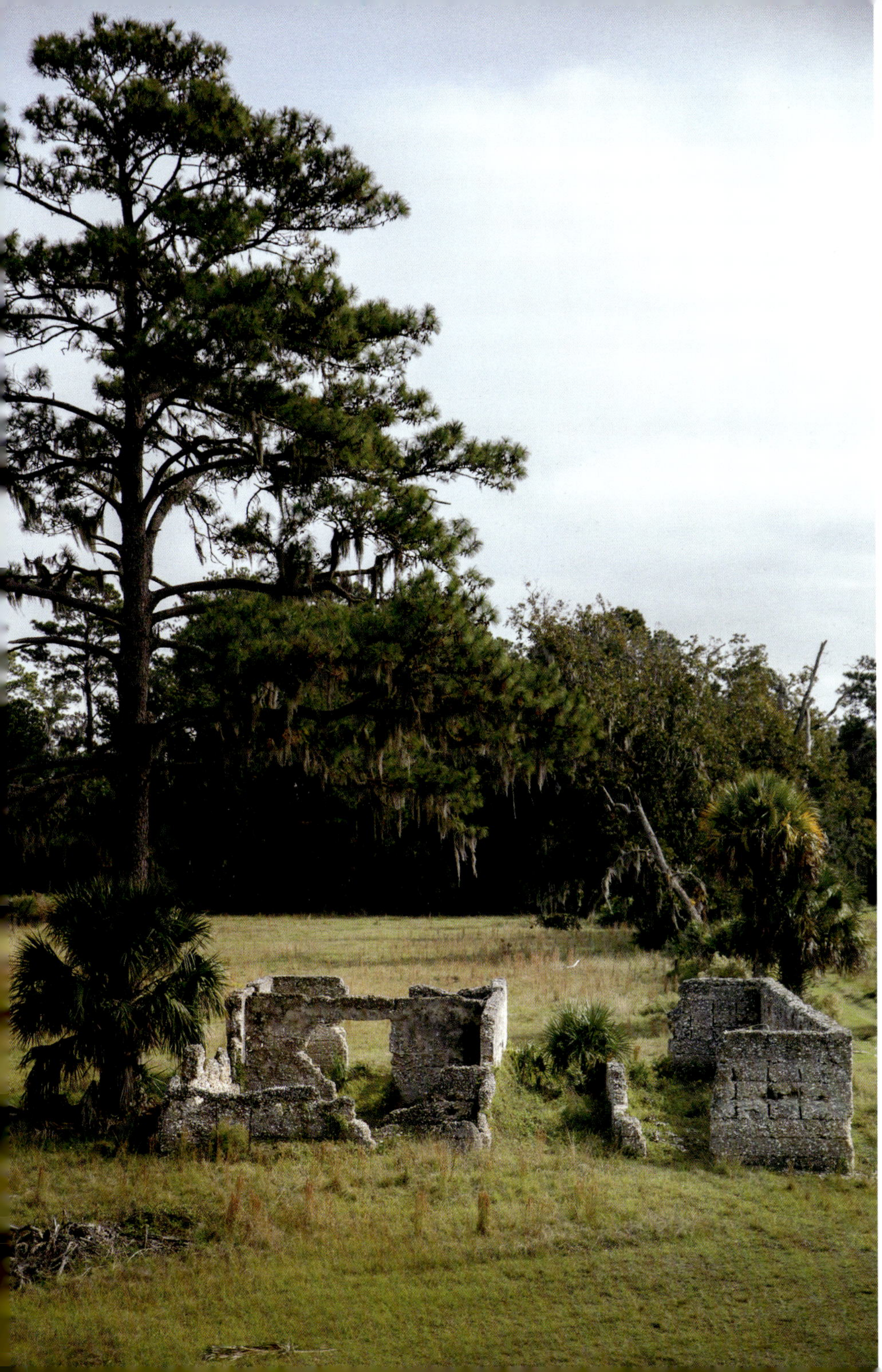
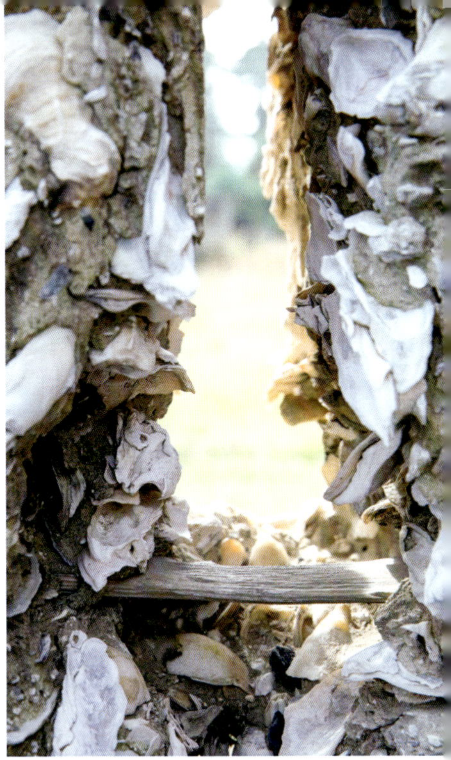
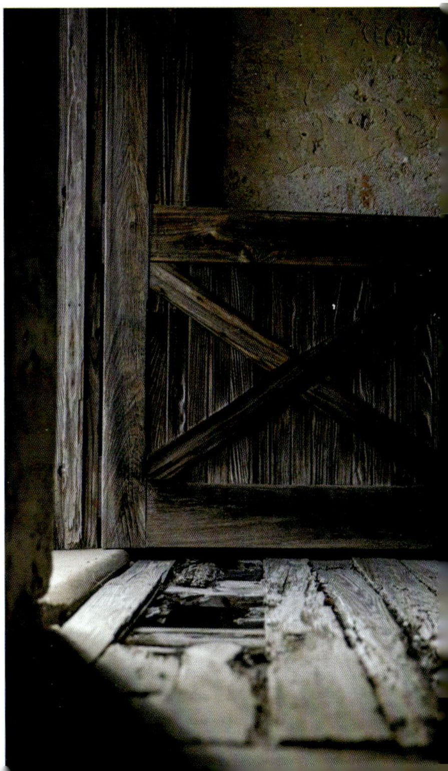

Sapelo. Swarbreck, a Danish sea captain and slave trader retained Chocolate.

Swarbreck was the first to build with tabby at Chocolate. His home and several rows of slave cabins were constructed of the oyster-shell concrete. Tabby was used for his two-part cotton house, which had been ingeniously designed to allow wagons to load and unload cotton bales with ease. The building featured ventilation slots, still visible in the weathered tabby walls, to keep the cotton from overheating and catching fire. Most of Swarbreck's tabby buildings were constructed between 1815 and 1819.

Swarbreck's use of tabby was encouraged by Spalding, who preferred the oyster-shell concrete to other building materials because it was strong and long lasting, and the materials to make it were readily available and free.

Swarbreck said he favored the concrete because his slaves were more comfortable in tabby cabins and the structures required less maintenance.

Swarbreck's newly imported Africans were at first given jobs making tabby that did not require special skill. They were put to work collecting oyster shells, mixing the concrete, and pouring and pounding the wet mixture into wooden forms under the supervision of experienced drivers. After about a year, the "wild" slaves were "generally tamed," according to Spalding's grandson.

When Swarbreck left Sapelo in 1827, he sold Chocolate Plantation to his agent, Dr. Charles Rogers. Rogers continued to grow sea island cotton, and he built a large tabby barn on the banks of the Mud River that was enlarged by a later owner. A west-facing window on the barn's second floor offers spectacular views of the salt marshes, tidal waterways, and the dark line of trees marking the distant mainland.

Thomas Spalding purchased Sapelo's north end in 1843 and deeded Chocolate to his newly married son, Randolph. For the next decade, the Randolph Spaldings lived at Chocolate and grew sea island cotton. When fire destroyed their house, the family moved for a time into Thomas Spalding's tabby mansion, called South End House, and later relocated to the mainland.

Howard Coffin, who purchased the bulk of Sapelo in 1912, turned Chocolate's tabby slave cabins into guest houses, converted one building to a hunting lodge, and used the others for storage. R. J. Reynolds, the tobacco magnate who later bought most of Sapelo, used one of Chocolate's tabby buildings as a stable. After Reynolds's death, the State of Georgia bought the bulk of the island. Chocolate Plantation is now part of the R. J. Reynolds Wildlife Management Area, run by the state's Department of Natural Resources. The department has stabilized Chocolate's crumbling tabby walls with bracing. State employees and volunteers try to keep vines and other weeds from crowding and damaging the tabby. Wild turkeys, feral pigs, and white-tailed deer are now Chocolate's most frequent visitors.

Getting to Chocolate is a challenge. The plantation is a bumpy seven-mile-long drive over rutted dirt roads from the state ferry dock at Marsh Landing. Tours of the island are available, and private transportation can be arranged with residents of Hog Hammock, the small Gullah Geechee community on the south end.

Bilali Muhammad, c. 1770–1857

Literacy was rare among the enslaved because teaching them to read and write was illegal. Bilali Muhammad was a well-educated multilingual Muslim before he was captured in Africa and sold in the Caribbean. Thomas Spalding found Bilali and his family there, bought them, and brought them to Sapelo.

Experts now hail Bilali as the first Muslim American scholar. Bilali's thirteen-page document, written from memory in Arabic during his decades on Sapelo, is considered the first book on Islamic jurisprudence ever penned in the Americas. It is now housed in the Hargrett Library of Rare Books, Maps, and Manuscripts at the University of Georgia in Athens.

A large sector of the slave trade focused on West Africa, including the kingdoms of Mali and Songhai, longtime centers of Islamic culture. About 20 percent of the estimated twelve million Africans captured and brought to North America as slaves were Muslim.

In his book *Sapelo's People: A Long Walk into Freedom*, the esteemed historian William S. McFeely reported that slave owners were inclined to consider Muslim slaves superior to others, in part because of their European-like facial features. Their religion forbade them to drink alcohol. In addition, most enslaved Muslims were educated and responsible. On Sapelo, Bilali and his family, according to McFeely, "held themselves aloof" from non-Muslim slaves.

Bilali Muhammad was born around 1770 in the West African city of Timbo, now in the Republic of Guinea. His family was well educated, and Bilali was instructed in several branches of Islamic study—hadith (the sayings and customs of the Prophet and his companions), sharia (Islamic law based on the Qur'an), and tafsir (explication of the Qur'an). He spoke Fula, French, and Arabic by the time he was captured and taken to a plantation in the Caribbean, where he probably learned some English. On the coast of Georgia, he acquired Gullah Geechee, the unique creole language of slaves in the coastal Southeast. Gullah Geechee is the only English-based creole spoken in the United States.

Bilali arrived on Sapelo in 1802 with his wife, Phoebe, seven daughters, and an unknown number of sons. The couple eventually had nineteen children. Thomas Spalding recognized Bilali as exceptional. He was disciplined, intelligent, literate, and dignified. He always dressed in the long black coat and red fez of his culture. During the hurricane of 1824, Bilali saved the lives of hundreds of Spalding's enslaved workers by forcing them to take refuge in sturdy tabby structures on the island.

Bilali Muhammad was a West African man enslaved by Thomas Spalding on Sapelo Island. Upon Bilali's death in 1857, it was discovered that he had written a thirteen-page Arabic manuscript transcription of a Muslim legal treatise and part of West Africa's Muslim curriculum. It is widely considered the first Islamic text written in the United States.

Spalding made Bilali his overseer, a rare position for a slave. Slave drivers were Black, but almost all overseers were white. Overseers managed the drivers, who were trusted slaves assigned to supervise the day-to-day labor of the field hands. White overseers often had reputations for brutality, drunkenness, and poor management. Bilali not only managed the plantation but also kept the account books for the Sapelo plantation. Thomas Spalding's grandson later referred to Bilali as Spalding's chief executive officer.

Bilali was a leader in Sapelo's large Muslim community, but kept himself and his family apart from slaves he called "Christian dogs." Slaves on other plantations were often forbidden to practice the religions of their home countries in Africa, but Spalding allowed Bilali and his other slaves to follow their faiths. Bilali and Phoebe prayed several times a day, kneeling on small rugs and facing east toward Mecca.

Bilali kept prayer beads and a copy of the Qur'an, and constructed a small mosque on Sapelo, perhaps the first one built in the United States. Some scholars consider Sapelo Island the home to the nation's first Islamic community.

Bilali's wife and daughters made traditional African rice cakes called saraka, which were eaten to break the fast on Muslim holy days. The cakes are still prepared by Hog Hammock residents on special occasions.

During the War of 1812, when British troops were invading the southeastern coast and liberating slaves, Spalding distributed more than eighty rifles to Bilali so that he and the other slaves could defend Sapelo against a possible British invasion. Spalding's action shocked other slave owners, but he had no qualms about trusting Bilali with guns when the Spalding family retreated to the mainland for the duration of the conflict. Bilali agreed to distribute weapons to Sapelo's Muslims but not to non-Muslims. It marked the only known instance in Georgia of slaves being armed en masse by their owner.

Especially notable is the fact that the British were offering freedom to slaves who escaped to their ships or raiding parties. Bilali and Sapelo's other slaves made no attempt to leave the island. Either Bilali forbade them to escape, or else they chose to remain on Sapelo for other reasons. One historian says the British did not raid as far north as Sapelo, so Spalding's slaves may not have had the opportunity to escape.

For many years, the brief book written by Bilali was believed to be his diary. It was translated only in recent years. He misquoted certain passages of Islamic law and misspelled words, possibly because he was captured as a schoolboy and wrote the text from memory. In places, ink bled through the pages, making the manuscript difficult to read. Bilali's book includes directions for worship under Islamic law: the call to prayer, the proper method for praying, and the method of washing before prayer.

Before he died in 1857, Bilali, then probably in his eighties, gave the document to his friend the Reverend Francis Robert Goulding of Darien, a well-known white southern writer and minister. Bilali had wrapped the book in a thin piece of leather and tied it with a leather thong. One scholar says that despite its brevity, the document carries considerable weight because it is among a very small number of original Arabic documents predating the Civil War that are now preserved in the United States.

The descendants of the Islamic slaves were usually subsumed into the majority Christian culture. For the past century or so, the nation's Muslim population has begun to rise again, albeit slowly.

Almost every resident of Sapelo's Hog Hammock community today claims kinship to Bilali. His great-great-granddaughter Cornelia Bailey, who died in 2017, was Sapelo's historian and island advocate. Her book, *God, Dr. Buzzard, and the Bolito Man*, is a memoir of growing up on the remote island in a Gullah Geechee community. Some scholars think the name Bailey may derive from "Bilali."

SITE 29

South End House

c. 1810–1812

1100 Autobahn

HISTORIC SIGNIFICANCE: The first South End House was an antebellum mansion built of tabby by Thomas Spalding, who revived the art of tabby construction on the southeastern coast. Unlike many multistory mansions of the era, Spalding's house was only a single story; it was flat-roofed and built low to the ground to weather coastal storms. In 1824, it survived a major hurricane, the worst storm ever known to hit McIntosh County.

South End House was designed by its owner, Thomas Spalding, and built by "six men, 2 boys, and two mules (one White Man Superintending) in two years," according to Spalding, who was often called the "Laird of Sapelo" because of the imprint he left on the 16,500-acre island. The men and boys Spalding referred to were his slaves. At one time, Spalding owned nearly five hundred slaves on Sapelo.

Spalding knew how he wanted his house to look and function. His first requirement was that it should endure so that it could house future generations of his family. Wooden buildings seldom lasted for more than a generation in the damp coastal environment. Spalding's thick tabby walls not only kept the mansion warm in winter and cool in summer but were also still standing a century later.

South End House featured elements of Greek, Italian, and Renaissance architecture. The finished structure was clean lined and classic. Spalding had visited Thomas Jefferson at Monticello, and his design may have been influenced by Jefferson's residence. The central part of South End House was ninety by sixty-five feet, not counting the side wings connected to the main structure by colonnaded loggias. The roof was covered with tar and sand to make it waterproof. The unroofed portico was defined by a row of six marble columns. It was one of the first large antebellum homes in Georgia and one of the few coastal mansions to feature Greek columns, which were more common in mansions on upland plantations. The thirty-foot-long portico of the front façade was recessed twenty feet deep into the central block. Windows flanked the front door, flooding the large entry hall with light. The tabby walls on either side of the portico had bull's-eye windows.

Inside, the great hall led to the rear parlor, later replaced by an indoor pool during the twentieth-century tenure of Howard Coffin, another prominent island owner. The dining room was north of the great hall; Spalding's library was on the south side. There were four bedrooms, one on

South End House, built c. 1810 and demolished c. 1912. It was replaced by a modified replica in the Palladian style, with neoclassical nods to Thomas Jefferson's Monticello.

each corner of the house. Open loggias led to the wings. The south wing was the plantation office; the north wing served as the kitchen.

The house was noted for its overall look of permanence and strength as well as for its elegant furnishings and beautiful gardens. When the roof of South End House was inspected in 1844, more than thirty years later, it was reported to be as sound as the day it was built.

The mansion was damaged during the Civil War when it was used and abused by troops and others. It sat empty until 1910, when a group of hunters from Macon partially restored it as a sporting lodge. At that point, only the marble columns and tabby walls were still standing.

Howard Coffin of Detroit bought South End House as a retreat in 1912. Coffin was a wealthy pioneer in automotive and aircraft design who founded the Hudson Motor Car Company. Coffin, along with his young cousin Alfred W. Jones, founded the upscale Cloister Hotel and cottage colony on nearby Sea Island. Using the original design, Coffin rebuilt South End House into an elegant mansion, enlarging it with a second story and a basement. By 1925, the house had reached its present-day configuration. Four marble columns now define the portico instead of the original six.

Two presidents, Calvin Coolidge and Herbert Hoover, were guests at South End House. The famed aviator Charles Lindbergh flew in for a visit in 1929. In the paranoia that followed the kidnapping of the Lindbergh baby three years later, bars were installed on the windows of the children's wing. A floor-to-ceiling wrought-iron gate leading to the wing was locked at night.

The tobacco magnate Richard J. Reynolds Jr. bought the bulk of Sapelo during the Great Depression. He modernized South End House in stages between 1934 and 1964. He decorated a room upstairs he called the Circus Room with a red-and-white-striped canopy resembling an old circus tent draping the ceiling. Murals of circus performers, wild animals, and birds, painted by the late Atlanta artist Athos Menaboni, decorate the walls. The room boasts a bowling alley, a billiards table, and a small library.

The house, which has thirteen bedrooms and eleven bathrooms, is available for group rentals.

Thomas Spalding, 1774–1851

A noted coastal planter, Thomas Spalding owned most of Sapelo Island in the early nineteenth century. He was without doubt the most enthusiastic advocate for tabby ever to build with the oyster-shell concrete. He designed and built tabby structures, devised and published a recipe for tabby, and praised its qualities in personal letters and in journals of the day. Spalding's efforts were so effective that he is credited with sparking a tabby revival on the southeastern coast that continued until the Civil War.

Spalding learned to appreciate tabby's durable qualities on neighboring St. Simons Island, where the fortified British town of Frederica was established in 1736 by Georgia's founder, James Edward Oglethorpe. Oglethorpe used tabby to build fort structures and his own residence, Orange Hall, as did other Frederica colonists.

After the Oglethorpe era, tabby fell out of favor because of an Old World superstition that persisted across the Atlantic. Masonry buildings were rumored to attract miasmas—unhealthy mists—which were thought to cause deadly diseases such as malaria (literally, "bad air" in Italian) and yellow fever. Miasmas were said to creep out of polluted swamps in warm months, the times of year when yellow fever and malaria epidemics raged through coastal cities and towns, killing hundreds, even thousands, of people. Yellow fever's mortality rate ran as high as 80 percent.

It was not until a century later that mosquitoes were identified as the disease vectors, but Spalding, a well-educated man with a logical mind, had dismissed the rumors of swamp miasmas almost a century earlier when he began building with tabby.

Spalding's parents bought Oglethorpe's tabby house on St. Simons and reared their only child there. "I was born in the town of Frederica, in one of these Tabby houses," Thomas Spalding wrote later. "I had seen time destroy everything but them: I had seen them even sawed up into blocks, like a mass of living stone; and of such blocks, carved from Frederica, are the three first stories of the lighthouse built at St. Simon's."

The first St. Simons lighthouse, built in 1810, was razed by Confederate troops retreating from a Union advance during the Civil War. The lighthouse was rebuilt after the war, but not of tabby.

In an article for the *Southern Agriculturist* in 1830, Spalding published his formula and method for making tabby. The best mix, he said, consisted of lime, sand, and shells in equal proportions—by measure rather than weight—plus enough freshwater to mix the components to the desired consistency.

Spalding pioneered the sugar industry in Georgia. He planted acres of a hardier, sweeter variety called ribbon cane. He partnered with a cane planter on the McIntosh County mainland to build Georgia's first rum distillery.

Thomas Spalding

Among Spalding's most successful tabby designs were ones for the sugar mill and adjacent boiling house he built on Sapelo. In 1816, after his sugar operation was up and running, Spalding published a treatise that discussed the cultivation and processing of sugarcane, accompanied by detailed drawings. The article, which established Spalding as the region's sugar expert, is still considered a significant document in the agricultural history of the Southeast.

A number of other planters in Georgia and Florida copied the design of Spalding's sugar mill. One, John Houstoun McIntosh, built a large mill in Camden County and refined Spalding's design. McIntosh and Spalding were first cousins.

Spalding experimented with a variety of crops and shared his expertise with other planters. Noting the dangers of single-crop farming, he wrote articles advocating crop diversity and rotation. He considered sugarcane supplementary to his plantation's primary crop: sea island cotton. With the labor of hundreds of slaves managed by his Black Muslim overseer, Spalding produced more sea island cotton than any other plantation on the coast.

During Spalding's lifetime, he was respected for a number of accomplishments. He was a founder of the Bank of Darien and served as its first president. He helped establish regional schools, served three terms in the Georgia Senate, and represented Georgia for a single term in Congress. He was a member of the state constitutional convention and was appointed a Georgia commissioner to determine the disputed boundary between Georgia and Florida, which involved trekking through swamps and dense woodlands on surveying expeditions.

In 1810, he sold land on the south tip of Sapelo for one dollar to the federal government as the site for a lighthouse. The structure, striped in red and white, was restored in recent years and is listed on the National Register of Historic Places.

To improve transportation in the region, Spalding promoted railroads and canals. He organized agricultural, cultural, charitable, and social societies.

Spalding contracted with the federal and British governments to provide wood for masts and other ship components. Live oak timbers from Sapelo and neighboring Blackbeard Island provided the frameworks for two frigates. One source says the navy sent Spalding molds, or patterns, so that boards could be cut to match them. Spalding hired Captain James Swarbreck, a sea captain and experienced ship's carpenter, to supervise the work.

When a new county was formed in Middle Georgia, it was named for Spalding. He died at age seventy-six at his mainland home, Ashantilly, in January 1851, and was buried in the Spalding family plot.

CHAPTER 10 *Savannah*

THIS CHARMING COASTAL CITY is steeped in history. It perches on a high bluff on the south bank of the Savannah River about twenty miles inland from the Atlantic Ocean. Savannah is the birthplace of Georgia.

Georgia was chartered by George II in 1732 as the thirteenth and last of North America's original British colonies. A board of trustees governed the new colony.

In 1733, James Edward Oglethorpe, a British philanthropist, sailed from London to deliver the first group of colonists to the site he had selected for Savannah. By that time, Georgia's coastal Natives, the Guale and Mocama people, were long gone. So were the Franciscan friars who had established Spanish missions along the Georgia coast to convert the Indigenous people to Catholicism.

Native peoples in the coastal Southeast, the first part of North America settled after contact, bore the brunt of the Euro-African invasion. Thousands, perhaps hundreds of thousands, died of common European and African diseases, enforced labor, or conflict with the foreigners and one another as they fought for survival in a catastrophically changed world.

When Oglethorpe arrived, the coast had been depopulated of its Native people by the Yamasee War of 1715. A mixed group of Lower Creeks and Yamasees occupied the bluff where Oglethorpe planned to site Savannah. The Lower Creeks, who lived inland, still claimed the Georgia coast and went there to hunt and fish. Oglethorpe negotiated for land with the Yamacraw leader Tomochichi, aided by the half-Creek, half-Scottish translator and trader Mary Musgrove.

Oglethorpe and William Bull of Carolina laid out Savannah in the style of an English town, with numerous green squares. Lots on the east and west sides of the squares were reserved for churches and public buildings; residences were located to the north and south.

The British king envisioned Georgia as a buffer between British Carolina and Spanish Florida. Georgia would also protect British territory from the French in Louisiana. Spain, which initially claimed a vast territory in North America, had been pushed south by British expansion almost to the Florida Peninsula. Savannah's original boundary stretched about fifty miles south from the Savannah River to the north bank of the Altamaha River.

Oglethorpe, a social reformer and idealist as well as a soldier, planned to populate Georgia with debtors imprisoned in England. One of his good friends had died in debtor's prison in London. Colonists who became merchants and businessmen would settle in town, while farmers would be granted acreage in the countryside. Oglethorpe's plan to populate Georgia with debtors was expanded to include England's "deserving poor." As it turned out, only a handful of Georgia's first settlers were poor, deserving or otherwise. Most were solidly middle class.

A number of houses and other buildings in Savannah's large National Register Historic District date to the colonial era. The city's design is considered an outstanding example of eighteenth-century municipal planning in North America.

When Georgia was founded, the trustees banned Catholics, Jews, and Frenchmen as well as slavery. A group of Jewish colonists who arrived in the colony's early days were allowed to stay, however. A decade later, Georgians were lobbying to legalize slavery. Their Carolina neighbors were making fortunes by growing rice and indigo with slave labor. Georgia's ban on slavery was lifted in 1750. Wealthy planters from Carolina and the West Indies, their lands worn out from continual heavy planting, rushed to obtain land grants and establish large plantations in and around Savannah. Enslaved laborers in rice fields toiled in brutal conditions in the marshy delta fields, where untold numbers died of illness, injuries, and overwork.

At the start of the American Revolution, most Georgians sided with the British. Savannah's Liberty Boys, on the other hand, supported the Patriot cause. In addition to raiding British munitions stores and staging other acts of rebellion, they tarred and feathered a "disrespectful" Loyalist and paraded him through the streets of Savannah. Three of the Liberty Boys signed the Declaration of Independence.

During the war, Georgia Loyalists fled to Spanish Florida, Caribbean islands, or other British-friendly locales, abandoning their businesses and plantations. Some were granted amnesty after the war and returned to become U.S. citizens. Savannah became Georgia's first state capital.

After the war, planters were introduced to a strain of Caribbean cotton that flourished only near the coast. Silky sea island cotton brought top prices in European markets and made the planters rich. Rice and cotton were Savannah's economic mainstays. The town became an international shipping port. Cotton factors' warehouses, now converted to restaurants, shops, and picturesque inns, still line Bay Street, the main thoroughfare along the Savannah River's upper bluff, and the cobblestoned River Street along the lower bluff.

General Nathanael Greene, commander of the Patriot forces in the South, was granted Mulberry Grove plantation in Savannah for his Revolutionary War service. Eli Whitney was staying at the plantation when he invented the cotton gin, which allowed inland growers to increase production. By ramping up the demand for African slaves, and thereby keeping alive the hope of slavery's expansion, the widespread use of the cotton gin contributed to the coming of the Civil War.

The first steamship to cross the Atlantic from the United States to Europe was the ss *Savannah*, which debarked from the Georgia coast in 1819 and made the trip in a record twenty-nine days. The Central of Georgia Railway, which ran from Savannah to Macon, allowed huge quantities of cotton to be transported from Middle Georgia to the port.

Many free Blacks in Savannah became successful businessmen, farmers, landowners, and even slaveholders. By 1860, Savannah had become Georgia's largest city, and one of America's most beautiful. During the Civil War, when the Union general William Tecumseh Sherman blazed a trail through Georgia from Atlanta to the coast, he did not burn Savannah. (His reason: the city had no military value.) Instead, he jokingly presented it to President Abraham Lincoln as a Christmas gift.

The Reconstruction period in Savannah was difficult, especially for thousands of freed slaves who flocked to the city in search of work. High rents forced most of them to live in squalid conditions. Although northern teachers provided education for Black children, Savannah's first public school for Blacks was not established until 1878.

The Girl Scouts of America were founded in 1912 by the Savannah resident Juliette Gordon Low.

As Savannah's port expanded in order to ship naval stores as well as cotton, the city prospered. During the 1920s, boll weevils destroyed southern cotton crops, ending the region's cotton economy. New industries opened, including a sugar-processing plant and pulp and paper companies. The military established Hunter Army Airfield in Savannah as a branch of the sprawling Fort Stewart Army Post in nearby Hinesville.

Historic tourism is now an economic mainstay of Savannah. Hundreds of lovely houses and public buildings have been carefully restored in the colonial and Victorian districts. Savannah's National Historic Landmark District constitutes one of America's largest urban preservation programs of its kind. John Berendt's gossipy best-selling book *Midnight in the Garden of Good and Evil* still lures visitors to the old coastal town.

Wormsloe State Historic Site

c. 1737–1739

7601 Skidaway Road

National Register of Historic Places

HISTORIC SIGNIFICANCE: Wormsloe's fortified tabby home is the oldest standing structure in Savannah, and among the oldest in Georgia. It was built by one of Georgia's first British settlers, Noble Jones. Wormsloe is unique for being the only tract of land in Georgia owned by the same family from the time of British colonization in 1733 to the present.

Sprawling over more than eight hundred acres about ten miles southeast of downtown Savannah, the Wormsloe State Historic Site is a tidewater treasure. The oldest of Georgia's coastal plantations, Wormsloe is located on the Isle of Hope, which is actually a mile-wide peninsula about four miles long, flanked by tidal marshes and brackish waterways.

The first owner of the property, Noble Jones, was one of the 114 original English settlers who traveled to America with James Edward Oglethorpe on his mission to found the new colony of Georgia. Jones was granted a town lot in Savannah, and he leased five hundred untamed acres on the Isle of Hope as well as a smaller hammock, or marsh island, nearby. He later received a grant to the Wormsloe tract. Over time, he added more acreage to the property.

Wormsloe is one of the few large coastal plantations that has never been subdivided and developed. "Plantation" is probably a misnomer; Wormsloe was always a country estate in the British style more than a major agricultural operation. Jones was interested in horticulture rather than the mass production of row crops such as corn and cotton, and some of his descendants have continued to cultivate impressive gardens. At one time, Wormsloe's gardens were a tourist attraction, open to the public.

Wormsloe's maritime forest bears little resemblance today to the one that covered the eighteenth-century site. All the old-growth pine was killed by beetles during the 1970s. Researchers from the University of Georgia are conducting ongoing studies that include soil analysis, archaeological digs, and historical investigations in order to profile the ecology of the area over time.

The remains of Jones' fortified tabby home display a combination of European military and residential design. The rectangular residence was thirty-two feet long

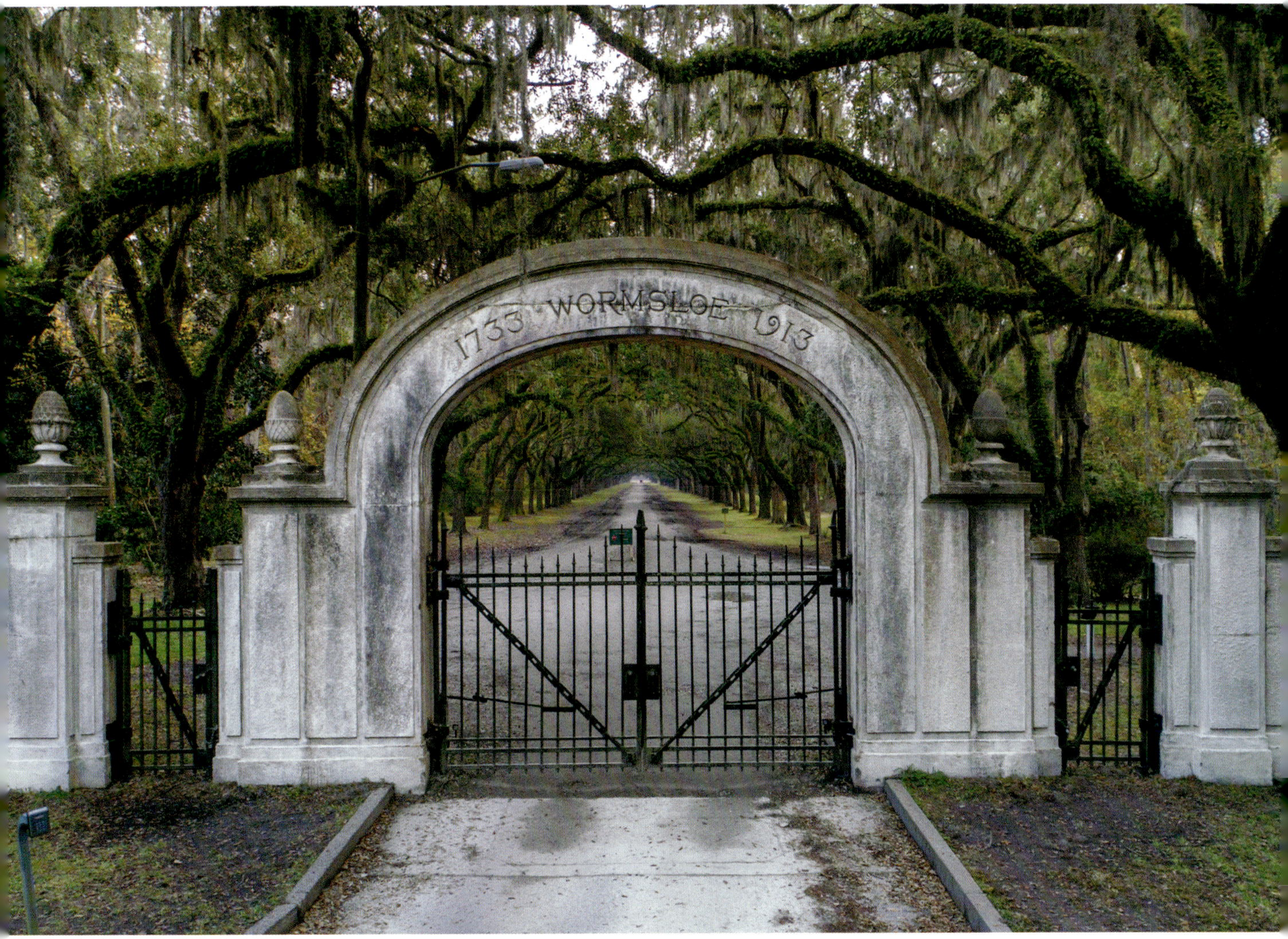
1733 WORMSLOE 1913

by twenty-four feet wide, about twice as large as the earliest Savannah houses. It was probably built in the roomier Georgian style, which Jones would have been familiar with in England. The structure may have had dormers and a catslide, or shed-style, roof, both common features of Georgian buildings.

For almost three centuries, Wormsloe has been connected with the wider world of national and international commerce, culture, and conflict. It was built primarily as a defense against the Spanish in Florida. Spain and Great Britain had long been involved in a fierce struggle to occupy land in North America. By the 1730s, the Spanish—who at one time claimed a vast territory that stretched from Newfoundland west to the Mississippi River—had been pushed south along the Atlantic Seaboard to the Florida Peninsula by British expansionism. Spain nonetheless still posed a significant threat to British settlements in the Carolinas as well as to the new town of Savannah.

Jones built his fortified tabby home in a strategic location overlooking tidal marshes and the Skidaway River narrows, originally named the Jones Narrows for him. Tidal waterways change course over time; in the 1730s, the Skidaway River provided access to Savannah's waterfront and could have offered a back door for a sneak attack on the fledgling city. Wormsloe was designed to prevent just such an assault. Ancient shell middens on the tract provided the raw material for tabby.

The original home built by Noble Jones was part of the tabby fortification. On three sides, the fort's eight-foot-high curtain walls surrounded the house and a parade ground or courtyard. Bastions at the four corners probably had raised shooting platforms. A recessed part of the east curtain wall provided entry to the fortress and to the five-room, story-and-a-half tabby house where Jones and his family lived. The house was floored with tabby. The curtain walls were pierced with openings so that Jones and his troops could fire at approaching enemies. An early observer described the fortification in an article published in 1745 in London as "a tolerable defensible Place with small Arms."

A brick well located partially under the west curtain wall indicates that the well was built before the fort, possibly by Jones when he cleared land and gathered materials to make tabby. The well was the only known source of freshwater at the site. When the curtain wall over the well was constructed, the builders made sure that the well shaft, where water was drawn, was inside the courtyard. In that way, the well would be out of enemy reach and accessible to Jones's family members and to the small garrison of colonial marines stationed at Wormsloe.

When the naturalist John Bartram visited Wormsloe in 1765, he described the house as "delightfully situated on a large tide salt creek where ye oisters is as thich as they can be within a stone's cast of his house."

The ten marines under Jones's command lived in wattle-and-daub huts around the tabby fort, close enough to take up arms inside if danger threatened. The same huts were later occupied by Wormsloe's slaves.

To improve Wormsloe's function as a defensive post, Jones directed the construction of a wooden watch house on nearby Pine Island—now Pigeon Island—where the marines' scout boat was kept.

William M. Kelso, an archaeologist who surveyed Wormsloe during the late 1960s, said the tabby plantation structure with its defenses "is one of the few, if not the only, remaining examples of fortified domestic architecture more typical of coastal Georgia than has been formerly recognized." Kelso's book, *Captain Jone's Wormslow: A Historical, Archaeological, and Architectural Study of an Eighteenth-Century Plantation near Savannah, Georgia* (1979), presents an expert's detailed view of the property. The title of the book echoes the spelling of the property's original name, Wormslow, which was probably taken from the ancestral home of the Jones family on the Welsh border in the English county of Herefordshire at a site called Wormslow Hundred.

A mile-long avenue of four hundred live oaks was planted during the nineteenth century. Oak Avenue leads from Wormsloe's arched front gate past the turnoff to the private property and on to the park's visitor center and parking area. The twisted branches of the oak trees form a shady canopy over the unpaved road.

During the Civil War, Confederate troops built earthworks on the southern tip of Wormsloe to guard the Moon River, a name that later became familiar in song. The song, which is featured in the now-classic 1961 film *Breakfast at Tiffany's*, has music by Henry Mancini and lyrics by Johnny Mercer, a Savannah native who was familiar with the river.

Noble Jones, 1702–1775

The July 11, 1765, issue of the *Georgia Gazette* reported that a number of people had gone to Noble Jones's estate to see "an Agave plant, now in blossom there, which is said to be 27 and a half feet high, and had 33 branches, which contain a vast number of blossoms."

Jones was a man of many talents. He served the colony as a doctor, carpenter, constable, Indian agent, royal councilor, and surveyor. He laid out the towns of Augusta and New Ebenezer and platted new roads for the colony. He commanded a garrison of marines and led them into battle against the Spanish. Jones was also a horticulturalist and an early environmentalist. When he served as a provincial ranger, he refused to let anyone cut slow-growing cypress or live oak trees without a permit.

Wormsloe was never planted as extensively as other large coastal tracts. Jones cultivated traditional row crops on property he purchased inland, but at Wormsloe he concentrated on vegetable and fruit trees, including oranges, figs, pomegranates, peaches, and apricots.

Like the other original Georgia colonists, Jones was encouraged to grow white mulberry trees to feed silkworms. Oglethorpe thought his colonists could raise silkworms, unravel the cocoons—a tedious task done by hand—and produce silk for England, thus saving British textile merchants the expense of importing silk from China. Although Georgians produced more than enough material to make a dress for the queen, the silk project was not a success.

Wormsloe was not profitable as a plantation. Jones earned money from his medical services, his work as a constable, and his duties as a ranger and a soldier. He made his wealth by investing in real estate. He eventually owned about fifty-five hundred acres in and around Savannah, including five town lots in the coastal city.

Portrait of Noble Wimberly Jones,
Rembrandt Peale, c. 1804

Jones was an active member of Oglethorpe's forces. In 1740, he and his marines joined a raiding party led by Oglethorpe against the Spanish at St. Augustine. British ships shelled the Castillo de San Marcos for more than a month without ever breaching the fort's coquina-and-tabby walls. In 1742, when the Spanish retaliated against Oglethorpe at Fort Frederica on St. Simons Island, Jones and his marines again joined British troops to defend the island. Oglethorpe's greatly outnumbered soldiers turned back the invaders at two small but significant battles on St. Simons.

Noble Jones died at the beginning of the Revolutionary War, a Loyalist to the end. His son Noble Wymberly Jones joined the Patriot cause. Noble Jones left his property to his son Wymberly and his heirs in perpetuity.

The original tabby residence at Wormslow (as it was then spelled) was occupied by three generations of the Jones family. The house was razed in the 1830s, and the rubble was used in the construction of a new house farther north on the property. The new residence, Wormsloe House, was a frame structure built on a tabby basement. George Jones, Noble Jones's grandson, built the new house, which has since been enlarged and remodeled many times. It bears only a slight resemblance to the house built by George Jones. Now located on fifty acres of private property adjacent to the historic site, it is still occupied by Jones family descendants and is not open to the public.

George Frederick Tilghman Jones, the son of the George Jones who built Wormsloe House, changed his name to George Wymberly Jones De Renne. At the same time, he changed the spelling of the name of the property to Wormsloe. Wimberly Jones De Renne planted the live oaks, now grown to giant trees, that flank Oak Avenue.

A number of Jones family members collected rare books, maps, and near-priceless historic documents, many related to Wormsloe's past. The collection grew to the point that the family had a separate library constructed near Wormsloe House to store the material. The fireproof structure was ornamented with Greek columns. The bulk of the collection was later sold to collectors and institutions such as the University of Georgia.

Elfrida De Renne Barrow created the nonprofit Wormsloe Foundation, which publishes primary and secondary source material related to Georgia history. (Elfrida cowrote *Anchored Yesterdays*, a history of Savannah; see the section on William Greaner Haynes Jr. in Site 26: Ashantilly.) She presented 750 acres of Wormsloe to the foundation in 1961. After a 1970 court decision revoked the foundation's tax-exempt status, the property was purchased by the Nature Conservancy in 1972 and transferred the following year to the State of Georgia. The historic site opened in 1979.

SITE 31   *Short Take*

Fort Pulaski National Monument

1847

U.S. 80

The attack on Fort Pulaski near Savannah during the Civil War changed the way wars were fought and forts were built.

The Confederate-held fort on Cockspur Island guarded the entrance to Savannah's port. Isolated from Tybee Island by tidal marshes across the Savannah River, the brick fort was considered impregnable. Its walls were backed by massive masonry piers. Ammunition was stored underground in tabby bunkers that extended beyond the fort's walls. The chief of the U.S. Army Corps of Engineers commented on the futility of attacking Fort Pulaski: "You might as well bombard the Rocky Mountains."

The only place to set up a Union battery was on Tybee Island, a mile away. Traditional cannon and mortars had no chance of breaking through Pulaski's walls at a distance of more than one thousand yards. General Robert E. Lee reassured Pulaski's young commander, Charles Olmstead, that the fort would withstand the expected attack.

But the Union commander on Tybee, Captain Quincy A. Gillmore, opted to test the army's new experimental weapon: cannons with rifled barrels. Rifling consists of grooves machined into the inside of the gun's barrel to spin and stabilize the projectile, making it more accurate over long distances.

The bombardment began early in April 1862. After a day of shelling, most of Pulaski's guns had been dismounted, and one wall was almost down. On the second day, Union cannons blasted two huge holes through the fort's walls and killed several soldiers. Fearing that shells would hit the ammunition bunkers and blow up the fort, Olmstead surrendered in order to save the lives of his troop. He was criticized until reports of the rifled guns spread.

The Pulaski assault marked the first time that rifled guns were used in combat. The new weapons rendered existing coastal defenses obsolete. As one Union general said, "No works of stone or brick can resist the impact of rifled artillery of heavy calibre."

207

SITE 32

Owens-Thomas House

1816–1819

124 Abercorn Street

National Historic Landmark

HISTORIC SIGNIFICANCE: The tabby mansion is considered one of the finest examples of English Regency architecture in the United States. Designed by the famed British architect William Jay, it features advanced technology of the time, including a modern plumbing system that predated the one at the White House. Tabby walls flank the garden between the tabby slave quarters and carriage house.

The Owens-Thomas House was built for Richard Richardson, a wealthy Savannah bank president, slave trader, entrepreneur, and shipping merchant whose brother-in-law was married to the sister of the architect William Jay. At the time, Jay was a rising star in England, and Richardson's house was his first commission in the United States.

Not long after the residence was completed in 1819, Richardson lost it and his fortune in the panic that followed a series of bank failures. A yellow fever epidemic at the same time killed large numbers of Savannah residents, and a fire destroyed half the city. After Richardson's wife and two of his children died, he relocated what was left of his family to New Orleans.

His elegant house was purchased by Durham Hall, who lost it to the bank shortly afterward. The bank leased the house to Mary Maxwell, an enterprising widow with three children whose husband's death left her without income. Needing to support her family, she ran the place for eight years as a fashionable boardinghouse, akin to the elegant bed-and-breakfasts now located in Savannah's large National Register Historic District.

Maxwell was a lively, imaginative woman whose boardinghouse was known not only for its beauty and comfort but also for the sparkling conversations she encouraged among her guests. The marquis de Lafayette, a French nobleman who fought in the Revolutionary War on the side of the Patriots, boarded at Maxwell's for three nights during his 1825 tour of the United States on the fiftieth anniversary of the war. He arrived in Savannah with his son, Georges Washington Lafayette, and two of the large French briard herding dogs he bred. One was named Quiz.

Lafayette spoke from the home's ornate cast-iron balcony to an admiring crowd that had gathered on the sidewalk. He delivered his address twice: once in English and

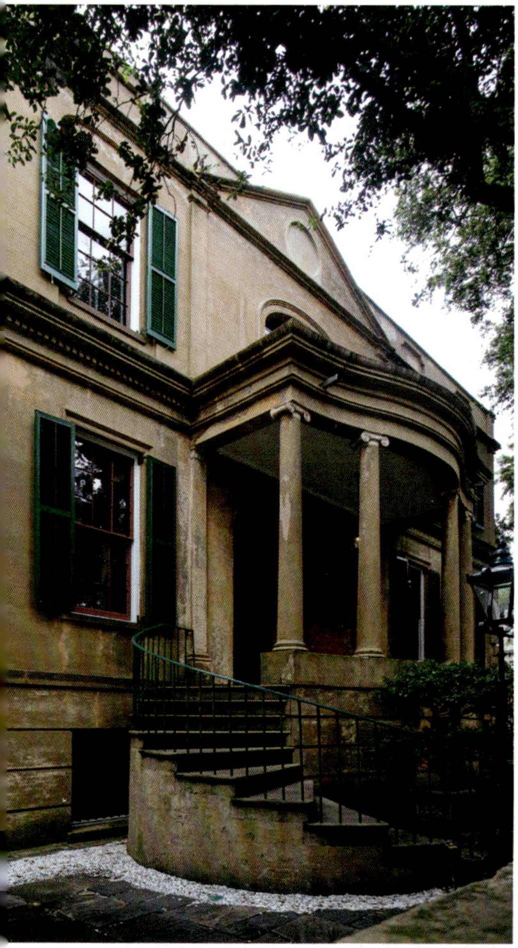

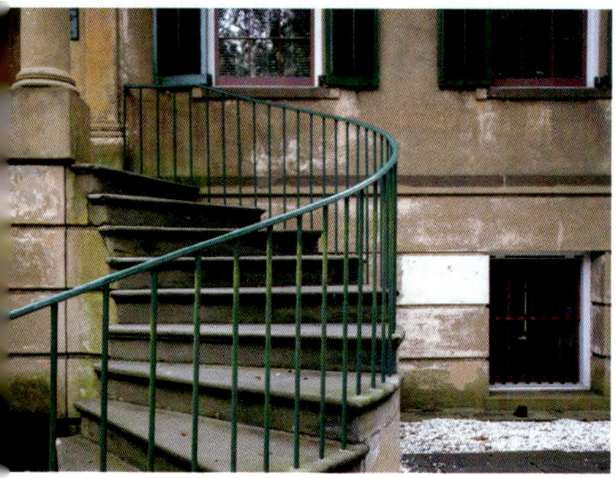

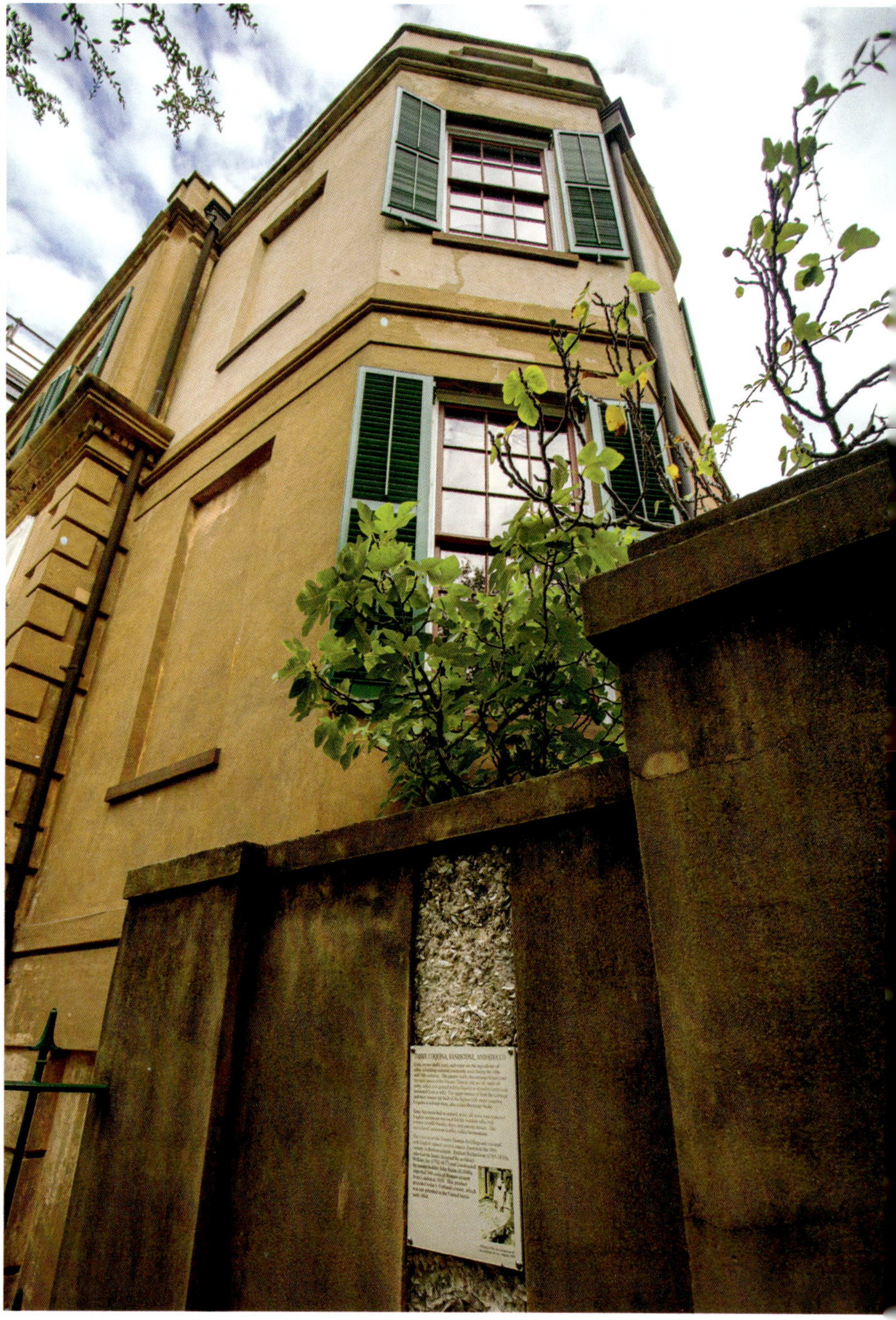

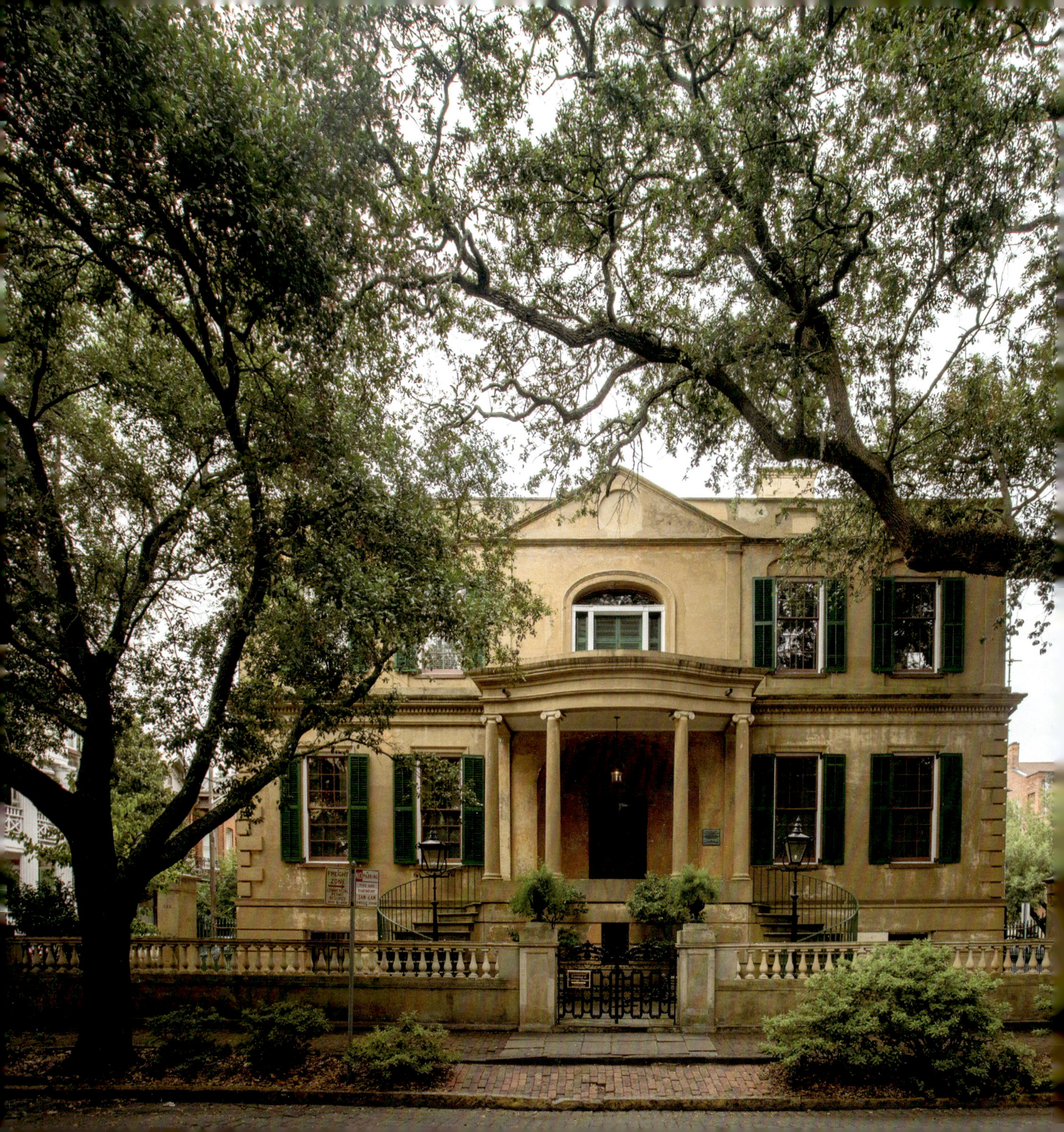
FREIGHT ZONE
NO PARKING
TUESDAY

once in French. The balcony was the first large structure of cast iron used in a building in the United States. Jay had had it shipped in pieces from England and put together on the building site. It may have inspired Savannah's long tradition of using cast iron and wrought iron for architectural ornamentation. Many of the city's historic buildings feature elaborate ironwork. Jay used iron for floor joists, columns, shutters, and windows in the Owens-Thomas House to give the structure additional strength and aesthetic appeal.

The third time the home was sold was the charm for its owner, George Welshman Owens, a Savannah attorney. Educated in England at Harrow and at Cambridge University, Owens served as a state legislator and senator, a congressman, and mayor of Savannah. He bought the property in 1830 for ten thousand dollars. His family occupied the house for the next 121 years. Owens owned several other houses in Savannah, plantations in North Georgia and South Georgia, and a plantation on St. Catherines Island.

His granddaughter Margaret Gray Thomas, the property's last private owner, willed it to the Telfair Museum of Arts and Science, established in the late 1800s. Thomas dedicated the gift in memory of her grandfather and father, a prominent Savannah doctor. Margaret Thomas died in 1951; the house opened to the public in 1954.

The Owens-Thomas House is an architectural and technological marvel. A pair of tabby cisterns in the attic could hold two thousand gallons of rainwater. Water moved throughout the house via gravity, including to the two rare indoor toilets. The cisterns fed water to another large tabby cistern in the basement that supplied water for the bathing chamber, laundry, scullery, and kitchen. To support the weight of the attic cisterns, the tabby walls of the first floor are twelve to eighteen inches thick; the raised basement's tabby walls are up to two feet thick. The basement may have been constructed on an earlier tabby structure built by William DeBraham, one of two royal surveyors who worked in Georgia in the 1700s.

The second floor walls are built of blocks of coquina, a semi-rare shellstone mined on the Atlantic coast of Florida. Coquina is lighter than tabby. Tabby mortar was used to lay the blocks.

Other architectural innovations include rooms designed in unusual shapes and of nontraditional materials. The large dining room was designed in the shape of a *D* with an amber window that bathes the room in a golden glow. William Jay's design for the house featured niches, demilunes for statuary, indoor column screens, and a unique bridge that connects the upstairs rooms.

Rooms feature period furniture, ornaments, and glorious decorative faux-painted marble Corinthian columns, painted sailcloth that mimics inlaid marble floors in the front entryway, and faux-painted oak walls. A flat ceiling is painted to create the illusion of a dome. The four-room master suite includes a bedroom, a bathing room originally fitted with a marble bathtub, a flush toilet, and a dressing room.

Brass inserts on the original mahogany stair rails and treads at one time reflected candlelight and helped illuminate the curved double stairway that bifurcates the second story. Jay designed an unusual bridge over the stairwell to provide access between the front and rear rooms of the upper floor. The bridge was the only one of its kind in the United States at the time.

The house occupies an entire block on Oglethorpe Square, one of the many lovely green spaces laid out under the direction of Oglethorpe.

The quarters once designed for house slaves occupy half a sizable two-story tabby structure at the rear of the back garden. The other half once accommodated horses and carriages. The first floor of the slave quarters, furnished as it might have been, has a coal-burning fireplace for heat; slaves cooked and ate in the main house. The ceiling of the quarters retains faded traces of the blue paint made from buttermilk, indigo, and lime used by the Gullah Geechee occupants to prevent evil spirits they called haints, or haunts, from entering. The color of the paint is still known as haint blue on the coast. The ceiling of the Owens-Thomas slave dwelling is the largest known that still retains its haint-blue ceiling. The loft of the slave quarters serves today as workspace for Telfair experts to study and interpret historic documents, artifacts, and other materials.

Experts have studied the lives of the enslaved workers who occupied the quarters, exploring the complex relationships between them and their owners. The researchers found that lives of urban slaves were very different from those of plantation slaves. Urban slaves may have had some freedom to move around the city and interact with other slaves and free Blacks. They had better access to material goods and were probably better informed about societal and political trends than their rural counterparts. After the Civil War, servants occupied the old slave quarters.

William Jay, c. 1792–1837

William Jay, who became Savannah's premier architect, was born in the English city of Bath to a family of stonemasons. He trained for several years in the classical style of architecture in London and later designed one of the city's iconic buildings: the neoclassical Albion Chapel in Moorgate. The square chapel has a recessed entry and a dome similar to that of the Pantheon, the famed temple to the gods in Rome. Jay was in his midtwenties in 1816 when he designed the structure.

Through a family connection, Jay received a commission that same year to design an elaborate home for Richard Richardson, one of the wealthiest residents of Savannah. It was his first commission in the coastal city but not his last.

Jay was the first professionally trained architect in the United States when he arrived in Savannah in 1817, and he became the city's resident architect. He had already sent plans for the Richardson house to the builder, who started construction a year before Jay arrived to oversee the project. Slaves and freedmen worked for three years to build the elaborate mansion.

Now called the Owens-Thomas House, the residence was the first of several fine neoclassical homes that Jay designed in Savannah. For the exterior walls, he had three coats of tabby-lime stucco stained a honey color and scored to look like the ashlar stone used in buildings in Bath. The pale stucco exterior of the mansion formed a sharp contrast to the traditional redbrick Federal style of many of its Savannah neighbors.

When Jay first arrived in Georgia, Savannah was a rich southern city. It was home to cotton merchants, planters, bankers, and other wealthy citizens. Many wanted to display their wealth and status by building imposing houses. The Regency style favored by Jay, modeled after sophisticated English townhomes, was admired by Savannahians who maintained close economic and social ties with England even after the American Revolution. Georgians were never passionate supporters of the Patriot cause. Most endorsed the struggle for independence out of sympathy for the other twelve American colonies in rebellion.

During his tenure in the city, Jay designed several private houses in the fashionable neoclassical style for some of the city's most prominent residents: William Scarbrough, Alexander Telfair, and the son and namesake of Archibald Bulloch, the first nonroyal governor of Georgia. Jay is sometimes credited with designing the Juliette Gordon Low House. As every Girl Scout knows, Gordon Low founded the Girl Scouts of America in Savannah.

Portrait of William Jay, William Etty, c. 1815–17

The Scarborough House is now home to the Historic Savannah Foundation, and the Telfair House is part of the Telfair Museums complex.

The Bulloch House was demolished a century after its construction by the city of Savannah, which replaced the historic mansion with a civic auditorium. The auditorium was razed during the 1970s, and a larger civic center was built in its place. The center's parking lot occupies part of the area where the Bulloch House once stood.

Jay designed the Savannah Theatre and the Savannah branch of the Bank of the United States. The bank featured a distinctive portico in what is called hexastyle, with six Doric columns. It was Jay's final commission in Savannah.

During his seven years in America, Jay worked across the Savannah River in South Carolina, too. He designed buildings in Columbia and Charleston and was appointed the official architect of the state's Board of Public Works, in charge of designing courthouses and jails.

After leaving his mark on the American Southeast, Jay returned to England in 1822. He married in London, and the couple had three children.

Jay designed a large, six-apartment row house called the Pittville Parade. The speculative development failed in 1829, and Jay was forced to declare bankruptcy in 1836. The bankruptcy forced him to take a job as a civil engineer and colonial architect on Mauritius, a British crown colony off the coast of Madagascar in the Indian Ocean. He died there the following year and was buried on the island.

PART III *South Carolina*

THE LOWCOUNTRY AND SEA ISLANDS of the Palmetto State were first occupied by people of the Late Archaic period about five thousand years ago. Like their counterparts in other parts of the coastal Southeast, the people fished and hunted in the estuaries and woodlands.

When the first Europeans arrived, in the 1500s, Carolina was occupied by twenty-nine Native chiefdoms, some of whose names are preserved in locales such as Edisto Island and the PeeDee, Catawba, and Santee Rivers. The Shawnee, Chicora, and Cherokee were also native to Carolina. Some of the groups remain culturally united in the state today.

In 1562, French Huguenots hoping to escape Catholic persecution at home built Fort Caroline in Florida and Charlesfort on Parris Island off the South Carolina coast, both in territory that had earlier been claimed by Spain. Charlesfort lasted less than a year; soldiers stationed there constructed a makeshift open boat and set off across the Atlantic toward France, though lacking both navigation experience and equipment. Before they were rescued, their boat had become becalmed, and they drew lots to see which one would be eaten by the others. The rest fared better than their Florida counterparts, most of whom were slaughtered by Spaniards.

The site on Parris Island was reoccupied in 1566 by Spanish colonists, who built a fort on top of Charlesfort's remains. They founded the town of Santa Elena, the first European colonial capital in what became the United States. The blend of French and Spanish artifacts found at the Parris Island site confounded modern investigators for decades until ongoing archaeological investigations unearthed the French fort and successive Spanish forts, along with portions of Santa Elena.

Almost a century later, Charles I of England granted the territory that became Carolina to eight lords proprietors to whom he owed money. The proprietors founded Charles Town in 1670 near the present-day site of Charleston.

Sites

HILTON HEAD ISLAND
33 Stoney-Baynard Plantation

ST. HELENA ISLAND
34 St. Helena Chapel of Ease

PORT ROYAL
35 Fort Frederick Hertiage Preserve

PARRIS ISLAND
36 Charlesfort–Santa Elena Site

BEAUFORT
37 Seawall
38 Arsenal
39 John Mark Verdier House
40 Parish Church of St. Helena
41 Barnwell-Gough House
42 Saltus-Habersham House
43 Old Baptist Meeting House
44 Tabby Manse

EDISTO ISLAND
45 Botany Bay Plantation
46 First Missionary Baptist Church

CHARLESTON
47 Horn Work

DORCHESTER
48 Fort

The Yamasees traded extensively with the English colonists, supplying them with deerskins and Native slaves. Conflicts between Natives and the colonists who cheated them, enslaved them, and took their land led to the Yamasees War (1715–17). The English prevailed, but the colony was almost destroyed.

Coastal towns and plantations were isolated by Carolina's geography. Rivers emptying into the Atlantic helped create dozens of barrier islands as well as hundreds of marsh islands called hammocks, large and small. A great deepwater sound named Porte Royale by the first French settlers plunges deep into the heart of Beaufort County, bifurcating it into northern and southern sectors. In lieu of making arduous weekly boat trips to attend mainland churches, planters worshiped nearby in small chapels of ease. The tabby chapel of ease near Beaufort boasts an unusual feature: an unsupported tabby arch.

After the Yamasee War, planters abandoned the practice of enslaving Native people in favor of importing African slaves to grow indigo and rice. Slave labor made South Carolina the wealthiest colony in British North America, and Charleston its richest city. By 1720, enslaved people of color greatly outnumbered the colony's free white population.

With the help of a free Black man from the Caribbean, a resourceful Carolina teenager boosted the colonial economy by learning to process indigo plants into a deep blue dye. The dye was so popular that England paid the colonists a subsidy for it.

When Great Britain taxed the colonies for tea, paper, wine, glass, and oil, Carolina colonists were outraged. Protestors staged a tea party in Charleston Harbor similar to the famous one in Boston. South Carolina was an active battleground between Patriots and the British during the Revolutionary War. More battles were fought there than in any other American colony. Francis Marion, the notorious Swamp Fox, used guerrilla tactics learned from Native Americans to defeat British troops.

After the revolution, a number of coastal planters abandoned worn-out lands and moved to Georgia, where slavery had been legalized in 1750. They became even wealthier by growing sea island cotton with enslaved labor. The silky, long-staple cotton fares best near the Atlantic Ocean, which moderates the climate and allows for a long growing season.

The rich planters built elegant summer townhomes in Beaufort and Charleston to escape the disease-carrying mosquitoes that plagued their coastal plantations in warmer months.

The first shots of the Civil War were fired in South Carolina when Confederate troops attacked a federal fort in Charleston Harbor. Most of the coast, with the exception of Charleston, was captured by northern troops early in the conflict. The Union soldiers confiscated some of the finest homes in Beaufort to use as hospitals for wounded troops, Black and white. A female doctor-abolitionist from the North wrote in detail about her experiences with treating Black patients in Beaufort.

The war ended South Carolina's agricultural economy. Black and white residents on the coast survived on subsistence farming, fishing, and, later, working on military bases in the region. Tourism is now a primary coastal industry. Sea islands such as Hilton Head and Pawleys Island lure visitors from all over the world.

CHAPTER 11   *Hilton Head Island*

ABOUT A DOZEN MILES LONG and an average of five miles wide, Hilton Head Island floats in the Atlantic like a bottle flung into the sea off the coast of South Carolina, its narrow mouth tilted toward the mainland. The wider part of the bottle is flanked by Port Royal Sound to the northeast; the southwest end faces Calibogue Sound and Daufuskie Island.

The island was home to Native people during the Late Archaic period, at least four thousand years ago. They and their descendants ate huge quantities of oysters and built four giant shell rings with the empty shells, for practical or ceremonial purposes, or both. Two of the shell rings still exist on Hilton Head: one in the Sea Pines Forest Preserve, accessible by hiking trails, and a younger ring, the Green's Shell Enclosure Heritage Preserve at 99 Squire Pope Road on Skull Creek, which is protected by the National Trust for Historic Preservation. The other two rings were destroyed by European settlers and later occupants, who used the clean, dry shells to make tabby and pave sandy island roads.

In 1521, Spanish explorers were the first known Europeans to visit the island, but they settled farther south on the Georgia coast in 1526. Huguenots (French Protestants) fleeing persecution in largely Catholic Europe settled on nearby Parris Island in 1562, but abandoned the area after less than a year because of food shortages and hostile natives.

In 1663, the English sea captain William Hilton sailed from Barbados in search of good land along the southeastern coast where West Indies planters could expand. In his journal, he described the island's sandy bluffs, which became known as Hilton's headlands, later shortened to Hilton Head.

John Bayley was granted several islands and a chunk of the mainland by William III of England in 1698. It was collectively called Bayley's Barony. Hilton Head was briefly renamed Trench's Island for Bayley's agent, who collected leasing fees.

In 1717, the famed Colonel John "Tuscarora Jack" Barnwell, an Irish immigrant who fought Tuscarora Indians in North Carolina, became the first European to settle on Hilton Head. For his efforts in the war, he received a grant of one thousand acres on the island's north end. Barnwell was among the founders of Beaufort. In 1721, he established Fort King George on the Altamaha delta in present-day Darien, Georgia, as an outpost against the Spanish in Florida. Two of Barnwell's grandsons, Robert and Edward, built a four-story tabby mansion in Beaufort that they shared. Edward had the more expensive taste; his side of the duplex was more elegant and cost twice as much to build as Robert's side. Nicknamed Barnwell Castle, the massive structure served during the Civil War as a hospital and as housing for Union officers. It later became a courthouse before it burned in the late 1800s. A new courthouse was built on the tabby foundation of the old one.

During the early 1700s, planters on Hilton Head grew indigo and rice. In 1790, William Elliott grew the first crop of sea island cotton on the island. Elliott and his neighbor Will Seabrook developed a new fertilizer that resulted in record crop yields. By the time the Civil War broke out, twenty-four plantations on Hilton Head were growing sea island cotton as well as smaller amounts of sugarcane, indigo, rice, and vegetables.

Union troops landed en masse on Hilton Head on November 7, 1861, just six months after the start of the Civil War. In the next five hours, twelve thousand Union soldiers and sailors captured Fort Walker on Hilton Head and Fort Beauregard near Beaufort. Island families fled inland, many taking their slaves with them. Hilton Head became a staging ground for Union ships blockading Charleston and Savannah. Enslaved people on the island, many with only the possessions in their gunnysacks, took refuge at the Union encampment. A year later, at least six hundred liberated slaves were living in Union contraband camps on the island.

The town of Mitchelville was founded on Hilton Head during the war as a home for former slaves who had been liberated but were not yet officially free. Mitchelville became the heart of a project known as the Port Royal Experiment, guided by northern missionaries who opened schools and helped the formerly enslaved make the transition to a life of freedom. During the war, many Mitchelville residents were employed by the Union military. When the soldiers left, Mitchelville people suffered from food shortages and the loss of regular wages. They lacked the land, finances, business connections, and management skills needed to grow profitable crops of sea island cotton. A few former planters who returned to the island to try to revive their plantations failed without slave labor.

During the 1880s, as more and more Blacks abandoned the island to find work, Mitchelville became a close-knit community of kinspeople rather than a town. Some stayed, surviving by farming, hunting, and fishing. Isolation helped preserve their unique Gullah Geechee culture.

During the 1940s, timber companies logged the island's dense forests of sea pines, an island species. More than twenty sawmills on the island prepared the wood for shipment. The first bridge to Hilton Head opened in the 1950s, providing a land link between the island and the wider world. Along with air-conditioning, the improved access prompted Charles Fraser, whose family was a major landholder on the island, to build a resort he named Sea Pines Plantation on the island's southwest end on Calibogue Sound. The ruins of the Stoney-Baynard Plantation are protected on a nine-acre tract in the Sea Pines enclave.

Most of the Gullah Geechee on the island were displaced by the upscale development that followed. Now about forty thousand full-time residents live on Hilton Head. The population swells during tourist season, which is now almost year-round. New island communities, several called plantations, feature golf courses, tennis courts, and man-made lakes attractive to the resident alligator population.

Stoney-Baynard Plantation

c. 1790–1810

Baynard Park Road and Plantation Drive

National Register of Historic Places

HISTORIC SIGNIFICANCE: Experts describe the architecture of the Stoney-Baynard Plantation as unusual, even unique. It is a part-tabby, part-timber mansion with a grand entry staircase that sits off center because the builders made an error in siting a basement door. The Stoney-Baynard ruins represent the only pre–Civil War planter's house built of tabby on Hilton Head. The slave cabin near the main house allowed modern researchers to study the lives of domestic slaves.

John "Captain Jack" Stoney, an Irish immigrant, and his wife, Elizabeth, came to South Carolina in 1774 on Stoney's merchant ship, the *Saucy Jack*. Stoney, who had made a small fortune as a privateer, sailed on the side of the Patriots during the Revolutionary War. By 1776, he had made enough money to buy the thousand-acre Braddock Point Plantation on the southwest end of Hilton Head. He built his house there, settled his family, and began growing sea island cotton.

Stoney built his house and outbuildings for comfort, not for show, in part because of the difficulties of living on a remote island. Hilton Head was isolated from the mainland and other populated islands by vast fields of Spartina marsh cut by a maze of tidal creeks. During the Stoneys' tenure, the island was not just isolated—it was a world apart, more akin to a frontier settlement than a rural community.

In the early nineteenth century, no bridges or causeways connected the island to the mainland or to more populated islands. Hilton Head's roads were so deep in soft sand that horses were forced to slow to a walking gait.

It was a long boat ride to the nearest town. As a result, it cost more to import tea, flour, china, glassware, cooking pots, and anything else needed than it did in places closer to civilization. Everyone on Hilton Head learned to make do. People scoured the beaches for lumber, iron spikes, copper hardware, and other usable salvage from shipwrecks.

Hilton Head averaged two tropical storms a year, and while most were not devastating, a day or two of heavy rain and above-normal winds could wipe out an entire sea island cotton crop—and a planters' annual income. The storms tended to come in late summer and early fall, critical times for harvesting cotton, sugarcane, and rice.

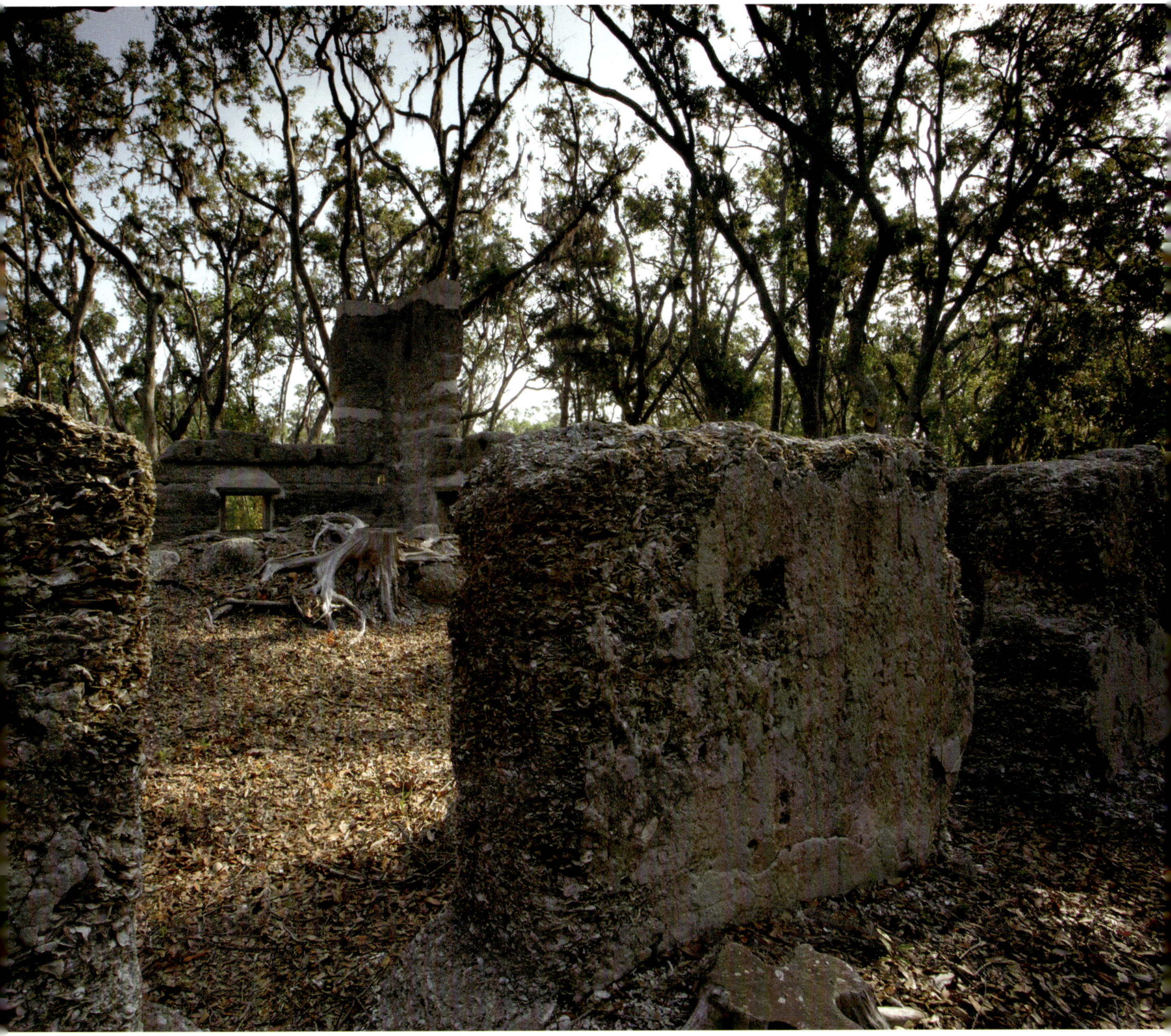

Island summers were hot, steamy, and thick with mosquitoes that transmitted malaria and yellow fever, ailments so prevalent that one woman noted: "The manufacture of coffins was the only business that was at all flourishing."

In spite of the drawbacks, Stoney invested his money on Hilton Head. He built his house on an old dune ridge about twenty-four feet above mean sea level. The ridge was a high point on the low-lying island, well out of range of storm tides. The south-facing structure was sited to catch breezes from nearby Calibogue Sound. When the Stoneys and, later, the Baynards occupied the dwelling, the land was cleared of most trees and other vegetation to give the occupants a view of the sound and the spreading fields of sea island cotton.

Stoney's residence was not elegant, but it was comfortable and spacious. Measuring about forty by forty-six feet, the almost-square dwelling provided almost nineteen hundred square feet on the main floor, with more room in the basement and the upper half story. The basement's tabby walls rose more than five feet above grade and elevated the main living areas even higher. Gable windows built into the pitched wood-shingled roof provided light and air to upstairs rooms.

The front façade and adjacent side wings were built of wood, perhaps covered by clapboard siding. The part-wood, part-tabby construction is rare, perhaps unique. Tabby is a strong building material except where it is weakened by openings cut for windows and doors. The wood framing may have allowed the builders to install multiple windows and French doors on the breezy wooden side of the house without endangering the integrity of the tabby walls.

A grand staircase was built slightly off center because builders misplaced a basement door. The staircase led either to a front portico or to a larger porch supported by brick columns and arcades. Like stairways in the West Indies, the stairs flared at the bottom and tapered as they rose to the entrance. The roof was probably hipped and wood shingled. Space under the porch was bricked, possibly to provide a sheltered walkway for the enslaved as they went about their daily labors or maybe to drain rainwater away from the structure.

Toward the end of their occupancy, the Stoneys used a simple method of trash disposal. They threw it down the slope off the front porch. Experts who explored the trash dump discovered sherds of expensive ceramics and gold-plated chains and cuff links, indicating that the owners were people of means. Researchers did not find evidence of goblets, finger bowls, or other bits of crystal, an absence suggesting that the owners did not engage in lavish entertainments as other planters did, probably because Hilton Head was far off the beaten track at the time.

A few items found in the ruins of the main house include the arm of a porcelain doll and a child's thimble, suggesting that a little girl lived there. Three clay marbles also turned up. At the time, marbles were most often used in adult games.

Three outbuildings shared the ridge. The ruins of one structure are probably the remains of a slave cabin that sat inside the fenced enclosure with the main house. The design of the cabin, with chimneys on either end, made it easier to build and required less labor than other options, but resulted in uncomfortable living quarters for the house slaves.

The tabby chimney block still standing at the site may mark the location of the overseer's house, where both the earliest and the latest artifacts were found. The other small foundation was probably a tent base dating from the Union occupation, made from blocks salvaged from

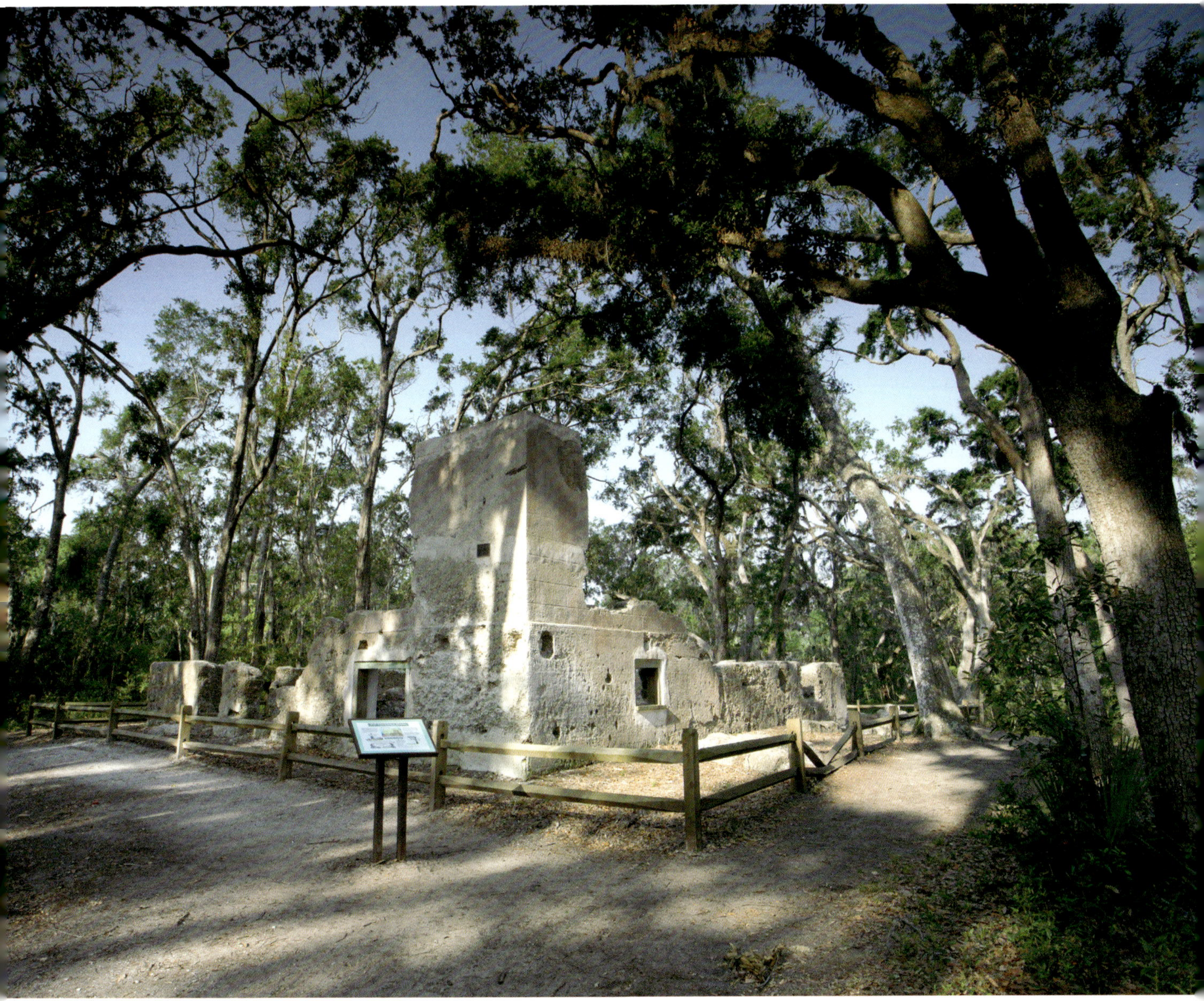

another structure. The kitchen was separated from the main house. It was small, fourteen by eighteen feet, with a foundation of tabby blocks. It faced south to allow the prevailing winds to help the chimney draft. The building was located at a distance from the main house to lessen the risk of a kitchen fire spreading, as well as to protect the planter and his family from smoke, cooking odors, heat, and noise.

During the Civil War, Union troops relocated the tabby-block foundation of the kitchen to build what may have been a fourth structure. Early builders, especially in remote locations, often recycled materials from abandoned structures for new construction. Little is known about how the military used the new building—if it was a building. The cast tabby blocks may have been used to build a raised dirt-filled foundation to accommodate a large tent where some of the soldiers stationed at the site were bivouacked.

The Stoneys occupied the home until about 1840, when the brothers sold the property to the bank. William E. Baynard, a wealthy planter, acquired the property and renamed it Braddock Point Plantation. Local legend says Baynard won the plantation in a late-night poker game, but historians say he purchased the property from the bank.

The plantation today is on the property of the upscale Sea Pines Plantation resort on Hilton Head's south end. Visitors are welcome; there is a fee to enter the Sea Pines complex.

Quarters for the Enslaved

On the ridge a short distance from the mansion, the enslaved who worked in the main house at Braddock Point Plantation occupied a cramped duplex tabby cabin designed to accommodate two families, each occupying a single twelve-by-fourteen-foot room that was used for all indoor aspects of their lives.

Their cabin was poorly constructed, possibly because the enslaved builders were inexperienced, careless, or under pressure from their owner to finish the structure quickly and cheaply. The problems started at the tabby foundation. To cast it in one continuous pour, the builders packed wet tabby into a rectangular form made of boards. Some of the interior boards were too long, which resulted in misaligned walls.

Imprints of timbers on the south wall indicate the tabby had not completely set when the wood framing was started. The foundation on the south side later broke apart, which probably caused the floor on that side to sink. The cabin's uneven floor was built at or below grade, which guaranteed that the duplex would be both hard to clean and plagued by dampness and insects.

Chimneys on the two gable ends were afterthoughts. Both developed major cracks. For the north chimney, floor joists were laid on the ground and tabby was poured around them to form the hearth. As a result, anyone entering or leaving the cabin had to step over the tabby footing.

It was probably a rare event for a doctor to visit Braddock Point Plantation. Researchers discovered that the house slaves attempted to ease their aches, pains, and fevers with patent medicines. The remains of patent medicine bottles were found in the ruins of the cabin; no such fragments were found at the main house. Embossing on one bottle indicated that it contained a syrup concocted by a druggist from Louisville, Kentucky. Other bottles held seaweed tonic and horse medicine.

The excavations turned up seeds and fruit of the chinaberry tree. Enslaved people used the plant to make a concoction for expelling the worms, especially roundworms, that plagued them in Carolina. Other concoctions were taken to increase urination, to relieve fever, or to treat eczema and dermatitis. Chinaberry fruit and seeds can be toxic, but either the variety that grew in the Lowcountry was less so than others, or else slave deaths were not attributed to chinaberry poisoning.

The lives of slaves who worked as field hands cultivating sea island cotton were even harder than those of domestic slaves, although the former may have had some small measure of relief by living in quarters distant from the main house. In early March, they would begin hoeing the fields to create good drainage for the crop. Planting would start about a month later. One worker would dig a hole for the seeds, another would drop them into the hole, and a third would cover them. When the plants had produced four or five leaves, enslaved workers would hoe the grass and thin the crop. The hoeing and thinning were done as many as eight times during a single growing season under the broiling sun and wilting humidity of a Deep South summer.

After the cotton flowered and the blossoms fell, woody brown pods, or bolls, would appear. When the plants were about five feet tall and the first bolls were ready, the picking would begin; it would continue over the next six months. Fields were harvested as many as a dozen times as the bolls continued to blow, or fully open. On some plantations, the fields were white until after Christmas.

Picking upland cotton was a backbreaking job. Sea island cotton was even harder to harvest because it was more delicate and required an expert touch. Debris that could stain the white fluff was gently pulled away, but if the fluff were handled too much, its value dropped sharply. Children and women were frequently impressed into harvesting the cotton. They were also expected to mote, that is, to separate stained cotton and seeds from the marketable fluff. Standard cotton gins were not used for sea island cotton, because they damaged the long-staple fibers that made the cotton so valuable.

Cleaned sea island cotton was gently pressed into bales of about three hundred pounds—a screw press was used to smash upland cotton into thousand-pound bales—then stored until it was shipped to the planter's factor, or salesman, in Charleston or Savannah, where it was graded and sold to European buyers.

Cotton production was a high-risk occupation. Any crop could be destroyed by plant diseases, insects, late frost, too much or too little rain, bad processing, poor storage, storms, or warehouse fires. Prices fluctuated from year to year. Planters took the risk because one good crop could make them wealthy beyond their wildest dreams—at least temporarily.

At Braddock Point Plantation, the enslaved would have been worked harder to produce more cotton as prices declined from a record high in 1820. By the time John Stoney died in 1838, leaving the plantation to his two sons, his cotton empire had been destroyed by depressed prices. The brothers tried hard to make the plantation profitable again, but lost it in 1845.

CHAPTER 12 — *St. Helena Island*

ST. HELENA—pronounced HEL-ena—is one of the largest of the South Carolina sea islands. Its history is diverse, and its natural beauty stunning, although time and modern development have taken a toll. The island is well known for its concentration of Gullah Geechee people, descendants of enslaved people who worked the island plantations and developed a distinct culture and language that have endured because the region was long isolated from mainstream culture.

The first known Europeans to reach the island were Spanish explorers who sailed the southeastern coast in search of natural resources and slaves. They lured Native Americans onto their ships to work the sugar plantations on the Caribbean island of Hispaniola. Like the Caribbean Natives, many of the kidnapped people died far from home of overwork, mistreatment, and common European diseases.

French Huguenots, who in 1562 became the first Europeans to settle in the area, named the island's giant natural harbor Porte Royale. The name was later anglicized to Port Royal by the area's first British settlers.

Port Royal's neighboring island, St. Helena, took its name from Santa Elena, the fortified Spanish town built on Parris Island in 1566.

The French, Spanish, British, and Native people fought over land in the coastal Southeast well into the eighteenth century. By then, the French had moved west, Native populations had collapsed, the Spanish had retreated to their stronghold at St. Augustine, and the British controlled the area. They still had to defend it from enemies and hack a homeland out of the semitropical wilderness.

From the earliest colonial days, the British imported slaves from Africa to clear land, harvest naval stores, raise livestock, grow indigo, and raise subsistence crops. Rice was never grown in quantity on St. Helena Island because there was not enough freshwater to support traditional Lowcountry rice-growing methods. After the Revolutionary War, island planters discovered sea island cotton, the crop that made them wealthy. More Africans were enslaved to work the giant plantations of the southeastern coast, where sea island cotton grew best.

St. Helena planters and their families fled their plantations in warmer months for higher, cooler places in order to escape malaria, yellow fever, and other ailments. Many spent summers at St. Helenaville, a small village in a pine forest on the northeast end of the island where ocean breezes and good drainage kept the mosquitoes at bay. The most affluent planters moved to the town of Beaufort on neighboring Port Royal Island, where they built elegant townhomes, many of tabby.

As many as 60 percent of all the African slaves imported to North America passed through Charleston, South Carolina, and other ports in the coastal Southeast. They came from scores of villages on the west coast of Africa, each with its own language, beliefs, and traditions. On the isolated sea islands and coastal mainland, the unique Gullah Geechee culture evolved, along with the only English-based creole in the United States. The name of the people and the language, originally called Gullah in South Carolina and Geechee in Georgia, are now used jointly.

It was unusual for the enslaved ever to leave St. Helena. Many spent their lives, from birth to death, on the isolated island. Because of the large slave population and its limited contact with whites, St. Helena slaves and their post–Civil War descendants retained much of their Gullah Geechee heritage.

When Union troops occupied the area, just six months after the start of the Civil War, white planters fled the island, leaving two thousand slaves behind. The federal Treasury Department was given the job of dealing with abandoned property, harvesting fields of valuable sea island cotton, and coping with the thousands of liberated slaves who were not officially freed until President Abraham Lincoln issued the Emancipation Proclamation on January 1, 1863, freeing all slaves in areas then in rebellion. Slaves in other parts of the country were freed by ratification of the Thirteenth Amendment in December 1865.

On St. Helena, treasury officials set up camps and schools to house and educate the contrabands and, later, the freed slaves, devising the Port Royal Experiment to deal with the needs of a population whose lives were undergoing radical change. Northern teachers established a school at The Oaks, a former island plantation. Laura Townes and Ellen Murray, abolitionists and teachers from Philadelphia, opened the first school in the plantation house, but soon relocated it to Brick Church as the school grew. Brick Church had the advantage of being more centrally located on the island. The school, named for the Quaker leader William Penn, continued to expand as more and more contrabands poured into the area. Additional classrooms were prefabricated in the North and shipped to St. Helena to be erected on the Brick Church property.

The Penn School educated the island's Black children until desegregation, a century later. It was renamed the Penn Center, which is still in operation and is credited with helping preserve the island's African American history and culture via its collections of artifacts, writings, recordings, and handicrafts. The fifty-acre complex is now listed as a National Historic Landmark. The center served as a retreat for Dr. Martin Luther King Jr., who came to St. Helena to plan civil rights actions and drafted his "I Have A Dream" speech in a cottage he occupied during his visits.

After the Civil War, freed slaves continued to grow sea island cotton until the arrival of the boll weevil in 1919, which wiped out cotton cultivation across the South. A phosphate mine opened in the late nineteenth century but closed after a devastating hurricane struck Beaufort in 1893. A newspaper writer reported that the storm, which left forty thousand people homeless, did more damage than Sherman's fiery march across Georgia.

At least fourteen hundred people died in the hurricane, three hundred of them on St. Helena Island. Most of the victims were freed people trying to build new lives on the sea islands. The banks of tidal waterways were stacked with their bodies. The famed Civil War nurse Clara Barton set up a Red Cross station in Beaufort to help care for the injured. It was the first major hurricane relief effort by the Red Cross.

As the Lowcountry recovered, farming and commercial shrimping propped up St. Helena's economy. A causeway to the mainland opened in 1927, giving the island and its people easier access to the wider world.

SITE 34

St. Helena Chapel of Ease Ruins

c. 1748

County Roads 45 and 37, MLK Drive

National Register of Historic Places

HISTORIC SIGNIFICANCE: The small structure built almost three hundred years ago is the only known tabby chapel of ease still standing. It features the largest known unsupported tabby arch. The chapel was constructed to serve members of the St. Helena Parish Church who lived a significant distance from the mother church in Beaufort.

Many wealthy planters in Beaufort County belonged to the St. Helena Parish Church in Beaufort. They moved to elegant Beaufort townhomes during warmer months to escape the deadly diseases that ravaged the Lowcountry in summer. After the first frost, the planters moved back to their sprawling island plantations, which were some distance from the church in Beaufort. Getting back and forth between town and the plantations was time consuming and difficult, especially in bad weather.

No bridges connected St. Helena Island to Beaufort, so a one-way journey to church involved crossing two tidal waterways plus transport in horse-drawn wagons or carriages. Slaves could row the planters and their families down twisting streams to Beaufort and back, but the lengthy trip sometimes required rowing against the tide both ways.

For that reason, the Anglican Church in colonial South Carolina authorized the establishment of four chapels of ease in today's Beaufort County, including the one in St. Helena Parish. The chapels, which had been popular in Great Britain for centuries, were designed to make it easier for parishioners to attend Sunday worship services.

The St. Helena Chapel of Ease was the only one of the four Beaufort County chapels built of tabby. Some experts say the light-colored oyster-shell concrete prompted the chapel's nickname, White Church. Others believe the enslaved Gullah Geechee forced to work on the plantations on St. Helena called it White Church because only whites were allowed to worship there. At many larger churches, Black worshipers sat in the balcony, or "slave gallery," but seats in the small chapel of ease were reserved for white congregants.

In 1850, the chapel was enlarged to the east and perhaps remodeled. The exterior skim coat of oyster-shell stucco was scored to look like stone, a common practice by immigrants who liked the solid look of stone structures in Europe. Stone was also considered more upscale

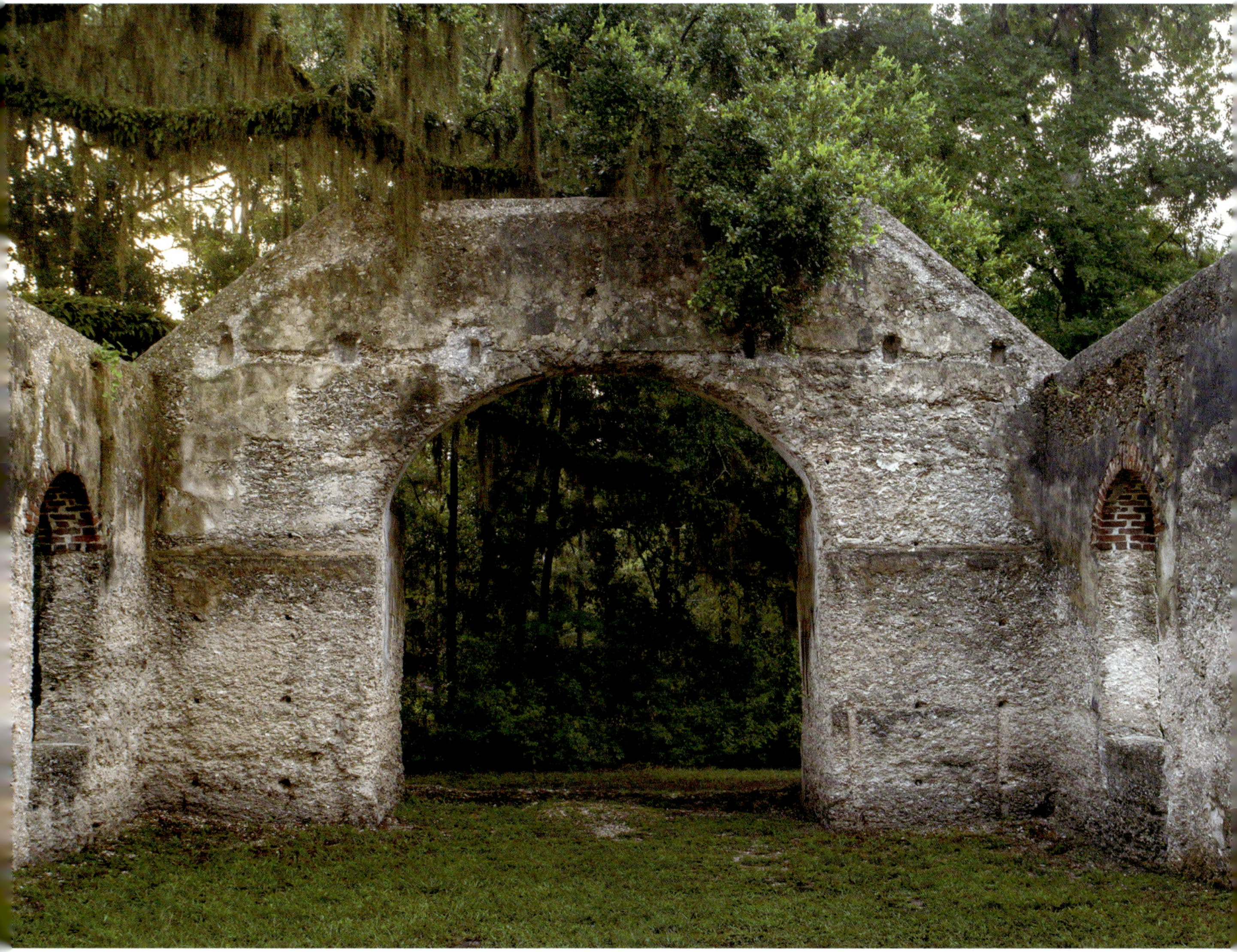

than tabby because it was more expensive and had to be imported.

The St. Helena Chapel of Ease has a rare and perhaps unique feature: a large tabby arch. The architectural historian Colin Brooker has stabilized scores of tabby structures but has never encountered a comparable arch. He explained that tabby has compressive strength, meaning that it holds up well when it is packed together, or compressed. But it lacks tensile strength: the ability to span distances without support. The chapel's arch continues to defy that principle, even after three centuries.

It was fairly common for chapels of ease to become full-fledged churches at some point. Because of population growth, the St. Helena chapel was designated a parish church in 1812, which gave it the right to conduct rituals such as baptisms, marriages, and funerals.

Members of the wealthy Fripp family, who had planted crops on St. Helena Island since colonial times, were major supporters of the chapel of ease and the church it later became. In his will, written in 1780, John Fripp III left £500 for its maintenance.

In 1852, Edgar Fripp, whose family owned twelve thousand acres on the island, commissioned a brick-and-stone mausoleum on the church grounds for himself and his wife, Eliza, who was also his first cousin. The mausoleum is considered an outstanding example of mid-nineteenth-century funerary art and architecture. Fripp hired famous stonemasons from Charleston to build entry columns that reflect the mausoleum's Egyptian Revival style. Locals claimed that Edgar Fripp wanted to be buried like the pharaohs of Egypt and take his wealth with him to the grave. In a diary written at the time, a local resident named Thomas B. Chaplin noted that the mausoleum "did not have to wait very long for its occupants Edgar & wife." Both died in 1852, the year the structure was built.

Union troops broke into the vault during the Civil War in hope of finding treasure, but discovered only the Fripps' remains. The soldiers left the mausoleum "somewhat out of order." They also carried away the organ that had been donated to the adjacent church by the Fripp family, Chaplin wrote.

The small church got its own satellite chapel of ease in 1840 in St. Helenaville, a summer retreat for wealthy island planters on the northeastern tip of St. Helena Island. The resort boasted a scattering of cottages on a bluff on Village Creek, overlooking the Morgan River and St. Helena Sound. The resort was adjacent to a pine forest—pine trees were believed to create a healthy summer environment—and was well situated to catch the summer breezes that reduced mosquito attacks. The proximity of the resort to island plantations allowed planters to check on their crops during the day and return to their families on the breezy bluff at night.

St. Helenaville has since succumbed to erosion, but bricks and chunks of tabby littering the banks of Village Creek testify to its former existence.

In 1861, services at the church were interrupted when Confederate captain William Oliver Perry Fripp was notified that Union forces were positioned to invade the Port Royal area. Three days later, the invasion began. Liberated slaves later referred to the action as the "Day of the Big Shoot" because of the noise of the guns during the Union bombardment.

During the Union occupation, Quakers and other northern abolitionists flocked south to aid and educate newly freed slaves. They held meetings, social gatherings, and religious services at the St. Helena chapel.

Nearby, what is today the Penn Center was built in 1862 as the Penn School, the first school in the South for the education of the formerly enslaved. The building is designated a National Historic Landmark and now serves as an African American cultural center. Martin Luther King Jr. often retreated there to write. The York W. Bailey Museum and Welcome Center on the site highlights the Gullah Geechee people's rich culture and history. A permanent exhibition showcases some of the oldest extant photographs of African Americans, the original school bell from 1863, and many artifacts related to Black life on the island.

After the war, freedmen established a Methodist congregation at the church until an 1886 forest fire destroyed the roof, gutted the interior, and damaged the exterior.

In recent years, Brooker, the architectural historian, stabilized the St. Helena Chapel of Ease with a modern version of tabby compatible with the historic material.

CHAPTER 13   *Port Royal*

THE NAME "PORT ROYAL" applies to several different geographic features in Beaufort County.

It is the name of one of the deepest natural harbors on the Eastern Seaboard, Port Royal Sound, which bifurcates the county into north and south sectors.

It is the name of the historic village of Port Royal.

It is also the name of the island complex that includes Parris Island, location of the Santa Elena National Historic Landmark and the U.S. Marine Corps Recruit Depot, as well as the restored historic town of Beaufort.

"Port Royal" has been used to describe almost any area on or near the sound; today it usually means the incorporated town of Port Royal.

St. Helena, another large Beaufort County island, lies adjacent to Port Royal Island. Although St. Helena is the English translation of Santa Elena, the Santa Elena National Historic Landmark is located in the Parris Island–Port Royal Island complex rather than on St. Helena Island.

Yes, it is confusing.

Santa Elena played a central role in the sixteenth-century struggles between Spain and France for control of territory in North America. Two of the first Europeans to found colonies in the New World were associated with the site: Jean Ribault, a French Huguenot naval officer, and Pedro Menéndez de Avilés, a Spanish commander sent to drive the French from the area.

Santa Elena was designated the capital of Spanish Florida in 1566, making it the first European colonial capital in North America. The site had been briefly settled by French Protestants in 1562, forty years before the English established Jamestown, Virginia.

During the Civil War, the Port Royal Experiment was established by northerners to help newly liberated slaves adjust to their new status and prepare for citizenship. Land owned by southern planters was given or sold to former slaves, and northern educator-abolitionists founded schools for freedmen. The town of Mitchelville was established on nearby Hilton Head Island as a freedmen's settlement.

Like the other sea islands of the southeastern coast, Port Royal was home to Late Archaic people at least four thousand years ago. They were drawn to the area by the bountiful, high-protein seafood they harvested from the Atlantic Ocean, tidal waterways, and marshes.

By the time the first Europeans arrived, eleven groups of Indigenous peoples lived between the Savannah and Edisto Rivers, including the Ahoya, Escamacu, Orista, and Witcheough. They supplemented their seafood-based diet by growing the traditional "three sister" crops: corn, beans, and squash or pumpkins.

The Spanish explorer Pedro de Salazar, the first European known to reach the island, arrived in 1514. He came in search of people to enslave as laborers on plantations on the Caribbean island of Hispaniola, where most of the Native islanders had died of European diseases and overwork.

Explorations along the coast and inland, including the famous winding trek of Hernando de Soto from the Gulf Coast of Florida to the Mississippi River, continued for decades.

By the mid-1600s, the British were exploring the coastal Southeast. They founded Charles Towne—today's Charleston—in 1670 and established indigo and cotton plantations on many of the sea islands, including Port Royal.

In 1715, Colonel Alexander Parris bought Santa Elena and several other smaller islands and grew sea island cotton there. During the Civil War, Union troops that took over the area renamed the island for Parris.

Both Charlesfort, the French fort, and the first Spanish fort, San Marcos, have been reinterred under a golf course, but artifacts recovered from the sites are on display at the Santa Elena Museum on the Marine Corps base, which also features military memorabilia and artifacts from other periods on the island. More material is housed at the Santa Elena History Center at 1501 Bay Street in Beaufort. The museum and the history center are open to the public.

SITE 35

Fort Frederick Heritage Preserve

1730–1734

Adjacent to Naval Hospital Beaufort, 1 Pinckney Boulevard
South Carolina Department of Natural Resources

National Register of Historic Places

HISTORIC SIGNIFICANCE: Camp Saxton, home of the first Black regiment in the Union army to be composed of the formerly enslaved, was established on the grounds of Fort Frederick, a tabby colonial fort built more than a century earlier. Liberated slaves at Camp Saxton were among the first to feel the full effect of the Emancipation Proclamation, read aloud at the camp on the date of its issuance, January 1, 1863. The remains of the fort may be the oldest tabby structure in South Carolina.

During the early 1700s, the English population of Beaufort County plummeted because of a series of bloody wars between South Carolina settlers and Native Americans. The Yamasee and other Indigenous people were fighting for survival in a world undergoing radical change. During the conflicts, British farms and plantations in the Port Royal area were raided, cattle were stolen or slaughtered, and the colonists' lucrative trade with local Natives was disrupted. Many colonists were killed in the attacks.

In 1727, the danger of a seaborne attack on Port Royal Sound prompted the construction of a small wood-and-earth fort on the Beaufort River, a major tributary of the sound. A few years later, Governor Robert Johnson of Carolina recommended replacing the fort with a stronger structure. "[It would be] much more serviceable with oyster shell and lyme than with earth and timber," Johnson commented in his request for a tabby fort.

The colonial government at first failed to provide sufficient funds to build the tabby version of Fort Frederick and even dragged its heels in paying garrison troops. The fort was built when funds were appropriated. It was named Fort Prince Frederick in honor of Frederick Louis, the Prince of Wales and eldest son of George II. Completed in 1735, the fort's tabby walls were only five feet high and could not have withstood a serious naval attack.

The fort was relatively small as well, measuring only 125 by 75 feet. One corner bastion projected toward the southwest; cannons lined the east wall. After almost three centuries, erosion has eaten away at the fort site. The northeast bastion now extends well into the Beaufort River. Part of the tabby is visible at low tide. An ammunition

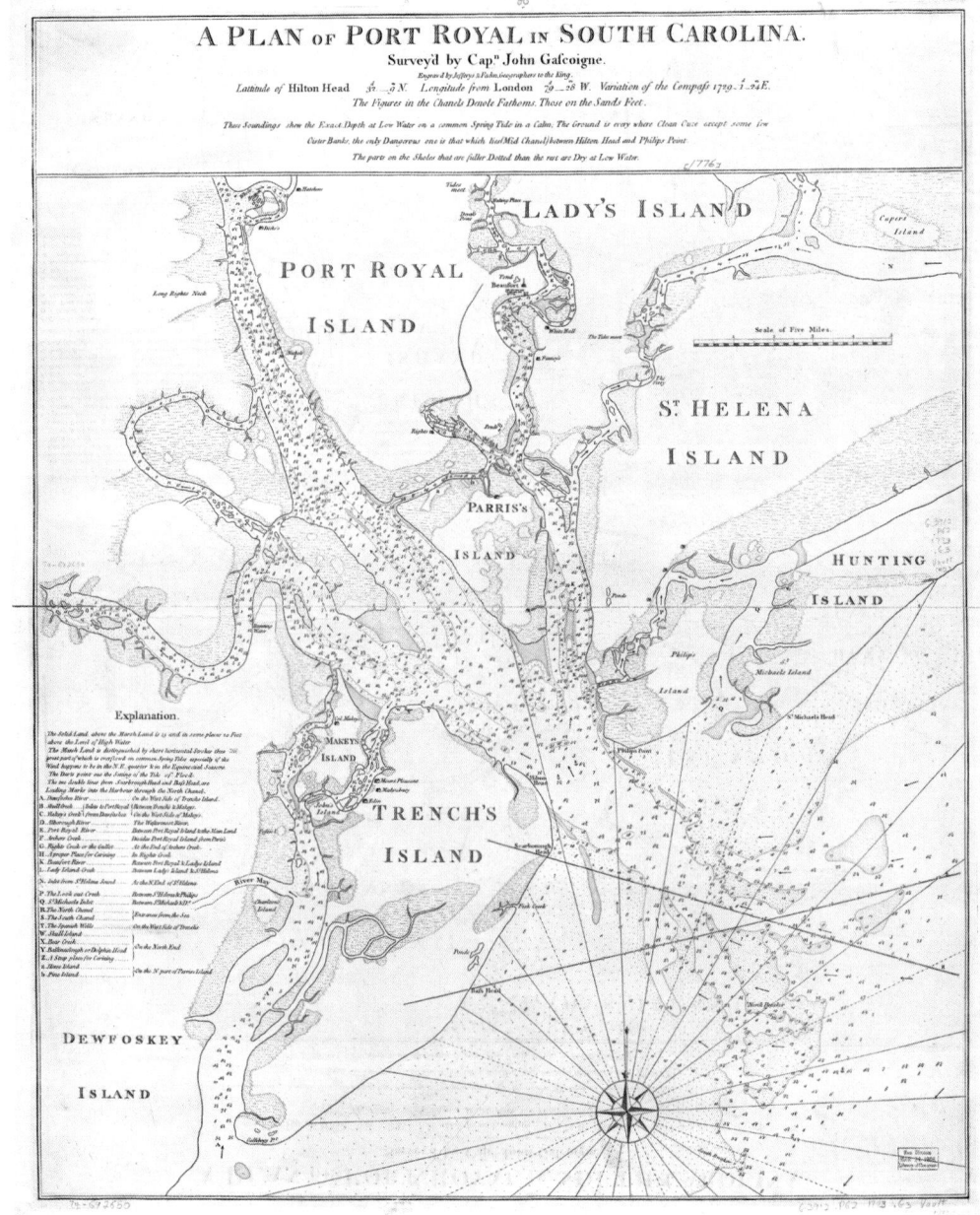

"A plan of Port Royal in South Carolina," map by John Gascoigne, printed by Jeffreys and Faden, London, c. 1773

magazine was built inside the fort walls, along with barracks to accommodate British regulars of the Independent Company of Foot who were stationed there. The Carolina scouts who patrolled the inland waterways of the coastal Southeast often docked their small boats at Fort Frederick. The famed Yamasee fighter Colonel John "Tuscarora Jack" Barnwell, who commanded the Carolina scouts, said they needed constant supervision to prevent them from being "wild idle people and continually sotting if they can get any rum."

During its first years, Fort Frederick served primarily as a lookout post. Its troops fired cannons whenever unidentified ships appeared in Port Royal Sound to warn the people of Beaufort and other upriver settlements of a possible attack from the sea. The tabby gun emplacements were damaged by the frequent juddering of cannon fire and deteriorated faster than the rest of the fort.

Fort Frederick's importance diminished in 1736 when James Oglethorpe built Fort Frederica on St. Simons Island, Georgia, almost a hundred miles south of Fort Frederick. The garrison of troops assigned to Fort Frederick was reassigned to the new Georgia fort. The transfer of the soldiers signaled Fort Frederick's demise. By 1740, it had fallen into disrepair, and by 1758 it was abandoned.

Before the Civil War, Fort Frederick and its surrounding acreage were part of a plantation owned by John Joyner Smith, a planter wealthy enough to own an elegant bay-front home in Beaufort. His farm was called the Old Fort Plantation or Smith's Plantation. It was sold during the war for unpaid taxes.

The Smith property and the tabby fortress were conscripted by Union troops, who occupied most of the South Carolina coast during the Civil War. They named the property Camp Saxton after Union brigadier general Rufus Saxton, who served as quartermaster of the South Carolina Expeditionary Corps. Saxton, a staunch abolitionist, was in charge of supplying food and other necessities to contraband communities in the area.

Camp Saxton accommodated thousands of fugitives: enslaved people liberated during the Union advance who had not yet been officially freed by the federal government. Before the signing of the Emancipation Proclamation, their status was unclear. The Union characterized them as contraband, or spoils of war, to prevent their former owners from demanding their return.

General Saxton directed the recruitment of the first Union regiments of freed slaves, including the First South Carolina Volunteers, who were based at Camp Saxton. The regiment's name was later changed to the Thirty-Third U.S. Colored Regiment.

In a ceremony held at Camp Saxton on New Year's Day 1863, the just-signed Emancipation Proclamation was read aloud to hundreds of contrabands, notifying them that they were officially free. It may have marked the first time the proclamation was read aloud to contrabands anywhere in the Deep South. Thousands of people, Black and white, gathered for the reading, including Susie Baker King Taylor, a literate contraband from Georgia who described the event in her memoir:

> It was a glorious day for us all, and we enjoyed every minute of it, and as a fitting close and the crowning event of this occasion we had a grand barbecue. A number of oxen were roasted whole, and we had a fine feast . . . The soldiers had a good time. They sang or shouted "hurrah!" all through the camp, and seemed overflowing with fun and frolic until taps were sounded, when many, no doubt dreamt of this memorable day.

The Fort Frederick property, adjacent to the Beaufort Naval Hospital, is now owned by the State of South Carolina. Because the old tabby walls were continuing to crumble, Colin Brooker, an architectural historian and tabby expert from Beaufort County, was hired to stabilize the fort with a tabby mixture compatible with the original tabby, which was made with oyster-shell lime and ancient oyster shells. The site is open to the public under state guidelines.

Susie Baker King Taylor, 1848–1912

Born on the Valentin Grest plantation on the Isle of Wight south of Savannah, Georgia, Susie Baker was a favorite of her owners. When she was a small child, the plantation mistress treated her like an adorable puppy, having the little girl sleep on the foot of her bed, giving her treats, and dressing her like a doll.

Later, when Baker and her younger brother were old enough, the Grests sent them to live with their grandmother, a free African in Savannah. They attended a series of illegal underground schools, called bucket schools because the students carried their books in pails to disguise the fact that they were attending school. Laws prohibited teaching slaves to read and write and mandated severe penalties for those who broke them.

At age fourteen, with Union forces attacking nearby Fort Pulaski east of Savannah, Baker and about six hundred other enslaved people who had been liberated along the coast by Union forces were relocated to contraband camps on St. Simons Island, Georgia. When officers learned that Baker was literate, they persuaded her to teach the children of other liberated slaves to read and write. She agreed as long as Union army officials provided her with books and other materials.

When adults begged her to teach them too, the teenager held night classes. Her schools, the first funded by the federal government during the war, were among the first schools for freed slaves in the Deep South.

For the rest of her time on St. Simons, Baker taught about forty children during the day and a similar number of adults at night, "all of them," according to her memoir, "so eager to learn to read, to read above anything else."

On St. Simons, Susie Baker, then fifteen, married Robert King, a contraband from Darien. King joined the First South Carolina Volunteers. In October, King and the other recruits were sent to Beaufort. They arrived just as the First South Carolina Volunteers merged with the Thirty-Third Regiment of U.S. Colored Troops. Susie King noted that she and her husband had a number of relatives in the regiment, where she was officially enrolled as a laundress. She traveled with the soldiers to campaigns in South Carolina, Georgia, and Florida, washing and cooking for the men.

After Susie King showed a talent for nursing, most of her time was spent caring for ill and injured soldiers. Once after a battle, a number of badly wounded soldiers unable to eat solid food begged for soup. None was available, so Baker made a soft custard for the invalids, improvising with a few cans of condensed milk and turtle eggs.

For more than a year, the men of the Thirty-Third received no pay. While the soldiers could depend on the commissary for food and supplies, wives and children traveling with them received nothing. They survived by doing washing for officers on the Union gunboats and baking cakes and pies to sell to "the boys in camp." Although a number of Union officers lobbied the government on behalf of the contraband soldiers, they were not paid until 1864, a year and a half after joining the army. Baker and other women who served the troops were never paid for their work.

Some of the Union officers lobbied for the Black troops to receive wages equal to those paid white Union troops. Offered half that amount, the soldiers refused; they nonetheless continued to perform their duties without compensation. After eighteen months, the Black soldiers finally received full wages as well as back pay.

While Susie King was visiting wounded soldiers from her regiment at a hospital for Black troops in Beaufort, she met the famed Civil War nurse Clara Barton. "Miss Barton was always very cordial to me, and I honored her for her devotion and care of those men," King wrote, noting that Barton at first declined to nurse Black troops but soon moved past her bias and cared for all the ill and wounded.

In Beaufort, King helped nurse soldiers from the Fifty-Fourth Massachusetts, the first all-Black regiment in the United States, after they launched their futile attack on Fort Wagner on Morris Island, east of Charleston. The fort guarded Charleston, the only southern port not under Union control. The Fifth-Fourth Massachusetts was composed of Black men from New England who were free before the war, unlike the recently liberated slaves recruited as Union troops in the South. The Fifty-Fourth was led by Robert Gould Shaw, a young New England abolitionist who died in the attack on Fort Wagner and was buried along with his troops, who exhibited extraordinary

Susie King Taylor, who served as a nurse with the Thirty-Third U.S. Colored Troops Infantry Regiment during the Civil War. She also taught children and adults to read in the three years she served with the regiment. Taylor is shown here between 1862 and 1866.

courage in the assault. Their story was told in the 1989 film *Glory*, based in part on the wartime letters written by Shaw to his mother.

After the war, the Kings moved to Savannah, where Robert King died in a work-related accident on the docks shortly before their only child, a son, was born. Baker took a series of domestic jobs and then left her son with her mother and traveled to Boston with a wealthy family as a housekeeper. She later married Russell M. Taylor of Boston and devoted the remainder of her life to the organization she helped found: the women's auxiliary of the Grand Army of the Republic, later serving as the organization's president.

In 1902, at the urging of a former Union officer, Susie Baker King Taylor published a memoir about her experiences with the Thirty-Third Regiment of U.S. Colored Troops. It is the only known document written by a Black woman who served in the Union army, and one of the few memoirs written from an African American perspective during the Civil War.

CHAPTER 14   *Parris Island*

ALTHOUGH PARRIS ISLAND is just four miles long and three miles wide, its size gives no hint about its importance in the history of the United States, especially its military history. Best known today for the U.S. Marine Corps Recruit Depot, Parris Island was home to French and Spanish military establishments 450 years ago.

Parris Island's location made it appealing to long-ago military leaders. The island is tucked into the throat of Port Royal Sound, the deepest natural harbor on the Atlantic Seaboard. Sea islands flanking the mouth of the sound protect it from ocean winds and waves, providing sheltered anchorage. The Inland Waterway, a natural maritime corridor of tidal rivers and inlets that runs through Port Royal Sound offered safe passage for dugouts, scout boats, and other small crafts traveling along the coast. The corridor later became the Intracoastal Waterway.

The first military establishment on the island was Charlesfort, the fortified Huguenot settlement founded in 1562. It marked the first attempt by the French to claim territory in the future United States. Santa Elena, founded four years later at the same site, was among the earliest Spanish settlements on the continent north of Mexico. It was also North America's first European colonial capital. By 1580, the Spanish were burning ancient oyster shells on Parris Island to make lime, the hardening ingredient in tabby. Neither Charlesfort nor Santa Elena lasted very long, but the site on Parris Island where the French and Spanish staked their claims, hopes, and dreams is now a National Historic Landmark, the highest designation of importance for historic sites.

Although Spain and France were the first European countries to struggle for territory in the coastal South, Great Britain eventually prevailed. Charles II granted land to eight men as a reward for helping him regain the throne. The eight became the lords proprietors of the Carolina colony.

Colonel Alexander Parris, treasurer of the colony, in 1715 bought the island later named for him. Until the outbreak of the Civil War, Parris and other planters grew indigo and sea island cotton on the island.

In 1861, southerners launched the Civil War by firing on federal Fort Sumter in Charleston Harbor. Only a few months later, Union forces captured Port Royal Sound and turned it into a coaling station for navy ships involved in the Union blockade of southern ports. The blockade, called the Anaconda Strategy because it curved like a giant snake as it followed the coast from Virginia to the Mississippi River, marked the Union's attempt to damage the economy of the rebel states by preventing southerners from exporting sea island cotton and other goods, and from importing food, troops, and armaments.

During and after the war, freed slaves attended Parris Island schools built by northern abolitionists. Clara Barton, the well-known Civil War nurse and founder of the Red Cross, taught at one of the schools.

Congressman Robert Smalls, a former slave who became a folk hero by stealing a Confederate ship and making a daring escape to Union ships blockading the southern coast, pushed for a new federal establishment on Parris Island after the war. Designated the Naval Station, Port Royal, the small security detachment initially consisted of thirteen men. They made a name for themselves by saving lives and property during hurricanes that flooded the island in the late 1800s.

In 1915, Parris Island was designated a Marine Corps training depot. During the depot's first fourteen years, marine recruits and everyone else rode a ferry back and forth to the island. In 1929, a causeway provided a land link to the mainland. The causeway crosses Horse Island, the highest point of land in the Parris Island complex. The point rises twenty-one feet above sea level.

A tragedy that occurred at the depot in April 1956 caused the corps to rethink some of its training methods. Six recruits drowned when a seasoned combat veteran but rookie drill sergeant marched a platoon of seventy-four men into Ribbon Creek at night. He was found guilty of negligent homicide by a court of inquiry, but information that came out during the investigation indicated that the corps had no prohibition at the time against night marches into tidal waterways. As more information emerged, the press and the public vilified the corps for brutal training practices.

The drill sergeant was court-martialed but later acquitted of serious charges when the most decorated marine in corps history testified in his behalf, calling the tragedy a "deplorable accident" rather than a criminal offense. The sergeant, whom the court found to be a good man filled with remorse over the drownings, was allowed to remain in the marines but was demoted to private. Several books were later written about the tragedy at Ribbon Creek. The corps reviewed its training practices and made significant changes.

Today, the marines train about seventeen thousand recruits every year on Parris Island. The corps takes an active role in protecting the island's wildlife, which is spectacular. Seabirds and shorebirds—bald eagles, ospreys, seagulls, oystercatchers, snowy egrets, great white herons, and many more species—soar above and stalk prey in creeks that wind through the island's extensive salt marshes. Bottlenose dolphins cavort in Port Royal Sound's olive-green waters, its color similar to the olive-green fatigues worn by the young recruits.

The occasional manatee makes it this far north in summer, drawn by the freshwater outflows from five coastal rivers that feed into the sound. Large alligators lumber casually across the Marine Corps' golf course, where the remains of the French and Spanish forts and the town of Santa Elena lie hidden underground. The site is still being excavated and studied by archaeologists. It is open to visitors, along with a museum of artifacts uncovered during the dig.

Other historic sites on Parris Island are buildings constructed in the Marine Corps complex between 1891 and World War I. The commanding general's house, a wooden dry dock from the 1800s, and a gazebo are all listed on the National Register of Historic Places.

SITE 36

Charlesfort–Santa Elena Site

Charlesfort, 1562; Santa Elena, 1566

Parris Island, South Carolina
U.S. Marine Corps Recruitment Depot
283 Boulevard de France

National Historic Landmark

HISTORIC SIGNIFICANCE: Charlesfort, founded by the French in 1562, and the Spanish town of Santa Elena and its series of five forts are sites of great Franco Hispanic American historic significance. Charlesfort was the first Protestant settlement and first French settlement in the future United States. Santa Elena, founded in 1566, was the first colonial capital in North America. The forts are among the earliest European military installations on the continent north of Mexico.

The young marines recruit who undergo arduous training on Parris Island today might sympathize with the grueling lot of the first European troops stationed on the island more than 450 years ago. The French Huguenot soldiers who staffed Charlesfort in 1562 suffered hardships so great that they abandoned their post in less than a year, willing to risk crossing 3,500 miles of the Atlantic Ocean in a crude open boat rather than remain on the island. The Spanish built a town and fort in 1566 on the site of Charlesfort. Although St. Augustine had been founded on the northeastern coast of Florida a year earlier, Santa Elena was named the first capital of La Florida, the vast territory claimed by Spain in North America.

Charlesfort, Santa Elena, and the five Spanish forts built on Parris Island between 1562 and 1587 disappeared after the sixteenth century as France and Spain began a centuries-long battle to become the dominant presence in North America.

The Huguenots had a strong incentive to settle in the New World: they were tortured and killed as heretics in France by Catholics. The Spanish had their own reasons for wanting to command territory on the Eastern Seaboard. They were mining gold and silver in Mexico and Peru and hauling it home on enormous ships. Twice a year, the treasure fleet rode the newly discovered northbound Gulf Stream along the southeastern coast from the Straits of Florida to North Carolina's Outer Banks before turning east to cross the Atlantic. The heavy, slow-moving ships were vulnerable to pirates and other enemies. Like the Spanish colonists and soldiers at St. Augustine, the people of Santa Elena were charged with protecting the

IHS
RELIGION FREEDOM ...
HERE STOOD
CHARLESFORT
BUILT 1562
BY JEAN RIBAUT
FOR ADMIRAL COLIGNY
A REFUGE
FOR HUGUENOTS
AND TO THE
GLORY OF FRANCE

treasure fleet, rescuing shipwreck victims, and salvaging sunken treasure.

The Spanish soldiers at Santa Elena did not have an easy time on Parris Island. With help from St. Augustine, their sister town, they survived violent storms, mosquitoes, food shortages, and attacks by Native Americans. They persisted from 1566 to 1587, except for a yearlong hiatus in 1576 when they fled to Florida after Native people set fire to Santa Elena and its fort. The capital of La Florida was then relocated to St. Augustine, where it remained, although some of the former settlers returned to Santa Elena a year later to rebuild.

By 1580, the wood-and-mud houses of Santa Elena were being plastered with lime, inside and out, and topped with flat lime roofs. That same year, the Spanish began burning ancient oyster shells to make lime on site, according to a letter to the king of Spain sent from Santa Elena.

The Spanish abandoned the settlement for the final time in 1587 under threat of an attack by Sir Francis Drake, who had been knighted a few years earlier by Queen Elizabeth I for being the first seaman to circumnavigate the world. The notorious British privateer, who had ravaged St. Augustine and Spain's other major settlements in the New World, was working his way north. Drake was a privateer, not a pirate. Pirates were freelance criminals; privateers sailed with letters of marque from their monarchs that allowed them to burn and pillage enemy ships and towns with royal sanction. They shared the spoils with their leaders.

Considering the historic significance of Charlesfort and Santa Elena, it is confounding that they were not unearthed and correctly identified until the late twentieth century.

After the marine training base opened during World War I, a marine major excavated a site he identified as Charlesfort, prompting Congress to erect a monument to the French leader Jean Ribault. When the artifacts discovered at the dig were reexamined decades later, experts identified them as Spanish, not French.

In 1979, the archaeologist Stanley South of the South Carolina Institute of Archaeology and Anthropology began the first academic search for Charlesfort on Parris Island. A decade later, the archaeologist Chester DePratter, also with the institute, began another search. The two joined forces in 1991 and discovered the remains of the Spanish town. Smith and DePratter determined Santa Elena's layout, now recognized as the nation's best surviving example of a Spanish colonial town design. They identified the central plaza, shops, three forts, and two Spanish houses, and excavated eight wells. They unearthed North America's oldest pottery kiln and its first known scientific instrument, an alembic used for distilling.

In 1993, they resumed the search for Charlesfort. Using old maps and documents, DePratter determined what he thought was the fort's location. Three years later, the archaeologist James Legg and DePratter examined an old collection of artifacts and found French pottery at the site that DePratter had pinpointed. They soon discovered the French fort hidden under the Marine Corps' golf course, buried beneath the remains of the Spanish Fort San Felipe. Parts of both forts had eroded into a tidal creek and marshes. Rising sea levels now threaten both historic treasures.

The digs continue. DePratter says only a tiny portion of the site has been excavated. Team members hope to locate Santa Elena's church and the home of Governor Pedro Menendez.

The Charlesfort–Santa Elena site is open to the public. A path with interpretive signs leads through the complex. Museums at the Marine Corps base on Parris Island and in Beaufort display artifacts and information from the discoveries.

Jean Ribault, c. 1520–1565

The celebrated French sea captain Jean Ribault was eager to found a settlement in North America. He was a Huguenot, as French Protestants were called, at a time when most Europeans were Roman Catholic. Protestants were considered heretics, tortured to renounce their faith, and often burned to death if they refused.

Ribault took two ships and a crew of about 150, including his second in command, René de Laudonnière, and crossed the Atlantic in 1562. They made landfall east of today's Jacksonville at the mouth of the St. Johns River, which Ribault named the River May. The travelers, sick of hard tack and salted meat, were delighted with the freshwater, seafood, beans, and meal cakes offered by the friendly Timucua Natives, whose territory covered a large swath of northern Florida and southern Georgia.

Ribault erected an ornate stone column, one of six he brought from Europe, to claim the land for France. He then sailed north, giving French names to the coastal rivers and sea islands he passed. The beauty of the southeastern coast provided him with "unspeakable pleasure." A storm and fog forced the ships to land on today's Parris Island at the mouth of the great sound discovered a few decades earlier by a Spanish explorer and named St. Helena. "St. Helena" is one of the oldest European place-names in the United States. Ribault renamed the sound Porte Royale, describing it as "one of the fayrest and greatest Havens of the worlde." Now anglicized to Port Royal, it is also among the nation's oldest European place-names.

The expeditioners erected a second stone column and built Charlesfort, naming it in honor of the twelve-year-old French king, Charles IX. None of the columns have been found.

Leaving a few dozen soldiers behind, Ribault and Laudonnière sailed back to France for additional colonists and supplies, promising to return in six months. When Ribault arrived in France, the country was embroiled in a civil war between Catholics and Protestants. He fought alongside fellow Huguenots in his hometown of Dieppe. When the town surrendered, he fled to England. An entrepreneur helped him organize his return expedition to Charlesfort, but when Ribault discovered the man's shady reputation, he feared he might persuade the queen, Elizabeth I, to require his French colonists to swear allegiance to England. Ribault tried to embark in secret but was caught and imprisoned for two years.

When he failed to return as promised in six months, his soldiers at Charlesfort ran short of supplies. At first, the Natives provided them with food, but as winter approached, they had no surplus to share. Irritated by the soldiers' constant demands, the Natives dispersed to distant woodlands to hunt and forage, leaving the Charlesfort men to fend for themselves. The Charlesfort commander made dreadful conditions even worse by imposing harsh punishments on his men for small infractions. After he hanged one man and exiled another to a small nearby island to starve, the soldiers mutinied and killed him.

When most of Charlesfort's remaining food burned, the desperate soldiers built a crude boat and caulked it with pine pitch and Spanish moss. They stitched sails from their shirts and sheets, destroyed the fort, and sailed for France, rescuing the exiled man along the way.

They were unprepared to make the 3,500-mile voyage across the stormy wintertime Atlantic in an open boat. They were soldiers, not sailors. The experienced

At the mouth of the St. Johns River, the explorer Jean Ribault erected a stone column carved with the French royal coat of arms and claimed it as French territory. When René Goulaine de Laudonnière (*right*) returned to Florida in 1564, he visited the column with Athore (*left*), son of the Timucua chief Saturiwa. The scene is imagined here in a 1591 engraving by Theodore de Bry after Jacques Le Moyne de Morgues.

249

seamen had all returned to France with Ribault and Laudonnière.

The cabin boy, Guillaume Rouffi, may have spent enough time at sea to realize the expedition was probably doomed. He stayed behind, living with the Natives near Charlesfort until a Spanish commander arrived belatedly from Cuba to oust the French, who had departed two years earlier. The Spaniard took Rouffi with him back to Havana.

Rouffi's fears were well founded. The Charlesfort soldiers' boat was becalmed for weeks. The men ran out of food and water and resorted to eating their leather shoes and jerkins and drinking seawater and urine. A storm blew them along, but when the wind died, land was still not in sight.

The desperate mariners drew lots to decide which one would be eaten by the others. The unlucky victim was the same man who had been exiled to the small island by the hated Charlesfort commander. An English ship rescued the rest of the emaciated men in time to prevent another grim lottery.

In 1564, Laudonnière resumed the Huguenot settlement effort. He set sail for North America with three ships, three hundred men, and four women. They landed on the Florida coast in the same place where Ribault had landed on their first voyage. They found the Timucua honoring, perhaps worshiping, the ornate stone column with tributes of food and flowers. The Natives kissed the column and insisted the French follow suit. To promote good relations between the two cultures, the Huguenots complied.

With the Natives' help, the French built Fort Caroline on the south bank of the St. Johns River. A year later, when promised supplies from France had failed to arrive, the people at Fort Caroline, like their counterparts at Charlesfort, leaned too heavily on the Natives for food. Tired of the Europeans' demands, the Timucua killed several Frenchmen. Laudonnière, ill and discouraged, prepared to sail with the other settlers back to France. Ribault, fresh out of prison, arrived at Fort Caroline in 1565 with supplies on the eve of the colonists' departure.

Pedro Menéndez, the Spanish commander aiming to establish colonies in La Florida, reached the coast within days of Ribault. Menéndez was under orders from his king to "kill and burn" any Protestants he encountered in North America. He attacked Fort Caroline, killing more than 140 Huguenots and seizing the fort. Laudonnière was wounded but escaped with a handful of others and sailed back to Europe.

Menéndez murdered the rest of the Huguenots at an inlet south of St. Augustine after they were shipwrecked on coastal beaches during a storm. Ribault was among the victims. The inlet, the tidal river it fed, and the tabby-and-coquina fort built there centuries later were all named Matanzas, the Spanish word for "massacres."

In 1566, Menéndez sailed north to Parris Island and built Fort San Salvador, in part to prevent the French from returning to the site. He laid out Santa Elena according to a design approved by the king for all of Spain's colonial towns in the New World. Because Santa Elena was named the capital of La Florida, Pedro Menéndez as governor was based there. Archaeologists excavating the site hope to identify his house at Santa Elena.

CHAPTER 15 *Beaufort*

BEAUFORT IS HOME to significant treasures of southern architecture built in what is called the Beaufort style. The town is a National Historic Landmark, the highest designation of historic importance awarded by the federal government. Together with the town of Beaufort, Beaufort County, which encompasses sixty-five islands and marsh hammocks, boasts more historic tabby than anywhere else in the United States.

Experts say the quality of Beaufort's historic buildings are the equal of the structures in better-known historic northern towns such as Salem, Portsmouth, and Providence. The Beaufort style, while similar to that of neighboring Charleston and Savannah, is unique in large part because of its abundance of old tabby buildings.

Beaufort was founded in 1711 by the wealthy planters John Barnwell and Thomas Nairn. Three years later, the Yamasee War erupted. It was one of the deadliest conflicts between Native Americans and European settlers in colonial America. Yamasee warriors, their bodies painted in red and black rays to symbolize war and death, were described by terrified townspeople as looking like "devils coming out of hell."

A settler named Seymore Burroughs was shot in the back and through the cheek but managed to swim several miles down the Broad River to John Barnwell's plantation and warn him about the attack. Barnwell sent riders to neighboring settlements and loaded about three hundred people, including African slaves, on a ship and sailed it to the middle of Port Royal Harbor. The Yamasees launched arrows at the ship, but it was out of range, so they burned the settlers' farms and plantations.

British exploration of Beaufort County dates to the 1600s. Captain William Hilton was the first to describe the sandy headlands of the island now known as Hilton Head. Robert Sanford landed on the coast in 1666 and then sailed away in search of colonists and supplies for a new colony on Port Royal Sound. The ship's doctor, Henry Woodward, stayed behind to establish trade with the Natives. Woodward, South Carolina's first British settler, got to know the Native people and the land as he traveled around the area.

When ships carrying the first group of English settlers arrived in 1670, Woodward warned them against settling near Port Royal Sound, since the Spanish were still active in the area. The colonists headed north and founded Charleston instead. By the late 1600s, British settlers in Beaufort County had begun to clamor for a center of commerce. A location on the Broad River was chosen as a site for the town because it was considered the best place in the Carolina colony for ships to load and unload cargo.

Woodward was among the first to grow rice on the Carolina coast. When a foreign ship took refuge from a storm in Charleston Harbor in 1685, the captain gave the doctor rice seed, which he planted. It grew well in the Lowcountry and soon became colonial Carolina's most valuable crop, followed by indigo, a plant used to make an inky-blue dye. Growing rice and indigo required a huge labor force. Between 1720 and 1740, forty thousand Africans were enslaved and brought to Carolina, most of them through the port of Charleston.

A scandal erupted in Beaufort when the wife of a prominent indigo grower abandoned her husband and child and ran off to the Caribbean with another man. In 1757, she bore a son, Alexander Hamilton, who overcame the stigma of his birth and played a leading role in early American history.

Beaufort flourished as wealthy planters built mansions on a bluff overlooking the river of the same name. They occupied elegant townhomes in summer to escape the mosquito-borne fevers that plagued their low-lying plantations. The mansions were designed in an English style but adapted for the climate and built with indigenous materials. Tabby was a favored building material.

During the American Revolution, British ships attempted to capture Port Royal Sound but were repelled in the Battle of Beaufort. Later, the British took coastal Carolina.

After the creation of the United States, Beaufort planters added sea island cotton to their crops. Cotton and rice made the Carolina coast one of the richest, most aristocratic regions in the new nation. Beaufort boasted some of the south's best libraries and prep schools, including Beaufort College, which sent graduates to Harvard, Yale,

Princeton, and West Point. Every white resident of age and ability in Beaufort could read and write.

Because of its elegant homes, well-educated residents, and natural charm, Beaufort was often called the Newport of the South. The good times ended in April 1861 when the first shots of the Civil War were fired by Confederate troops on a federal fort in Charleston Harbor. The historian Lawrence S. Rowland calls November 7, 1861, the most important day in the history of Beaufort. Slaves who heard the cannon fire as Union troops advanced called it the "Day of the Big Gun Shoot." Beaufort's white residents fled in a mass evacuation nicknamed the "Great Skedaddle." The Union army may have spared Beaufort's historic buildings because it met no opposition from the town. A number of Beaufort's large houses were converted into hospitals, dormitories, and officers' quarters.

Beaufort was left in economic ruin after the war. A powerful earthquake in 1886 destroyed many buildings. A phosphate mine opened and boosted the economy for a while, but it closed after Beaufort was devastated by a major hurricane in 1893. The storm killed more than two thousand Lowcountry residents, most of them formerly enslaved people scratching out a living on the sea islands. Beaufort was still rebuilding in 1907 when a fire broke out and damaged most of the downtown area.

The boll weevil almost ended cotton production in the South in the 1920s. Almost half of Beaufort's residents relocated. Beaufort joined the ranks of the state's poorest communities, dependent on truck farming and shrimping.

World War II led to the establishment of a naval air station, a naval hospital, and a Marine Corps training depot, all in Beaufort County. Resort development on Hilton Head and Fripp Islands helped create a thriving tourist industry.

Beaufort citizens launched a major revitalization project aimed at restoring the town's historic houses and public buildings. Beaufort's Bay Street was proclaimed one of the most beautiful in the nation, and tourists flooded in, eager to explore colonial and antebellum mansions and outlying plantations. Retirees, attracted by the mild winters and gentle pace of life, moved to town. New businesses opened to serve the newcomers and tourists.

SITE 37   *Short Take*

Seawall

dates unknown

East end of Bay Street between Cartaret and Stephen Elliott Park

Stretches of Beaufort's historic seawall run intermittently along Bay Street. The wall was built in sections over time to protect private and public properties from tidal flooding. The oldest sections of the wall were built with original tabby made with oyster-shell lime; portland cement was added to seawall segments constructed after the Civil War.

Three of Beaufort's first families built waterfront townhomes side by side during the 1850s and combined their considerable resources to build one stretch of the seawall along the 600 block of Bay Street. The three families owned the vacant lots between their homes and the Beaufort River. They dedicated the lots to the city with the provision that nothing would ever be built on them to spoil their views of the river and tidal marshes.

The oldest parts of the seawall were built at Black's Point, named for James Black, who owned a shipbuilding enterprise there at the start of the American Revolution. The shipyard was one of the most successful businesses in the region. One house on the point had a garden that sloped down to the water. The owners built a seawall around three sides of the garden to keep salty tidewaters out of their flower beds.

Other stretches of the tabby seawall were added from time to time. Even after centuries of weathering, the wash of daily tides, and storm surges, many parts of the seawall still stand.

A long section of the structure can be viewed at Stephen Elliott Park at the foot of the Woods Memorial Bridge downtown where Cartaret and Bay Streets intersect. Other stretches of the seawall are visible at King and Short Streets, and East and Craven Streets.

The seawall is considered a good example of tabby's suitability for large public works. It also exhibits the transition from original tabby to revival tabby made with portland cement instead of burned-oyster-shell lime.

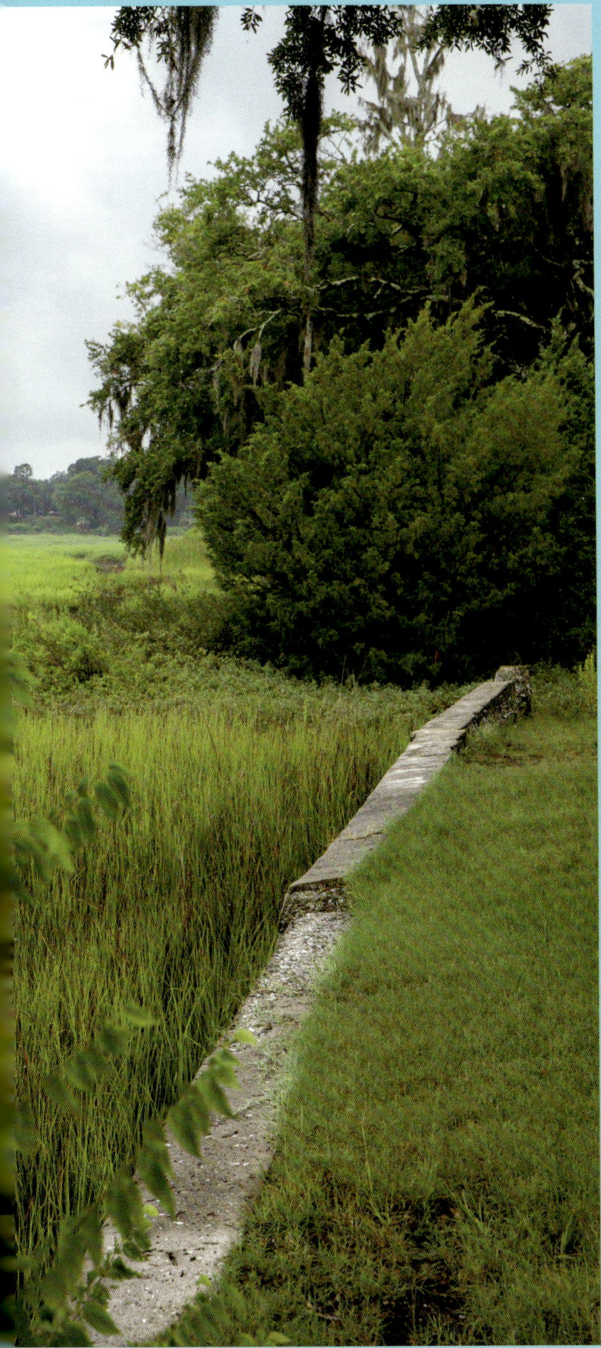

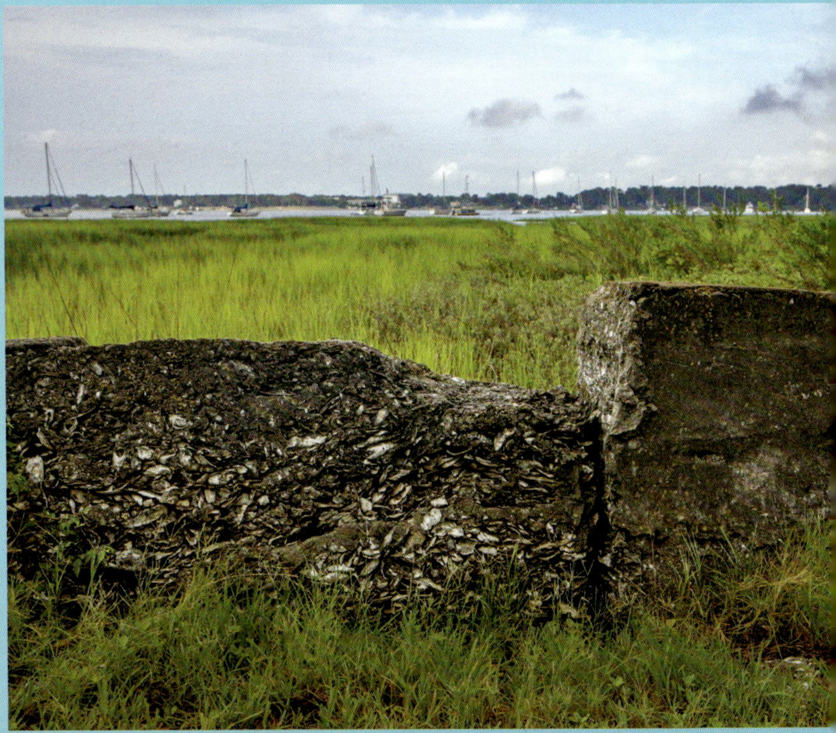

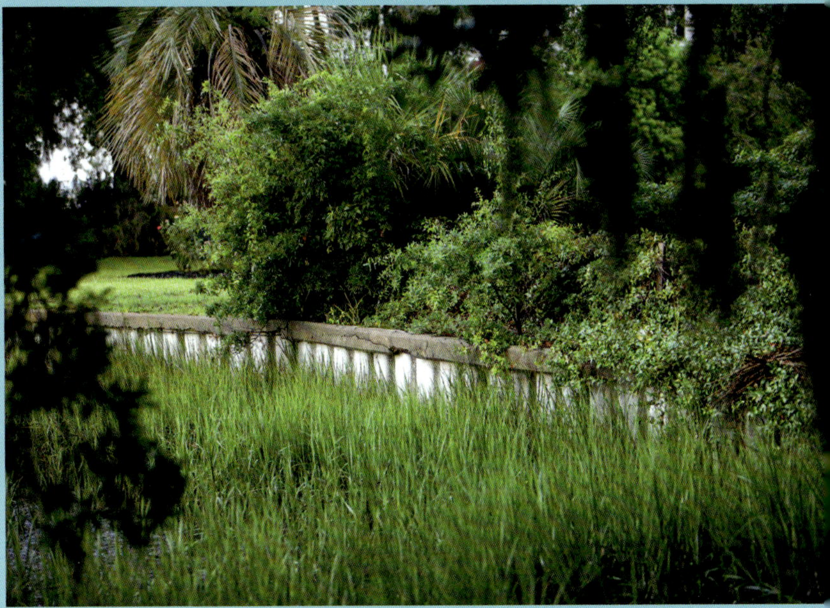

SITE 38 *Short Take*

Arsenal

1798; rebuilt 1852

713 Craven Street

National Register Historic District

Troops with the Beaufort Volunteer Artillery, the fifth-oldest militia in the United States, were organized well before the Revolutionary War to fight pirates, Spanish invaders, and Indigenous peoples. The volunteers, all well-trained and well-equipped prominent local citizens, fought alongside the Continental Army against the British during the American Revolution. They fought in the Battle of Port Royal in 1861, one of the earliest amphibious actions of the Civil War.

After the revolution, the volunteers raised money to build a tabby fortress on the old courthouse square where they could store weapons and have their headquarters. Armed with six cannons, the Arsenal accommodated a garrison of 250 men, who received no government support.

The mission of the volunteers was to protect Beaufort and its ports in wartime, but they also used the Arsenal to hold upscale social events such as banquets and balls. Women were usually not invited to events that featured large quantities of alcohol.

Before the Civil War, volunteers patrolled the area for runaway slaves and forced them back to the Arsenal to be punished. Secessionists rebuilt the tabby Arsenal with brick shortly before the Civil War. Only a corner of the original tabby structure remains.

During the Great Depression, the Arsenal was renovated under the auspices of the federal Works Progress Administration, an agency that employed an estimated 8.5 million out-of-work people.

The Volunteer Artillery later became the National Guard of Beaufort, whose troops were housed in parts of the Arsenal until the late twentieth century. The imposing crenellated building, limewashed a pale yellow, now houses the headquarters of the Beaufort History Museum, a gift shop, and a visitor center.

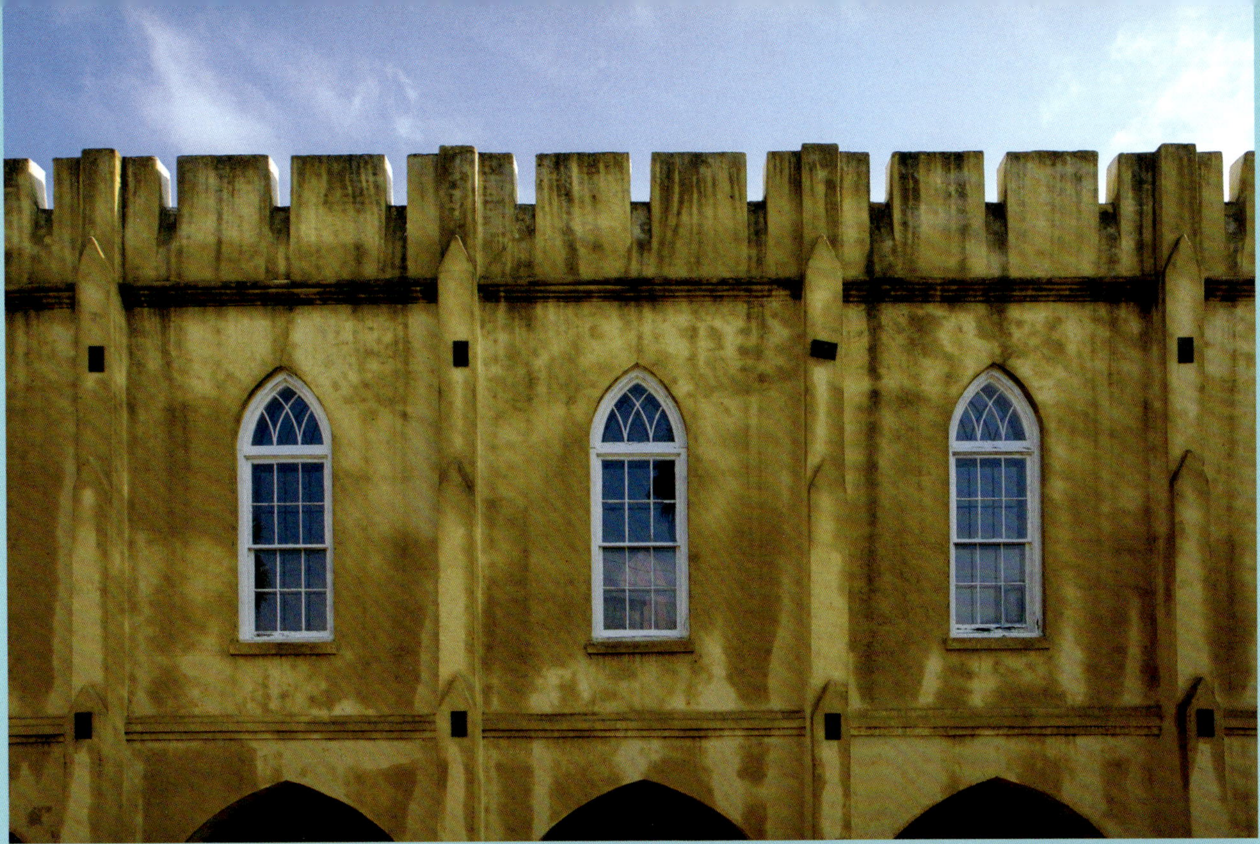

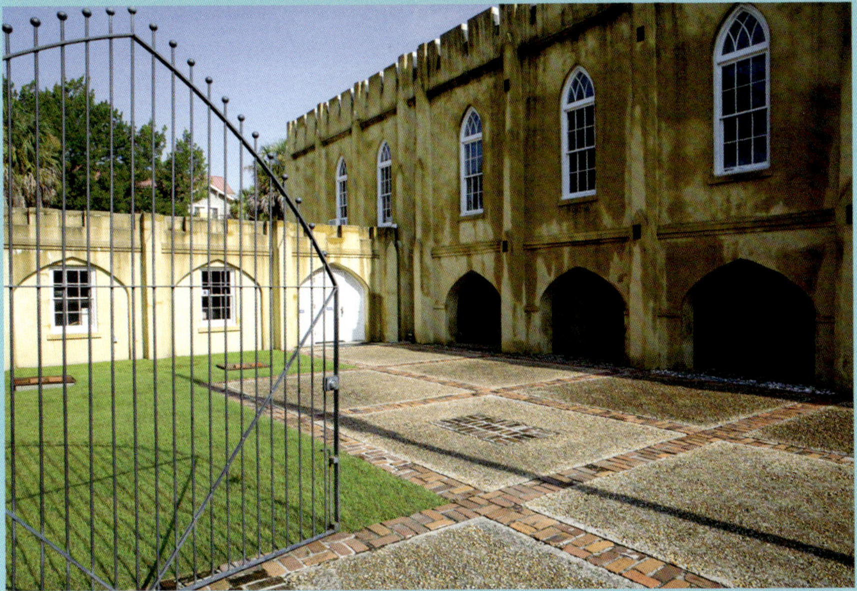

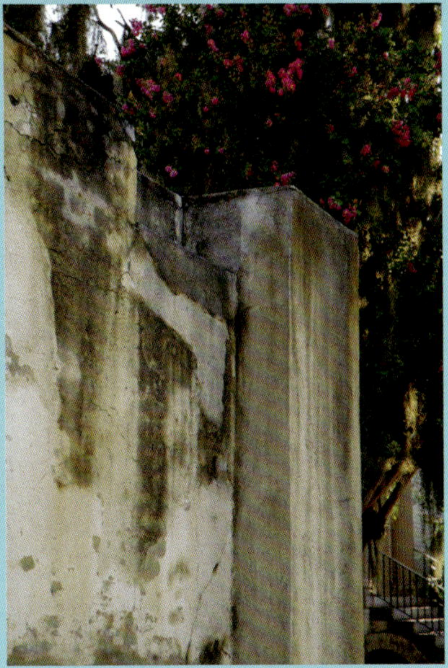

John Mark Verdier House

c. 1804

801 Bay Street

National Register of Historic Places

HISTORIC SIGNIFICANCE: Now a museum run by the Historic Beaufort Foundation, the Verdier mansion is the only antebellum planter's mansion in Beaufort open to the public. Permanent exhibits include a diorama of Bay Street c. 1863, built to scale, and a model of the CSS *Planter*, a Confederate ship commandeered during the Civil War by Robert Smalls, a slave who piloted himself, his family, and his friends to freedom.

The John Mark Verdier mansion on Bay Street is one of the grandest old houses in a town of exceptional historic properties. It is a blend of vernacular building materials and sophisticated European design. Its basement is constructed of tabby made with burned-oyster-shell lime. Pattern books from Europe provided the design of the residence's traditional appearance.

The Verdier mansion sits on a raised original-tabby foundation topped by a two-story structure, a style transferred to South Carolina by planters from Barbados. Because it is higher, the main house is cooled by prevailing breezes during sultry Lowcountry summers. It is also out of reach of all but the most extreme hurricane flooding.

The mansion was designed in the classic Federal style with a double-tiered columned portico that extends forward from the façade from the lower level to the hipped roof. The interior is Adam in design (a neoclassical style associated with the Scottish architect William Adam and his sons), with a center hall flanked by a drawing room and dining room in front and two additional rooms behind. Mantels were elaborately hand carved with ribbons, fruit, flowers, wheat sheaves, and allegorical figures. A graceful archway frames the staircase, and a Palladian window lights the landing. On the second floor is a large ballroom where Beaufort's first telephone was later installed.

Moldings carved to look like rope reflect Verdier's involvement in shipping, and the elegance of the mansion indicates his rise from middle-class indigo trader to upscale planter. At the time, Beaufort was one of the wealthiest towns in colonial America, and the richest planters built their summer townhomes on Bay Street to reflect their prosperity, social standing, and taste.

The planters' wealth came from sea island cotton, which reached record production levels between 1790 and 1825. The silky, long-staple cotton, which fetched record prices

259

on international markets, grew best on the sea islands of the Southeast.

   Verdier, the son of a French Huguenot immigrant, got his start as an indigo trader at a time when Great Britain paid the colonies a subsidy for producing the rich blue dye. Before the revolution, Verdier speculated in forfeited land, but when the British indigo subsidies ended at the start of the war, he was overextended and unable to pay his bills. After a brief incarceration in debtor's prison in Charleston, he returned to Beaufort and began growing sea island cotton on some of his acreage, with the forced labor of more than two hundred enslaved people. Soon he was wealthier than ever.

   In 1825, the Verdier mansion hosted the marquis de Lafayette, the French hero of the American Revolution. As a teenager, Lafayette had joined the Patriot cause; after the war, he delivered a speech from the Verdier mansion's portico. The home was then called the Lafayette House.

   Verdier died in Charleston two years later. Very few possessions were listed in his estate. He had already given most of his assets to his children.

   During the Civil War, Union commanders appropriated the mansion as their headquarters.

   In the 1930s, the building was occupied by a fish market, a fruit stand, an art school, and a stenographer. The paint was peeling and repairs were needed. It was a mighty comedown for a mansion once lauded as a Beaufort landmark. By World War II, the structure had been condemned. When it was purchased by a developer, word circulated that the Verdier mansion would be replaced by a gas station. A group of Beaufort residents came to the rescue and collected donations to restore the property. They formed the Historic Beaufort Foundation and restored the house to serve as the organization's headquarters, a museum, and an interpretive center.

A Beaufort resident named Dennis Cannady, a retired mechanical engineer and history buff, spent more than a year creating a scale-model diorama of Bay Street buildings as they were in 1863. It is now on permanent exhibition in the Verdier House. Cannady also created a model of the css *Planter*, the Confederate ship stolen by Robert Smalls to escape to the Union during the Civil War. The model is also on permanent exhibition there.

Robert Smalls, 1839–1915

Born in Beaufort in 1839, Robert Smalls was the son of a slave, Lydia Polite, and an unknown white man. His heroism during the Civil War prompted President Abraham Lincoln to open the Union army to Black soldiers and ask Smalls to recruit them. After the war, Smalls served in both houses of the South Carolina legislature and was the first Black man elected to the U.S. Congress, where he served for eleven years. He was convicted of taking a bribe as a state senator but was later pardoned. The charges may have been trumped up because of his race.

Growing up in Beaufort, Smalls lived with his mother, a nanny to the children of John McKee, in a small structure behind the McKee house at 511 Prince Street. Some historians believe Smalls's father may have been his enslaver's son or grandson. The McKees favored Robert to the point that his mother worried he would grow up unaware of the horrors of slavery. She sent him to McKee's cotton fields to observe the enslaved being whipped.

Robert Smalls was sent to Charleston to be hired out. He worked on the docks, learning to rig and run workboats. By the time he was nineteen, he was an expert boatman, familiar with Charleston Harbor and adjacent coastal waters. He was allowed to keep one dollar of his weekly pay; the rest went to his owner.

In Charleston, Smalls married Hannah Jones. Aware that his enslaved wife and three children could be sold away from him at any time, Smalls tried to buy them out of slavery, but it was impossible to raise the $800 purchase price.

At the outbreak of the Civil War, Smalls was conscripted into the Confederate military as a wheelman on the css *Planter*, described as a coastwise vessel built of live oak and cedar. The ship was converted to transport ammunition between Confederate forts in Charleston Harbor. Smalls learned the signals used by Confederate captains to pass through security checkpoints in the mined and heavily guarded harbor.

During the war, Union ships blockaded the southern coast to keep the South from sending goods to European markets and importing guns and other war supplies. The Union ships offered freedom for slaves willing to risk their lives to escape.

On a spring night in 1863, the *Planter*'s white captain and two or three white shipmates went ashore, leaving Smalls and the enslaved crewmen on board. It was the chance Smalls had waited for. He sent word for his family and friends to meet the *Planter* at a rendezvous point. Because the penalty of being caught was death, two of the

The Honorable Robert Smalls, photograph by Matthew Brady, c. 1875–1900

enslaved crewmen aboard the *Planter* were too frightened to make the attempt and got off the boat before it left the dock. At the rendezvous point, Smalls picked up fourteen more enslaved people: six men, five women, and three children, including his wife and daughters.

Over the next several hours, as the *Planter* steamed through the harbor past Fort Johnson and Fort Sumter, Smalls blew the ship's whistle, flashed the appropriate lantern signals, and folded his arms to imitate the usual stance of the white captain. With his face hidden by the captain's wide-brimmed straw hat, Smalls passed through the checkpoints with ease. Smalls and his passengers were so determined to reach freedom that they had agreed to blow up the ship if they were stopped. The Confederates were clueless until the *Planter* cleared the mouth of the harbor, but by then it was too late. As the vessel approached the Union blockade, it was spotted by the crew of the USS *Onward*, which prepared to fire.

Smalls ordered the Confederate and South Carolina flags lowered and a white bedsheet hoisted in their place. It was sunrise and just light enough for the *Onward*'s crew to see the *Planter*'s white sheet of surrender and the Black faces aboard the Confederate ship. The people on the *Planter* held their breath; the Union crewmen held their fire. As the *Planter* escapees gathered on deck, singing, shouting, and dancing, Smalls swept off the straw hat and announced to the captain of the *Onward* that he had brought the Union "some guns."

In addition to a twenty-four-pound howitzer and a thirty-two-pound pivot gun, the *Planter* carried four other guns, including one dented in the original Confederate attack on Fort Sumter, and two hundred rounds of ammunition. On board the ship, Union sailors found documents detailing Confederate shipping routes, the location of mines in the harbor, and timetables for ships docking and departing. Smalls delivered all that, plus seventeen enslaved people, including himself, to freedom. The next day, a Union officer wrote to the secretary of the navy, praising Smalls's skill and bravery in engineering the escape. Smalls was awarded $1,500 for his effort; his crew also received compensation.

Smalls was celebrated as a hero in northern states. He lobbied Edwin Stanton, the secretary of war, to begin enlisting freed slaves in the Union forces. President Lincoln agreed and sent Smalls on a recruiting tour. It is said that Smalls's Gullah Geechee creole language helped him recruit more than five thousand Black troops in the coastal Southeast. He joined the battle himself in late 1862 when he returned to pilot the *Planter* and the USS *Keokuk*, an ironclad. He took part in well over a dozen military actions, including the Union assault on Fort Sumter in April 1863. During the attack at Folly Island Creek, South Carolina, the *Planter* took such heavy fire that the white captain hid in the coal bunker. Smalls took command and saved the ship and crew. He was promoted to the rank of captain for his bravery, with a salary of $150 month, which made him one of the highest-paid Black troops during the Civil War. Even before the war ended, Smalls had served a number of times as a delegate to the state constitutional convention in Union-held South Carolina. In Philadelphia to have the *Planter* repaired in 1864, he was evicted from an all-white streetcar. Smalls then led one of the nation's first mass boycotts of segregated public transit. Three years later, the city passed a law permitting integrated streetcars. After the war, Smalls was promoted to brigadier general in the South Carolina militia. With freedom and funds, he purchased the McKee House, the Beaufort home where he grew up and where his mother had worked as a slave. When members of the McKee family became destitute during Reconstruction, Smalls took them in and supported them. He started a school for the children of freed slaves, founded a newspaper called the *Beaufort Southern Standard*, and opened a general store.

He served in both houses of the state legislature and was elected to Congress in 1874, where he became a champion of civil rights. Partisans accused him of taking a $5,000 bribe during his term as a state senator. He denied the charge but was convicted in 1877 and sentenced to three years in prison. He was pardoned by the governor in 1879.

After Hannah's death, Smalls married Annie Wigg in 1890. They had one son, William Robert; Annie died in 1895. Smalls served as a U.S. customs collector in Beaufort from 1889 until 1911. He stayed active in politics until he died in 1915 at age seventy-five.

SITE 40

Parish Church of St. Helena

1724

505 Church Street

National Register of Historic Places

HISTORIC SIGNIFICANCE: The Parish Church of St. Helena is one of the oldest active churches in North America. Its congregation dates to 1712; the tabby foundation of the first sanctuary dates to 1724. Tabby walls flank part of the churchyard and some of the burial plots. During the Civil War, the church served as a hospital for Union troops; doctors reportedly used marble grave slabs as makeshift operating tables.

The original Parish Church of St. Helena was established in 1712 by South Carolina's governing body, the Commons House of Assembly, under the lords proprietors. It is the second-oldest church in South Carolina and one of the oldest still active in North America. It is a decade older than the celebrated Old North Church in Boston, where Paul Revere saw two lanterns lit in the belfry, indicating that the British were attacking by sea.

During St. Helena's first dozen years, services were conducted in the homes of parishioners because church construction was delayed. Beaufort was a pioneer town in the early 1700s, subject to attacks from Natives, pirates, and enemies from European countries competing for territory on the continent.

In 1715, Indigenous people, aggrieved at being pushed from their land, enslaved, and cheated by Europeans attacked Beaufort, destroying property and killing townspeople. This was the start of the Yamasee War. Most of the parishioners escaped on flatboats to Charleston up the coast, remaining there until the bloody conflict ended, three years later.

Beaufort recovered after the war and began to grow again. The town's prosperity was fueled by indigo. Planters who grew the plant and processed the leaves into a vivid blue dye received generous subsidies from England for producing cakes of indigo dye.

Construction of the first St. Helena church began in 1724. Walls built of bricks brought to Beaufort as ballast on sailing ships rose on a tabby foundation. The walls were finished with stucco made from oyster-shell lime to make the church look more refined.

Over the next four decades, the church deteriorated. Charles Woodmason, an Anglican minister, noted in his writings in 1766 that Beaufort, the second town in the province, "boasts the very meanest church in it." This

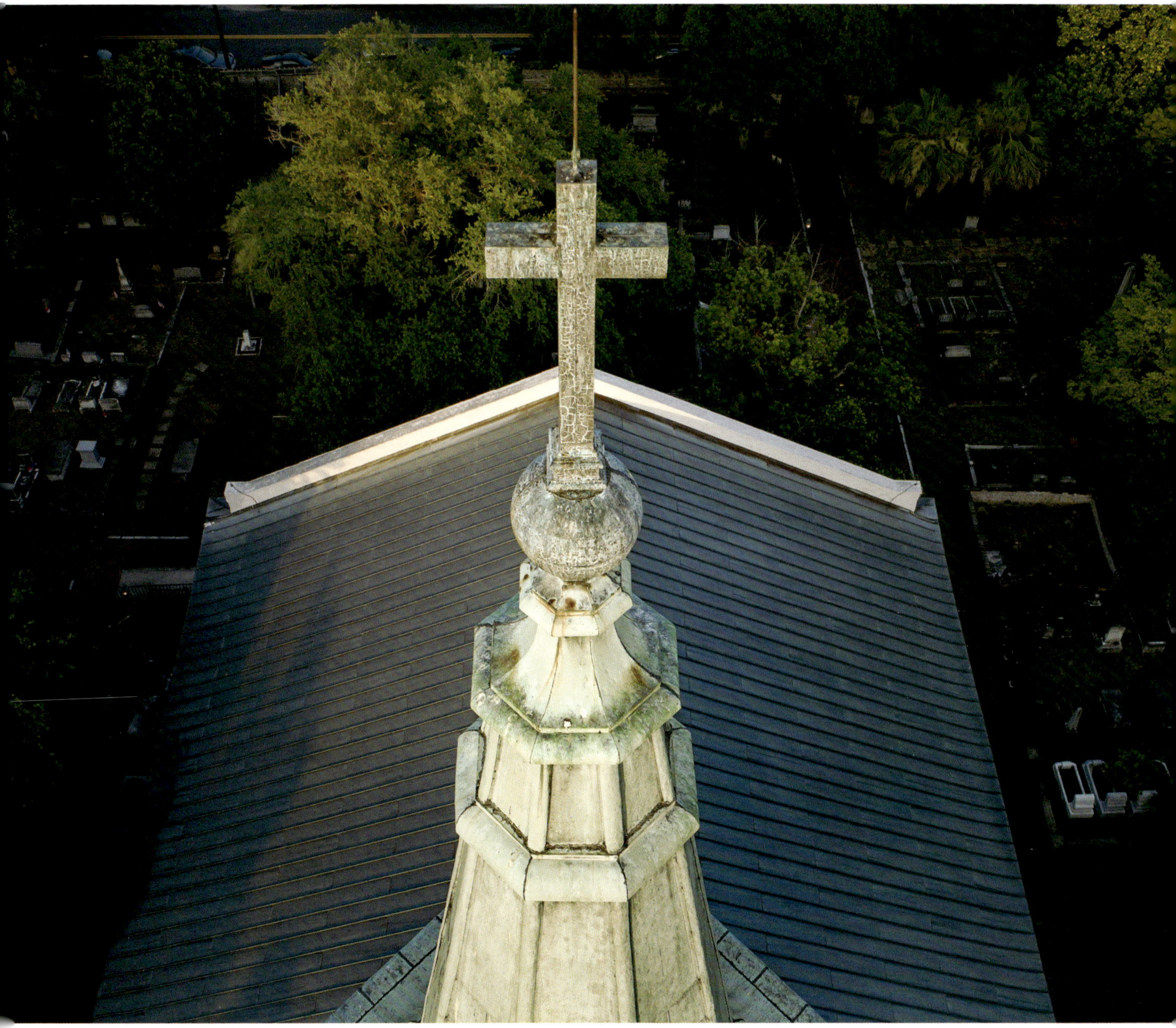

criticism may have prompted the St. Helena congregation to enlarge and improve the structure three years later. Woodmason's account of his travels, *The Carolina Backcountry on the Eve of the Revolution*, is considered one of the most complete and vivid portraits of the American colonial frontier. He was a caustic critic of frontier conditions; his writings have been compared to those of the Irish satirist Jonathan Swift.

In 1817, an addition to the west side of the church enlarged the sanctuary again. When most of the church was razed in 1842, the extension was the only part retained, aside from the tabby foundation. The St. Helena church was rebuilt with the original bricks, heart pine floors, and mouth-blown glass panes in the graceful Palladian windows. The church façade today dates to the 1842 reconstruction. The bells, installed in the 1800s, still call the faithful to worship.

During the church's early years, children newly confirmed there climbed the narrow stairway to the top of the steeple to symbolize their spiritual journey. The charming

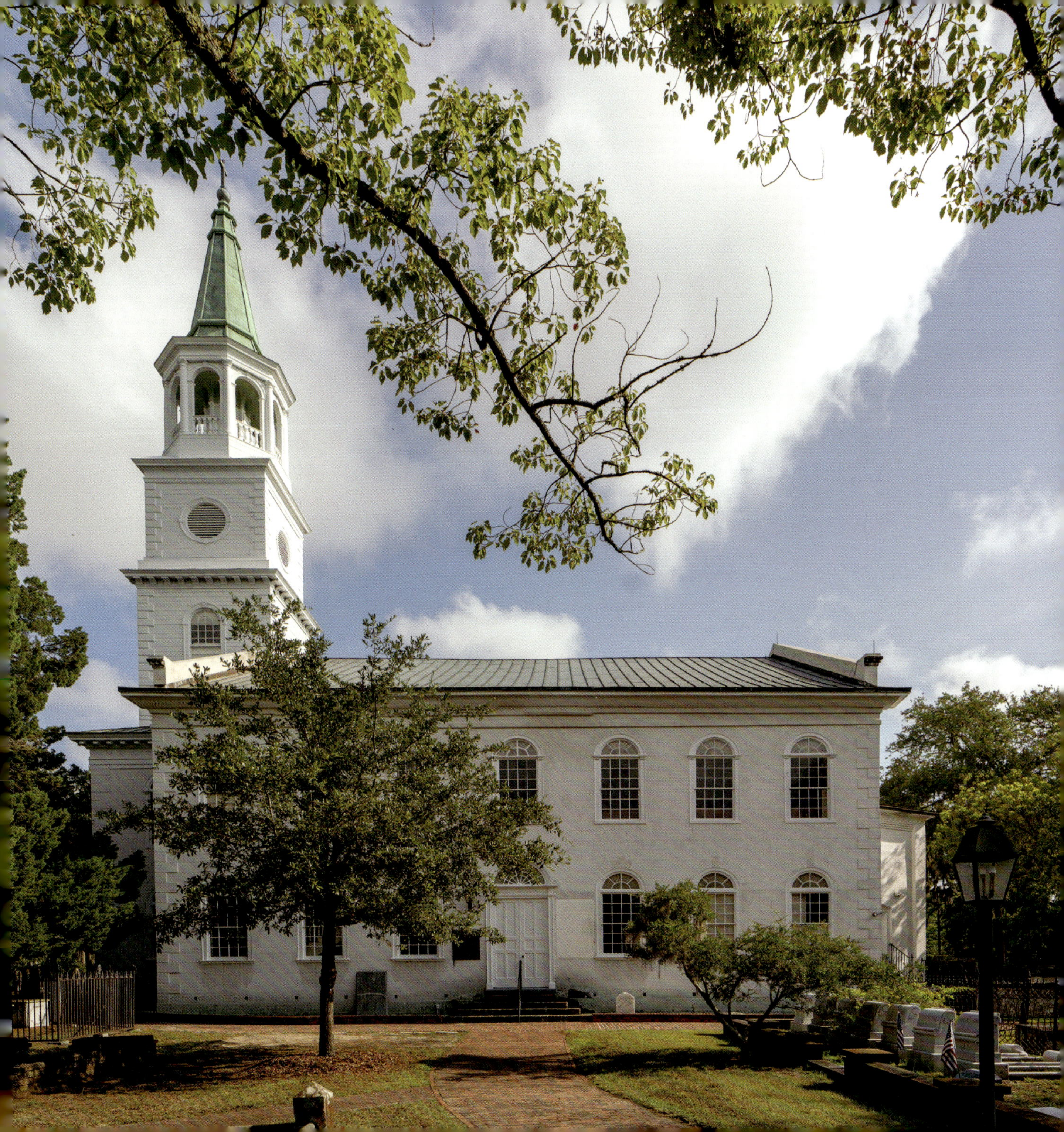

custom was banned later by the company that insured the church.

St. Helena began life allied with the Anglican Church of England. After the revolution, an assembly met in Philadelphia to unify Episcopal congregations in America that had abandoned the state-supported Anglican Church and no longer swore loyalty to the British Crown.

St. Helena remained an Episcopal church until the Civil War. Episcopalians in secessionist states changed the name of their denomination to Protestant Episcopal and pledged their loyalty to the Confederacy. After the fall of Richmond in 1865, the Protestant Episcopalians disbanded without fanfare and returned to their status as mainstream Episcopalians.

From its earliest days, the church served as an important meeting place. Vestrymen, churchwardens, and commissioners met there to discuss the construction of roads, educational needs, tax collections, orphaned children, poor people, and voting. Civil records were kept along with the church books. One of the early vestry members was Thomas Heyward Jr., a signer of the Declaration of Independence.

The church was damaged during the revolution when the British occupied Beaufort. During the Battle of Beaufort, in February 1779, British forces attempted to drive Patriot troops from town but were turned back by militiamen and a few Continental Army troops. The bodies of three British officers killed in battle and buried in shallow graves were later exhumed and reburied with full honors in St. Helena cemetery. Beaufort's townspeople were sharply divided between Patriots and Loyalists. After the Patriots won the war, many South Carolina and Georgia Loyalists fled to the Bahamas, where they discovered a special strain of Anguilla cotton. They shipped the seeds back to relatives on the southeastern coast, and sea island cotton soon became the south's most valuable crop.

The church was occupied again during the Civil War after Union forces took over Beaufort in late 1861. Union soldiers destroyed the organ to prove that the church no longer belonged to southerners. The invaders used the church for religious services and as a meeting place but soon converted it to a hospital for Black troops. Pews were ripped out and balconies were decked over to increase floor space; the pews were burned for firewood.

When congregants returned after the war, it took several years to repair the church sufficiently to hold services. Complete repairs took even longer. Town craftsmen hand carved heart pine pews, and Union sailors stationed in Port Royal Harbor during Reconstruction donated the hand-carved altar as a gift of reconciliation.

The St. Helena church was damaged again in the hurricane of 1893, known locally as the Great Sea Island Storm. The wind almost blew away the east end of the church.

Women of St. Helena's Parish made needlepoint kneelers and cushions to symbolize the links between the three historic churches. In recent years, parishioners raised money for a new pipe organ patterned after the seventeenth-century organs of Europe.

St. Helena manages the tabby Chapel of Ease at Frogmore on St. Helena Island and the brick Old Sheldon Church in Gardens Corner.

St. Helena Cemetery

Veterans of the American Revolution, colonial wars against Native Americans, the Civil War, and every other major conflict through the Korean War are buried at St. Helena Parish Church. Over more than three centuries, 740 people have been laid to rest in the old churchyard.

Tabby was used to construct mausoleums and tombstones, including the tomb of a former rector. Rectors were usually buried under marble slabs.

A few British officers were buried at St. Helena during the American Revolution. Interred initially on the battlefield, the bodies were recovered and reburied at the church cemetery. A Patriot officer who spoke at their funeral commented: "We have now shown our enemies . . . that we have the humanity to give their dead a decent and Christian burial."

The remains of John "Tuscarora Jack" Barnwell occupy the oldest grave. Barnwell was the first to be buried in the cemetery after it opened in 1724. He was a major general in the South Carolina militia and led troops against the Native Tuscarora in the early 1700s. (For more on Barnwell, see the overview to chapter 11, "Hilton Head Island," and chapter 15, "Beaufort.")

Captain John Bull, another early St. Helena parishioner buried in the old churchyard, was a captain in the provincial forces. The forces were formed by the lords proprietors of Carolina, who governed the province from 1670 until 1729, when South Carolina became a crown colony. While Bull was fighting in the Yamasee War, his wife disappeared and was never found. The silver communion set that he commissioned in her honor is still in use at the church.

Another gravestone honors William Elliott II, who was captured by the British during the fall of Charleston in 1780. After the war, he was the first to grow sea island cotton commercially in the Southeast. The cotton brought

St. Helena Parish Church cemetery, which dates to 1724

undreamed-of prosperity to area planters and prompted the importation of thousands of African slaves through the port of Charleston. An obelisk rises above the Elliott family plot at the front of the churchyard.

William Henry Cory served in the British Army in the Crimean War (1853–56), which pitted the Russian Empire against an alliance of England, France, the Ottoman Empire, and the Kingdom of Sardinia. The war made Florence Nightingale a household name. Cory survived the Charge of the Light Brigade. The frontal assault, ill conceived and impossible from the start, resulted in numerous British casualties. The doomed action was memorialized by the poet Alfred, Lord Tennyson with the memorable lines: "Theirs not to reason why, / Theirs but to do and die." Cory later came to America and fought against the United States in the Civil War, again surviving a bloody conflict. He died in his own bed and was buried in the St. Helena churchyard in 1893.

In 1924, Elizabeth Macdonald Wilkinson and her husband were deployed as missionaries to Nigeria by the Church Missionary Society. For nine years, she worked to decrease the high levels of infant mortality among the Igbo people in remote villages in southern Nigeria by combining her Gospel message with lessons on modern sanitation and hygiene. After returning to England in 1933, she wrote *Easy Lessons on the Care of Babies*, thought to be the earliest instructional text written from firsthand knowledge of Igbo customs and culture. She was interred in the churchyard after her death in 1991.

The cemetery is filled with tombstones bearing the names of some of South Carolina's oldest and most illustrious citizens, many of whom appear in contemporary history books. State and federal government officials, celebrated military officers, and respected religious leaders and educators all lie beneath the great live oak trees of the peaceful old graveyard.

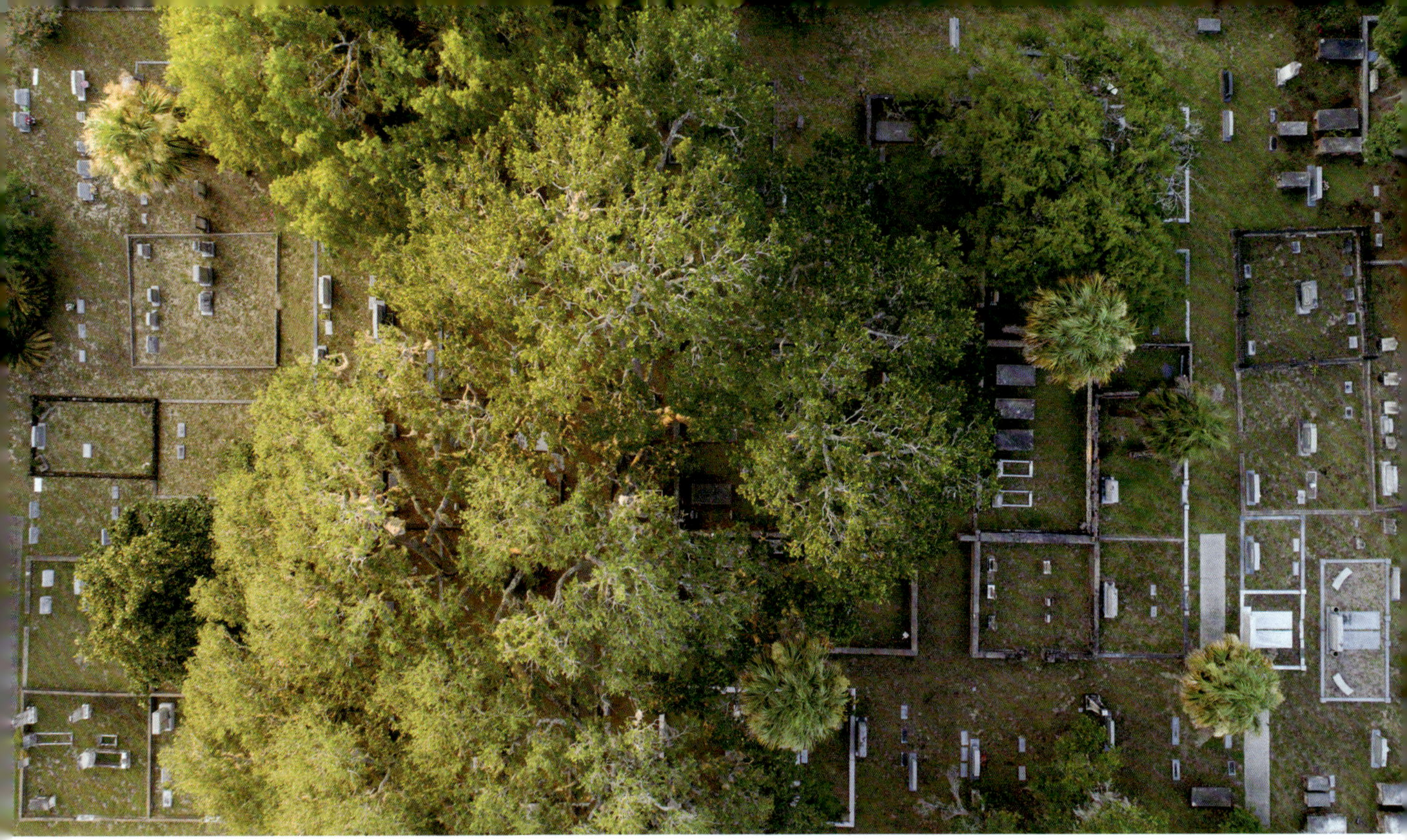

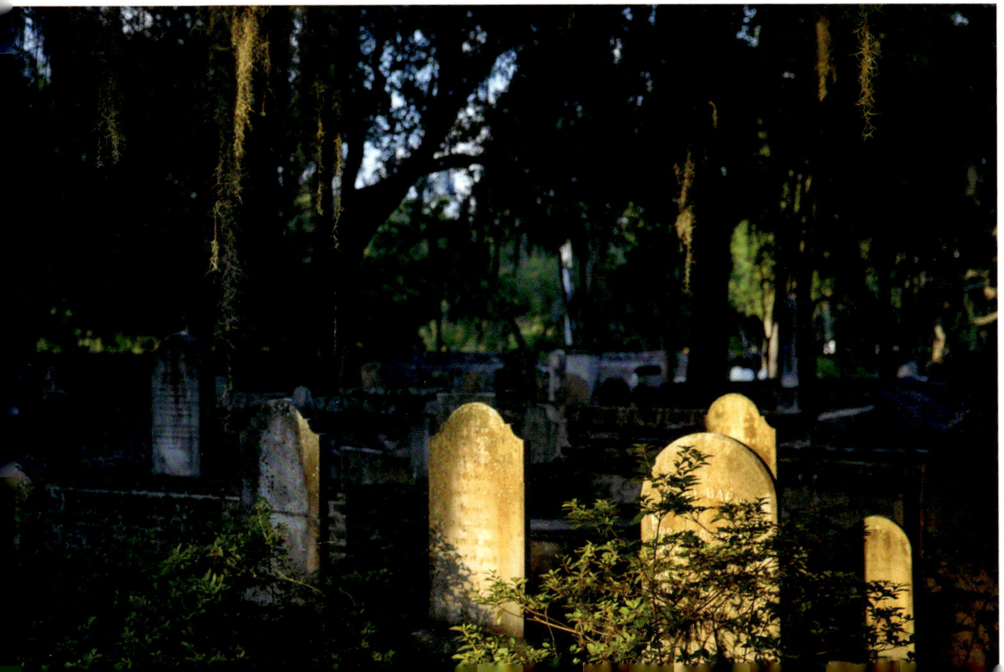

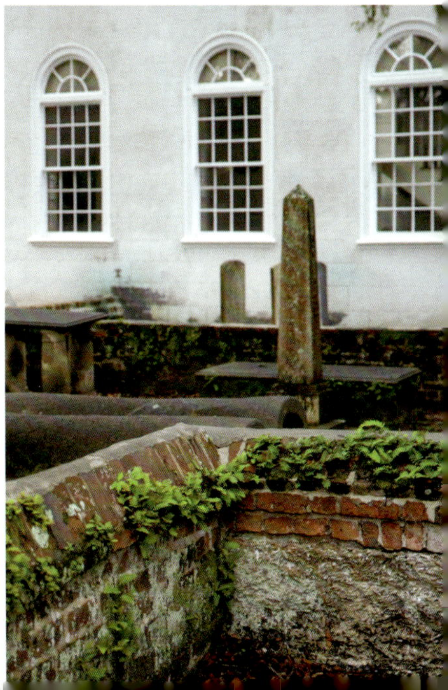

SITE 41

Barnwell-Gough House

c. 1789

705 Washington St.

National Register of Historic Places

HISTORIC SIGNIFICANCE: Designated Hospital #10 in 1862, the Barnwell-Gough House served as the first Civil War medical facility dedicated to the care of Black patients, including troops from the Fifty-Fourth Massachusetts Infantry, the first all-Black regiment in the U.S. Army. Their story was made famous in the award-winning 1989 film *Glory*.

The elegant tabby home was built around 1789 for Elizabeth Barnwell Gough, a member of one of South Carolina's founding families. Her grandfather was Colonel John "Tuscarora Jack" Barnwell, who battled Indigenous Tuscarora in North Carolina and built Fort King George, the first British enclave in today's Georgia. All eight of the South Carolina delegates sent to ratify the U.S. Constitution were related to Elizabeth Barnwell Gough by blood, marriage, or both.

Experts consider the house a treasure of southern architecture of the late eighteenth and early nineteenth centuries. It is listed on the National Register of Historic Places and is a contributing property to Beaufort's National Landmark Historic District.

The design of the house was inspired by neoclassical Palladian architecture, which was based on the clean symmetrical lines of ancient Greece. It was one of the largest tabby buildings of its time, similar in exterior style to the Tabby Manse, another historic residence in Beaufort. The façade of the Barnwell-Gough House is lovely. A pair of slender columns rise high to the second story eaves from the front portico, and the broad, temple-like porch leads to the main entry.

The sides of the portico steps are aligned with the columns, giving the appearance of extended pillars curving and widening as they descend to the lawn. To emulate the grand and dignified homes of Europe that were constructed of quarried stone, Beaufort's colonial builders used a trompe l'oeil technique of scoring the exterior coat of lime mortar covering the original tabby walls to resemble blocks of dressed stone.

The Barnwell-Gough House was among Beaufort's earliest T-shaped, double-pile-plan houses, which became the signature style of the old coastal town. Big windows front and back provide natural ventilation and give the home a light, airy look in spite of its imposing size.

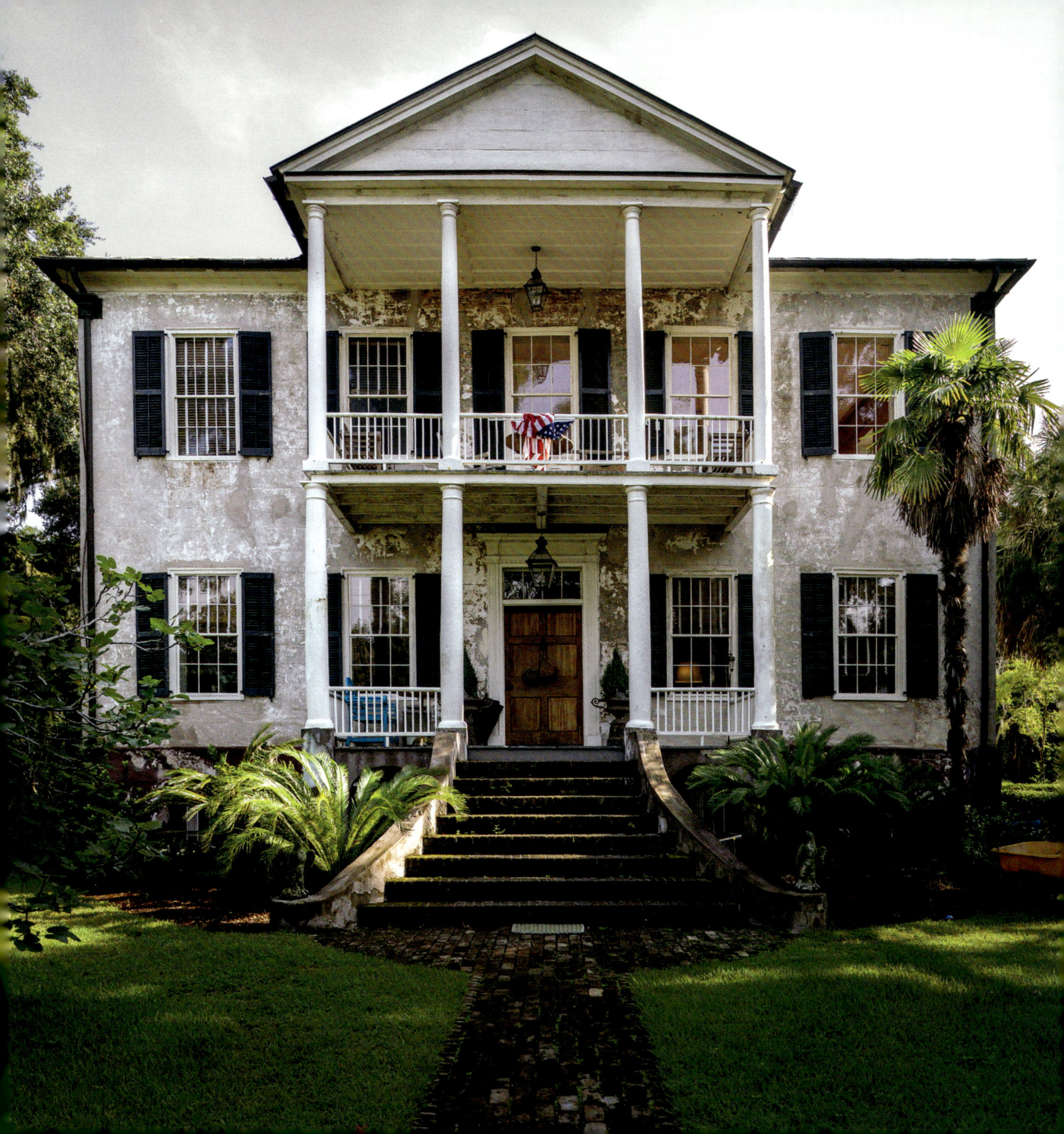

The T-shape is formed by two-story side wings at the rear of the house, a design considered superior to simple rectangular structures because it allowed better airflow to the back rooms. The large tripartite windows in the wings are alterations thought to date to the 1820s or later. They were probably installed to give the building a more fashionable look as well as to improve ventilation.

Built high off the ground on an elevated tabby basement, the house features first and second floors in the classic Beaufort double-pile style, each with a central hall flanked by spacious rooms. One large upstairs room served as a reception room or ballroom.

Unlike the crowded townhomes of Savannah and Charleston, Beaufort's grand houses were built on estate-sized lots. They were owned by wealthy residents whose sprawling indigo and cotton plantations were on nearby islands and the mainland. One expert calls the planters' second homes in Beaufort "plantation houses come-to-town."

Elizabeth Barnwell's parents opposed her desire to marry Richard Gough of James Island (near Charleston) and sent her to London with family chaperones in hope she would get over him. Elizabeth's family believed that Gough was "intemperate"; local lore says he drank and gambled to excess.

Gough followed Elizabeth Barnwell to Europe, where she ignored her family's wishes and married him. When they returned to South Carolina, they settled on James Island. Both Elizabeth and Richard were said to have fiery tempers. Two months after the birth of their only child, Marianna, Elizabeth left her husband and returned to Beaufort with her daughter. Neither Elizabeth nor Marianna ever lived with Gough again.

Elizabeth's father left her inheritance with her brother, Edward Barnwell, to prevent Gough from claiming it, with instructions that Edward build his sister a suitable house.

One of Elizabeth's grandsons was Robert Barnwell Rhett, a South Carolina politician and leading Fire-Eater, as vehement southern advocates of slavery and secession were known. Rhett may have been born in the Barnwell-Gough House.

Over the years, the elegant house has been carved into apartments, occupied by Union troops, and pressed into service as a hospital. It now faces another threat. Because of changes in the local water table caused by golf courses and other new development, saltwater has crept into the groundwater and is wicking upward into the porous tabby walls of the basement. Salt weakens tabby.

The architectural historian Colin Brooker and his wife, the architect Jane Bruce Brooker, stabilized and renovated the Barnwell-Gough House and its parklike setting during their ownership of the property. Brooker has restored more historic tabby structures than anyone else in the world.

The house is still privately owned and is off-limits to the public. Parts of the exterior of the house and its gardens are visible from Washington Street.

Esther Hawks, 1833–1906

One of three large structures collectively designated Hospital #10, the Barnwell-Gough House was the first Civil War hospital dedicated to the care of Black soldiers who were barred from facilities where white Union troops were treated. John Milton Hawks, a New England doctor, agreed to run the hospital. He and his wife, Esther Jane Hill Hawks, readied the tabby mansion to receive patients. Esther Hawks was also a doctor. Female physicians were rare at the time and often practiced—if at all—under the supervision of a male doctor.

Both staunch abolitionists, the Hawkses came to the Union-occupied lower South Carolina coast in 1862 to volunteer their services. Esther Hawks was in charge of opening schools and teaching Black children and adults. She collected clothing and other necessities from northern donors on behalf of the formerly enslaved.

Until the signing of the Emancipation Proclamation on January 1, 1863, those who had been enslaved were in legal limbo; liberated but not yet technically free. Called contrabands—which meant that they were spoils of war and thus the property of the Union—the desperate refugees poured into Beaufort and other Union-held southern locales in need of clothes, food, housing, and medical treatment.

As she helped her husband convert the Barnwell-Gough House into Hospital #10, Esther Hawks noted that months of Union occupation had left the home "nothing but a filthy shell." The graceful mahogany railing for the main stairway had been torn out. Four months after the hospital opened in April 1862, Hawks and her assistants armed themselves with soapy rags to continue cleaning the building as they made rounds.

Esther Hawks circulated through the wards, prescribing treatments and medicines, changing bandages, and moving patients with gangrene to outside shelters to prevent the odor of decomposing flesh from spreading through the hospital. She sat, sometimes for hours, with dying soldiers, holding their hands.

Accustomed to cool New England summers, Esther Hawks suffered in the heat of the Deep South, often working while she was sick with fever. Mosquitoes, fleas, and other insects plagued her and her patients. The thunder of guns provided grim background noise day and night. Confederate soldiers conducted regular raids in the Beaufort area to try to reclaim lost territory.

Union troops provided the hospital with some of its first patients. In the early days of occupation, white Union soldiers stationed in the Port Royal area routinely raped contraband women and girls. One soldier attacked a woman who tried to shield her daughter. He grabbed the mother by her hair, and when she struggled, he shot her in the shoulder. The woman spent weeks in Hospital #10. Hawks said other contrabands were hospitalized after being raped or shot when they resisted the soldiers' "vile demands." In the early days of occupation, rape and other crimes went largely unpunished. Some Union officers tacitly endorsed the behavior by keeping contraband women and teenage girls hostage themselves.

The Port Royal area was initially under the management of a special agent within the U.S. Treasury Department, sent south to oversee the harvesting and sale of valuable long-staple sea island cotton to help fund the Union war effort. The agent in charge of the Port Royal area had no experience in managing civilians or troops in a war zone. When the Union general Rufus Saxton assumed

Dr. Esther Hill Hawks

command, conditions rapidly improved. Offending soldiers, including officers, were dispatched to the front lines or drummed out of the army.

In July 1863, Esther Hawks helped care for survivors of the Battle of Fort Wagner, a Confederate stronghold on Morris Island that guarded Charleston Harbor. Esther Hawks said wounded men flooded Beaufort in the days following the battle. About 150 of the "brave boys" were brought to Hospital #10, "mangled and ghastly" with life-threatening wounds, many missing arms and legs. There were not enough beds, so the patients lay on blankets on the floor. Food was scarce, but area contrabands, proud of the bravery of the Black troops, brought provisions to the hospital every day: "Buckets full of nice broth and gruel, pitchers of lemonade, fruit, cakes, vegetables . . . everything needed." The contrabands did this even though they had scant rations themselves.

The troops who attacked the fort were with the Fifty-Fourth Massachusetts Volunteer Infantry, an all-Black regiment composed of freedmen from the North. The Fifty-Fourth was the first Black regiment in the United States. The soldiers were led by Colonel Robert Gould Shaw, a young white officer who died in the assault on Fort Wagner. When a Union general inquired about Shaw's body, he was told by Confederates that the young man had been buried with his Black soldiers, the Confederates using a racist slur to describe them. Shaw's father later wrote that he and his wife "would not have his body moved from where it lies surrounded by his brave & devoted soldiers."

After the war, the remains of the soldiers buried in a trench by Fort Wagner were reinterred at the National Cemetery in Beaufort, their graves all marked "unknown."

When Milton Hawks was detailed temporarily to Florida, Esther Hawks was left in charge of Hospital #10, although female doctors were considered unfit to manage anything as complex as a hospital. When her husband was not immediately replaced, Esther Hawks credited her promotion to an oversight as well as to a shortage of doctors, particularly ones who would treat Black patients.

In September 1863, Hospital #10 was placed under the command of a doctor described by Esther Hawks as young, dissipated, inefficient, and a racist "tyrant." When a nurse complained of being insulted by the new doctor, he excused his behavior by saying he was drunk. The doctor and his steward confiscated goods intended for the patients. "Fowl which I had obtained for the sick were all eaten by those in the Office . . . A box of luxuries sent out to the 54th wounded—by the friends in Boston—consisting of fruits, jellies[,] wine and some clothing were disposed of in the same way," Hawks reported.

Furious but unable to change the situation, Esther Hawks left Hospital #10, much to the sorrow of her patients, and returned to teaching and organizing schools. She later noted that the new doctor at Hospital #10 soon "ran his course," but not before he had had most of the patients jailed for trivial offenses.

In 1870, Esther Hawks returned to New England where she practiced medicine. She died in 1906.

SITE 42   Short Take

Saltus-Habersham House

1796

802 Bay Street

Beaufort National Register Historic District

When it was built, the residence now known as the Saltus-Habersham House provoked an outcry from residents who complained that it and similar structures then under construction encroached on the ends of town streets that terminated at the river and thereby blocked access to the water. The General Assembly agreed and enacted legislation mandating that Beaufort's streets "should be open and free, to the river."

Captain Francis Saltus was a wealthy cotton planter from Charleston whose exceptionally tall tabby home in Beaufort was set among wharves, warehouses, and other commercial buildings related to maritime enterprises.

While living in the house during the early 1800s, Saltus built five gunboats for the U.S. Navy, all of which were in service during the War of 1812 in waters off the coasts of Georgia and South Carolina. The commander of one of the boats was kin to Saltus.

His house, built originally with three floors over an elevated basement, is a rare example of a late eighteenth-century merchant's home. It was a rectangular structure with gable ends, with living accommodations above the basement on the upper floors. Architectural embellishments, including a domed stair hall and an elliptical staircase added later, are both unique in Beaufort County.

During the Civil War, the house was used as a commissary for Union troops. Since then, it has endured neglect, abuse, and numerous alterations that damaged its structural integrity, according to a report from the Historic American Buildings Survey of the National Park Service, which lists the property as endangered. Uprights were installed along interior walls to protect occupants of the building in case it collapsed. The building now houses a restaurant and other commercial enterprises.

Local legend says the house was owned by John Habersham. If so, those records have been lost, although a man of that name did live in Beaufort.

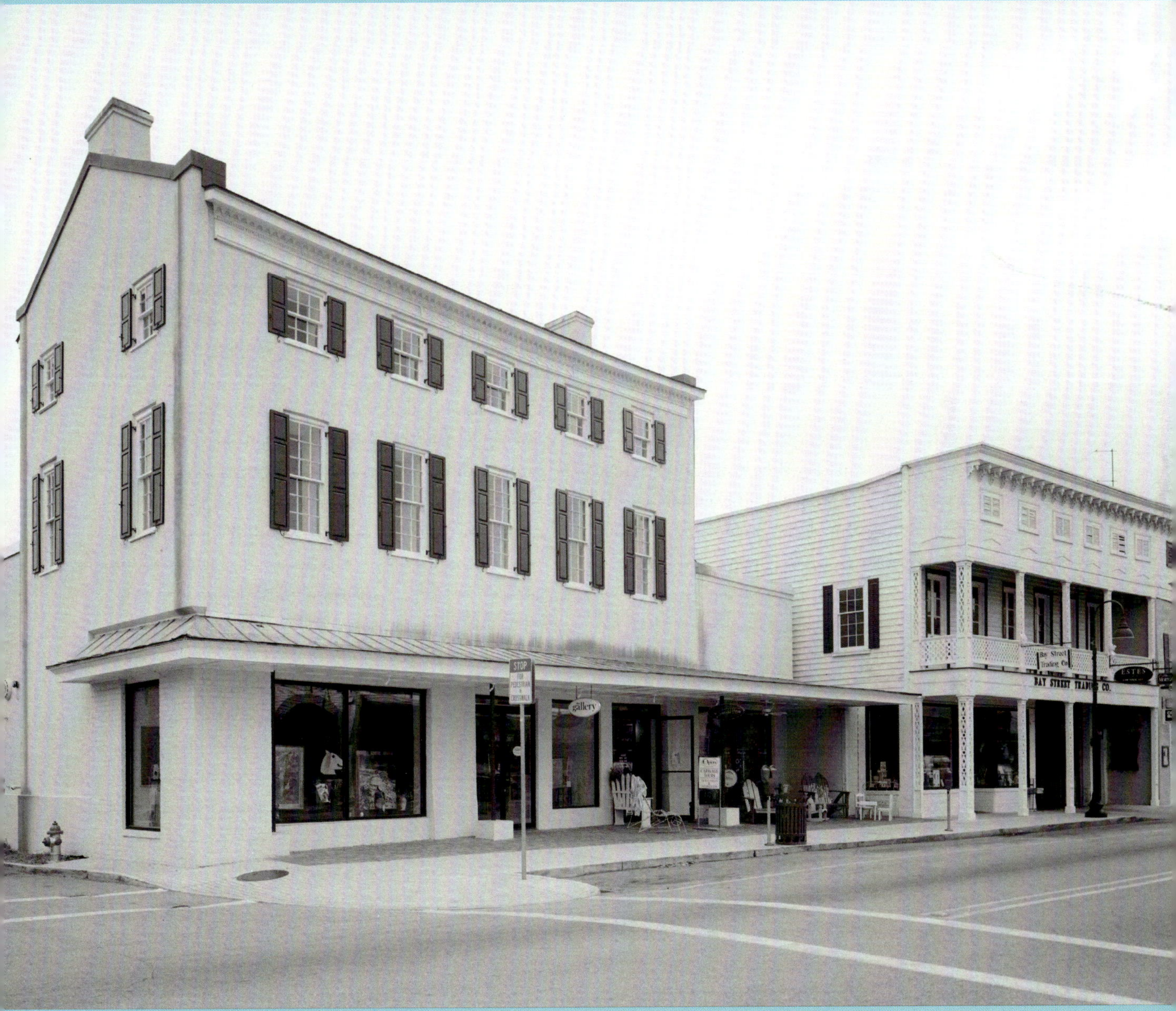
STOP
gallery
Bay Street Trading Co.

Old Baptist Meeting House (Baptist Church of Beaufort)

1794–1844

600 Charles Street

HISTORIC SIGNIFICANCE: The church is considered a major force in the growth of the Baptist Church in the United States. Built on the site of the earlier Baptist Meeting House, the structure is considered one of the nation's finest examples of Greek Revival architecture. Part of the church retains its original eighteenth-century tabby foundation; the adjacent cemetery features tabby gravestones and walls dating to the original structure. The ornate molded-plaster ceiling was crafted by enslaved artisans before the Civil War.

The Baptist Church of Beaufort was founded in 1794 as a mission of the Euhaw Baptist Church, founded in 1745 in today's Jasper County. The Beaufort mission, first called the Baptist Meeting House, was just over one thousand square feet, but in 1794 that was space enough to accommodate its small congregation.

In a series of letters, the first pastor, the Reverend Henry Holcombe, wrote about how happy he was to lay the foundation for a place of worship that ranked with the "most neat and commodious" Baptist meeting houses in the nation. A decade later, the church was no longer commodious enough to seat all the new members it attracted during a series of revivals in the area. The congregants had not only outgrown their sanctuary but were also ready to become an independent church with a new name: the Baptist Church of Beaufort. The 1805 addition doubled the size of the original building.

By 1842, one of the sanctuary walls was bulging, and the roof was threatening to cave in. Richard Fuller, the pastor at the time, directed construction of a new church over the next two years. The original building was torn down to the old tabby walls, which were leveled to a matching height. The new structure was built of brick on part of the leveled walls. The first floor featured pew boxes—waist-high boxed-in seating sections, each with its own gate-like door—that were rented for prices ranging from $12 to $30; the cheap seats were in the front row and the last three rows. A bell in the new bell tower called congregants to Sunday services and rang to celebrate weddings and other events.

An upstairs gallery built on three sides of the sanctuary was supported by fluted Doric columns. The gallery accommodated the large number of Black people who attended services but were forbidden to sit with white

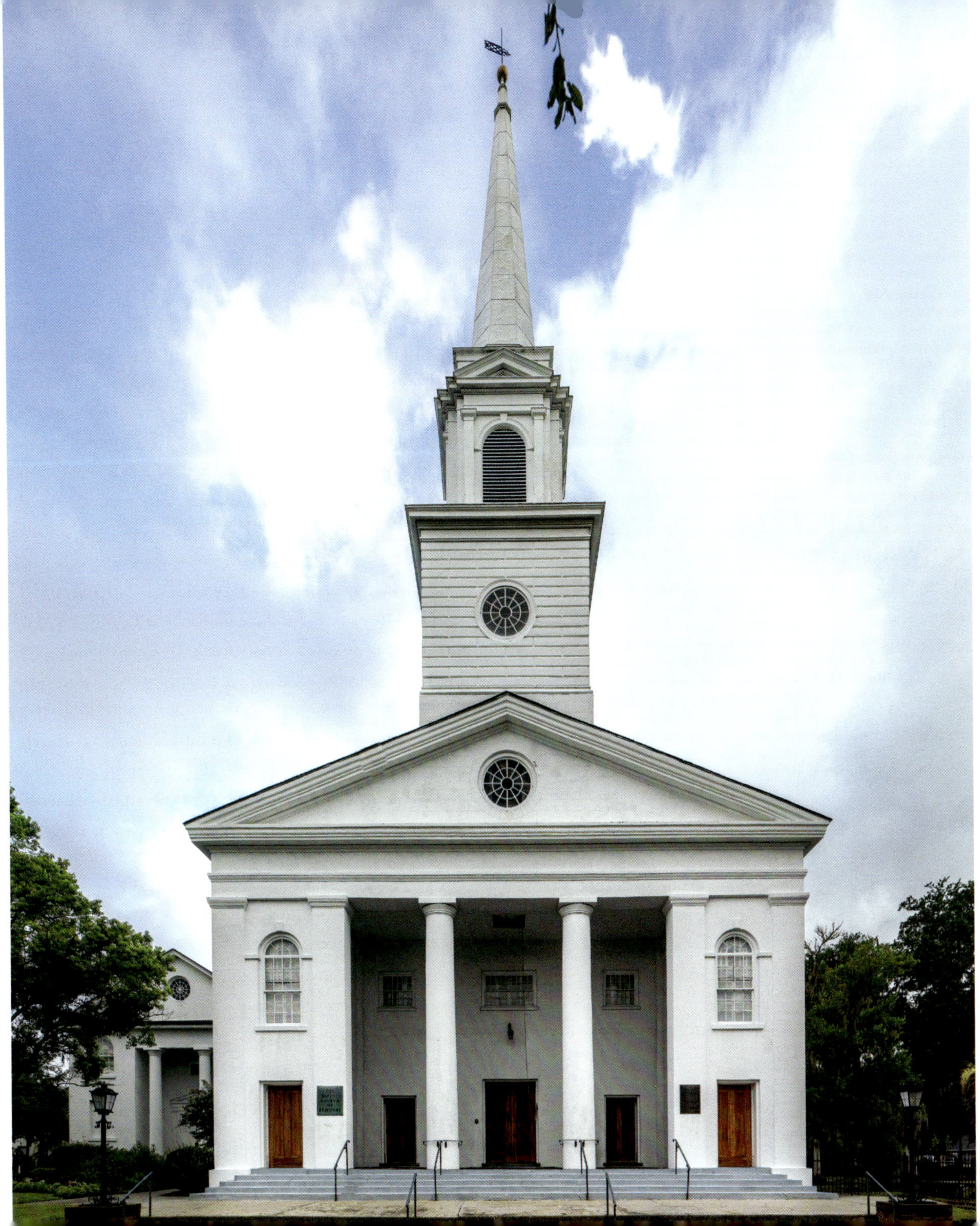

congregants downstairs. The gallery seats, however, offered the best views of the ornate oyster-shell-plaster ceiling, which had been molded by highly skilled enslaved artisans. The rosettes, medallions, and band of leaves that circles the entire ceiling are classed among the finest plasterwork in Beaufort, a town known for architectural ornamentation.

The present-day Greek Revival building was completed in 1844, except for the steeple. Although it was part of the original design, the steeple was not added until more than a century later, in the early 1960s, when a local couple donated the needed funds.

After the rebuilding, burial lots in the churchyard were assigned to five prominent white members of the church. In the cemetery today, a series of low tabby walls capped with brick and concrete define the location of parts of the original structure and the 1805 addition. Some of the oldest grave markers are made of tabby.

Until the early 1800s, most of the faithful in the Beaufort area were Anglican, a religion brought to America by the English lords proprietors who governed the South Carolina colony. In the late 1700s, laws that prohibited the practice of any other faith were expunged, giving rise to a series of evangelical movements that led to the establishment and growth of Baptist, Methodist, and Presbyterian churches. During the Beaufort Great Revival of 1831, hundreds of souls were converted. Six lawyers and the president of Beaufort College left successful professions to enter the ministry.

By the 1820s, Baptists in the Beaufort district outnumbered every other denomination. The Baptist Church of Beaufort played an important role in spreading the faith around the United States. Leading Baptist churches in large cities—Atlanta, Baltimore, Charleston, Houston, Philadelphia, and Washington—at one time were led by pastors who had trained at the Beaufort church.

Some members of the Baptist and Methodist denominations in the Deep South questioned the morality of slavery. Although their voices were drowned out by the opposite-thinking majority, some white Baptists and Methodists encouraged enslaved men to become licensed ministers in order to foster the growth of Christianity throughout the Black community. The enslaved brought their African religions to North America and, over time, blended many of those beliefs with the beliefs of their white enslavers.

A few years before the Civil War, the congregation of the Baptist Church of Beaufort numbered 183 white people and more than 3,500 Black people, although many of those enslaved members attended affiliated mission churches on the sea islands. When Union forces invaded the Port Royal area seven months after the war's first shots were fired, the church, along with many other large Beaufort houses and public buildings, was converted for use as a hospital. Graffiti from the era has been preserved on beams in the belfry and on one wall of the sanctuary.

The Baptist Church of Beaufort was occupied by freedmen and freedwomen after the war. They worked hard to bring the church back to its prewar condition. One formerly enslaved man who had served as a deacon in the earlier iteration of the church returned the communion silver. He had hidden the silver in his feather bed for the duration of the Civil War to keep it from being stolen during the Union occupation.

The communion table turned up in Charleston and was brought back to Beaufort. The pew boxes, which had been removed to make space for hospital patients, were reinstalled, but the doors were left off, possibly to make the church seem more democratic and welcoming.

The church complex has continued to expand. A Sunday-school building was added in 1917, followed by more educational buildings. Ongoing restoration work has preserved some of church's unique features. When the ceiling of the sanctuary was carefully restored in the mid-1950s, almost all the original plaster rosettes were saved and reinstalled. Hurricane Gracie in 1959 damaged the roof, walls, and carpet, but the crowning glory of the church—the beautiful ceiling—was unharmed.

A church restoration during the final years of the twentieth century was done at a cost of more than $2.2 million. Workers replaced most of the exterior stucco with matching material and restored the interior walls. Old carpet was removed, revealing the original heart pine floors, which were refinished to an amber glow.

The Reverend Richard Fuller, 1804–1876

Richard Fuller, who began his career as an attorney, was one of the founders of the Southern Baptist movement.

At sixteen, Fuller entered Harvard University. He developed health problems, possibly tuberculosis, and dropped out of school after two and a half years. His academic record was so impressive that the faculty voted to allow him to graduate with his class in 1824. His grades put him at the top of his class of eighty students.

Fuller returned to Beaufort to study law. He practiced for a time, earning a reputation as a respected, successful attorney. Fuller's career in law was short-circuited by his decision to enter the ministry during the Beaufort Great Revival of 1831. He believed it was his Christian duty to become a preacher. The day he was ordained in 1833, Fuller baptized more than one hundred ministerial candidates. His sermons were so inspiring that he came to be known as the "Prince of Preachers."

Fuller had been reared and baptized in the Protestant Episcopal Church, but after he converted to Baptism, he insisted that he be baptized a second time by submersion, a Baptist practice. Several Black people were baptized in the river along with him, which caused some of his white friends to shun him.

Fuller received his religious education from one of the most celebrated Baptist preachers of his time, W. T. Brantley Sr., who excelled in classical scholarship and was known for his impressive oratory. Fuller preached for fifteen years at the Baptist Church of Beaufort and led the 1844 effort to rebuild the church. Because the majority of the more than two thousand church members were slaves with little or no money to donate

The Reverend Richard Fuller

toward the project, Fuller raised $17,000 in restoration funds by giving sermons in nearby communities and states. After his marriage to Charlotte Bull Stuart, a wealthy widow whose affairs he had handled as an attorney, Fuller donated family money to help fund church construction.

During his tenure at the Beaufort church, Fuller was named chairman of the by-laws committee for the new

Southern Baptist Convention, which split from the national church over the issue of slavery. He preached the sermon at the first annual convention, served as its third president, and was a featured preacher for the next thirty years at every annual meeting of the Southern Baptist Convention. Fuller was a spellbinding speaker whose reputation for drawing crowds to religious revivals spread far and wide. He likewise inspired congregations with his preaching. His voice was described as "soft and gentle," but capable of sounding with "trumpet power" when the need arose.

In 1847, Fuller moved to Baltimore as pastor of the struggling Seventh Baptist Church. He made the move in part to observe slavery "with a calm and impartial judgment" in a border state such as Maryland. While he was pastor of the Seventh Baptist Church, the membership grew from about ninety congregants to about twelve hundred.

During the Civil War, Fuller preached to congregations where half of the male members wore gray uniforms and the other half wore blue. Like many of his congregants, Fuller was conflicted about slavery. A slaveholder himself from a slave-owning family, Fuller wrestled for most of his life with the question whether slavery was moral. He debated the issue at length in correspondence with the Reverend Francis Weyland, the president of Brown University. Both men quoted the Bible to support their positions. Fuller argued that slavery was moral as long as slave owners treated their slaves humanely. Weyland disagreed, saying it was immoral to own human beings. In spite of the men's strong opinions, the tenor of their letters was always reasoned and cordial.

Fuller baptized and mentored Annie Armstrong, who served as the first executive of the Women's Missionary Union, an organization within the Southern Baptist Convention, now the largest Protestant women's mission organization in the world. Armstrong's great-great-grandfather Henry Sater helped found Maryland's Baptist church.

Fuller also founded the Eutaw Place Baptist Church in Baltimore, a mission church of the Seventh Baptist. He preached his final sermon there in 1876, the year of his death.

Tabby Manse (Thomas Fuller House)

c. 1786–1788

1211 Bay Street

National Register of Historic Places

The Tabby Manse was built by the prosperous planter Thomas Fuller as a wedding gift for his bride, Elizabeth Middleton. The dwelling is remarkable as one of the few large eighteenth-century houses in South Carolina with exterior walls built entirely of tabby. The walls are two-feet thick, skimmed with stucco and scored to look like stone. It is one of Beaufort's oldest houses and an outstanding example of the Beaufort style.

Homes built in the Beaufort style featured large lots, formal gardens, and piazzas supported by stuccoed piers or arches. Exterior stairs were usually centered at the front of the house. Paneling, wainscoting, mantels, cornices, and high ceilings created a look of airy elegance inside. Beaufort-style houses were designed to be breezy and cool while incorporating elements of Georgian, Colonial, Greek Revival, and Spanish architecture.

The interior of the Tabby Manse consisted of eight perfectly proportioned rooms, three paneled in heart pine and cypress. Architecturally, the building is modeled on the Elizabeth Barnwell Gough House in Beaufort, which was in turn adapted from the design of a house in Charleston. Today the Tabby Manse retains its original appearance. Although the house is privately owned and not open to the public, it is listed in Beaufort tour guides and featured on public tours. Visitors can admire the imposing two-story façade from the public sidewalk. Thomas Fuller was the father of the Reverend Richard Fuller, a charismatic preacher instrumental in the founding of the Southern Baptist Convention.

The house was sold for taxes during the Civil War. It was converted into a guesthouse in 1870 and remained in that capacity for a century. The writer Francis Griswold, who wrote *A Sea Island Lady* (1939), a 960-page novel set during the Civil War, lived in the Tabby Manse during its days as a guesthouse.

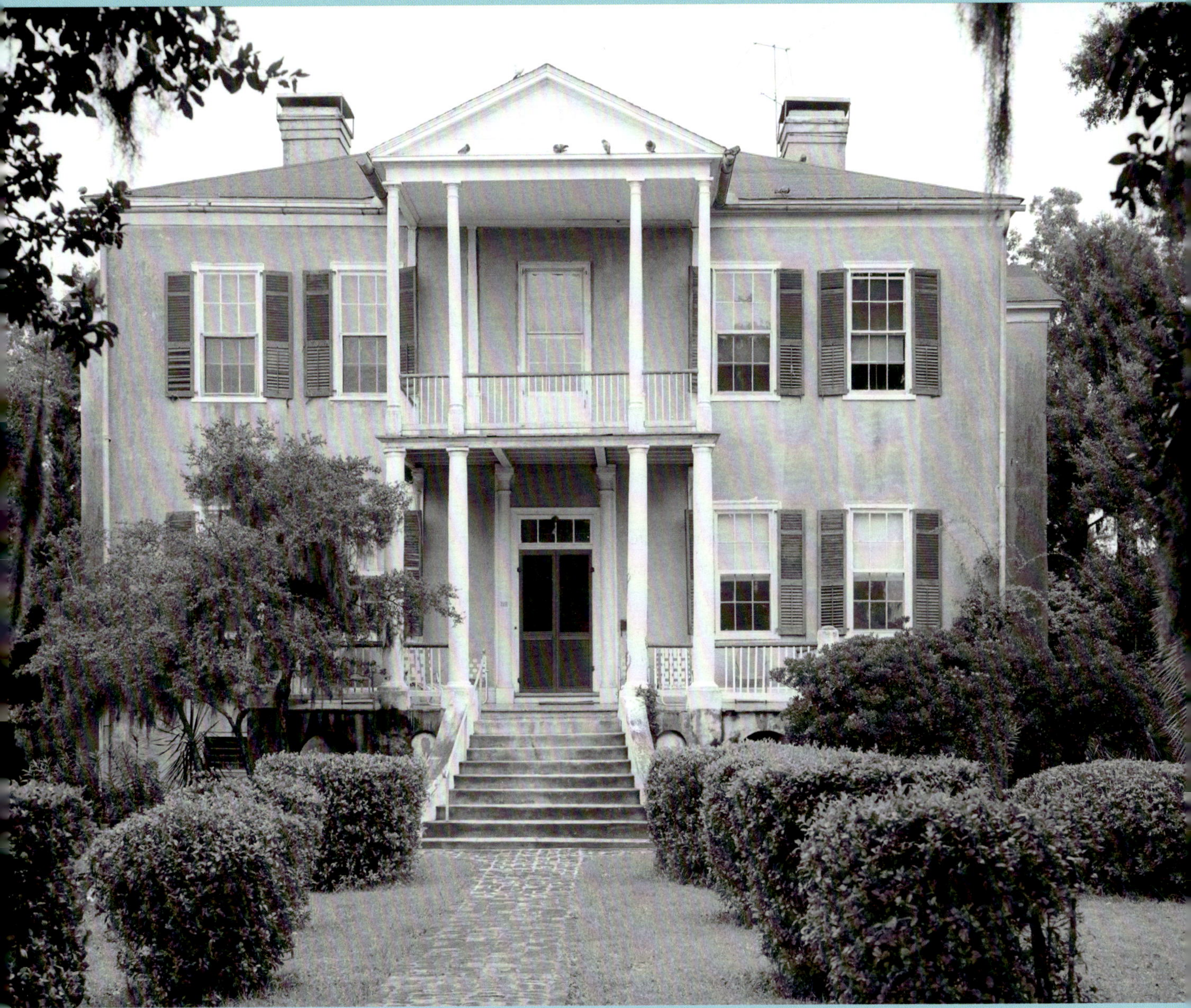

CHAPTER 16 *Edisto Island*

EDISTO ISLAND is a breath of fresh briny air, so far unspoiled by the overabundance of chain hotels, high-rise condominiums, and other resort developments that mars many of the larger islands in the sea islands chain of the coastal Southeast.

Live oaks, many of them belonging to the bifurcated subspecies that grows only near the ocean, stretch their limbs above quiet two-lane roadways. Filtered sunlight leaks through the leafy tree canopy, dripping onto the lush foliage below. A so-called mystery tree decked out with an American flag and items scavenged on the island sits in the high marsh just off the main road, perhaps to notify visitors that Edisto is not your ordinary sea island.

Almost half of Edisto's acreage is protected natural land. The island offers uncrowded beaches and bike trails, along with the necessary overnight amenities for visitors: rental cottages, villas, and campsites. Daytime attractions include a museum, an environmental learning center, and a serpentarium as well as markets, shops, restaurants, and golf.

Edisto Beach, on the island's south end in Colleton County, is the only incorporated municipality, with just over four hundred full-time residents. Edisto Beach State Park, in Charleston County farther north, offers hiking and camping with ocean views. The Botany Bay Heritage Preserve and Wildlife Management Area is a 4,600-acre enclave that includes the tabby remains of two antebellum plantations: Bleak Hall and Sea Cloud.

Like most of the sea islands of the southeastern coast, Edisto is a composite of islands, each separated from the others by tidal waterways and marshes. As its name implies, Big Edisto is the largest; Little Edisto, Botany Bay, Jehossee, Edisto Beach, Edington Beach, and other islands complete the Edisto complex. Edisto's boundaries are defined by the North Edisto River, the South Edisto River, and the Atlantic Ocean.

Its earliest human occupants settled on the sea islands thousands of years ago. On nearby thirty-eight-acre Fig Island lie the remains of an archaic shell ring built by Indigenous inhabitants. Because of this archaeological treasure, the small island is off-limits to the public.

The first European known to spend time on the island was Father Juan Rogel, a Jesuit missionary from Spain who arrived along with the first Spanish immigrants, who came to colonize the area. Father Rogel reached Edisto in 1569, hoping to convert the Natives to Catholicism. He abandoned his effort because he could not convince the Oristas, or Edistows, to stay in one place year-round. The Natives abandoned their village for months at a time to practice swidden (slash-and-burn) agriculture, growing corn, beans, and squash on isolated plots of land, clearing and planting new tracts every few years after the soil of the old tracts was worn out. In winter, they left the island on hunting expeditions.

A century later, English explorers sailing along the Eastern Seaboard reported on its merits to eight loyal supporters of Charles II of England. The king granted them the rights to all the land between Virginia and Spanish Florida. To populate the area, the lords proprietors recruited wealthy British sugar planters who had run out of plantation land on the Caribbean island of Barbados and wanted to expand.

In 1680, Natives sold the island to the English for £100. Paul Grimball, an English merchant, received a six-hundred-acre land grant on the north end, where he established a farm and became the first Englishman to settle on Edisto.

Grimball built a tabby house, planted Indian corn, peas, tobacco, and onions, and raised pigs. In 1686, Spanish troops from Florida fighting to reclaim land in the Southeast attacked Edisto. They burned houses, kidnapped slaves, and killed Grimball's brother-in-law. The rest of the family escaped by hiding in the woods. A wall of Grimball's tabby house still stands, but it is on private property and not open to the public. The ruins may be the oldest surviving tabby in the state and among the oldest in the coastal Southeast.

Rice became a money crop on Edisto in the 1700s, especially on Jehossee Island. By diking marshlands to create rice fields, the farmers could regulate the flow of freshwater to the crop. Early settlers also grew and processed indigo on Edisto, but when the British subsidy for the vivid blue dye ended with the American Revolution, they shifted to sea island cotton. The silky long-staple cotton made island planters wealthy. By 1850, there were more than sixty plantations spread over Big Edisto and other islands in the complex. Some of the old plantation houses, all built with slave labor, still stand.

In 1800, Joseph Edings offered beachfront lots for sale. Planters and wealthy Charlestonians built two rows of resort cottages, most of them roomy two-story structures of brick or tabby with large verandahs. The developer built a causeway to Edingsville Beach across the marsh from Big Edisto. His development was a hit. For several decades, Edingsville Beach was known as the area's most upscale summer resort. Since sea breezes kept the heat, humidity, and mosquitoes at bay, Edingsville Beach evolved into a small resort community. During its heyday, two chapels, a small store, a school, and a billiard parlor opened. Some cottage owners began staying year-round.

The marquis de Lafayette, the French hero of the American Revolution, visited in 1825 during his American tour.

Before the Civil War, a third of the Edingsville Beach cottages were lost to storms and erosion. On the eve of the war, 329 white people lived on Edisto Island, along with 5,082 enslaved Black people and 4 freedmen. In the absence of enslaved labor after the war, Edisto's cotton economy collapsed. The planters were in no position to rebuild their vacation houses on Edingsville Beach. Many white people left Edisto, but most of the freed Gullah Geechee people remained. They planted subsistence crops, fished and hunted, and made cast nets and sweetgrass baskets to use and to sell at roadside stands.

Transportation around Edisto traditionally involved boats and mule-drawn wagons or horses. Getting off Edisto was difficult. Until the early 1900s, when a regular ferry service opened, islanders could travel to the mainland or other islands only in private boats.

In 1893, a powerful hurricane made landfall in Savannah, devastating the sea islands and the coastal mainland of South Carolina. Besides wiping out the last vestiges of development at Edingsville Beach, the storm killed as many as two thousand people in the Lowcountry, most of them African Americans living on the sea islands, who drowned in the sixteen-foot storm surge.

Tabby Outbuildings at Botany Bay Plantation

c. 1845–1850

Botany Bay Plantation Heritage Preserve and Wildlife Management Area
1066 Botany Bay Road

National Register of Historic Places

HISTORIC SIGNIFICANCE: Three historic tabby structures built in the Gothic Revival style are survivors of Bleak Hall plantation, now part of the sprawling Botany Bay Plantation Heritage Preserve and Wildlife Management Area. Botany Bay features a diversity of habitats and twenty-one listed historic sites, including the remains of a Japanese garden that is said to be the first in the United States.

Before the Civil War, the prominent Townsend family assembled 3,360 acres on Edisto Island by combining the land of two plantations, Bleak Hall, established in 1798, and Sea Cloud, established around 1825 when Ephraim Seabrook built his house there. Sea Cloud may have been named in honor of two former property owners after a Seabrook and a McLeod married.

Bleak Hall and Sea Cloud remained in the Townsend family until the 1930s, when the property was purchased and renamed Botany Bay Plantation. It was sold again in 1968 to the real estate magnate John E. "Jason" Meyer, who built an illegal pond on state-owned wetlands. To avoid prosecution, Meyer agreed to will all the Botany Bay acreage to South Carolina after he and his wife died. Margaret "Peggy" Meyer, Jason's widow, was an ardent conservationist who cared for the property for the rest of her life.

South Carolina opened the property to the public in 2008 under the management of the state's Department of Natural Resources. Because it is a wildlife management area, its mission is to accommodate wildlife rather than people. Facilities are limited—no drinking water or toilets—and overnight stays are banned, as are drones, alcohol, and dogs on the causeway or beach. Strong currents and sharp oyster shells make Botany Bay's beach dangerous for swimming. Sometimes beach sections are closed because rare or endangered seabirds are nesting. The refuge is closed every Tuesday and during managed hunts.

Botany Bay, a heritage preserve, embraces twenty-one historic sites listed on the National Register, including a beehive-shaped brick well.

Daniel Townsend began building the plantation structures in 1798, shortly before his marriage to Hephzibah

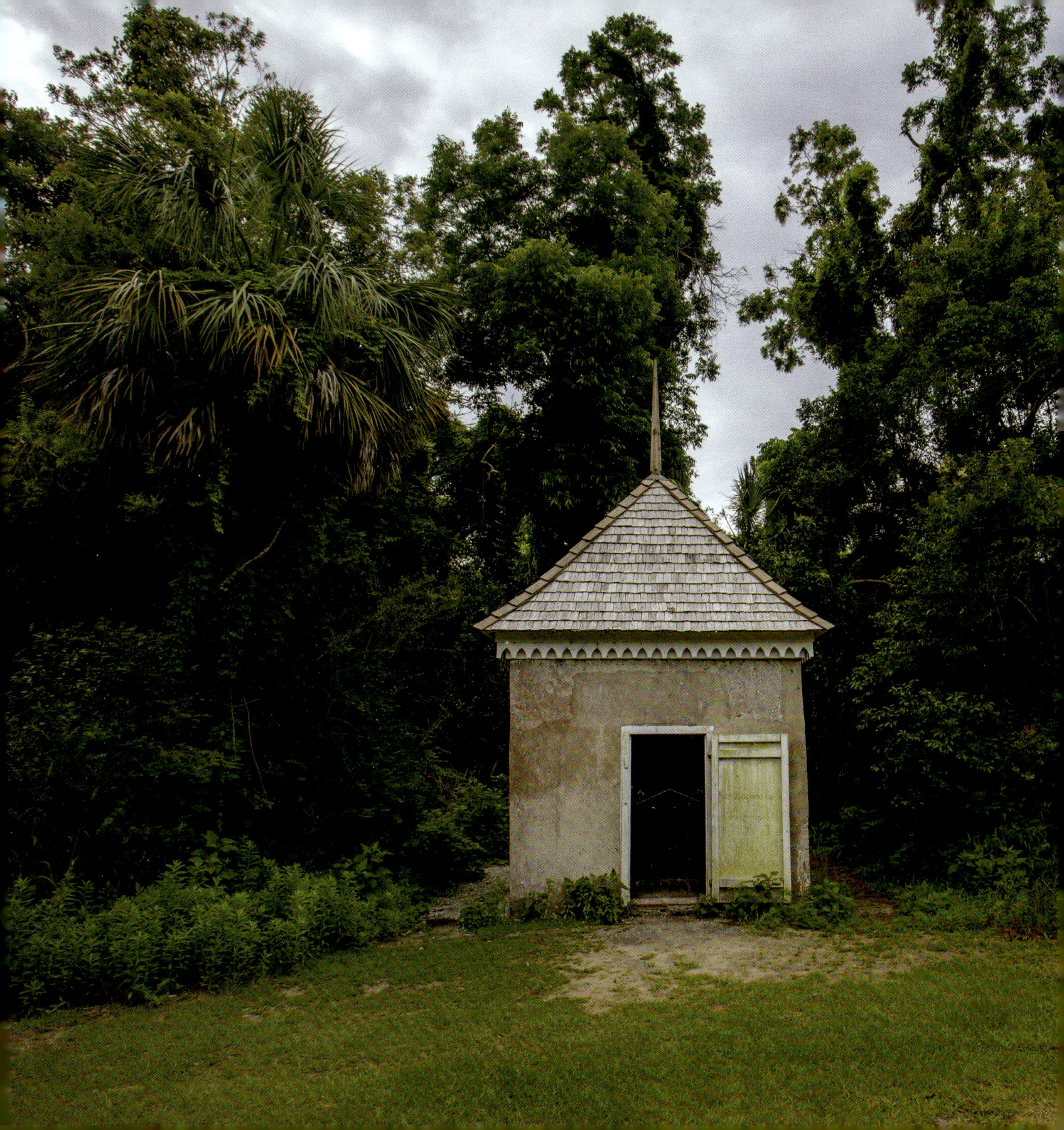

Jenkins Townsend. She was renowned for raising funds, against her husband's wishes, to build the first Baptist Church on Edisto Island by baking goods in custom-built tabby ovens and selling the breads and pastries in Charleston. She also started a women's missionary society on the island that evolved into a still-active worldwide organization. According to local legend, Bleak Hall was named after Charles Dickens's novel *Bleak House* because a family member was a Dickens fan. But the serialization of Dickens's novel began in 1852, well after Daniel Townsend named his plantation Bleak Hall.

In 1845, John Townsend inherited Bleak Hall from his father. He built the three still-standing outbuildings entirely or in part of tabby, probably during the late 1840s. They were designed in the same Gothic Revival style that Townsend chose for his own house. During the Civil War, the cupola of Bleak Hall was used, at different times, as a lookout point by both Confederate and Union forces. The house burned during the war years.

The well-preserved icehouse, an ornamented one-and-a-half story structure, is the most prominent of the tabby outbuildings. It features mock tracery windows and a faux door, as well as real doors set in the gable ends. The steep roof is shingled with cypress in typical Gothic style. A triangular dormer has twin twelve-light windows. A tiny decorative balcony under the windows has supports done in a double diamond design. The basement has tabby walls filled with charcoal insulation; sawdust was used to insulate the upper wooden walls of the structure. The interior of the building stays cool even on the hottest summer days.

Ice packed in sawdust was shipped in from the North and kept in the insulated building. On one gable end of the structure, an affixed ladder runs beside the two plank doors, one above the other, to give access to ice from the upper

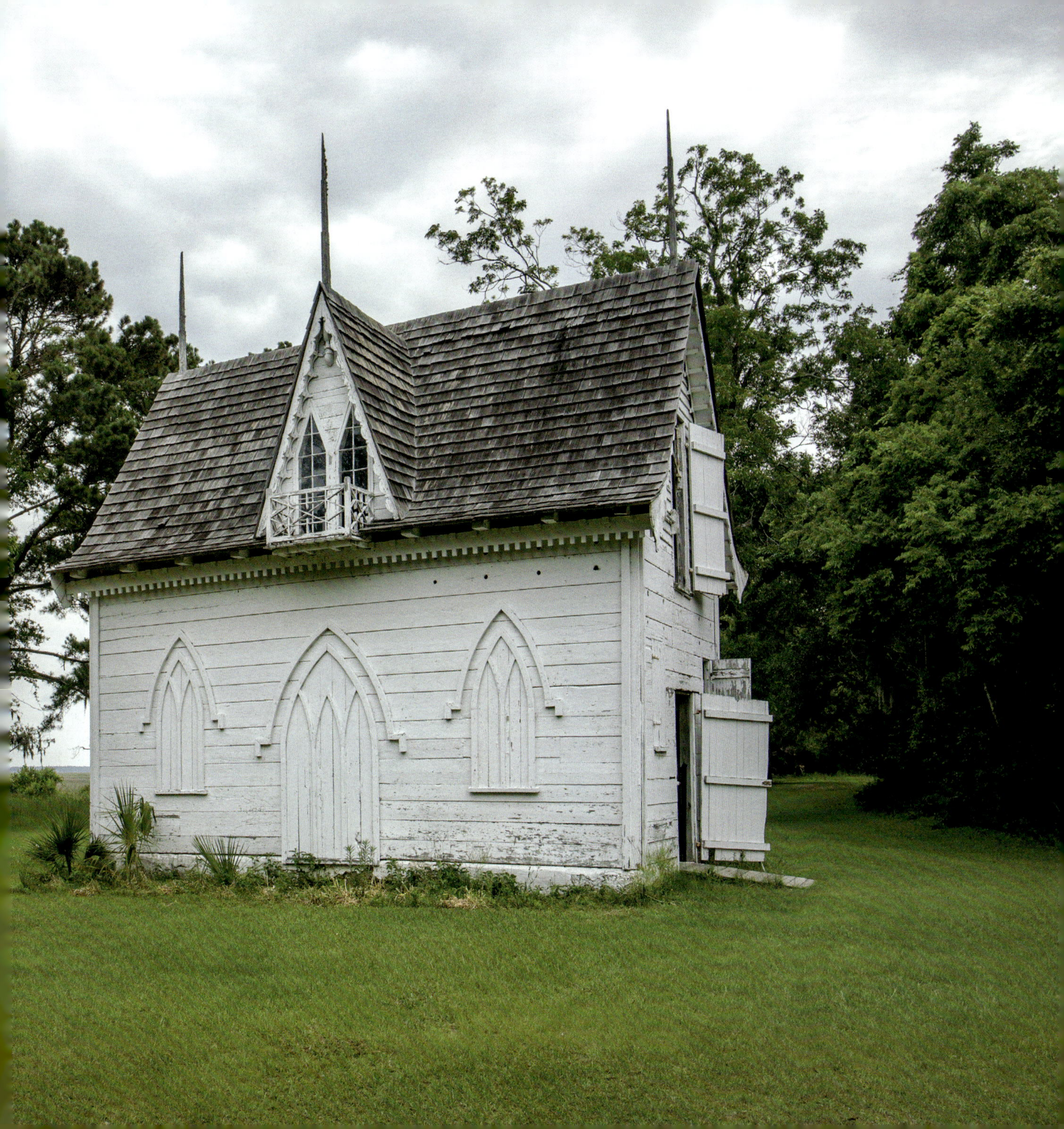

level. At the roof peaks, three-level wooden spires are finished with decorative pendants. The intricate detail of the building is unusual, considering its prosaic function.

A rectangular shed that probably served as a barn during the colonial era was later used as an equipment shed, possibly for the formal Asian-style gardens nearby. The building was constructed entirely of tabby with a high, cypress-shingled gable roof. Modern sliding doors open at the south end of the structure; the original plank door flanked by a fixed ladder gives access to the north end. The roof is topped with wooden spires echoing those of the icehouse.

The third outbuilding probably served as a smokehouse. It is a small tabby cube with a single planked door and no windows. Its hipped roof of cypress shingles supports wooden spires like those of the larger outbuildings. A decorative board with serrated dentil molding runs under the eaves.

Before the Civil War, enslaved workers at Bleak Hall and Sea Cloud produced some of the largest and finest crops of sea island cotton in South Carolina. The silky, long-staple cotton was favored by French and Belgian lace makers because of its quality. John Townsend was able to sell his entire crop even before the seeds were planted each year.

Botany Bay encompasses a variety of habitats: marine and estuarine wetlands, upland pine and hardwood forest, freshwater and brackish ponds impounded by dikes, and fields planted with food for wildlife. Managed dove and deer hunts are held periodically.

The beach at Botany Bay is a narrow strip of sand that includes a small maritime forest that is losing ground to erosion, leaving a boneyard of dead trees sprawled like giant sun-bleached skeletons on the beach. Really a separate island, the beach is accessed by a half-mile-long causeway, closed to motorized vehicles, that crosses the marsh and separates the beach from the main part of Edisto Island. The causeway was inaccessible for a time because of severe damage from Hurricane Matthew in 2016 and storm surge from Hurricane Irma in 2017. The storms gobbled up thirty more feet of forest and washed away one of the most picturesque and photographed of the boneyard trees. Because visitors are not allowed to collect seashells to take home, they often hang the best specimens they find from limbs of the dead trees.

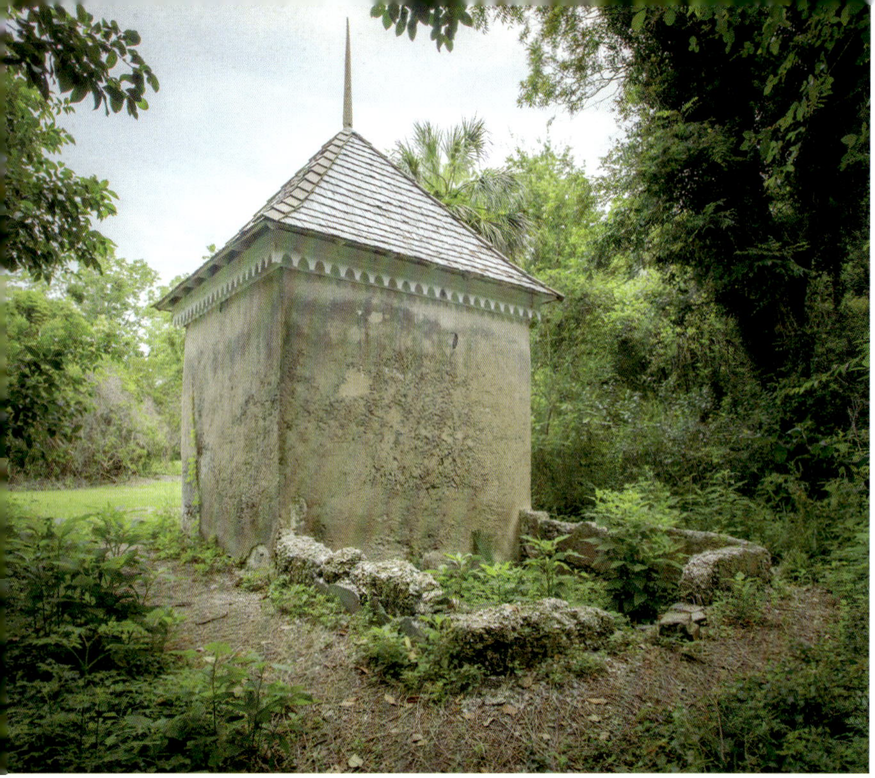
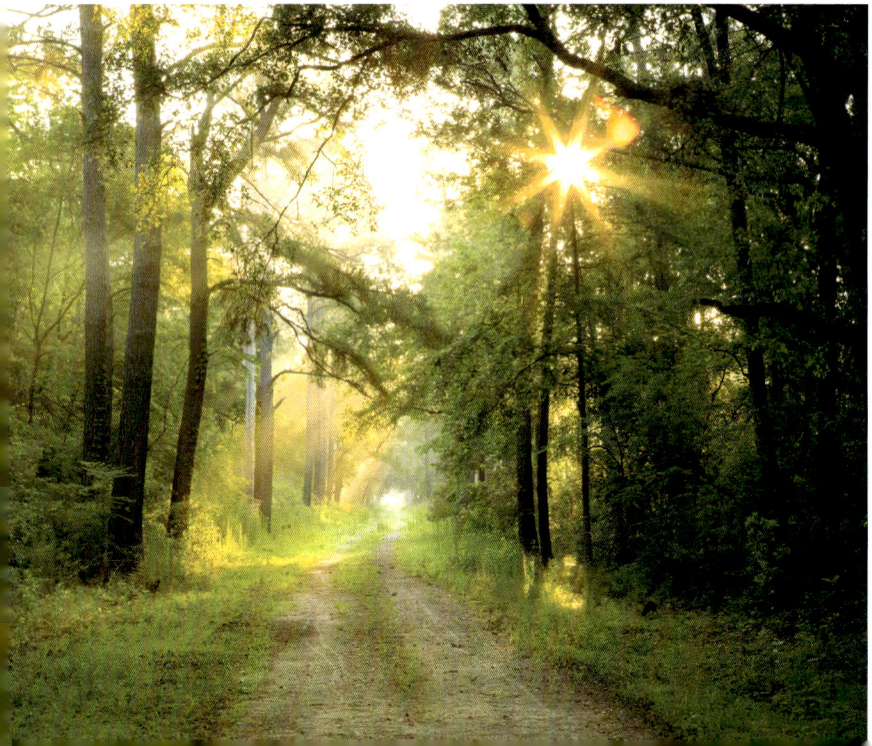
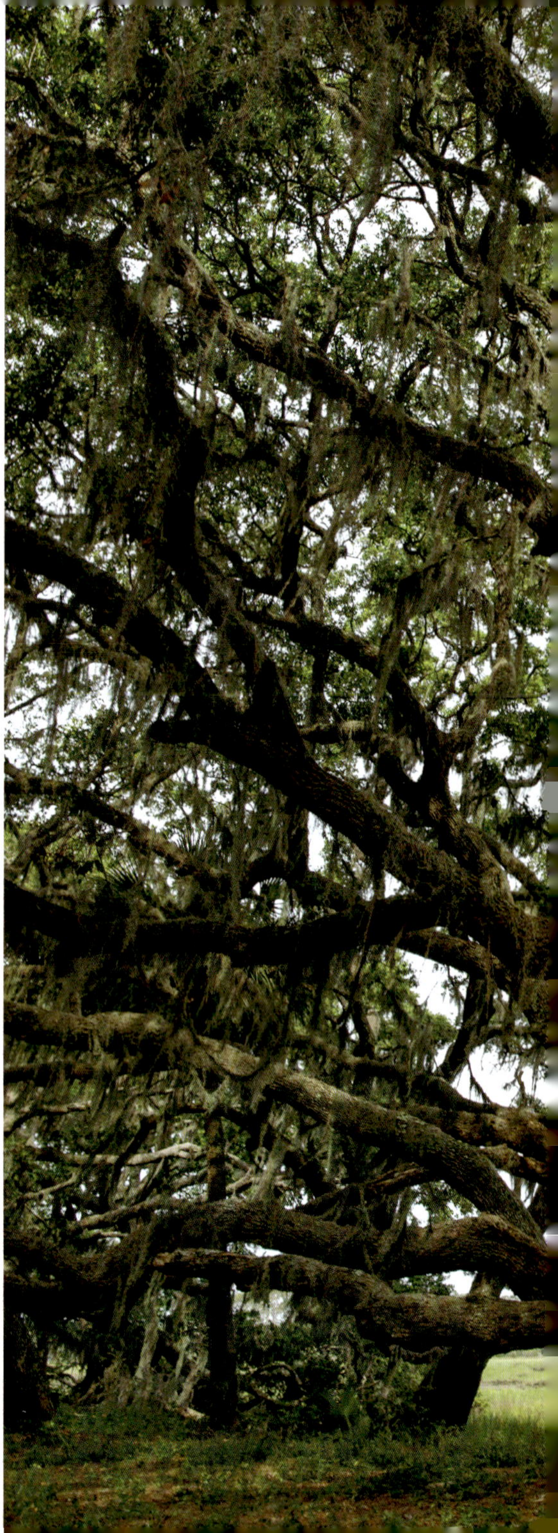

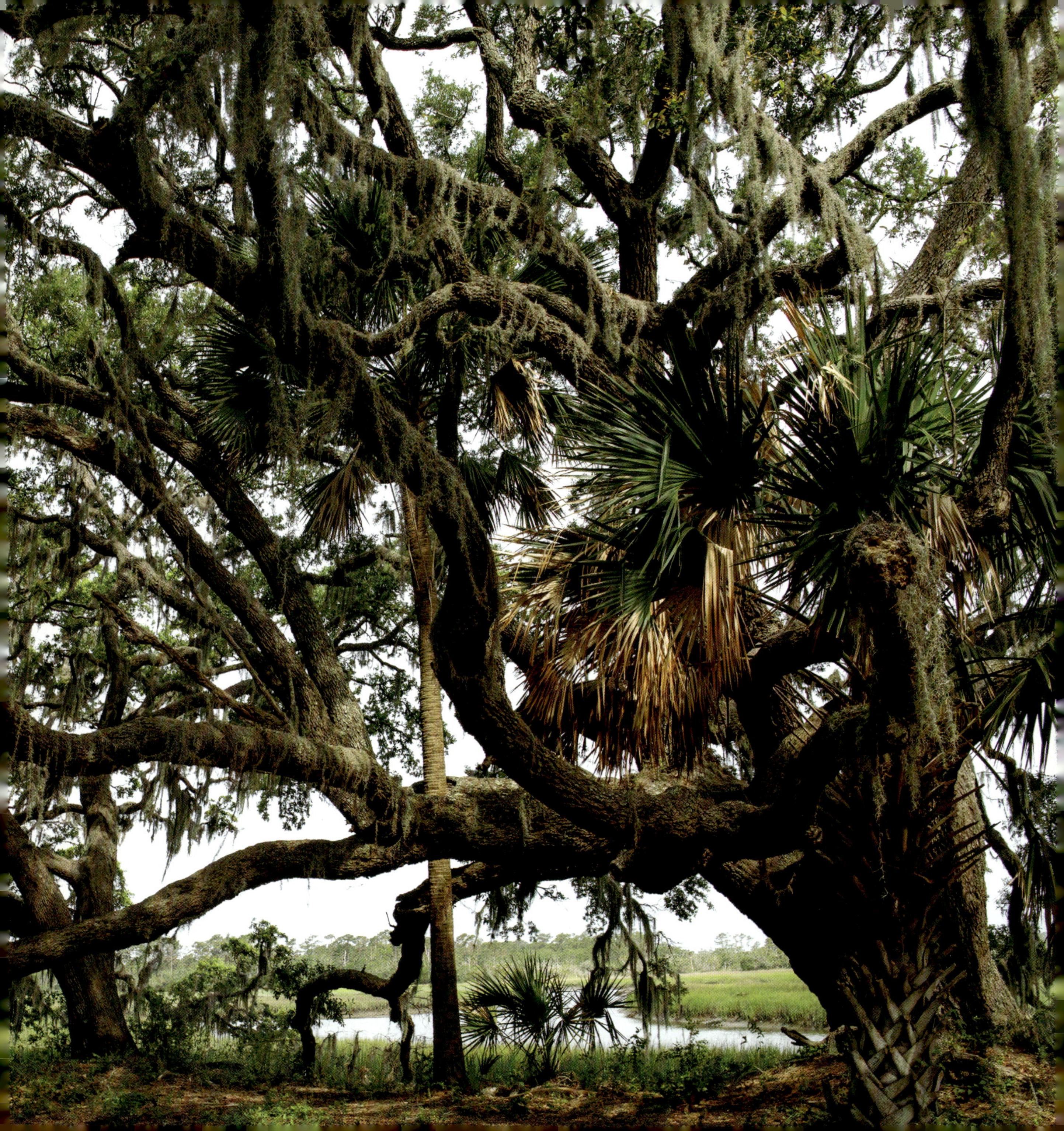

Oqui, c. 1835–?

Oqui, who hailed from the Guangdong region in southern China, created a magnificent garden at Bleak Hall, although the garden was always described as Japanese rather than Chinese. He came to Edisto Island after traveling in Asia with Commodore Matthew Perry, who secured his place in history by opening Japan to Western trading in the mid-1850s. Perry succeeded in his mission by using what came to be called gunboat diplomacy.

Perry was sent to Asia because the United States wanted to trade with Japan, arrange protection for America's whaling fleet in Japanese waters, and establish coaling stations to supply U.S. ships. Under the Tokugawa shogunate, Japan's ruling family for 250 years, the country was a closed society. Outsiders were barred from entering Japan, and citizens were forbidden to leave the country on pain of death.

James Morrow, a medical doctor and botanist, had joined the Perry expedition to deliver plants, seeds, and agricultural equipment to Japan, where, it was expected, they would be welcomed because of the importance of agriculture to the Japanese. While Perry traveled around Asia, Morrow collected botanical specimens and agricultural tools to bring back to America. During the course of the expedition, Morrow collected 1,500 to 2,000 living plants. He often used locals with botanical knowledge to help him find different species, which may explain how he met Oqui in China.

Morrow must have been impressed with the young man because he persuaded him to assist in caring for the living plants on the return voyage to America. On the trip over, Morrow had experienced great difficulty in keeping specimens alive because they were often soaked with saltwater as waves washed over the ship in rough seas.

Oqui landed in New York on the *Lexington*, an event that rated an article in the *Baltimore Sun* on February 22, 1855. The newspaper noted that the ship's captain had brought home "a real live Chinese from Hong Kong," who, as a florist and gardener, was to care for the plant specimens brought from Asia. The story reported that Oqui was a twenty-year-old Cantonese who had learned a little English on the voyage to America and was "tolerably good-looking."

Oqui tended the Asian specimens in the U.S. Botanic Garden on the National Mall, founded in 1820 at the urging of George Washington, James Madison, and Thomas Jefferson. Horticulture was becoming popular with Americans at the time. Oqui, who soon became unhappy with the Washington climate, announced plans to return to China.

John Townsend, Bleak Hall's owner and a state legislator, was attending a legislative session in Columbia, South Carolina, when he ran into his old friend Dr. Morrow, a fellow South Carolinian. When Townsend told Morrow of his dream to create a unique garden at Bleak Hall, Morrow advised him to contact Oqui.

Townsend went to Washington and offered to build Oqui an Asian-style house at Bleak Hall, similar to the one he lived in in China. Some reports say that Oqui named the house Celestials. No trace of it remains today. Townsend also promised to spare no expense on the plantation's garden. A tabby barn built by the Townsend family on the plantation sometime in the 1840s was probably converted into an equipment shed for Oqui's gardening tools. The shed still stands next to the remains of the garden.

Considering Oqui's heritage, the garden may have been more Chinese than Japanese, but since Japan had been closed for centuries to Westerners, it is doubtful that many Americans would have known the difference. Because of Perry's expedition, Japan was much in the news at the time, and anything Japanese was considered exotic and fascinating.

Townsend's slaves who worked on the garden performed well under Oqui's leadership. They planted domestic as well as Asian plants, including white poppies, which now grow wild on the sea islands. Chinese tobacco bloomed with trumpet-shaped yellow flowers favored by hummingbirds. Oqui's orange grove bordered the large vegetable garden that fed Townsend's family and slaves. It was not unusual for Oqui to harvest more than a thousand sweet oranges from a single tree. Townsend had an orange house built with tray-like shelves filled with beach sand to cover the fruit and keep it fresh for months. Oqui planted other trees: olive, fragrant gardenias, puffy pink mimosas, and golden coreopsis had taken their place. Hephzibah noted that Oqui's poppies and narcissus "bloom with unchanging beauty."

She wrote that she intended to send Phoebe "a little heliotrope and rose-geranium" from Oqui's hot bed. Rose-geranium, which smells like old roses with hints of citrus, spices, herbs, and resin, is said to calm anxiety, lift the spirits, and soothe irritated skin. It can also be used to flavor sweets and beverages. Heliotrope, which is said to smell like a grape Popsicle, vanilla, or cherry pie, is toxic if ingested, but its large pink, purple, and white blossoms and sweet scent are a favorite with gardeners.

Hephzibah understood that the garden, which attracted scores of admirers, was more than a showpiece to Oqui. She wrote to her daughter that he would be horrified to know that the plantation horses had to be brought through the garden to drink because a summer drought had ruined the water at the usual watering places.

SITE 46

First Missionary Baptist Church

1818

1650 Highway 174

National Register of Historic Places

HISTORIC SIGNIFICANCE: The church was built through the efforts of a planter's wife and a freedwoman. The oldest part of the structure has a tabby foundation. The only known tabby baptismal font was built behind the church. A gallery upstairs was designed to accommodate Black church members, but most sat wherever they liked. After the Civil War, white trustees turned the church over to the Black congregants.

Until 1818, there was no Baptist church on Edisto Island. Hephzibah Jenkins Townsend, the wife of the planter John Townsend and a woman of forceful character, was determined to build one. To fund the project and a women's missionary society, Townsend and a free Black woman, Bella, baked goods in outdoor tabby ovens and sold them in Charleston. The commercial-size ovens were erected in 1815 on property that Hephzibah Townsend owned. Her husband, a Presbyterian elder, was not in favor of his wife's church-building project. It was not the only time that she defied him during their long and apparently happy marriage.

The original church was a square two-story building on a tabby foundation. When it was enlarged in 1865, brick piers instead of tabby supported the new construction. The original building was sheathed in beaded weatherboard. An addition, which doubled the size of the church, was covered in plainer weatherboard.

Triangular pediments were installed at the gable ends at the front and back of the original church. The front pediment was removed and reinstalled after the expansion. The rear pediment was permanently lost when a pair of one-story bathrooms sheathed in shiplap siding were added during the twentieth century. A two-story covered portico, supported by four simple wooden columns, was added to the façade in about 1880. With its arched louvered vent, the portico provided a dramatic entry to the sanctuary as well as a shelter for congregants during inclement weather. Above the portico, a small square belfry was crowned with a decorative finial. The belfry and church have tin roofs.

The main entry features double doors topped with ten-light transoms. Inside the sanctuary and in the gallery upstairs, large windows with transoms flood the church with light, illuminating the simple frieze and wall pilasters. The

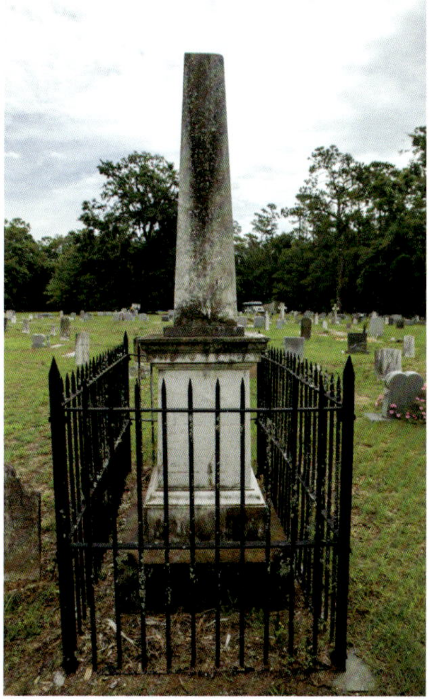
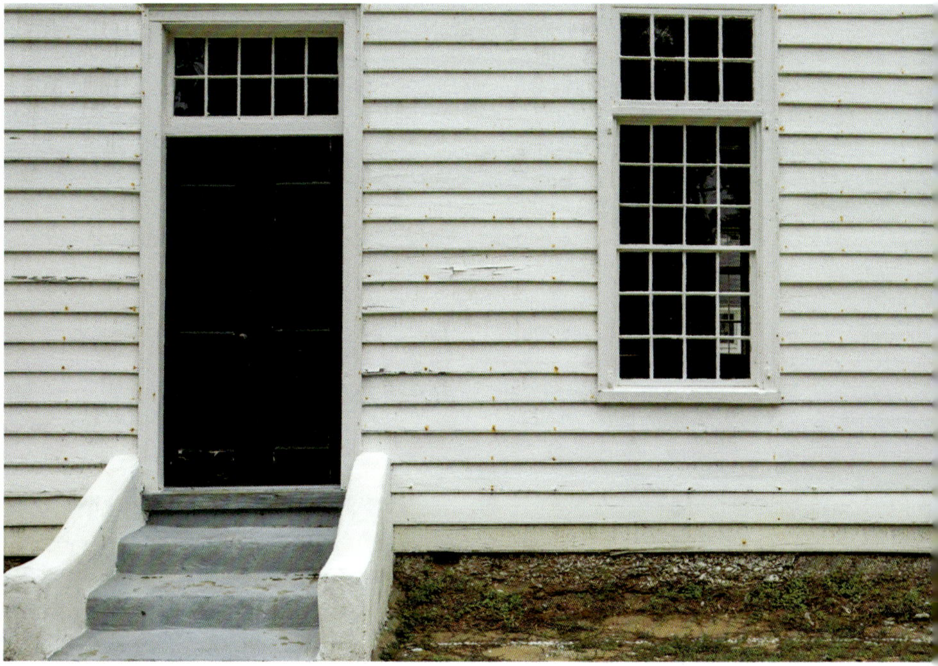
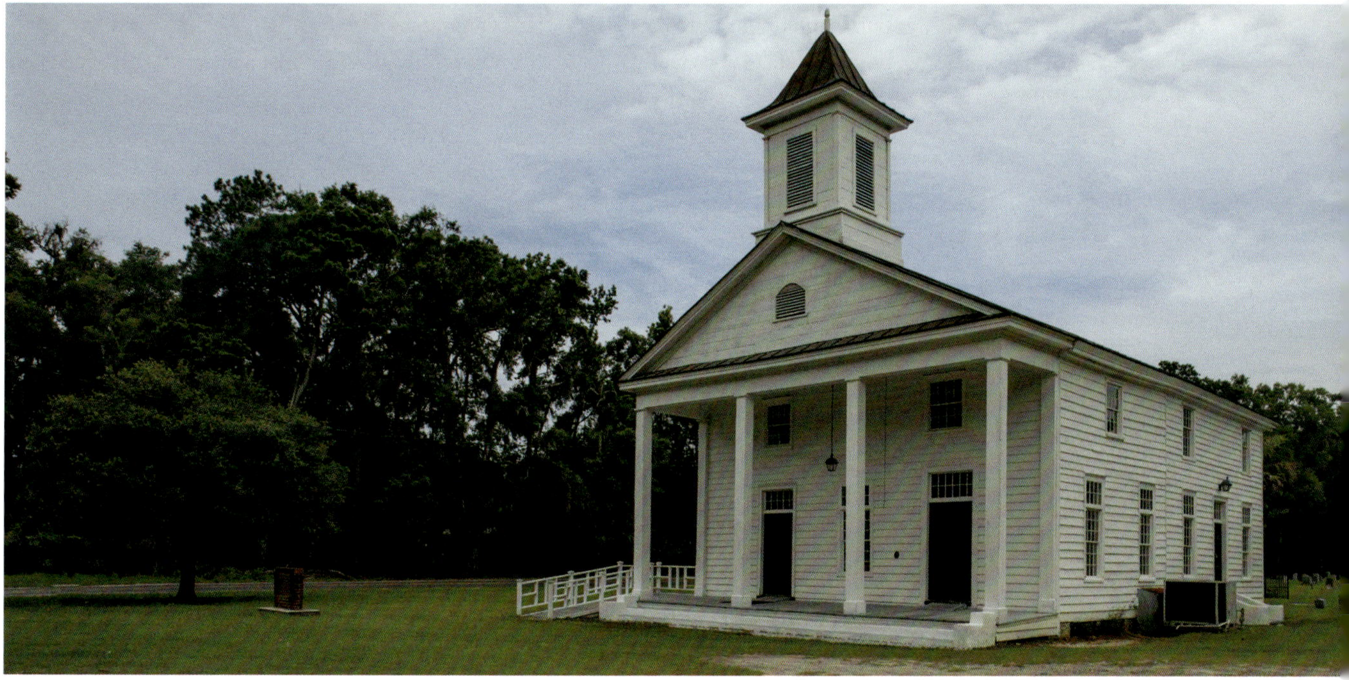

rare recessed-panel slave gallery flanks both sides of the nave. It was designed to accommodate Black church members, but as it turned out, only 5 percent of the congregants were white, so enslaved and free Black congregants sat downstairs as well.

Black members were treated with a degree of dignity by white members of the church. They were ordained as deacons and had a voice in church business. No other house of worship on Edisto—and possibly in the rest of the Deep South—offered such benefits to Black members in a church built and attended by white congregants well before the Civil War.

The church pulpit rests on a raised platform at the rear of the sanctuary. It is a replacement for the original mahogany pulpit, which was relocated when congregants built a new Baptist church next door. The windows behind the pulpit are finished with shelf architraves and dentil molding. A decorative vault sheathed in narrow beadboard and bordered with diagonal beadboard forms a pyramid over the pulpit.

In 1940, a tropical storm ripped off most of the shutters and destroyed original window sashes. They were replaced by larger windows, along with a transom above the door on the northeast side.

The baptismal font, the only one known built of tabby, may have been constructed at the same time as the original church. The font, seven feet wide and ten feet long, was sunk two and a half feet into the ground with an above-grade brick coping and rounded ends. The interior was smoothed with tabby stucco to protect the people being baptized from the sharp oyster-shell aggregate in the rough tabby.

Some of the stucco flaked off over the years, exposing the tabby construction. Two parallel ghost marks on the bottom and continuing up the ends of the font indicate that at one time tabby blocks divided the pool into three vertical compartments, which would have allowed for multiple baptisms at the same time. A metal water pipe extended about eighteen inches out of the pool's east side. Water was supplied by an artesian well and would have been as cold as spring water year-round.

For many years, the Edisto Island Baptist Church, as it was first called, was the island's only Baptist church. The name was changed to the New First Missionary Baptist Church after the congregation moved into its new church next door. A predominantly white Episcopal congregation later took over the historic church. The Episcopal and Baptist congregations now hold joint services on special occasions.

The remains of Hephzibah's outdoor ovens still stand, although they are in poor repair. Possibly the only tabby ovens in existence, they are listed on the National Register of Historic Places. They are located near Wilkinson's Landing, a little over three miles from the church that Hephzibah built. The property is privately owned but accessible to people who arrange kayak rentals or boat tours at the dock near the ovens.

Hephzibah Jenkins Townsend, 1780–1847

Hephzibah Townsend was an independent women in an age when women were expected to be subservient to their fathers, brothers, husbands, and even their sons. Although her father was an Episcopal church elder and her husband was an elder in Edisto's Presbyterian church, Hephzibah Townsend was a committed Baptist who wanted to build a Baptist church on Edisto. She needed money for construction of the church and for her missionary work.

Hephzibah Jenkins was born in Charleston in 1780 during the Revolutionary War, a day or so before the coastal city was captured by the British. Her father, Daniel Jenkins, a captain in the Patriot forces, was taken prisoner. Her mother died shortly after giving birth to her.

Before Hephzibah's mother died, she arranged to have two slaves take her infant daughter to relatives at Bleak Hall plantation on Edisto Island, where she would be safe from the dangers and turmoil of war.

The trip to the island from Charleston by rowboat took six hours. Hephzibah grew up at Bleak Hall, but even as a young girl, she often made the long boat trip back to Charleston to attend services with relatives at the First Baptist Church.

The Baptist pastor in Charleston, Richard Furman, a prominent theologian of the day, told congregants the story of a disabled woman in Boston who started a mission to raise money for poor people in India. The mission was referred to as a "mite society," from a biblical passage in which Jesus praises a poor widow who gave all she had to charity, a tiny contribution known as a mite. Hephzibah Townsend was inspired to act. In 1811, she started the Wadmalaw and Edisto Female Mite Society, modeled after a similar group in Boston. Wadmalaw is an island just north of Edisto.

As a girl and young woman, Hephzibah Jenkins was described as brilliant and beautiful, with a sense of justice as strong as her will. At fifteen, she married her distant cousin Daniel Townsend, who by then owned Bleak Hall. The couple had fifteen children, but only six lived to adulthood. Hephzibah may have taken refuge from those tragedies in her religion.

When she married, Hephzibah's father gave her four thousand acres of valuable sea island cotton land as a dowry, but under antebellum law, she could not borrow against the property or sell it without Daniel Townsend's consent. This restriction became a problem when Hephzibah Townsend asked her husband for money for the mite society and to fund the construction of a Baptist church on Edisto. He refused.

Hephzibah was undaunted. She sent her confidant, a freed slave named Bella, to Charleston to learn how to bake fancy pastries—gingerbread and special cakes—from the city's top chef. While Bella was in training, Hephzibah had other enslaved people build two commercial-size outdoor tabby ovens on waterfront land that her brother had willed specifically to her.

When Bella retuned, the two women fired up the ovens. They baked during the week and on Saturday transported their goods to Charleston, where they sold them, no doubt to Daniel Townsend's embarrassment and displeasure.

He and his wife disagreed again over Daniel's plan to will the plantation to the couple's eldest son, a common practice at the time. Hephzibah thought the inheritance should be divided equally among all the children, and she moved out of the house when Daniel refused to rewrite his will. Daniel got his way, but the couple reconciled and Hephzibah moved back home.

A year after Hephzibah founded the Wadmalaw and Edisto Female Mite Society, the first one in the Deep South, she and the other members presented $122.50 to the Charleston organization that funded foreign missions. The success of the effort inspired women in other southern states to found mite societies to raise mission funds. The societies evolved into the Women's Missionary Union, now the largest such association in the world.

Hephzibah then turned her attention to fund-raising for the construction of the church, in part because she was concerned that many slaves on the island had limited access to Edisto's white churches. She and Bella started a catering business, providing food for island weddings and other events. In a few years, the women had raised $2,000, enough to build the church.

Hephzibah was a progressive woman. After her husband's death, she welcomed all church members, including Black ones, to Bleak Hall. During a Christmas revival in 1844 that continued through the holiday season, congregants met every night in her parlor for evening services that lasted until midnight. On the final night, she helped the pastor baptize sixty new church members.

Hephzibah Townsend died in 1847. She is said to be the only white person buried in the churchyard of the Baptist church that she built. A monolith marks her grave. In her will, she made sure that church members would retain ownership of the land on which the church was built.

During the Civil War, the building was occupied by Union troops. After the war, the white trustees turned the church over to its Black members.

Raising funds for missions and a church was not Hephzibah's only talent. The National Museum of American

Child's quilt appliquéd by Hephzibah Townsend, c. 1840–50, with a Tree of Life pattern that features peacocks, butterflies, and large flower blooms. It is now in the Smithsonian Museum in Washington, D.C.

History, located on the National Mall in Washington, D.C., acquired her hand-stitched child's quilt, appliquéd with a Tree of Life motif featuring peacocks and other colorful birds. The tree's branches and birds, as well as the flowers and butterflies, are cut from blocks of cotton in different prints and colors. The diagonal grid quilting pattern is closely worked at thirteen stitches an inch.

CHAPTER 17   *Charleston*

CHARLESTON, FOUNDED IN 1670, is one of the nation's oldest municipalities. Designated a National Historic Landmark, the city embraces more than 2,800 historic structures, many fronting cobblestone streets. Charleston had the first taxpayer-supported public library in America, the first museum, and the nation's first municipal college. Charleston was the birthplace of the Reform branch of Judaism in America. The Civil War began with the bombardment of Fort Sumter in Charleston Harbor by Confederate forces on April 12, 1861.

The Carolina colony and Charleston were founded at the same time. In the late 1600s, Charles II needed to compensate eight of his generals for helping him regain the throne. Cash-strapped, he paid them with property in North America.

The eight generals became the lords proprietors, or overseers, of the Carolina territory, which originally encompassed modern North Carolina, South Carolina, and Georgia. The king got a bonus: he was interested in expanding England's settlements in North America and claiming its riches for the Crown.

The famed British philosopher John Locke was the principal author of the Fundamental Constitutions of Carolina. The documents provided the basis for Carolina's early government and created a climate of tolerance that led to immigration to Carolina by French Huguenots, Sephardic Jews, and other diverse communities.

The colonists had planned to establish their settlement at Port Royal, farther south, but Native Americans and Dr. Henry Woodward, South Carolina's first English inhabitant, warned them that Spanish and Indigenous people were guarding the area. The settlers sailed up the coast and landed near the Charleston of today. They settled at Albemarle Point on the south bank of the Ashley River, which the Lord Proprietor Anthony Ashley Cooper named for himself. The proprietors called the settlement Charles Towne in honor of the king.

About a decade later, the town was outgrowing its available land. Many of the settlers and governmental officials relocated across the river to the nearby peninsula between the Ashley and Cooper Rivers. There was more room on the peninsula for the town to expand, and the site also offered better access to the deep harbor formed by the confluence of the rivers as they approach the Atlantic Ocean. Lord Ashley predicted accurately that the settlement in its new location would become "a great port towne."

By the late 1600s, Charleston colonists were establishing rice plantations in coastal tidewaters, using methods developed on the west coast of Africa. The vast rice fields required slave labor to be profitable. As a result, hundreds

Anthony Ashley Cooper, 1st Earl of Shaftesbury, by Jacobus Houbraken, after a painting by Sir Peter Lely, mid-eighteenth century

of thousands of Africans, most of them from Africa's rice coast—present-day Senegal, Gambia, Guinea-Bissau, Guinea, Sierra Leone, and Liberia—were enslaved and forcibly imported through Charleston's port. In 1710, a decade before Carolina became a crown colony, Africans outnumbered Europeans in the Lowcountry.

The notorious pirate Edward Teach, better known as Blackbeard, blockaded Charles Towne's harbor in 1718, capturing and ransacking a number of ships and taking hostages. Blackbeard threatened to behead the hostages and burn their ships unless the colonial government provided him with a chest filled with medicines and medical supplies. When the ransom was late in arriving because two of the pirates sent to get the chest got drunk in a Charles Towne bar, Blackbeard sailed his fleet upriver toward the city to learn the cause of the delay, which terrified the settlers. The medicine chest was soon delivered, and Blackbeard kept his word. He released the hostages, but only after stealing everything of value they had, including the clothes they were wearing.

Indigo became an important colonial crop after a Charleston teenager developed the method of growing the plant and processing it into a vivid blue dye. Eliza Pinckney was just sixteen when she was left in charge of three family plantations near Charleston. Determined to find additional crops to make the plantations profitable, Eliza settled on indigo. The British offered colonial planters a generous subsidy to produce the dye. Until the American Revolution, indigo was a staple of the colonial economy.

After the war, Charleston prospered as one of the most important seaports on the East Coast. Its economy grew even more after planters—many from Barbados—migrated to the coast of Carolina to grow rice, indigo, and the most profitable crop of all: sea island cotton.

Wealthy planters and merchants built magnificent houses along the Battery, Charleston's old seawall. Important buildings of the era include the Exchange Building, the Fireproof Building, and Society Hall. The privately owned Coming Street Cemetery is now ranked as the oldest Jewish cemetery in the South.

By 1710, diasporic Africans outnumbered Europeans in the Lowcountry. A few decades later, Africans represented 70 percent of the population. In 1739, Carolina slaves organized a rebellion on the banks of the Stono River south of Charleston. They hoped to escape to Spanish Florida, where slaves received better treatment and had a chance at freedom. They broke into a store, seized firearms, and killed a number of white settlers as they moved south. White authorities caught them as they reached the Edisto River, killing many of the rebels, hanging others, and shipping survivors off to the West Indies.

After the Stono Rebellion, the Carolina Assembly enacted a law requiring a ratio of one white person for every ten enslaved people on each plantation. The Negro Act of 1740 banned the enslaved from growing their own food, assembling in groups, earning money for themselves, or learning to read. The new laws were accompanied by penalties for slaveholders who imposed brutal punishments or demanded excessive work from their enslaved laborers.

In 1822, Denmark Vesey planned and led another slave uprising. The failed effort prompted the establishment of a military garrison in Charleston's Marion Square, where a remnant reminds locals and visitors of the famous hornwork that surrounded the city to control future rebellion attempts. In 1842, the state legislature converted the Charleston garrison into the Citadel, South Carolina's noted military college. By 1918, the Citadel had outgrown its downtown site and was moved to its present location on a larger tract on the south bank of the Ashley River.

Wars usually destroy the cities in their paths, but the Civil War is credited with helping save much of Charleston's historically significant architecture, including houses, commercial buildings, and public structures. For one thing, General William Tecumseh Sherman spared the city, despite relentless pressure from the North to torch it for having started the Civil War. Charleston surrendered as soon as Sherman neared its outskirts, which probably weighed in its favor. Second, the war destroyed the Lowcountry economy, and for many years near-destitute Charlestonians were forced to repair their damaged buildings rather than raze and replace them.

SITE 47   *Short Take*

Horn Work

1757–1784

Marion Square
Meeting and King streets

A chunk of historic tabby about six feet high and ten feet long marks the sparse remnants of a once-massive structure built to protect the British in Charleston from invasion by the Spanish in Florida. Started in 1757, the hornwork, or as it came to be written in Charleston, Horn Work, was in place by 1780 when Charleston was attacked—not by the Spanish, but by the British during the Revolutionary War.

By that time, the fortress enclosed five acres of land, boasted eighteen cannons, and had a moat thirty feet wide that could be flooded by tidewater. The Horn Work was the focal point of a wall that stretched across the Charleston Peninsula between the Ashley and Cooper Rivers.

For many years, the Horn Work guarded the main road into Charleston. Named for twin half bastions that resembled horns, it was gated and equipped with a drawbridge. During the siege of Charleston, Major General Benjamin Lincoln, the Patriot commander, attempted to hold the city with six thousand troops against a force of more than ten thousand soldiers.

British ships took control of Charleston Harbor in April 1780. The British offered Lincoln a chance to surrender, but he declined and the British bombardment began. The Horn Work could not withstand the ongoing assault. The Patriots were running out of food and supplies. Patriot officers favored the surrender; civilian officials did not. Lincoln negotiated a deal that allowed his troops to retreat inland unharmed, and he surrendered the town in early May. The capture of Charleston was the worst Patriot defeat of the American Revolution. It gave the British a foothold from which to attack the southern colonies.

Three years later, the Treaty of Paris ended the war, and the Horn Work was dismantled. The eastern section of the Horn Work is now buried beneath Marion Square; the western side of the fortress wall is covered by buildings on King Street.

The colonial fortification built over King Street in Charleston in 1759 to protect the only road into town was razed in 1784. The Horn Work remnant in Marion Square is all that is left. The old Citadel Academy, built in 1829 to operate as the state's arsenal, is seen in the background.

CHAPTER 18 *Dorchester*

THE COLONIAL TOWN was founded in 1696 on a 4,000-acre peninsula by Congregationalists, dissenters from the Church of England. The swampy neck of land, named Bo-Shoe-ee by Native Americans, lay between the Ashley River and today's Dorchester Creek at the upper limit of navigation on the Ashley. The location made Dorchester ideal for shipping rice, indigo, and other goods to the coast and for receiving coastal goods for sale or trade to settlers and Natives inland.

The Congregationalists came to South Carolina from the Massachusetts Bay Colony to "settle the gospel" among the people. They had named their Massachusetts town Dorchester, after a town of the same name in England, and then passed the name along to their southern settlement.

The settlers spent several days designing the town. They set aside about 50 acres for Dorchester's place of trade, or commercial center. Individual congregants staked out lots. The process was conducted without controversy in an atmosphere of "love and amity and peace," one elder reported. Near the mouth of Boshoe Creek, 123 acres were reserved for a mill, and 50 acres were set aside for a commons. Streets and a public square were laid out, and an area of about 20 acres between the town and creek was dedicated to public use.

The colonists' first priority was to establish a place of worship. They built St. Andrews Anglican Church in 1696, probably of wood. They replaced it a few years later with a brick church that was renamed St. Andrews Parish Church after the Carolina colony established parishes. When the parishes were reconfigured, Dorchester was reassigned to St. George's Parish, and the church was renamed accordingly. A tall brick bell tower was added in 1751. The epicenter of the 1886 earthquake, among the most destructive natural events in Carolina history, was about a mile from Dorchester. The quake devastated Charleston, the nearby colonial capital, and split the bell tower almost in half lengthwise, which may have been its salvation. Because it was unstable, scavengers were afraid to take bricks from the structure for fear it might fall on them. Metal straps held the halves together until the tower was restored in the 1960s.

In its heyday, Dorchester was a commercial success. The town bustled with activity on weekly market days. Even more exciting were the twice-yearly fairs. The colonial government authorized Dorchester to hold four-day fairs in spring and fall. Colonial fairs were outgrowths of the old English custom of holding cattle, cloth, or hay fairs, which, over time, expanded to include a variety of offerings. In addition to stalls offering food, crafts, trinkets, tools, toys, and other items, the fairs featured a variety of entertainments and commercial opportunities. To encourage attendance, the town fathers offered incentives for outlying residents to bring farm animals for sale or trade. The person who brought the most horses was awarded a "pistole." The attendee with the best draft horse received a horse whip. The person who brought "the most fat hogs, and . . . offers them for sale" was paid eight pence per hog. In addition, colonial fairs featured participatory events: wrestling matches, foot and horse races, beauty contests—no swimsuits—cockfights, and target shooting. Competitors chased a pig with a soaped tail around the fairgrounds. The person who caught and lifted the pig off the ground by its slippery appendage was declared the winner. People who won competitive events received a variety of prizes. One was a hunting saddle embellished with "a fine broadcloth housing, fringed and flowered." A series of fiddlers competed on a Cremona violin; the best one won the instrument. "The handsomest maid upon the green" received a pair of silk stockings. Men danced for a pair of pumps. Traveling showmen and women staged awe-inspiring entertainment. At one fair, a female acrobat elicited gasps as she performed high above the crowd on the "roaps." Puppeteers presented dramas and comedies. Trained animals leapt and twirled and somersaulted on command. Children loved the merry-go-round.

Among the more unusual fixtures at colonial fairs were pipowder (pronounced "pie-powder") courts, which date to the Middle Ages in England. Historians speculate that pipowder meant "dusty foot," indicating a traveler, peddler, or vagrant. Pipowder courts were convened during the fairs to settle small problems, with town merchants acting as judges. The courts handed down swift justice and avoided the expense and delay of litigation in traditional courts. At one colonial fair, a vendor sold a ring of "purest gold" to a buyer who discovered it was brass. The pipowder court found the seller guilty and ordered him to make restitution. The seller was poor but pledged to work for the buyer until the debt was satisfied. Another defendant found guilty was allowed to pay the fine with his overcoat.

Dorchester's location was its ultimate downfall. The nearby swamps were infested in summer with mosquitoes carrying malaria and yellow fever. Even more important was the fact that the site was too small for Dorchester to expand. The Congregationalists began pulling up stakes in 1752 and relocated to Liberty County in coastal Georgia. For about fifteen years, Dorchester was a ghost town, but by 1768, new residents had moved in. The colonial government chartered a free school, and residents built a brick school and house for the schoolmaster and his family. Citizens helped fund the school and support and educate poor children.

Dorchester ceased to be a Congregationalist settlement and functioned as a supply depot for wealthy planters. New roads were built and commerce increased on the Ashley River. Planters began dealing directly with merchants and factors in Charleston. During the Revolutionary War, Dorchester was again abandoned when British troops marched into town. They burned the interior of the large brick church as Patriot forces were massing to drive them out.

After thriving for almost a century, Dorchester never recovered from the war. Wealthy planters began building summerhouses in the nearby pine barrens, which offered high, well-drained ground. Planters named their resort town Summerville. The pine-scented air was fresh and cool, and mosquitoes were seldom a problem. A number of Summerville houses were built of bricks scavenged from Dorchester's remains. By 1788, only ruins marked the location of the once-prosperous town. The only recognizable remnants of Dorchester today are the bell tower, a scattering of graves, and the nearby tabby fort on the Ashley River.

SITE 48

Fort

1757

300 State Park Road

Colonial Dorchester State Historic Site

HISTORIC SIGNIFICANCE: The fort at Dorchester is the only one of its design ever constructed in North America, and it is the best-preserved tabby fort still standing. It served as a strategic point and supply depot during the American Revolution for both Patriot and British troops. It was abandoned after the war, but the tabby ruins on the banks of the Ashley River remain in remarkably good shape.

The outbreak of the French and Indian War in 1754, along with rumors of a French naval invasion, prompted the South Carolina governor to recommend housing a powder magazine in Dorchester. At the time, the colony's only public magazine was in Charleston. The brick magazine was built partly underground to shield the soldiers guarding it from harm in case of an accidental explosion.

The tabby fort was built around the magazine. It was situated on a bluff on the Ashley River in the southwestern corner of Dorchester. The tabby walls, some now darkened by centuries of weathering, were built by enslaved people, who used thousands of bushels of oyster shells barged upriver to the fort site as aggregate for the concrete. Oyster-shell lime, the hardener, was made on the coast and transported to Dorchester in bushels to cut down on shipping bulk.

The structure's pinwheel design appears to duplicate a flanked fortress in Great Britain. Half bastions projected from the corners of walls that enclosed about ten thousand square feet. The faces of the bastions were angled inward so that troops could direct fire down the adjacent walls.

The structure took about three years to complete. By that time, the threats to South Carolina had eased, so there was no rush to install cannons. An area planter later willed his "great guns" to be used at the fort, specifying that they should be fired to celebrate holidays, especially the king's birthday and the feast day of St. George.

The fort first saw action during the Revolutionary War, when Dorchester became a military depot. Legislative records were transferred from Charleston to the fort for safekeeping. Because of fears that Loyalists allied with the British might attack the town, the garrison was reinforced with two companies of the Second South Carolina Regiment under the command of Francis Marion, whose

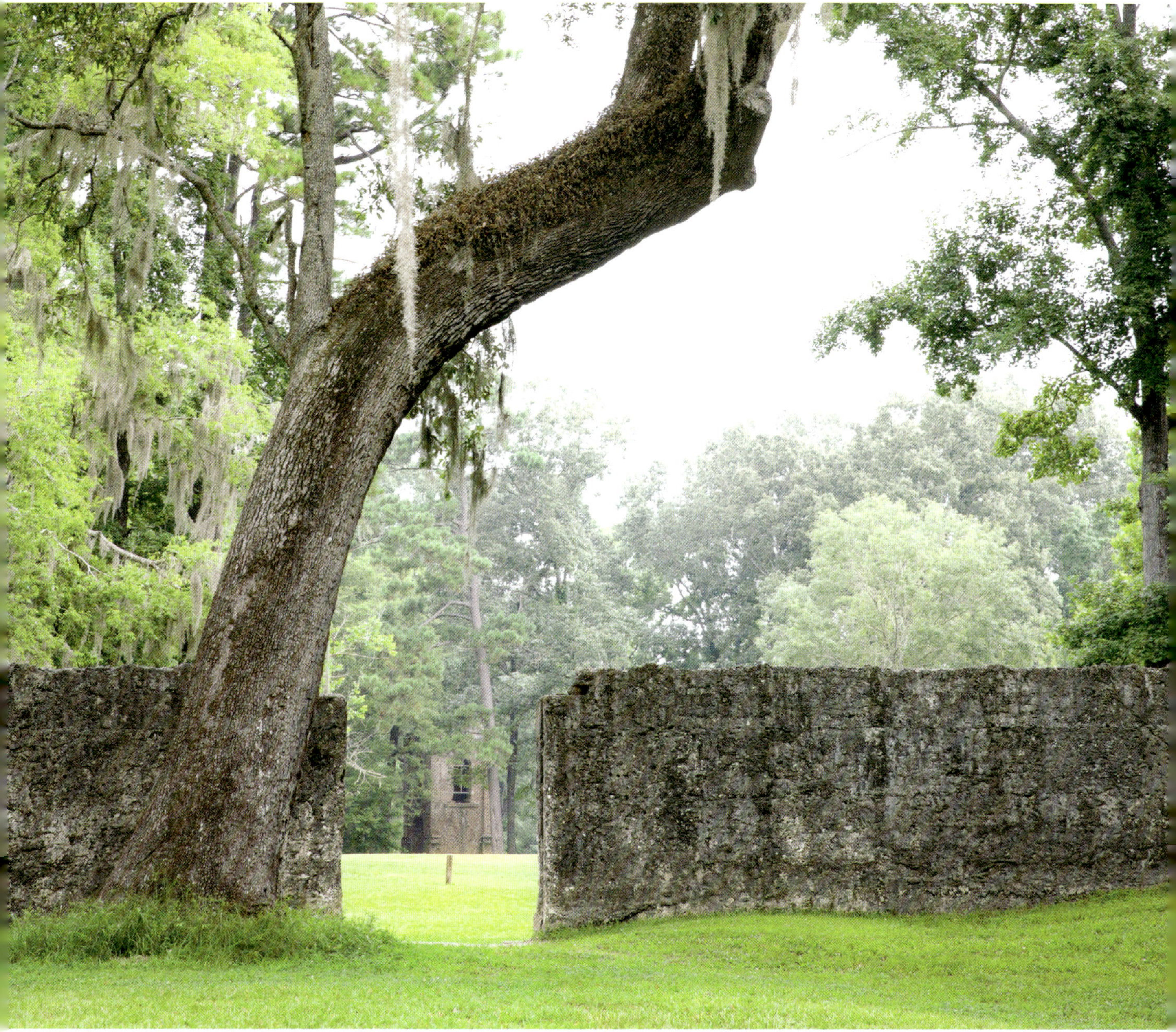

unorthodox military tactics earned him the nickname the Swamp Fox. Provisions were brought in to feed a thousand soldiers for a month.

Lieutenant Colonel Owen Roberts of the First South Carolina Regiment was ordered to make the fort strong enough to resist a major assault. The rows of bricks that top the tabby walls on one side of the fortress may represent Roberts's efforts. Authorized to use any means necessary to make Dorchester an armed encampment, he had plans drawn up to fortify even the church. The troops garrisoned at the Dorchester fort suffered most from boredom, since no attacks were forthcoming. In 1780, British troops frustrated by their lack of success in the North turned toward Charleston, the most important city in the Southeast.

When the siege of Charleston began, Patriot troops assembled at Dorchester for the march to the coast. In spite of the Patriots' efforts, Carolina's capital soon fell to the British. Dorchester was briefly occupied by the British, but the town and fort were abandoned before being raided by the Patriot commander Henry "Light-Horse Harry" Lee, father of Robert E. Lee. After Lee's forces were diverted to other battles, British soldiers retook the fort.

British and Patriot commanders wanted the fort because of its strategic location on the Ashley River. As a consequence, the Dorchester fort passed back and forth between the rival armies during the war. Although it is sometimes called Fort Dorchester now, that name does not appear in historic documents, in which it is always called "the fort at Dorchester."

General Nathanael Greene, the commander of Patriot forces in the South, planned a surprise attack on Dorchester. The British garrison there included 400 infantry soldiers, 150 mounted troops, and a number of Loyalist militiamen. The British discovered the plan and sent a patrol to investigate. Greene's vanguard met and attacked the patrol, and the British suffered heavy casualties. The Redcoats' cavalry rode out to help but retreated as Greene's troops advanced. Before the British abandoned Dorchester, they destroyed supplies, burned the interior of the church, and wrecked the school buildings.

For the rest of the war, skirmishes broke out in and around Dorchester whenever enemy patrols and raiding parties happened to meet. In December 1782, the British gave up Charleston, which marked the end of the Revolutionary War in South Carolina.

The fort was damaged by the earthquake of 1886, which devastated Charleston. It cracked the tabby walls of the fort but did not bring them down, although the epicenter was just a mile away. Someone who visited the fort afterward commented that the tabby walls were "as fresh and hard as newly-cut granite."

Every year, about fifty thousand visitors explore the historic site, the brick church tower, the historic cemetery, and the lovely, shaded three-hundred-acre grounds overlooking the Ashley River.

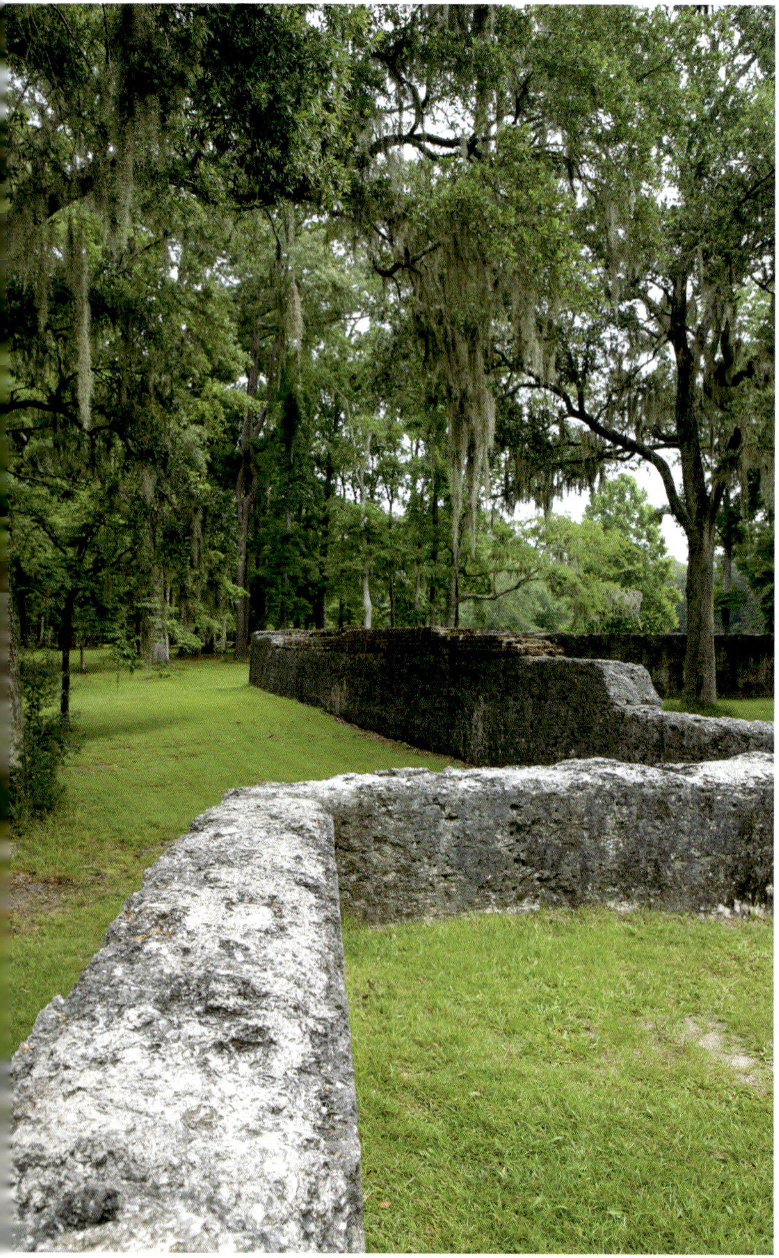

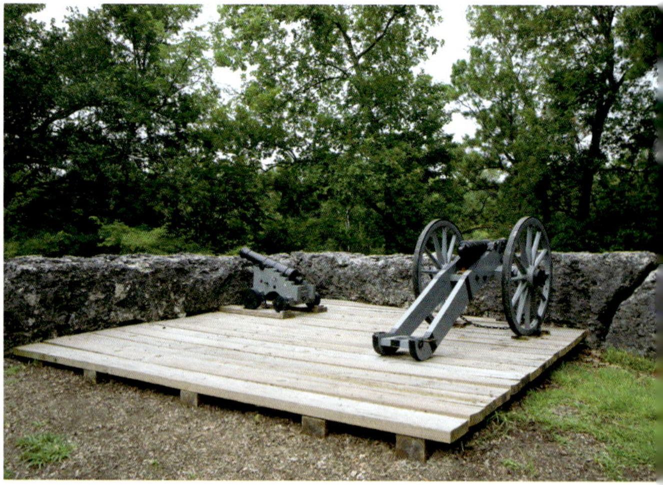

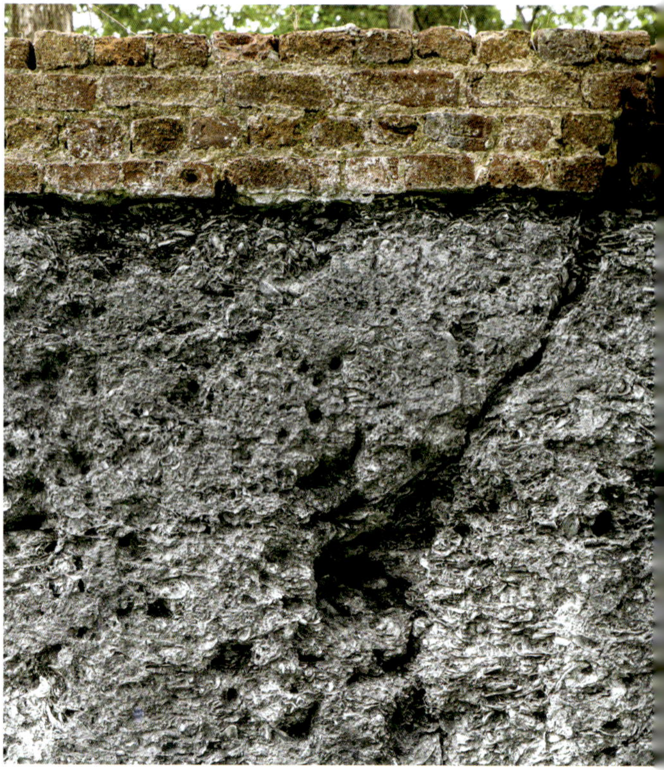

Francis Marion, c. 1732–1795

The tabby fort at Dorchester was briefly under the command of Francis Marion, the notorious Swamp Fox. Marion was a native South Carolinian, born at his family's plantation in Berkeley County. Short of stature in part because his legs were deformed at birth, Marion never let the handicap slow him down.

Seeking adventure at fifteen, he sailed on a ship bound for the West Indies. The ship sank; it was rumored that a whale rammed it. The men escaped in the lifeboat but floated for a week before drifting ashore. Marion decided he preferred life on land and came home to manage the family plantation.

At the outbreak of the French and Indian War, Marion, then about twenty-five, joined the South Carolina militia. During the fighting, he observed the guerrilla tactics of the Cherokee, who used the Carolina landscape to their advantage, hiding in woods and ambushing enemy soldiers. When battles were in danger of being lost, the Cherokee escaped into near-impenetrable swamps to regroup. European troops, trained to fight in conventional styles, confronted their enemies head-on, often with poor results.

After the war, Marion saved enough money to buy his own property, which he named Pond Bluff. In 1775, he was elected to the first South Carolina Provincial Congress, a group supporting self-determination for the American colonies. At the outbreak of the American Revolution, Marion joined the colonial militia, taking his enslaved manservant, Oscar, along with him to war.

Marion wanted to lead combat troops, but instead was assigned to captain the regiment in charge of building Fort Sullivan in Charleston Harbor, a job that took several years. Once the fort was built, his troops were given the job of guarding it. Marion found the task frustrating. He reported that he spent his time trying to control unruly, drunken soldiers who showed up barefoot for inspections.

During the revolution, Marion adopted the Cherokee style of warfare, which focused on stealth and speed rather than on marching formidable but sometimes inefficient lines of men directly at the enemy. He led fifty men in a raid against a much larger British force. His troops hid in dense underbrush and ambushed the British soldiers, routing them and rescuing 150 Patriot prisoners.

His memorable nickname, Swamp Fox, is credited to a British officer, Banastre "Butcher" Tarleton, who chased Marion and his men for twenty-six miles over seven hours until Marion's troops escaped into a swamp. The Patriots were mounted on marsh tackies, small feral horses that still run wild in the salt marshes and river swamps of the Lowcountry. "Taki" is a Gullah Geechee word for horse. The sure-footed marsh tackies were accustomed to picking their way through rough, swampy terrain. Tarleton, whose troops were mounted on heavy British horses that foundered in the wetlands, called off the pursuit, angrily exclaiming: "As for this damned old fox, the Devil himself could not catch him." Marion's nickname was thus established.

Marion's exploits as the Swamp Fox have inspired many stories, no doubt some of them apocryphal. One reported that Marion was dining with friends at an officer's home in Charleston. According to custom, the host locked the doors to prevent diners from slipping out after the meal in order to avoid the traditional toasts that continued for hours.

Marion did not drink, and as the toasts continued and his companions got louder and drunker, he felt trapped. He jumped from a second-story window and broke his ankle. Marion's injury turned out to be fortuitous, or so the story goes. While he was at home recuperating, the British took Charleston, and all of Marion's dinner party companions were captured.

He commanded several forts during the revolution but preferred to launch attacks from encampments in woods and swamps. His favorite camp was on Snow's Island, a remote bit of high ground surrounded by the swampy wetlands of the Pee Dee River. In the winter of 1781, Marion and his men were camped there when a British officer, under a flag of truce, arrived to discuss an exchange of prisoners.

It was breakfast time, and Oscar was roasting sweet potatoes in the open fire. The British officer shared the simple meal. He observed that Marion's men were dressed in tatters and that the camp was short on food and other supplies. In spite of the shortages, Marion's men showed dedication to their unorthodox leader. According to legend, the Redcoat was so impressed that he switched loyalties to the American side. Snow's Island is now listed on the National Register of Historic Places.

A painting of the breakfast encounter, done around 1810 by the South Carolina artist John Blake White, now hangs in the U.S. Capitol. The only Black man in the painting is the enslaved Oscar Marion, who accompanied Marion on all his campaigns.

Marion's Oak near Dorchester was once rumored to mark the spot where his forces had camped to defend a bridge while Oscar roasted sweet potatoes. A number of other Carolina oaks were said to mark trees where Marion's troops had assembled to eat before a battle. So many trees were designated as Marion's oaks that some claimed the Swamp Fox would have had no time to fight if Oscar cooked sweet potatoes under every one.

One modern author credits Marion as a major factor in America's victory over the British. He commanded a brigade of militia at the Battle of Eutaw Springs in 1781. It was the last large battle fought in the south before the siege of Yorktown.

For the most part, Marion was known for guerrilla tactics similar to those of today's special forces. He spied on enemy encampments and listened to gossip from locals. Marion's men were apt to show up anywhere, which forced British commanders to divide and divert their troops from other campaigns. The colorful exploits of the Swamp Fox boosted the morale of South Carolinians, who were captivated by tales of a contemporary Robin Hood fighting to free them from British rule.

Marion's unorthodox style of warfare was at first criticized by his superior officers, including General Nathanael Greene. Over time, Greene came to admire the Swamp Fox's tactics.

In 1779, Marion and his troops were called to fight at the siege of Savannah, which the British had taken the year before. A Polish nobleman, Count Casimir Pulaski, led a joint force of French and Patriot cavalry, but when he was killed, the siege was abandoned. Marion led a daring rescue of American prisoners at Parker's Ferry, South Carolina, and in 1781, Congress elevated him to the rank of brigadier general.

Fort Pulaski, later built east of Savannah and named in the nobleman's honor, was defended by Confederate troops during the Civil War. The brick fort was considered

Oscar Marion cooking a breakfast of sweet potatoes in John Blake White's *General Marion Inviting a British Officer to Share His Meal*, c. 1810. According to the South Carolina artist's son, Octavius A. White: "The figure of Marion is a portrait from memory, as my father, when a boy, knew him well. Marion's farm adjoined the plantation of my grandfather."

nearly impregnable but fell to a Union bombardment that used cannons with rifled barrels, which sent the shot much farther and with more force than did older-style guns.

After the Revolutionary War, Marion took charge of a peacetime brigade, served in the South Carolina Assembly, and helped write the state constitution. He opposed punishing Loyalists after the war, recommending amnesty and the return of their confiscated property.

Marion married for the first time at age fifty-four. His wife was his forty-nine-year-old cousin Mary Esther Videau. Marion died at Pond Bluff Plantation in 1795.

In December 2006, President George W. Bush recognized Oscar Marion as an "African American Patriot" in a ceremony at the U.S. Capitol, in a proclamation expressing the appreciation of a "grateful nation" for Oscar Marion's "devoted and selfless consecration to the service of our country in the Armed Forces of the United States."

Acknowledgments

Daniel J. Bell, guide, Fort at Dorchester, S.C.
Carol Belser, descendant of Hepzibah Townsend, Edisto Island, S.C.
Colin Brooker, architectural historian and tabby expert, Beaufort, S.C.
Craig Buckley, architect, Camden County Library, Kingsland, Ga.
Patricia Cofer, historian and writer, St. Simons Island, Ga.
Allison Conboy, Kingsley Plantation, Fort George Island, Fla.
Aaron Daughtry, computer wizard, Darien, Ga.
Kathleen Deagan, archaeologist, expert on Fort Mose, St. Augustine, Fla.
Chester DePratter, archaeologist, expert on Charlesfort–Santa Elena, Parris Island, S.C.
Anne Meyers Devine, rare books outreach coordinator, Hargrett Rare Book and Manuscript Library, University of Georgia, Athens
Allie Daughtry Ellis, interpretive ranger, Fort King George, Darien, Ga.
Dan Elswick, tax incentives, income-producing historic buildings, architectural assistance, South Carolina Department of Archives and History, Columbia, S.C.
Jim Gilbert, attorney and reader, St. Simons Island, Ga.
Leslie and Phil Graitcier, traveling companions, St. Simons Island, Ga.
Gretchen Greminger, manager, Wormsloe State Historic Site, Isle of Hope, Ga.
Gilbert Head, archives associate, Hargrett Rare Book and Manuscript Library, University of Georgia, Athens
Harriet Langford, president of the board of directors, Ashantilly Center Inc., Darien, Ga.
Frank and Amy Lesesne, owners and managers, Anchorage 1770 historic inn, Beaufort, S.C.
Fred Marland, ecologist, marsh and beach expert, Darien, Ga.
Andrea Marroquin, curator of historic resources, Jekyll Island State Park, Ga.

Jim Renner, geologist, manager of environmental stewardship, Southern Ionics Minerals, Patterson, Ga.

Janice Rodriguez, chairman of the restoration committee, tabby slave cabins, Hamilton Plantation, St. Simons Island, Ga.

Mike Russo, archaeologist, National Park Service, Florida State University, Tallahassee

Edward Smith, ranger, Fort George Island Cultural State Park, Fort George Island, Fla.

Gretchen Smith, director, Edisto Island Historical Society Museum, Edisto Island, S.C.

Brad Spear, blacksmith shop restoration, St. Augustine, Fla.

Denise Spear, cultural resource specialist, Fort Frederica National Monument, St. Simons Island, Ga.

Frankie Strother, membership vice president at Sea Island, Sea Island, Ga.

St. Simons Library staff, especially Jim Orser-Schwalm, St. Simons Island, Ga.

Buddy Sullivan, Sapelo Island expert, historian, and writer, McIntosh County, Ga.

Charles Tingley, librarian, St. Augustine Historical Society, St. Augustine, Fla.

Linda Wallis, docent, Owens-Thomas House, Savannah, Ga.

Magen Wilson, executive director, St. Augustine Historical Society Museums, St. Augustine, Fla.

Linda Wood, traveling companion, St. Simons Island, Ga.

For general support, encouragement, and first readings: Books Without Borders book club members; Frankie Ansley; Frankie Bulfer; Claire Cofer; staff of the Glynn Visual Arts Center; Jim Gilbert; John Griffin; Shelley Renner; and as always, my family

Appendix   *Chronological List of Site Construction*

CHRONOLOGY

Following the Tabby Trail presents sites by geographic location rather than by date, which can be confusing for some readers. A chronological listing of tabby constructions follows, along with the country of origin of settlers before the American Revolution and the site's current cultural or historical listing, if any. Settlers from Ireland and Scotland are referred to as British, since neither of those countries ever claimed the southeastern coast.

5,000–3,000 BCE, Paleo-Indians—Oyster-shell mounds, middens, and rings constructed over time on the southeastern coast of North America

SIXTEENTH CENTURY

1562, French—Charlesfort, Parris Island, S.C. National Monument

1564, French—Fort Caroline, St. Johns River near Jacksonville, Fla. National Memorial

1565, Spanish—St. Augustine, Fla. National Historic District

1566, Spanish—Santa Elena (overbuilt Charlesfort), Parris Island, S. C. National Monument

SEVENTEENTH CENTURY

1672–98, Spanish—Castillo de San Marcos, St. Augustine, Fla. National Monument

EIGHTEENTH CENTURY, BRITISH AND SPANISH

Date unknown (possibly begun before the Revolutionary War and enlarged before or during the Civil War), British, American—Tabby seawall, Beaufort, S.C. National Historic District

1724, British—St. Helena Parish Church and Cemetery, Beaufort, S.C. National Historic District

1726, British—Fort Frederick ruins, Port Royal, S.C. National Heritage Preserve

1733–90, Spanish—González-Álvarez (Oldest) House, St. Augustine, Fla. National Historic Landmark

1736, British—Fort Frederica ruins, St. Simons Island, Ga. National Monument

1738, Spanish—Fort Mose, Fort Mose Historic State Park, north of St. Augustine, Fla. National Historic Landmark

1740, Spanish—Fort Matanzas, Rattlesnake Island, Fla. National Monument.

1740, British—Chapel of Ease ruins, Frogmore, St. Helena Island, S.C. National Register of Historic Places

c. 1742, British—Horton House ruins, Jekyll Island, Ga. National Register of Historic Places

1745, British—Wormsloe Plantation Fortified House ruins, Isle of Hope, Ga. State Historic Site

1758, British—Horn Work, Marion Square ruin, Charleston, S.C. City park

1760–1785, British—Father Miguel O'Reilly House, St. Augustine, Fla. National Historic District

c. 1764, Spanish—Fernandez-Llambias House, St. Augustine, Fla. National Historic District

1771, British—Fort at Dorchester, Old Dorchester, S.C. State Historic Site

1774, British—Hampton Plantation, St. Simons Island, Ga. Privately owned; some ruins viewable via public street. Unlisted

EIGHTEENTH CENTURY, AMERICAN

c. 1748—Sea Cloud plantation, Edisto Island, S.C.; later combined with Bleak Hall plantation as Botany Bay plantation. South Carolina Heritage Preserve and Wildlife Management Area

c. 1749—Bleak Hall plantation, Edisto Island, S.C.; later combined with Sea Cloud plantation as Botany Bay plantation. South Carolina Heritage Preserve and Wildlife Management Area

1786—Tabby Manse (Thomas Fuller House), Beaufort, S.C. Privately owned; façade viewable via public street. National Historic District

1789—Barnwell-Gough House, Beaufort, S.C. Privately owned; façade viewable via public street. National Historic District

1790—Arsenal, Beaufort, S.C. National Historic District

1793—Stoney-Baynard House, Hilton Head, S.C. National Register of Historic Places

1793—Cannon's Point Plantation, St. Simons Island, Ga. St. Simons Land Trust Preserve

1796—First Dungeness Mansion, Cumberland Island, Ga. National Seashore

1796—Saltus-Habersham House, Beaufort, S.C. Beaufort National Register Historic District

c. 1790s–1802—Chocolate Plantation, Sapelo Island, Ga. Sapelo Island National Wildlife Reserve.

NINETEENTH CENTURY: 1800–1850

1803—Miller-Greene House, Cumberland Island, Ga. National Seashore

c. 1804—John Mark Verdier House, Beaufort, S.C. National Register of Historic Places

1805—Retreat Plantation slave cabin, St. Simons Island, Ga. Privately owned, operated as gift shop. Unlisted

1805—Old Baptist Meeting House, cemetery walls and tombs, Beaufort, S.C. National Historic District

c. 1807–10—South End House, Sapelo Island, Ga. Group rentals, some tours. Sapelo Island National Estuarine Research Reserve

c. 1821o—Ashantilly Plantation, Darien, Ga. Foundation owned; operated as a historic and cultural learning center. National Register of Historic Places

1820–30—Kingsley Plantation slave cabins, Fort George Island, Fla. Talbot Island State Parks, National Timucuan Ecological and Historic Preserve

1816—The Thicket sugarcane mill, Darien, Ga. Private subdivision, not open to public; some ruins viewable via public street. Unlisted

1816–18—Owens-Thomas House, Savannah, Ga. National Register Historic District

1818—New Missionary Baptist Church and Cemetery, Edisto Island, S.C. National Register of Historic Places

c. 1820s—Darien River wharfs and Adam-Strain Building, Darien, Ga. Privately owned, viewable via public street. Darien Historic District

1825—McIntosh Sugar Mill, New Caanan Plantation, St. Marys, Ga. Camden County Historic Site

1827—Altama Plantation Sugar Mill, near Brunswick, Ga. State Wildlife Management Area

1829—Fort Pulaski, Cockspur Island between Savannah and Tybee Island, Ga. National Historic Monument

pre-1833—Hamilton Plantation slave cabins, St. Simons Island, Ga. Privately owned, open to public on Wednesday mornings or by appointment. National Register of Historic Places

1854–55—Thomson House (never completed), Fort George Island, Fla. National Register of Historic Places

NINETEENTH CENTURY: 1851–1899

1872–76—St. Cyprian's Episcopal Church, Darien, Ga. National Historic District

c. 1874—St. Athanasius Protestant Episcopal Church, Brunswick, Ga. National Historic District

1886–87—Grace United Methodist Church, St. Augustine, Fla. National Historic District

1887–89—Hotel Ponce de León, Flagler College, St. Augustine, Fla. National Historic District
1887–89—Hotel Alcazar and Casino, St. Augustine, Fla. National Historic District
1889—Memorial Presbyterian Church, St. Augustine, Fla. National Historic District
1890—Hollybourne Cottage, Jekyll Island Club, Jekyll Island, Ga. National Historic Landmark District, Jekyll Island State Park
1893—Second Dungeness Mansion, Cumberland Island, Ga. Cumberland Island National Seashore

TWENTIETH CENTURY

1900—St. Mark's Episcopal Church, Kingsland, Ga. Episcopal Diocese of Georgia. Unlisted
1910—Dairy silo, Jekyll Island, Ga. Jekyll Island State Park

Illustration Credits

All images are by Ben Galland except those listed below:

ii	Mapping Specialists Ltd.
8	Mapping Specialists Ltd.
19	British Library
27	Library of Congress Prints and Photographs Division
35 both	Sandra Foyt / Alamy
45	Library of Congress Prints and Photographs Division
47	Library of Congress
48	Courtesy of Jillyan Corrales, Fort Mose Historical Society
49	Courtesy of Jillyan Corrales, Fort Mose Historical Society
62	Library of Congress Prints and Photographs Division
66	Mapping Specialists Ltd.
78	*Century Magazine* (January 1878)
90	State Archives and Library of Florida
92	Florida Map Collection, State Archives and Library of Florida
109	Based on original plans by William Day in Southern Historical Collection, Library of the University of North Carolina, Chapel Hill
111	Southern Historical Collection, Library of the University of North Carolina, Chapel Hill
129	Courtesy of Coastal Georgia Historical Society. Original portrait in the private collection of a family member
136	National Portrait Gallery, Smithsonian Institution
144	Library of Congress Prints and Photographs Division
150	Hargrett Rare Book and Manuscript Library, The University of Georgia
151	© National Portrait Gallery, London
160	Wikimedia Commons

170	Episcopal Diocese of Georgia Archives, Wikimedia
176	Library of Congress Prints and Photographs Division
182	Alamy
183	Michael Rivera
190	Alamy
193	Jud McCranie
195	Hargrett Rare Book and Manuscript Library, The University of Georgia
204	Gift of the Wormsloe Foundation, Inc., 1981.14.1, Telfair Museum of Art, Savannah, Georgia
214	Courtesy of York Museums Trust
216	Mapping Specialists Ltd.
237	Library of Congress Geography and Maps Division
240	Library of Congress Prints and Photographs Division
249	National Portrait Gallery, Smithsonian Institution
262	Library of Congress Prints and Photographs Division
276	Library of Congress Prints and Photographs Division
284	From *Baltimore: Past and Present. With Biographical Sketches of Its Representative Men* (1871)
287	Library of Congress Prints and Photographs Division
299	Metropolitan Museum of Art. Gift of Robert Hatfield Ellsworth, in memory of La Ferne Hatfield Ellsworth, 1986
304	National Museum of American History, Smithsonian Institution
306	National Portrait Gallery, London. Gift of Mary Elizabeth Fleming Stopford
309	The Charleston Museum, Charleston, South Carolina
319	U.S. Senate Collection

Index

Acadians, 83
Adam-Strain Building, 163
Adelantado, 19
African American archaeology, 56
Alexander, Anna, 154
Altamaha delta: Anna Alexander rows across, 169; Butler's plantation on, 146–48, 166; crossed for church services by former slaves, 168; diked by slave labor, 148, 160, 164, 168; featured in Fanny Kemble's journal, 151; flatboats cross, 159, 168; at Fort King George, 219; rice growing on, 115, 138; tabby misidentified as Spanish mission ruins, 182
Altamaha River: boundary between indigenous coastal chiefdoms, 87, 184; Brunswick-Altamaha canal link, 152; as colonial Savannah's southern boundary, 197; cotton barged down, 164; Darien River distributary of, 162; Hopeton Plantation location on, 158–59; as natural resource; 177; as southern limit of Georgia colony, 185
Arsenal, 256
Avilés, Pedro Menéndez, 16, 18–21; founds San Miguel de Gualdape, 87; founds St. Augustine, 11

Ballast stones, 70, 94; as marsh hammock foundation, 70, 122; in rock garden, 122

Baptist Church of Beaufort, 283; ornate plaster ceiling, 280
Barnwell, Col. John "Tuscarora Jack," 251; buried in St. Helena Cemetery, 269; saves residents from Native American attack, 252; as Yamasee fighter, 238, 272
Barnwell Castle, 219–20
Barnwell-Gough House, 272–74; as Civil War hospital, 272–77
Battery, Charleston, 307
Battle of Beaufort, 252; Parish Church of St. Helen damaged during, 268
Battle of Bloody Marsh (Moosa), 137
Battle of Fort Mose, 162
Battle of the Grenadiers (Battle of Bloody Marsh), 137
Beaufort, S.C.: architectural style of, 251; Civil War hospitals in, 218; planters' summer homes in, 217
Beaufort County, S.C., 121; bifurcated by Port Royal Sound, 217; chapels of ease in, 217, 230; exploration and settlement of, 251; St. Helena Island in; as locale of most historic tabby, 251
Bella, 300, 303–4
Blackbeard (pirate Edward Teach), 306
Blackbeard Island, 177, 184; source of live oak timbers, 196
Black drink, 12, 185

Black militia: ally with Spanish militia, 91; Menéndez named captain of, 51; plot to destroy, 91; raid Georgia plantations, 90; run amok after Patriot War, 91; Spanish governor forms, 90
Black Seminoles, 90
Bleak Hall Plantation, 294; in Botany Bay, 288; tabby outbuildings at, 292
Bilali Muhammad, 189–91
Botany Bay, 290–97; Heritage Preserve and Wildlife Management Area, 288
Braddock Point Plantation: lost to Stoney brothers, 227; slave quarters, 226–27; as Stoney-Baynard Plantation, 222–26
British period, St. Augustine, 12–13, 26
Brunswick, Ga., 84, 111, 152–54; yellow fever epidemics, 110
Burr, Aaron, 144
Butler, Fanny Kemble, 150; appalled by slavery, 150–51; describes John Couper residence, 141; pens plantation journal, 146, 151; as wife of Pierce Butler, 150
Butler, Major Pierce, 146–49; builds tabby structures, 146–48; establishes Hampton Plantation, 146
Butler, Pierce Mease, 141; holds country's largest slave sale, 151; inherits Hampton Plantation, 150; as slave owner, 151

Butler's Island: in Fanny Kemble journal, 150; largest Georgia tidewater rice plantation, 148; mortality in rice fields on, 69; religious services at, 168; slaves on, 148–49

Cabins, tabby, 9, 55
Calibogue Sound, 224; Sea Pines Plantation on, 219
Camps, Father Pedro, 31–32
Camp Saxton: contraband camp, 238; Emancipation Proclamation first read aloud at, 236; First South Carolina Volunteers based at, 238; Fort Frederick at, 236; home to first Black Union regiment, 236
Cajuns (Acadians), 83
Campbell, Tunis, 163
Cannon's Point Plantation, 138–45; agricultural experiments at, 143; kitchen of, 141–42; slaves escape from, during War of 1812, 161; USS *Constitution* stern post cut at, 144–45
Cassina (black drink), 12, 185
Castillo de San Marcos, 38–40; escaped British slaves employed at, 42; Fort Mose outpost of, 7, 46; ledger art at, 42; as prison, 9, 27, 34, 42; as refuge for St. Augustine, 7, 14; tabby and coquina construction of, 5, 7
Catholic missions: in Guale and Mocama villages, 7, 68; under siege, 68; tabby misidentified as, 181–83
Chapel of Ease, 230–33; largest unsupported arch, 230; mausoleum site, 233
Charlesfort–Santa Elena site, 12; plantation, 235; significance of, 244–47
Charleston (Charles Towne), S.C.: Beaufort residents escape to, 264; blockaded, 221; first rice seed imported into, 252; first shots of Civil War fired from, 218; founded, 215, 235, 305–7; Hephzibah Townsend sells baked goods in, 303; Horn Work location, 308; house inspires Beaufort's Tabby Manse, 286; planters' summer homes in, 217; richest colonial city, 217; Robert Smalls works in, 261; settlers bypass Beaufort for, 251; slaves imported through, 228

Chato, 44–45
Chefs, plantation, 141–42
Chocolate Plantation, 186–89
Cockburn, Admiral Sir George, 76, 83; liberates slaves, 102
Colonial Dorchester State Historic Site, 310–12; as fort location, 312–16
Colonial fairs, 310–11
Constitution, U. S., Third Amendment to, 31
Contrabands, 121; in Beaufort, 275; status prior to Emancipation Proclamation, 238; on St. Helena Island, 229; on St. Simons Island, 121
Coquina, 3, 9; in Castillo de San Marcos, 38–42, 46; in Father O'Reilly House, 34–35; in Fernandez-Llambias House, 28; in Flagler tabby, 36–38; in Fort Matanzas, 250; in González-Álvarez house, 24–26; homes built of, 12; in John McQueen's basement, 56; in Owens-Thomas House, 211; rarity, 14
Counting coup, 42
Couper, James Hamilton, 118, 123, 160–61; builds tabby slave cabins, 158; builds tabby sugar mill, 180; sister Ann, 123; son of John, 144; use of tabby at Hopeton, 156
Couper, John: at Cannon's Point, 138–45; as James Hamilton partner, 122–23, 143, 156; sells to James Hamilton, 161

Cuba: British capture of, 52; Castillo builders from, 38; First Spanish Period exodus to, 31; importance to Spanish, 9, 12; Mary Peavett goes to, 26; Menéndez dies in, 52; ships from run blockade, 14; Spanish swap for Florida, 26
Cumberland Island National Seashore, 71–73; Carnegies on, 77; Father Pareja on, 72; federal wilderness, 71; ferry to, 82; homes on, 72; Miller-Greene oldest house on, 73; mission foundation, 69; missions raided by pirate, 54; Mocamas village-mission on, 72; naming of, 73; Nathaniel Greene granted land on, 74; sea turtles nest on, 71; ship torpedoed near, 153

Dairy silo, 112
Datil peppers, 33
Debatable land, 69, 100; book, 181
Distillery, rum, Georgia's first, 178–80; Spalding as partner in, 195
Donax. See Coquina
Dorchester colonial town and fort, 310–18; commanded by Francis Marion, 317
Double-pile plan Beaufort houses, 272–74
Drake, Sir Francis, 38; as privateer, 246
Dungeness I, 74–76; as Caty Green Miller home, 78; Gen. Cockburn occupies, 76; Lighthouse Harry Lee dies at, 77; Millers build, 74; in National Register Historic District, 73; Oglethorpe brings name to Cumberland, 73
Dungeness II, 72

Earthquake: damages Dorchester bell tower, 310; damages fort at Dorchester, 315; destroys Beaufort buildings, 253;
Edingsville Beach, 289

Edisto Island, 288–89; embraced by Botany Bay, 290; Father Rogel visits, 288; name of Native chiefdom, 215; prehistoric shell rings discovered on, 4

Elizafield Plantation (Mission Santo Domingo de Talaje), 182–83

Emancipation Proclamation: first read, 229; slaves feel first effect, 236

Enslaved: African countries imported from, 306; build with tabby 1–2, 4–6, 80; freed by Gen. Cockburn, 76; hospital for, 124–27; laws restricting, 307; move with Spanish to Cuba, 12; Muslims, 189–91; outnumber white population, 217; return to plantations post–Civil War, 70; Spanish law regarding, 46; take refuge at Hilton Head, 221; uprising, 307

Father Miguel O'Reilly House Museum, 34
Fernandez-Llambias House, 28; original style of, 28–31
Fernandina, 83, 84, 91
Ferry. See Cumberland Island National Seashore; Fort Matanzas; Sapelo Island
Fifty-Fourth Massachusetts, 240; based at Hampton Plantation, 148; burns Darien, 148; featured in film *Glory*, 272; first Black Union regiment, 149; soldiers treated at Hospital #10, 272, 277; Susie King Taylor nurses, 121
First Missionary Baptist Church, 300–304
Flagler tabby, 10, 36–37
Fort at Dorchester, 11; under command of Francis Marion, 317; in Revolutionary War, 312–16; town of Dorchester, 310–11; unique design, 312
Fort Caroline, 14, 16, 215; failed attempt to attack Spanish, 20; French massacred at, 16; Spanish destroy fort, 20

Fort Frederica National Monument, 4; in battles on St. Simons, 105; Horton leads, 96, 104; location of Mary Musgrove tabby house, 68; Oglethorpe's home at, 105
Fort Frederick Heritage Preserve, 34, 236
Fort George Island Cultural State Park, 53; Oglethorpe renames, 54
Fort King George, 162
Fort Marion. See Castillo de San Marcos
Fort Matanzas, 11, 14–18; massacres, 20–21
Fort Moosa. See Fort Mose Historic State Park
Fort Mose Historic State Park, 46–50; Menéndez named commander, 51
Fort Pulaski National Monument, 206–7
Fort San Mateo. See Fort Caroline
Fountain of Youth, 22
Franciscan friars, 7; on Cumberland Island, 72; establish missions, 68; retreat to Spanish Florida, 185; on St. Simons Island, 114; in western states, 181
Fripp, Edgar, 232–33
Fuller, Rev. Richard, 280, 284–85
Fuller, Thomas, House (Tabby Manse), 272, 286–87

Gascoigne Bluff: contraband camp at, 121; Hamilton Plantation on, 122–23; naming of, 122; sawmills at, 121–22; tabby slave cabins at, 118–20
George II: charters Georgia colony, 197; father of Duke of Cumberland, 73; father of Frederick, Prince of Wales, 236; Fort George Island named for, 54
George III: grants land to William Hopeton, 156; monarch when Brunswick founded, 151
Georgia Bight, 1, 4
Georgia colony: aim of, 69; founding, 50, 72; John Wesley as minister for, 135; Oglethorpe absent from, 135; Oglethorpe negotiates for land, 114; predated by Darien, 162; in relation to Spanish Florida, 83; slavery banned in, 146
Geronimo, 44
Glory (film), 149, 241, 272
González-Álvarez (Oldest) House, 22–27; naming of, 24; remodeled, 24
Good Shepherd Church and School, 154; congregational donations, 170
Gough, Elizabeth Barnwell, 272–74
Gracia Real de Santa Teresa de Mose (Fort Mose), 46–50
Greene, Catherine "Caty" Littlefield, 69, 74, 77–79
Greene, Brig. Gen. Nathaniel: acquires land on Cumberland Island, 74; Miller-Greene house, 80. See Dungeness I
Green's Shell Enclosure Heritage Preserve, 219
Gullah Geechee, 6, 69; Bilali Muhammad as, 189; Cultural Heritage Corridor, 1; displaced by Hilton Head development, 221; festivals, 122; hired at Hamilton Plantation, 122; at Hog Hammock, 184; settle in Pennick after Civil War, 170; songs of, 115; on St. Simons Island, 114–15; task system preserved culture of, 149; in Weeping Time, 151

Haint blue: in Owens-Thomas House slave quarters, 212; recipe for, 212; in St. Simons slave cabins, 120
Hamilton, James, 118–22; wealth, 123
Hamilton Plantation slave cabins, 118–22
Hampton Plantation, 115, 148–51; Aaron Burr flees to, 144, 146–49; enslaved work at, 149; Fanny Kemble Butler visits, 146–50
Hawks, Dr. Esther Jane Hill, 275–77

Haynes, William Greaner, Jr., 175–77; founds Ashantilly Press, 177
Highlanders: fight Spanish with Oglethorpe, 162; John Houstoun McIntosh as descendant of, 86; settle Darien, 162
Hilton Head Island, 218–21
Hollybourne Cottage, 106–11
Hopeton Plantation, 156–61; chef at, 141; John Couper dies at, 146; rice fields of, 159–60; sugar cane, 88–89, 180
Horn Work, 307–8
Horton, Major William, 100–105; granted land on Jekyll Island, 69; second in command to Oglethorpe, 96
Horton House, 99–102; Jekyll Club members donate funds to restore, 108; rebuilt of tabby, 69
Huguenots: build Charlesfort and Fort Caroline, 215, 244; establish Charlesfort, 12; first European settlers, 228; Jean Ribault as, 149; massacred at Matanzas inlet, 250; migrate to Charleston, 305; put to death at Fort Caroline, 20; relationship with Timucua, 250; Spanish king learns of settlements in La Florida, 16, 19
Hurricane: Aaron Burr describes, 149; Baptist Church of Beaufort damaged by, 280; Beaufort devastated by, 253; Bilali saves other slaves during, 189; Brunswick slaves die in, 153; crop failures caused by, 161; damages Edisto Beach causeway, 295; damages Old Baptist Meeting House, 229; destroys roof of Dungeness I, 74; destroys St. Augustine wooden forts, 38; destroys sugar works, 180; destruction at Cannon's Point, 143–44; first Red Cross relief effort, 229; kills thousands in South Carolina, 289; Morris saves slaves during, 149; Port Royal Naval Station saves people during, 243; sand dunes protect against, 71; South End House survives, 192; tabby resistance to, 2; wrecks French ships, 20

Indian Training School (Carlisle, Pa.), 44
Indigo: Minorcans imported to grow, 9, 31–32; slaves grow, 6; tabby vats, 2
Indigo snake, 166

Jay, William, 208–14
Jekyll Island: DuBignon slaves speak French on, 97; Horton granted land on, 69; imported on slave ship Wanderer, 97; naming of, 96–102
Jekyll Island Club, 70
Jekyll Island State Park, 96
John Mark Verdier House, 258–63
Jones, Noble, 69, 200–205

King, Anna Matilda Page, 127–28
King, Roswell, Jr., 149; father of slave Daphne, 169; wife punishes slave mothers, 151
King, Roswell, Sr., 149
Kingsland, 82–85
Kingsley, Anta Madgigine, 59–63
Kingsley, Zephaniah, 55–63

Lafayette, Marquis de: Caty Greene and, 77–78; speaks at Owens-Thomas House, 208; stays at Verdier mansion, 260; visits Edingsville Beach, 289
La Florida, 11–12, 16, 19, 21, 244–50
Lanier, Sidney, 152; Lanier's Oak, 153
Late Archaic Period, 3–4; Carolina lowcountry occupied during, 215; on Cumberland Island, 71; on Edisto Island, 288; on Fort George Island, 53; on Hilton Head Island, 219; at Port Royal, 234; on Sapelo Island, 184
Laudonniére, René de, 14, 16, 20, 248
Laurel Grove Plantation, 62–63; Ring Lardner, 24
Lee, Henry "Light-Horse Harry," 76–77, 314
Liberty Boys, 198
Lighthouse: first female keeper at St. Augustine, 33; Sapelo Island, 184; St. Simons, 114, 115–16, 126, 127, 134, 145, 195
Lime, burned shell, 2–4
Limelight (quicklime), 4, 5
Little San Felipe. See Minorcan
Lopez, Father Francisco: celebrates first Mass in La Florida, 11; chronicles Matanzas massacre, 20

Magundo, Mansillo, 59, 61, 64–65
Mandinga, 50–52
Márquez, Don Francisco Menéndez, 51
Mary Ross Park, 153, 183
Menéndez, Francisco, 50–52
Marine Recruit Depot, Parris Island, 242, 243
Marion, Francis, 9, 40, 128, 217, 312, 314, 317–19
Manse, Tabby, 272, 286–87
Maurice, Charles Stewart, 108–11
Maurice, Charlotte, 108, 110, 111
McIntosh, James Houstoun, 54, 63, 70, 86–93, 195
McIntosh Sugar Works, 86–89
McQueen, John; 54, 56; renamed Don Juan, 54, 186
Miller-Greene House, 73, 80
Minorcan, 9, 13, 28, 31–33
Missionary Baptist Church, First, 292, 300–302
Mission San Juan del Puerto, 53–54

Mission Santo Domingo de Talaje, 182–83
Mitchelville, S.C., 221, 234
Mocama, 53, 67, 96, 181, 197; missions, 68, 72, 114
Montiano, Manuel de, 48, 52
Morris (slave), 149
Morrow, Dr. James, 298
Mulberry: Grove Plantation, 69, 76–79; trees, 68, 203
Museum of Coastal History, St. Simons, 123
Musgrove, Mary, 68, 134
Muslims, enslaved, 189–91

Nelson, Admiral Horatio, 180
Nombre de Dios Mission, 22
Nuestra Senora de Guadalupe de Tolomato, 181–82; ruins, 178–80

Oglethorpe, Gen. James Edward, 54, 68–69, 102; in battles on St. Simons Island, 105; builds forts on Cumberland Island and at Frederica, 114, 126, 130–37; names Jekyll Island, 96; Orange Hall, 126, 136; siege of St. Augustine, 50; Tomochichi and, 68, 73; and William Horton, 104–5
Okra, 181
Old Baptist Meeting House, 280–83
Old Ironsides, USS *Constitution*, 144–45
Oqui, 298–99
Orange Hall, 126, 136
Oscar, 318; in portrait, 319
Ovens, tabby, 292, 300, 302–3
Owens-Thomas House, 208–13
Oyster shells, 1–4

Paleo-Indians, 53; on Cumberland Island, 71; on Jekyll Island, 96; on Sapelo Island, 184; on St. Simons Island, 114, 146
Pareja, Father Francisco, 54, 72

Parish Church at St. Helena, 230–33
Parris Island, 12, 14, 234, 235; Charlesfort on, 213, 242, 248–50; Marine Corps Recruit Depot, 243–47; National Historic Landmark, 242–47, 244; Santa Elena on, 215, 228, 242, 250
Patriot rebellion, 54–56, 62, 90–91, 93
Peavett, Mary "Maria" Evans, 24, 26–27
Penn Center, 229, 233
People of the Sea. *See* Mocama
Philip II, 14, 18, 19
Pinckney, Eliza, 306
Pipowder courts, 311
Plaçage (plaçée), 9
Pleistocene ice ages, 96
Ponce de León, 11, 14, 16, 67; Fountain of Youth, 22
Ponce de León Hotel, 36
Portland cement, 1, 10. *See also* Revival tabby
Port Royal (Porte Royale), 163, 228, 236–38; Fort Frederick, 34, 236; Union invasion, 233. *See also* Taylor, Susie Baker King
Port Royal Experiment, 221, 229
Port Royal Sound, 219, 235, 238–39, 242

Quicklime, 4, 5

Retreat Plantation, extent of, 124
Revival tabby, 36; in Beaufort seawall, 254; Dairy silo, 112; Darien's First Presbyterian Church rebuilt with, 162; Dungeness II, 74; Flagler tabby, 46; Hollybourne, 97, 106–11; Fort Frederica merlons, 130; Miller-Greene House stucco, 80; Retreat Plantation buildings restored with, 126–27; St. Mark's Episcopal Church, 94
Ribault, Jean, 14, 16, 20–21
Rice, 6, 33, 50, 86, 115; on Butler's Island, 148, 150; James Couper's dikes, 158–59, 160–61; mills, 2, 86; Shakers grow, 85; tidewater growing of, 69, 138, 160; value of, 163–64
Rollins Shell Ring, 53
Ross, Mary Letitia, 181–83; park, 153, 183

Saltus-Habersham House, 278–79
San Buenaventura de Guadalquini, 114
San Miguel de Gualdape, 67
Santa Elena, 12, 21, 215, 228, 234, 242; Charlesfort–Santa Elena site, 244–50
Sapelo Island, 86, 122, 141, 143, 172, 184–85; Bilali Muhammad, 189–91; Chocolate Plantation, 186–89. *See also* South End House
Savannah, 1, 54, 70, 97, 104, 120, 127; founding of Georgia colony, 69; John Couper in, 143; John Wesley in, 135; underground schools in, 121; Weeping Time slave auction in, 115, 151
Savannah River, 68, 69, 76, 78
Sea Cloud Plantation (Botany Bay), 290–97
Seawall, Beaufort, 254–55
Seminole, 54, 93; ally with Spanish against United States, 91; Black Seminole, 90; origin of name, 90
Sephardic Jews, 305
Shakers, 85
Shaw, Col. Robert Gould, 149, 240–41, 277
Shell Ring: on Fig Island, 288; Rollins, on Fort George Island, 53; on Sapelo Island, 184
Slave cabins, tabby, 2, 9; at Chocolate Plantation, 186–89; at Hamilton Plantation, 118–22; at Hampton Plantation, 146; at Hopeton Plantation, 158; at Kingsley Plantation, 55–59, 61; at Retreat Plantation, 124, 127
Smalls, Robert, 243, 258, 261–63

Index   333

South End House, 172, 174, 184–85, 188, 192–94
Spalding, Thomas, 86, 143, 186–88; Bilali Mohammad, 189–91; father James, 126; formula for tabby, 195; public service, 196; Thicket Sugar Mill and Rum Distillery, 178–83. *See also* Hopeton Plantation; Sapelo Island; South End House
Spanish periods, St. Augustine, 12, 26
Spartina, 3, 53, 184, 185, 222
St. Andrews Anglican Church, 310
St. Athanasius Protestant Episcopal Church, 154–55
St. Augustine, 1, 5, 7, 9, 10, 11–13
St. Cyprians Episcopal Church, 166–69
St. Helena Island, 228–29, 234; Chapel of Ease, 230–33. *See also* Port Royal
St. Mark's Episcopal Church, 94–95
St. Marys, 9, 71, 82–84, 85
St. Marys River, 83, 90, 91, 93
Stoney-Baynard Plantation, 221, 222–27
Stono Rebellion, 46, 307
St. Simons Island, 4, 50, 69, 76, 114–17; battles on, 105, 114–16; causeway, 96

Sugar, 2, 6, 143, 156, 158, 199; Thicket Sugar Mill and Rum Distillery, 178–83; Thomas Spalding and, 195–96. *See also* Hopeton Plantation
Swamp Fox. *See* Marion, Francis

Tabby Manse, 272, 286–87
Tacatacuru, 72
Taki, 48
Talbot Islands State Park, 53
Tapia, 3
Taylor, Susie Baker King, 121, 238, 239–41
Thanksgiving, first, 11
Thicket Sugar Mill and Rum Distillery, 178–83
Thomas Fuller House (Tabby Manse), 272, 286–87
Thomson House, 56, 59, 64–65
Timucua, 5, 11, 53, 82, 96, 114, 181, 248–50
Timucuan Ecological and Historic Preserve, 56, 72
Townsend, Hephzibah Jenkins, 290–92, 299; First Missionary Baptist Church, 300–304
Treaty of Ghent, 76
Treaty of Paris, 9, 308

Underground Railroad Network to Freedom, 7, 46

Valley Forge. *See* Greene, Catherine "Caty" Littlefield
Vesey, Denmark, 307

Wadmalaw and Edisto Female Mite Society, 303, 304
War of Jenkins' Ear, 105, 134, 136
Washington, George and Martha. *See* Greene, Catherine "Caty" Littlefield
Waterfront warehouses, 163–65
Wayne, Gen. "Mad Anthony," 77, 79
Whitney, Eli, 69, 77, 78–79, 198
Woodbine, 82, 84–85
Woodward, Dr. Henry, 251–52, 305
Wormsloe State Historic Site, 200–205

Yamacraw, 68, 73, 114, 134, 185, 197
Yamasee, 51, 68, 90, 114, 132, 185, 217, 236
Yamasee War, 51, 197, 217, 251, 264, 269; Col. John Barnwell, 238
Yazoo land frauds, 145

BOOKS BY JINGLE DAVIS AND BENJAMIN GALLAND

Island Passages
An Illustrated History of Jekyll Island, Georgia

Island Time
An Illustrated History of St. Simons Island, Georgia